Adolf Hitler

Significant Figures in World History

Charles Darwin: A Reference Guide to His Life and Works,
by J. David Archibald, 2019.

Leonardo da Vinci: A Reference Guide to His Life and Works,
by Allison Lee Palmer, 2019.

Michelangelo: A Reference Guide to His Life and Works,
by Lilian H. Zirpolo, 2020.

Robert E. Lee: A Reference Guide to His Life and Works,
by James I. Robertson Jr., 2019.

John F. Kennedy: A Reference Guide to His Life and Works,
by Ian James Bickerton, 2019.

Florence Nightingale: A Reference Guide to Her Life and Works,
by Lynn McDonald, 2020.

Napoléon Bonaparte: A Reference Guide to His Life and Works,
by Joshua Meeks, 2020.

Nelson Mandela: A Reference Guide to His Life and Works,
by Aran S. MacKinnon, 2020.

Winston Churchill: A Reference Guide to His Life and Works,
by Christopher Catherwood, 2020.

Catherine the Great: A Reference Guide to Her Life and Works,
by Alexander Kamenskii, 2020.

Golda Meir: A Reference Guide to Her Life and Works,
by Meron Medzini, 2020.

Karl Marx: A Reference Guide to His Life and Works,
by Frank Elwell, Brian Andrews, and Kenneth S. Hicks, 2020.

Eva Perón: A Reference Guide to Her Life and Works,
by María Belén Rabadán Vega and Mirna Vohnsen, 2021.

Adolf Hitler: A Reference Guide to His Life and Works,
by Steven P. Remy, 2021.

Adolf Hitler

A Reference Guide to His Life and Works

Steven P. Remy

ROWMAN & LITTLEFIELD
Lanham • Boulder • New York • London

Published by Rowman & Littlefield
An imprint of The Rowman & Littlefield Publishing Group, Inc.
4501 Forbes Boulevard, Suite 200, Lanham, Maryland 20706
www.rowman.com

86-90 Paul Street, London EC2A 4NE, United Kingdom

Copyright © 2021 by Steven P. Remy

All rights reserved. No part of this book may be reproduced in any form or by any electronic or mechanical means, including information storage and retrieval systems, without written permission from the publisher, except by a reviewer who may quote passages in a review.

British Library Cataloguing in Publication Information Available

Library of Congress Cataloging-in-Publication Data

Names: Remy, Steven P., author.
Title: Adolf Hitler : a reference guide to his life and works / Steven P. Remy.
Description: Lanham : Rowman & Littlefield, [2022] | Series: Significant figures in world history | Includes bibliographical references and index. | Summary: "Adolf Hitler: A Reference Guide to His Life and Works captures Hitler's life, his works, and his legacy. The volume features a chronology, an introduction, a bibliography, and a cross-reference dictionary section that includes entries on people, places, and events related to him"— Provided by publisher.
Identifiers: LCCN 2021022523 (print) | LCCN 2021022524 (ebook) | ISBN 9781538139103 (cloth) | ISBN 9781538197608 (paper) | ISBN 9781538139110 (epub)
Subjects: LCSH: Hitler, Adolf, 1889–1945—Encyclopedias. | National socialism—Encyclopedias. | World War, 1939–1945—Encyclopedias. | Germany—History—1933–1945—Encyclopedias. | Germany—Politics and government—1933–1945—Encyclopedias.
Classification: LCC DD247.H5 R434 2022 (print) | LCC DD247.H5 (ebook) | DDC 943.086092 [B]—dc23
LC record available at https://lccn.loc.gov/2021022523
LC ebook record available at https://lccn.loc.gov/2021022524

Contents

Preface	vii
Acronyms and Abbreviations	xi
Chronology	xiii
Introduction	1
THE DICTIONARY	9
Appendix: Reichstag Elections, 1919–1933	247
Endnotes	251
Bibliography	253
Index	263
About the Author	273

Preface

Adolf Hitler was hardly the modern world's only murderous tyrant and imperialist. Yet he and the regime he ruled over for 12 years exerted an enormous impact on the 20th century. We are still living with the consequences. Interpretations of his life and legacy continue to extert a range of influences—some beneficial and others deleterious—on our politics and popular culture. "For the world to be done with Hitler," German journalist and historian Sebastian Haffner wrote in 1979, "it had to kill not just the man, but the legend as well."[1] That legend has proven to be like the mythical hydra.

Beginning in the 1930s, scholars, journalists, diplomats, politicians, and filmmakers compared Hitler to other tyrants, ancient and modern, with references to the devil or various villains of Western mythologies thrown in for good measure. As one American historian pointed out recently, when the full, seemingly unprecedented horrors of the war were revealed after 1945, Hitler became historically incomparable, "western civilization's new archetype of evil."[2] To a certain extent, he has retained that position to the present day, though now it is common to compare sitting or would-be dictators to Hitler. Neither form of comparison has been helpful for understanding his life and impact on the world.

Serious biographies began appearing in the 1950s. They tended to present Hitler as a kind of political gangster, a charlatan and master manipulator for whom ideology was nothing more than window dressing. A pervasive weakness in the first wave of biographies was their tendency to accept much of Hitler's self-mythologizing as factual. This tendency included a willingness to believe rumors peddled by his political opponents. Historians working within a Marxist framework could offer little illumination, as their conceptual framework characterized Hitler and national socialism as nothing more than expressions of capitalist imperialism in crisis. At the same time, influential thinkers like Hannah Arendt theorized about totalitarian political systems and suggested a fundamental similarity between Hitler's regime and Joseph Stalin's in the Soviet Union. But this was not an approach that revealed much of anything about Hitler the person and the specific circumstances in which he ascended to power and ruled Germany.

Far less well known to this day are the observations of intellectuals and activists in the Black Atlantic tradition—notably Ralph Bunche, W. E. B. DuBois, and Aimé Césaire—who saw something depressingly familiar in Nazi Germany: namely, an attempt to do to other White Europeans what White westerners had been doing to non-White peoples around the world for the previous three centuries. The fact that these thinkers rarely receive acknowledgment for pioneering an interpretation of the Nazi regime that is now accepted widely by historians—that Hitler was an imperialist and national socialism was an imperial project driven by racism—reflects the deeply entrenched belief that the Nazis represented a form of evil that defies historical comparison.

Beginning in the 1960s, historians and social scientists turned their attention to German society and its relationship to Hitler, Nazi ideology, and the regime. At the same time, the study of the Holocaust became a major area of research. By the turn of the millennium, the body of research on seemingly every conceivable area of Germany and Europe before, during, and after Hitler's rule had reached enormous proportions and continues to grow. This flood of scholarship and popular writing both reflects and feeds into what has become a remarkably broad, though certainly not uncontested, consensus across most of the German political spectrum: that millions of Germans supported Hitler and the regime and that this fact must be memorialized in public, taught about honestly in schools, and never forgotten. Another salutary outcome of this remarkable convergence of historical research and public consensus involves changing perceptions of those relative few who resisted. People like Colonel Claus von Stauffenberg, the students of the White Rose, and the nameless Germans who protected Jews at enormous personal risk went from being seen as traitors by a majority of Germans to martyrs to the decent and humane nation that the Nazis and their supporters could never fully extinguish.

This outpouring of scholarship and the sea change in how most Germans think about the Nazi period implied a society-wide rejection of the idea of Hitler as a figure with almost supernatural powers, a mass hypnotizer who took advantage of a nation in crisis and led it into the abyss. And in contrast to the steady flow of research on Nazi Germany, the war, and the Holocaust, scholarly and popular interest in Hitler arrives in what Germans call *Hitlerwellen*, "Hitler waves." In 1998 and 2000, after a lull in the publication of new biographies, British historian Ian Kershaw produced a two-volume biography to great scholarly and public acclaim. It was the first to draw extensively on decades of international research on Nazi Germany and archival revelations from the former Soviet Union. What interested Kershaw—trained as a social historian—was less Hitler's personality (and whatever amounted to his personal life) and more the ways in which he exercised power and how the German public responded to him. Reflecting the current state of research on national socialism and German society, Kershaw's Hitler is no cynical gangster-type. Rather, he is an ideologue whose self-generated mythologizing as a leader destined to restore Germany to greatness proved to be a potent political weapon. Potent, of course, because so many Germans were willing to believe it.

The next Hitler wave began around 2010 with the first of two important studies by Thomas Weber of Hitler's experiences as a soldier and then in postwar Munich. These were followed by four new full-scale biographies, all of which take slightly different approaches to Hitler's life. The latest scholarly Hitler wave has finally fully disentangled what can be known reliably about his life from the influence of his own mythmaking. It has also given us an understanding of a dictator who was not remotely weak (as had been suggested by some German historians in the 1970s) and certainly not a power-mad tyrant for whom ideology played no significant role in his leadership of Germany and conduct of the war. We also now have a fuller understanding of Hitler the human being—his personality, his private life, and the state of his mental and physical health.

Perhaps the next task facing historians of this singularly important individual is how to contextualize his place and that of Nazi Germany and the Holocaust in modern history. Doing this necessitates making comparisons. It requires no longer treating Hitler, the regime, and the Holocaust as paragons of evil that somehow stand above history. But this is something many are still reluctant to do for fear of relativizing Hitler's criminality. For better and for worse, representations of Hitler in popular culture—in film, television, and especially across the internet—has already been "normalized" (as American historian Gavriel D. Rosenfeld puts it). Though cinematic satires of Hitler date back to the years of his rule, the last two decades have witnessed an explosion in Hitler memes that has greatly accelerated normalization. Or perhaps *debasement* is a better term. More ominous is the growing real-world idolization and fetishization of Hitler and Nazi symbols by a resurgent global Far-Right.

Normalization in popular culture, in short, has undermined Hitler's position as a transcendant symbol of evil to an extent that most scholars or mainstream politicians are unwilling to accept. To a certain extent, this reluctance is justifiable. But contextualizing Hitler's life need not diminish our appreciation for the magnitude of his crimes. The arc of contemporary politics is bending toward nationalist authoritarianism, and the history of Adolf Hitler and the Nazi regime has much to tell us about its trajectory.

I hope this book provides a useful and engaging source for anyone interested in Hitler's life. The introduction provides a brief biographical overview and highlights the main themes explored in the entries. Given the huge amount of scholarhip on Hitler and Nazi Germany, I am highly selective in my choice of entry topics. To my knowledge, this is the first English-language biographical encyclopedia on Hitler, and I have endeavored to see that it reflects the current state of research. The bibliography must also be highly selective, and I emphasize works published in English. But I hope it serves as a starting point for any reader interested in further exploring. To make this book as useful as possible, cross-references are inserted in the individual entries. Within each, terms that have their own entries are in boldface the first time they appear. Related terms appear in *see* and *see also* references. My greatest debt of gratitude is to the many historians upon whose work this book is based. I thank Jon Woronoff for his enthusiastic support. Thanks also to April Snider and Andrew Yoder. I am grateful to colleagues and friends whose comments, suggestions, and encouragement through a very difficult period were essential to the book's completion: April Henning, Steve Sachoff, Benjamin C. Hett, Thomas Weber, Richard Steigmann-Gall, Randall Bytwerk, and Jonathan Beard. Marybeth Tamborra and Robin Tainsh helped with the images and chronology, respectively. Miranda Brethour prepared the index. This book is dedicated to my father, Richard Remy, with love, gratitude, and respect.

Acronyms and Abbreviations

BDM	Bund Deutscher Mädel (League of German Girls)	NSDAP	Nationalsozialistische Deutsche Arbeiterpartei (National Socialist German Workers' Party or Nazi Party)
Comintern	Communist International		
DAF	Deutsche Arbeitsfront (German Labor Front)	NSV	Nationalsozialistische Volkswohlfahrt (National Socialist Welfare Organization)
DAP	Deutsche Arbeiterpartei (German Workers' Party)		
DNVP	Deutschnationale Volkspartei (German National People's Party)	OKH	Oberkommando des Heeres (Army High Command)
DVP	Deutsche Volkspartei (German People's Party)	OKW	Oberkommando der Wehrmacht (Armed Forces High Command)
FDJ	Freie Deutsche Jugend (Free German Youth)	OT	Organisation Todt (Todt Organization)
		POW	prisoner of war
GNF	German National Front	RAF	Royal Air Force
HJ	Hitlerjugend (Hitler Youth)	RNS	Reichsnäherstand (National Food Estate)
IMT	International Military Tribunal		
IOC	International Olympic Committee	RSHA	Reichsicherheitshaptamt (Reich Security Main Office)
KdF	Kraft durch Freude (Strength through Joy)	SA	Sturmabteilung (Storm Section, Stormtroopers, or Brownshirts)
KPD	Kommunistische Partei Deutschlands (Communist Party of Germany)	SD	Sicherheitsdienst (SS Security Service)
NASA	National Aeronautics and Space Administration	SIPO	Sicherheitspolizei (Security Police)
		SPD	Sozialdemokratische Partei Deutschlands (Social Democratic Party of Germany)
NCO	noncommissioned officer		
NKVD	Naródnyy komissariát vnútrennikh del (People's Commisariat for Internal Affairs)		
		SS	Schutzstaffel (Protection Squad)
		UN	United Nations
NMT	Nuremberg Military Tribunal	USAAF	US Army Air Force
NS	Nasjonal Samling	USPD	Independent Social Democratic Party
		WHW	Winterhilfswerk

Chronology

1889 20 April: Adolf Hitler is born in Braunau am Inn, Austria.

1895 Alois Hitler retires and buys a farm near the Austrian town of Fischlham. **May:** Adolf Hitler begins attending school.

1900 Adolf Hitler begins attending secondary school in Linz, Austria.

1903 3 January: Alois Hitler dies. Klara Hitler enrolls Adolf in another school in Steyr, Austria.

1905 Autumn: Hitler returns to live with his mother in Linz.

1906 May: Hitler's first visit to Vienna.

1907 September: Hitler moves to Vienna, takes the entrance exam for admission to the academy of fine arts, and is rejected. **21 December:** Klara Hitler dies.

1908 12 February: Hitler returns to Vienna. **September:** Hitler applies for the second time to the Academy of Fine Arts and is rejected.

1909 Autumn: Hitler moves into the Meidling homeless shelter and begins painting and selling small postcards.

1910 February: Hitler moves into a men's home on the outskirts of Vienna and spends most of his time painting and reading.

1913 25 May: Immediately after becoming eligible for a paternal inheritance, Hitler moves to Munich.

1914 January: Munich police take Hitler to the Austro-Hungarian consulate for failing to register for the draft in Linz. **5 February:** Hitler is given a military medical examination in Salzburg, is deemed unfit for service, and is allowed to return to Munich. **3 August:** Hitler volunteers to join the Bavarian Army. **5 August:** Hitler's first attempt to enlist is unsuccessful. **16 August:** Hitler is inducted into the Second Bavarian Infantry Regiment and undergoes basic training. **1 September:** Hitler is transferred to the 16th Reserve Infantry Regiment (List Regiment). **10 October:** The List Regiment departs Munich for training near Augsburg. **21–23 October:** The List Regiment is transferred to the western front. **27 October:** Hitler participates in the assault on Gheluvelt in Belgium (First Battle of Ypres). **1 November:** The List Regiment is withdrawn to village of Werwick after suffering high casualties. **3 November:** Hitler is promoted to private first class and is transferred to the regimental staff, where he will serve as a dispatch runner for the remainder of the war. **2 December:** Hitler is awarded the Iron Cross, second class.

1916 September: The List Regiment is transferred south to assist in the German response to the Anglo–French offensive on the upper reaches of the Somme River Valley. **5 October:** Hitler receives a shrapnel wound

CHRONOLOGY

in his left thigh and recovers in a Red Cross hospital until 2 December, during which time he visits Berlin for the first time. **2 December:** Hitler is sent to Munich and is assigned to a List Regiment replacement battalion.

1917 **5 March:** Hitler returns to the front in the region around Arras. **July:** The List Regiment participates in Third Battle of Ypres and is transferred to Alsace in August after suffering high losses. **17 September:** Hitler is awarded the Military Merit Cross, third class, and is given an 18-day furlough, which he spends in Berlin.

1918 **4 August:** Hitler is awarded the Iron Cross, first class. **21 August:** Hitler is sent to Nuremberg for training in telephone and radio operation. **10–27 September:** Hitler spends his furlough in Berlin. **13–14 October:** Hitler is wounded in a mustard gas attack near Comines, France, and recovers in a military hospital in Pasewalk, Germany (now Szeczin, Poland). **19 November:** Hitler is discharged from the hospital and returns to Munich, where he is assigned to the Seventh Company of the First Replacement Battalion of the Second Infantry Regiment. **December:** Hitler is assigned to guard duty at a prisoner-of-war camp in the town of Traunstein im Chiemgau, Bavaria.

1919 **January:** Hitler returns to Munich. **February:** Hitler is assigned to the Second Demobilization Company of the Second Infantry Regiment. **3 and 15 April:** Hitler's battalion elects him as liaison to the first and second Bavarian Soviet Republics (April–May 1919). **9 May:** Hitler serves on a three-person commission investigating other soldiers' actions during the two Soviet Republics. When his company is disbanded later that month, he is allowed to remain in the army. **June:** Hitler is assigned to the Second Infantry Regiment's demobilization office. **10–19 July:** Hitler participates in a training course in Munich for a special counterintelligence unit created to monitor and counter support for communism among soldiers. **20–25 August:** Hitler serves as 1 of 26 instructors in a course for soldiers on opposing communism at a camp in Lechfeld, Bavaria. **12 September:** Hitler attends his first meeting of the German Workers' Party and joins a week later. **16 September:** Hitler writes a former student in the course, Adolf Gemlich, a letter in which he states that Jews are a "racial and not a religious community" and that the "final aim" of anti-Semitism must be the "uncompromising removal of the Jews altogether." **October:** Hitler is assigned as assistant to the educational officer on the staff of the 41st Rifleman's Regiment in Munich.

1920 **24 February:** The DAP announces its 25-point program at the Hofbräuhaus in Munich and renames itself the National Socialist German Workers' Party. **31 March:** Hitler is discharged. **August:** At a conference in Salzburg, Hitler seems to support the idea of a merger of nationalist and non-Marxist socialist parties though has rejected the idea by the beginning of 1921. **13 August:** Hitler explains the party's anti-Semitism in a long speech in a Munich beer hall. **December:** Hitler leads the party's effort to acquire the *Munchener Beobachter* newspaper.

1921 **29 July:** The party selects Hitler as its chairman. **11 August:** The party creates the Gymnastics and Sports Department, which it begins referring to as the Sturmabteilung (SA, Stormtroopers) in October. **October:** Hitler is questioned by Munich police following multiple unauthorized party demonstrations and brawls between party members and police.

1922 **22 January:** Hitler is sentenced to three months' imprisonment for his role in a brawl in Munich between party members and leaders of the Peasant League the previous September, during which the league's chairman was injured. **24 June–27 July:** Hitler is imprisoned in the Munich-Stadelheim Prison. **14–15 October:** The German Day march in Coburg. **November:** NSDAP is banned in Prussia.

1923 **27–29 January:** The first Reich party rally is held in Munich. **1–2 September:** There is a German Day rally in Munich. **8 November:** Hitler leads an attempted seizure of power in Bavaria, which collapses over the following two days. **9 November:** Hitler is injured during a march with putschists in Munich and flees the city. **11 November:** Hitler is arrested at Ernst Hanfstaengl's home.

1924 January: Alfred Rosenberg creates the Grossdeutsche Volksgemeinschaft (GVG) to replace the banned NSDAP and SA. **26 February:** The trial of Hitler and nine other defendants in Munich begins. **1 April:** Hitler is convicted of treason and sentenced to five years' imprisonment. **20 December:** Hitler is released from Landsberg Prison.

1925 February: The ban on NSFB and SA is lifted. **26 February:** Hitler announces his return to politics and reestablishes the party in a speech to party members at the Bürgerbräukeller the following day. **March:** The Schutzstaffel (SS) is established. **9 March:** The Munich police ban Hitler from speaking in public. **11 March:** Hitler commissions Gregor Strasser to rebuild the party in northern Germany. **26 April:** Paul von Hindenburg is elected president following the sudden death of Friedrich Ebert on 28 February. **May:** Hitler completes work on the first volume of *Mein Kampf*. **3–7 July:** The party holds its first rally since 1923 in Weimar. **August:** Hitler begins working on the second volume of *Mein Kampf*. **10 September:** The Working Community of the North and West German Gaue of the NSDAP, led by Gregor Strasser, and its newsletter, edited by Goebbels, is established.

1926 14 February: Hitler ends a challenge to his authority at a meeting of party leaders in Bamberg. **1 July:** Hitler dissolves the Working Community, an informal group of party officials in northern Germany. **3–4 July:** The SS makes its first official public appearance at the party rally in Weimar. **September:** Hitler appoints Strasser as the party's propaganda chief. **November:** Hitler completes work on the second volume of *Mein Kampf*.

1927 5 March: The speaking ban on Hitler is lifted in Bavaria. **27 April:** Hitler addresses several hundred members of Germany's business elite in Essen in an effort to win their political and financial support. **19–21 August:** The third party rally is held in Nuremberg.

1928 20 May: The party does poorly in Reichstag and state elections. Hitler secludes himself over the summer in Berchtesgaden to write a second book, unpublished in his lifetime, focusing on foreign policy. **September:** The speaking ban on Hitler is lifted in Prussia.

1929 Hitler moves to a spacious apartment on Prinzregentenplatz in Munich. **1–4 August:** The fourth party rally held in Nuremberg. **8 December:** Following a strong showing in state elections in Thuringia, the party joins a governing coalition with the DVP and the DNVP.

1930 September: Hitler testifies in a treason trial of three Nazi officers accused of infiltrating the army and insists that the NSDAP was attempting to come to power by legal means. **1 September:** Hitler takes control of leadership of the SA following a revolt in Berlin. **14 September:** The Reichstag elections are held, resulting in the NSDAP becoming the second-largest party after the SPD. **30 November:** Hitler announces to party leaders that Ernst Röhm will become the head of the SA.

1931 1 April: Hitler convenes party leaders in Weimar, and Walther Stennes, SA leader for eastern Germany, is removed. **18 September:** Hitler's niece Geli Raubal commits suicide in Hitler's Munich apartment. **10 October:** Hitler meets with Reich president Paul von Hindenburg in Bad Harzburg, where delegations from Far-Right parties and groups representing the "nationalist opposition" were assembling to demand the resignation of the Prussian and Reich governments. **November:** Police in Hesse obtain party documents (the Boxheim documents) planning for an NSDAP counter–coup d'état in case of a communist seizure of power.

1932 26 January: Hitler addresses the Düsseldorf Industry Club, part of a longer-term effort to reassure business leaders that the NSDAP was not a truly socialist party. **22 February:** Hitler announces he will run for the presidency against Paul von Hindenburg. **26 February:** Hitler formally becomes a citizen of Germany. **10 April:** Hindenburg wins the second round of the presidential election. **24 April:** State parliament elections makes the NSDAP the largest party in Prussia. **29 May:** In Oldenburg, the NSDAP wins an absolute majority of votes in state elections. **30 May:** Hindenburg agrees to Hitler's conditions for supporting a new cabinet. **17 July:** A large-scale riot in Hamburg between SA and communists leaves 100 wounded and 18 dead. **31 July:** The NSDAP gets 37.4 percent of the votes in the Reichstag elections, making it the single largest party. **13 August:** Hitler demands the chancellorship in meetings with Schleicher, Papen, and Hindenburg and is unsuccessful. **30 August:** The NSDAP–Centre Party cooperation results in Hermann Göring being elected president of the Reichstag. **6 November:** The NSDAP gets 33.1 percent of the votes in the Reichstag elections. **19 and 21 November:** Hitler again demands the chancellorship in meetings with Hindenburg. **8–9 December:** Gregor Strasser resigns from his party offices, and Hitler further centralizes control in his own hands and reasserts his dominance over the party.

1933 **4 January:** Hitler and Franz von Papen meet for the first of several discussions about breaking the political logjam and removing Kurt von Schleicher as chancellor. **15 January:** The party receives 39.5 percent of the vote in state elections in the region of Lippe. **28–29 January:** In meetings with Papen, Hindenburg assents to appointing Hitler chancellor under certain conditions. **30 January:** The new government is sworn in with Hitler as chancellor. **8 February:** Hitler proclaims to government ministers that rearmament is the nation's highest economic priority. **27–28 February:** The Reichstag is set on fire, most likely in an operation involving the Gestapo and the SA, and President Paul von Hindenburg signs the Decree for the Protection of People and State. **5 March:** The NSDAP wins 43.9 percent of the vote in the Reichstag elections. **7 March:** The cabinet begins the process of Gleichschaltung by asserting the authority of the Reich government over the states. **10 March:** In a radio address, Hitler forbids attacks on non-Jewish-owned businesses. **11 March:** The cabinet creates the Reich Ministry for Popular Enlightenment and Propaganda, and Joseph Goebbels is appointed minister. **21 March:** Hitler uses the ceremonial occasion of the opening of the Reichstag to celebrate the joining of the Nazi "nationalist revolution" with the traditions of Prussian conservatism. Himmler announces the opening of the concentration camp at Dachau. **23 March:** The Reichstag votes overwhelmingly to pass the Enabling Act. Only SPD delegates vote against it. **28 March:** Triumph of the Will premieres in Berlin. **28 March:** Hitler announces a national boycott of Jewish-owned businesses to begin on 1 April. **7 April:** The Law for the Reestablishment of a Professional Civil Service is announced, and the Second Law for the Coordination of the Federal States the same day is followed by restrictions and exclusions in other professions. **1 May:** Hitler, Goebbels, and Hindenburg give speeches at a massive rally in Berlin in honor of the "day of labor," a new public holiday. **2 May:** The German Labor Front is created. **5 May:** Hitler approves the extension of the Berlin Treaty with the Soviet Union. **12 May:** Trade unions are replaced by the German Labor Front, a party organization. **17 May:** Hitler delivers a "peace speech" in the Reichstag. **6 June:** Hitler announces to Reich governors that the seizure of power was completed and the "National Socialist revolution" is over. **8 July:** A concordat between the regime and the Vatican is concluded. **14 July:** Cabinet approves forced sterilization law and law banning creation of new political parties. The Law for the Prevention of Genetically Diseased Offspring is announced. **15 July:** The regime signs but never ratifies the Four Power Pact with Italy, Great Britain, and France. **23 July:** On Hitler's orders, Protestant churches hold elections, producing a majority for regime supporters. **August:** Hitler backs off the attempt to topple Austria's government as a prelude to annexation. **1 September:** The first annual party rally since 1929 is held in Nuremberg. Leni Riefenstahl's film of this became *Victory of Faith*. **1 October:** Hitler and Richard Walther Darre announce the hereditary farm law. **14 October:** Hitler announces that Germany will leave the Disarmament Conference talks in Geneva and the League of Nations.

1934 25 January: Hitler meets with a delegation of Protestant church leaders to demand their allegiance to his regime. **26 January:** A nonaggression pact with Poland is announced. **25 February:** Party officials gather across Germany to swear personal allegiance to Hitler. **14 June:** Hitler makes his first state visit to Italy. **30 June–2 July:** The purge and murder of the SA's leadership and conservative opponents occurs. **18 July:** Hitler meets with German Christian leaders and issues a statement reconfirming his support for a unified Protestant Church. **25 July:** The Austrian SS unit begins an unsuccessful putsch attempt in Vienna on Hitler's orders. **2 August:** Hindenburg dies, and Hitler combines the offices of president and Reich chancellor. **19 August:** A nationwide plebiscite reveals a drop in the regime's popularity. **20 August:** Public officials and military personnel are required by law to swear allegiance to Hitler personally as "Führer of the German Reich and People." **5–10 September:** There is a party rally in Nuremberg. Leni Riefenstahl's film of this became *Triumph of the Will*.

1935 13 January: The Saar plebiscite occurs. **6 March:** German troops march unopposed into the Rhineland. **16 March:** The cabinet formally approves conscription, announced to the public on 18 March. **25–26 March:** Hitler meets with British foreign affairs minister Anthony Eden. **21 May:** Hitler delivers the second "peace speech" to the Reichstag, in which he promises to respect Austria's borders and signals a willingness to limit the size of Germany's navy vis-à-vis Britain's. **23 May:** Hitler undergoes a successful operation to remove a polyp from his throat. **18 June:** The Anglo–German naval agreement is concluded. **15 September:** A bundle of anti-Jewish measures are enacted as the Reich Citizenship Law (the Nuremberg Race Laws).

1936 6–16 February: The Winter Olympics are held in Garmisch-Partenkirchen, Bavaria. **7 March:** Hitler announces to the Reichstag that Germany will no longer honor the terms of the Locarno Pact, as small numbers of German troops march unopposed into the left bank of the Rhine River. **4 April:** Hitler gives Göring expansive authority to resolve Germany's foreign exchange and raw materials crisis. **17 June:** Hitler appoints Heinrich Himmler "Reich SS Leader and Head of the German Police in the Reich Ministry of the Interior." **25 July:** Hitler orders German support for Franco's forces in Spain. **1–6 August:** The Olympic Games occur in Berlin. **18 August:** Hitler appoints Göring to head the Four-Year Plan. **4 September:** Göring presents Hitler's memorandum to the cabinet demanding that Germany be prepared for war in four years' time. **1 November:** Mussolini proclaims creation of a "Rome–Berlin Axis." **25 November:** The Anti-Comintern Pact with Japan is signed.

1937 1 May: In a public speech, Hitler warns Germany's churches to stick to purely religious matters. **18 July:** Hitler opens the first Great German Art Exhibition at the new House of German Art in Munich. **25–28 September:** Mussolini visits Germany. **5 November:** Hitler signs the German–Polish Minorities Declaration and holds a meeting in Berlin with war and foreign ministers and armed forces commanders in chief to discuss rearmament and moving against Austria and Czechoslovakia. **6 November:** Italy confirms with Germany that it will join the Anti-Comintern Pact. **19 November:** Halifax visits Hitler in Berchtesgaden to discuss the future of cooperation between Europe's major powers.

1938 27 January: Reich minister of war Blomberg resigns, and Hitler sacks Wehrmacht commander in chief Fritsch. **4 February:** Hitler appoints himself commander in chief of the Wehrmacht, dissolves the War Ministry, and appoints von Ribbenstrop foreign minister. **5 February:** Hitler announces his government and military shakeup to military leaders and then at what would be the final meeting of the cabinet. **12 February:** Hitler meets Austrian chancellor Schuschnigg at the Berghof and forces him to legalize the activities of Austrian Nazis and appoint the pro-Nazi Arthur Seyss-Inquart as interior minister. **12 March:** German troops enter Austria, and Hitler signs the Law for the Reunification with Austria with the German Reich the next day. **28 March:** Hitler orders Sudeten German Party leader Konrad Henlein to make a series of unacceptable demands on the government of Czechoslovakia regarding the status of the German ethnic minority in the Sudetenland. **April:** With Hitler's encouragement, Goebbels launches a campaign aimed at driving Jews out of Berlin. **2 May:** Hitler pays a state visit to Italy, and Mussolini offers a verbal promise of Italian neutrality should Germany and Czechoslovakia go to war. **20 May:** The Czech government orders a partial mobilization, and Hitler appears to back down in the face of British and French warnings. **28 May:** Hitler meets with German military leaders and top diplomats and demands a quick victory over Czechoslovakia, followed by an attack on Western Europe. **30 May:** Hitler signs a war plan for attack on Czechoslovakia (Case Green). **18 August:** Hitler accepts Chief of the General Staff Ludwig Beck's resignation and replaces him with Franz Halder. **6 September:** German diplomat Theo Kordt holds a secret meeting with Lord Halifax and Harold Wilson and claims Hitler could be removed by a network of German conservative nationalists if Britain pledged to defend Czechoslovakia. **6–13 September:** There is a party rally in Nuremberg. **15 September:** British prime minister Neville Chamberlain meets with Hitler in the Berghof to resolve the crisis over Czechoslovakia. **22–23 September:** Chamberlain meets Hitler in Bad Godesberg, where Hitler demands the immediate annexation of the Sudetenland to Germany. **28 September:** Hitler agrees to more negotiations with Britain, France, and Italy. **29–30 September:** Chamberlain, Mussolini, and French prime minister and minister of defense Edouard Daladier meet with Hitler in Munich and agree to the German occupation of the Sudetenland to begin 1 October. **9 November:** Hitler authorizes a nationwide pogrom following the shooting of a German diplomat in Paris by a Polish Jew on 7 November. **10 November:** Hitler delivers a secret speech ordering the German population be prepared for war.

1939 7 January: Construction of a new Reich chancellery in Berlin is completed. **20 January:** Hitler fires economics minister and Reichsbank director Hjalmar Schacht. **30 January:** Hitler uses the occasion of his annual speech to the Reichstag to link "international Jewish financiers" with the outbreak of another world war, the result of which Hitler threatens would be the "annihilation of the Jewish race in Europe." **14 February:** In a speech in Hamburg, Hitler claims to have completed the work of national unity begun by Otto von Bismarck. **14 March:** Hitler meets with the Czech president and foreign minister in Berlin and compels them to agree to a German takeover. **15 March:** German troops enter Prague. **16 March:** Hitler signs a decree establishing the Protectorate of Bohemia and Moravia. **22 March:** Lithuania signs over control of Memel to Germany. **31 March:** Chamberlain issues a declaration of support for Polish territorial sovereignty in the House of Commons. **3 April:** Keitel issues a directive to the Wehrmacht to prepare for war. **13 April:** Daladier announces France has joined the Anglo–Polish mutual assistance pact. **28 April:** Hitler abrogates the Anglo–German Naval Agreement and the nonaggression pact with Poland. **14–19 May:** Hitler tours the Westwall fortifications. **22 May:** The Pact of Steel agreement is signed in Berlin. **23 May:** Hitler delivers a speech to military leaders demanding the acquisition of adequate "living space" within the following 10 to 15 years and articulates his plan for wars with Poland, Western Europe, and Britain. **20 August:** Hitler has a letter delivered to Joseph Stalin agreeing to the basic terms of a nonaggression pact. **21 August:** Stalin agrees to conclude a nonaggression pact. **22 August:** Hitler meets with German officers in the Berghof explaining the necessity of immediately launching a war against Poland. **23 August:** German and Soviet foreign ministers sign the nonaggression pact in Moscow. **31 August:** Hitler gives a final order for the invasion of Poland to begin the following day. **1 September:** German forces invade Poland. **27 September:** Germany and the Soviet Union sign a Treaty of Borders and Friendship. **2 October:** Warsaw is occupied by German forces. **6 October:** Hitler makes an offer of "peace" to Britain and France. **7 October:** Hitler appoints Himmler as Reich commissar for the Consolidation of German Nationhood. **9 October:** Hitler authorizes (in a note backdated to 1 September) the medical murder of physically and mentally handicapped people. **8 November:** A bomb in the Bürgerbräukeller beer hall in Munich set by Georg Elser, a carpenter acting alone, detonates shortly after Hitler delivers a speech, killing 8 and wounding 60. **23 November:** Hitler meets with military leaders and demands an expansion of the war to the West as soon as possible.

1940 **1 March:** Hitler authorizes the occupation of Denmark and Norway (Weserübung). **17 March:** Hitler selects Fritz Todt as Reich minister of munitions. **9 April:** The German invasion of Denmark and Norway begins. **10 May:** The attack on the Low Countries begins. **28 May:** Hitler approves Himmler's plan to transfer European Jews to Africa, and Madagascar becomes the target location; Belgium surrenders. **11 June:** Italy enters the war. **12 June:** Marshal Philippe Petain takes control of the French government and asks Germany for an armistice. **14 June:** Paris is occupied. **23 June:** Hitler tours Paris. **2 July:** Hitler orders the military to prepare for an invasion of Britain (Sea Lion). **1 August:** Hitler orders air and naval attacks on Great Britain. **25 August:** The first RAF raid on Berlin occurs. **14 September:** Hitler postpones the cross-channel invasion of the British Isles indefinitely. **27 September:** The Tripartite Pact is signed in Berlin. **23 October:** Hitler visits France, meets with Francisco Franco at Hendaye on the Franco–Spanish border, and fails to secure a Spanish pledge to declare war on Britain. **28 October:** Italian forces invade Greece from Albania, and the ensuing debacle forces Hitler to invade Greece the following April. **November:** Hitler orders the deportation of more than 150,000 Jews from the territory of Poland annexed to Germany to the General Government. **13 November:** Soviet foreign minister Molotov visits Berlin to discuss joining the Tripartite Pact. **20–24 November:** Hungary, Romania, and Slovakia join the Tripartite Pact. **18 December:** Hitler issues a war directive for the invasion of the Soviet Union.

1941 **Early January:** Hitler orders Reinhard Heydrich to devise a plan for the evacuation of all Jews from all German-controlled territory after the end of the war. **11 January:** Hitler orders the creation of what will become the Afrika Korps under the command of Erwin Rommel to prevent the British from routing Italian forces in Libya. **2 March:** German forces enter Bulgaria. **25 March:** Yugoslavia joins the Tripartite Pact, resulting in the overthrow of the Yugoslav government by pro-British officers and a decision by Hitler to invade the country. **30 March:** Hitler issues the Commissar Order in a meeting with his generals, confirmed by Keitel on 6 June. **6 April:** German forces attack Yugoslavia and Greece. **13 April:** The Japanese–Russian neutrality pact is signed. **30 April:** Hitler sets 22 June for the invasion of Russia (Operation Barbarossa). **10 May:** Rudolf Hess flies to Scotland on a self-proclaimed peace mission and is immediately arrested. **19 May:** OKW issues the "Guidelines for the Conduct for the Troops in Russia." **20 May–2 June:** The German operation to capture Crete from the British occurs. **4 and 6 June:** The Wehrmacht issues orders to troops to take extreme measures against soldiers and civilians in the forthcoming invasion of the Soviet Union. **22 June:** German forces invade the Soviet Union. **16–17 July:** Hitler outlines and puts in writing his plans for the administration of occupied eastern territories (Ostraum) to top officials. **Late July/early August:** SS Einsatzgruppen, police battalions, and other SS units begin executing Jews of all ages and both sexes. **31 July:** On Hitler's orders, Göring orders Heydrich to prepare a "comprehensive solution" to the "Jewish question in Europe." **18 August:** Hitler agrees to forcing Jews to wear yellow stars in public and, following public statements of protest by Catholic Church officials, orders a halt to the Euthanasia Program, though the killings continue. **1 September:** German Jews are required to display a cloth yellow star in public. **16–18 September:** Hitler orders the deportation of Jews from the "Old Reich" (Germany and Austria) and the Protectorate (Bohemia and Moravia) to ghettos in the occupied East. **19 September:** Kiev is captured by German forces. **2 October:** The German army's autumn offensives in Russia begin. **15 October:** The first wave of deportations begins. **8 December:** The Chelmno death camp in Poland begins operating. **11 December:** Hitler announces a declaration of war on the United States. **16 December:** Hitler prohibits any retreat on the eastern front, makes himself de facto commander in chief, and begins a major shakeup of the military's high command.

1942 20 January: Reinhard Heydrich convenes a meeting of SS and state officials (the Wannsee Conference) to discuss the future course of the "final solution." **9 February:** Hitler appoints Albert Speer Reich minister for armaments and munitions and head of the Todt Organization. **21 March:** Hitler appoints Fritz Sauckal general plenipotentiary for labor mobilization. **27 May:** Heydrich is injured in an attempted assassination in Prague and dies 4 June. **21 June:** Rommel captures Tobruk. **28 June:** The first summer offensive in Russia begins, with a second launched on 3 July. **16 July:** Hitler moves his eastern front headquarters to Ukraine. **8 September:** Hitler dismisses General Wilhelm von List as commander of Army Group A and makes himself commander. **8 November:** Allied forces land on the coasts of Morocco and Algeria. **11 November:** Hitler orders the occupation of southern France. **19 November:** The Red Army launches a winter offensive against German forces in the South and quickly encircles the German Sixth Army around Stalingrad.

1943 31 January–2 February: Stalingrad falls to Soviet forces. **18 February:** Goebbels give a "total war" speech in Berlin. **13 April:** The Propaganda Ministry announces the discovery of mass graves of Polish officers executed by the Soviet NKVD in 1940. **19 April:** The Warsaw ghetto uprising begins. **13 May:** 250,000 German and Italian soldiers surrender in Tunisia. **31 May:** Admiral Dönitz informs Hitler that German naval forces in the Atlantic have been forced to retreat to secure waters. **9 July:** The German offensive in the Kursk region opens (Operation Citadel). **10 July:** Allied forces land in Sicily (Operation Husky).

12 July: Hitler calls off the attack on Kursk. **24 July–3 August:** The RAF attacks Hamburg (Operation Gamorrah). **25 July:** Mussolini is deposed by the Fascist Grand Council and King Victor Emanuel III. **20 August:** Hitler appoints Himmler interior minister. **8 September:** Italy surrenders. **15 September:** After being freed from prison by German commandos, Mussolini announces establishment of the Social Republic of Italy, to be based at Saló. **November–March 1944:** An RAF bombing campaign targets Berlin.

1944 19 March: German forces begin the occupation of Hungary. **April–July:** Hungarian Jews are deported to Auschwitz. **4 June:** Allied forces capture Rome. **6 June:** Allied forces invade France at Normandy. **22 June:** The Soviet offensive against the German Army Group Center begins. **20 July:** A bomb planted by Colonel Claus Schenk von Stauffenberg at Hitler's East Prussian headquarters (the Wolf's Lair) detonates but fails to kill Hitler. **25 August:** Paris is liberated, and Romania declares war on Germany. **September:** German V-2 rocket attacks on Britain, France, and Belgium begin. **8 September:** Bulgaria declares war on Germany. **17 September:** American and British forces launch unsuccessful attempt to cross the Rhine River from the Netherlands (Operation Market Garden). **15 October:** Hungary is lost to Germany as an ally. **16 December:** The final German offensive of the war begins in the Ardennes, with the objective of capturing Antwerp and dividing American and British forces.

1945 15–16 January: Hitler moves his headquarters to Berlin. **3 February:** Hitler moves to a bunker complex beneath the garden of the Reich chancellery. **19 March:** Hitler issues the Nero Order for the destruction of infrastructure on German territory. **20 March:** Hitler makes his last official public appearance in the garden of the Reich chancellery to meet decorated Hitler Youth members. **28–29 April:** Hitler and Eva Braun are married in the bunker. **29 April:** Hitler dictates his "political testament." **30 April:** Hitler commits suicide in the bunker.

Introduction

Given Hitler's significance to the history of the modern world, it is easy to forget that he spent more than half his life in total obscurity. As a young person growing up in Upper Austria, he expressed a desire to become an artist, an inclination his father would hear none of. Adolf was much closer to his mother, who indulged his fantasies about a future as a great artist. But he remained indifferent at best to formal education, and as he dreamed of designing great public buildings or composing operas, he never developed the dedication and discipline necessary to learn how to do any of these things.

At an early age, Hitler exhibited the traits of a narcissistic personality. He lacked empathy and spent a great deal of time dwelling in a fantasy world. He had a single friend and demonstrated little interest in women. Hitler did become entranced with Vienna after a short visit in 1906. He moved to the imperial capital in September 1907 with the intention of being accepted to its great fine arts academy. His first rejection was followed by the death of his mother in December, a deeply traumatic experience for the 19-year-old Adolf. Rejected by the academy a second time, he eked out an existence on Vienna's margins, living on a modest inheritance, with loans from family members he otherwise kept at a distance, and by selling picture postcards he had painted.

Hitler had opinions about everything, but there is no evidence that he thought about a career as a politician while living in Vienna. Though he was awed by the city's grand neoclassical architecture and attended the theater as often as he could, he otherwise despised its multiethnic character, a reflection of his wider hatred of the sprawling empire. What passed for his political belief system was standard pan-German nationalism fueled by a bundle of personal resentments and insecurities and the belief that he possessed unrecognized artistic genius. Contrary to his claims in *Mein Kampf*, he did not become an anti-Semite in his Vienna years, despite the fact that the city was a cesspool of anti-Jewish sentiment.

Nor was there anything particularly remarkable about his military service. Though he had been deemed unfit for service in Austria, he enlisted enthusiastically in the German Imperial Army in August 1914 after moving to Munich a year earlier. He served for four years on the western front as a dispatch runner, a position that involved some physical danger but not of the kind faced by frontline troops. Throughout the war, he remained a loner. He received two decorations but actively resisted promotion. There is no evidence of political radicalization in any direction, and he got on well with his numerous Jewish comrades. When he later became a politician and boasted that he had been just a simple soldier, for once he was telling the truth.

Hitler claims in *Mein Kampf* that upon hearing of the armistice while convalescing in a military hospital, he experienced a quasi-religious revelation that he was destined to enter politics; this is nonsense. While there's no reason to doubt that he was as shocked at the news as anyone, the fact was his life had no more direction at that point than it did four years earlier. He had a limited formal education; no practical skills; and no close family, marriage prospects, or friends. Demobilization would have thrown him, at 29 years of age, back into his marginal existence. It was the first year after the war that proved to be the crucial one for Hitler, mainly because he was stationed in Munich after his discharge from the hospital.

The Bavarian capital city was a hothouse for political radicalism on the Left and Right. In February 1919, radical socialists established a "soviet republic," which held on until May, when it was overthrown by the army and right-wing paramilitaries. At the same time, dozens of small Far-Right groups sprung up around the city, its members energized by the armistice, Germany's revolutionary turmoil, and the shock of the new democratic government's ratification of the Versailles Treaty. In these months, a handful of military officers, middle-class professionals, veterans, exiles from revolutionary Russia, and a smattering of wealthy elites dominated the scene, giving some of the new groups access to money, weapons, and allies in the police and judiciary. It was a fractured and fractious scene, but three main objectives predominated: overturn the republic, destroy the Left, and avenge the humiliation and supposed betrayal of the armistice and treaty.

Hitler's route to one of these new parties, the German Workers' Party, was determined mainly by chance. Between February and May 1919, he served both the socialist-dominated government and the short-lived soviet republic. But there is no evidence that he was committed to anything more than doing what was necessary to stay in the army. Hitler still had no clear political ideology beyond a hazy, resentment-fueled nationalism. What was crucial was that after the fall of the soviet republic, he was mentored by Far-Right army officers who sensed he could be an effective anti-Bolshevik influence on returning soldiers.

After attending a training course that exposed him to prominent Far-Right thinkers, Hitler was ordered to attend a meeting of the German Workers' Party in September 1919. The party was created to draw working-class Germans away from the Left and to the nationalist cause. Renamed the National Socialist German Workers' Party (NSDAP) in February 1920, its program called for a strong national state, creation of a "greater Germany," rejection of the Versailles Treaty, the expansion of "living space," and a citizenship law based on race in which Jews were to be excluded. Much of the platform involved demands for the creation of a kind of socialism in which the state ensures the well-being of citizens. The nationalization of large-scale industries and some kind of land reform were intended to curtail the individualistic excesses of free-market capitalism.

Hitler had found his political home, though his initial impulse was not that he would become its leader or a leader of any kind. Rather, as he put it, he would be a "drummer"—a follower who would attract others to the cause. His "drum" would be his voice. Hitler could talk. As a young person, he had developed the habit of subjecting the very few people who could tolerate being around him to long monologues, mainly about history, art, and politics. Articulate and intelligent but also deeply insecure, he could nonetheless appear to be supremely self-confident in the rightness of his views on anything and everything. He developed a dramatic style of public speaking, with both the form and content of his tirades proving effective at whipping up audiences into gales of self-righteous anger. Soon he was one of the party's most popular speakers and then its leader. But the impact Hitler's speaking abilities had on early recruits to the party, particularly those who became his most important supporters, should not be overstated. In every important case, men (and they were all men) like Rudolf Hess, Alfred Rosenberg, Martin Bormann, Hermann Göring, Heinrich Himmler, and Joseph Goebbels were already deeply immersed in the culture of the Far Right when they first met him.

The army officers who mentored him in 1919 and the rabidly anticommunist and anti-Semitic exiles from the Bolshevik dictatorship were very important to shaping his ideology. The lectures by right-wing thinkers he attended that year also left an impression on him. It was in this immediate postwar period that Hitler channeled his resentments into a coherent worldview. At its core was pan-German nationalism and racist imperialism. Though in the early 1920s he briefly flirted with the idea of an anti-French alliance between Germany and a post-Bolshevik Russia, he soon embraced what would be an unshakable belief in the necessity of expanding German territory eastward to create "living space" for the German "race."

At the center of his conception of humanity divided hierarchically into races were the Jews. Of the world's races, he considered Jews to be the most inferior—and dangerous. Jews—all Jews—were part of a global conspiracy to take over the world and exterminate the German race. The center of this supposed conspiracy was the Soviet Union, hence the use of the term *Judeo-Bolshevism*. But the conspiracy extended across Europe and Great Britain and to the United States. For Hitler and committed Nazi ideologues, Jews were not only behind communism but also finance capitalism in general and the governments of the world's liberal democracies. As early as September 1919, Hitler was advocating what he called the "uncompromising removal" of Jews from Germany. An all-or-nothing approach became his characteristic approach to politics and then war: Either the Jews would be removed from Germany, or they would destroy the German race. Either communism would be vanquished, or Germany would be destroyed. Either he would become Germany's leader, or nothing.

We can divide the period from the founding of the NSDAP in 1920 to Hitler's appointment as chancellor on 30 January 1933 into three periods. The first runs from 1919 to 1924. In this period, the Nazi Party was a small organization and insignificant as a factor in local and national politics. Then in 1922, Benito Mussolini staged the "march on Rome" and took power in Italy. Hitler set his sights on doing the same in Germany by staging a coup attempt in Munich that he believed would spread to Berlin. But it quickly collapsed, and Hitler and most of the conspirators were arrested. He faced the very serious charge of high treason and potentially a long, career-ending prison term.

Instead, he was sentenced to five years and spent only nine months in prison. With a sympathetic judge presiding over the courtroom, Hitler put his speaking abilities to effective use, and the publicity generated by the trial brought him national and international attention. The leniency with which Hitler and the insurrectionists were treated by the conservative nationalist Bavarian judiciary was of incalculable importance for the future. Had he received a sentence more in line with the magnitude of the crime he and his party had committed or had he been deported to Austria, his political career would have ended in ignominy and obscurity.

In Landsberg Prison, Hitler served his sentence in relatively comfortable conditions, spending his time receiving visitors, writing the first volume of his memoirs, and thinking about the party's future. He did not attempt to run the now-banned party from his prison cell, preferring instead to let it fall apart and rebuild it from the ground up once he was released. But his most important decision in Landsberg was to abandon the idea of a "march on Berlin" and seek a legal route to power. In the second half of the 1920s—the next major period in his ascent to power—Hitler established his absolute authority over the party, while its able organizers and propagandists built it up as the new, national, and socialist alternative to the Left and the traditional conservatives. Data from elections in the 1920s show unusually broad, if uneven, support for the NSDAP across multiple sectors of the electorate. Parallel to the legal path to power was intensifying violence, much of it initiated by the party's paramilitary wing, the Sturmabteilung (SA; Stormtroopers or Brownshirts). Here, Hitler's authority was less absolute than it was over the party. But the SA was a necessary tool of recruitment to the party and for maintaining ideological militancy within the "movement."

The mid-1920s were tough years for political radicalism on the right and the left. The economy had stabilized after a traumatic bout with hyperinflation, and the German government was negotiating revisions of the Versailles Treaty through patient diplomacy. Election results in these years reflected this stability, with both the radical Left and Right seemingly stuck on the margins. It would take a major crisis to propel Hitler and the NSDAP to the center of national politics and to put Hitler in the chancellor's office. The Great Depression hit Germany with particular ferocity, but the economic crisis alone does not account for the surge in popular support that made the NSDAP the single largest party in the Reichstag by the summer of 1932. The party had already established itself across the country as the only viable nationalist and non-Marxist socialist alternative to the fatally divided Left, the liberals, and the establishment Right.

The third period culminated in President Paul von Hindenburg's appointment of Hitler as chancellor on 30 January 1933. Despite the electoral landslide in July 1932, Hitler's and the party's prospects had darkened by the end of the year. That summer, Hitler lost the presidential election to Hindenburg, who then steadfastly refused to put Hitler in the chancellor's office. The party lost seats in the November elections, leading many to suspect that it had reached its peak of popularity. It was also running out of funds, and frustration among rank-and-file activists at Hitler's refusal to consider anything other than the chancellorship was mounting. When one of the party's most effective organizers, Gregor Strasser, resigned in December, Hitler told Joseph Goebbels that he was contemplating suicide.

Then in January, everything changed. The role of conservative nationalists was crucial. Facing a resurgent communist party and shrinking representation in the Reichstag, they needed Hitler and the Nazi Party to form a majority coalition in the Reichstag. The two sides disliked and distrusted each other. But the conservatives assumed that should the inexperienced Hitler be appointed chancellor, he would have to rely on the well-connected nationalist conservative elite, which would thus be able to control him. This was the single most catastrophic political miscalculation in modern history. At the end of the month, a handful of conservatives with access to Hindenburg convinced him to break the impasse by appointing Hitler chancellor. Hindenburg's assent required that conservatives dominate the new cabinet, including the new post of vice chancellor, with Nazis occupying only two positions other than the chancellor's office. The president retained his extensive executive powers.

The conservatives' misjudgment was not immediately apparent. The destruction of the Weimar Republic took place over the following three months. The most significant turning point came on the night of February 27–28, when a deranged, half-blind Dutch communist was arrested for setting the Reichstag building in Berlin on fire. Debate over who was really responsible has raged ever since, though a recent meticulous investigation by an American historian suggests very strongly that it was a Nazi operation. There's no evidence that Hitler was involved in the attack. Regardless, he and Goebbels proclaimed it to be the opening move in a communist attempt to seize power. They seized on the moment to lay the legal groundwork for Hitler's dictatorship through an emergency decree and the passage of an enabling act by a truncated Reichstag. The rights of citizens guaranteed by the constitution were suspended, the central government asserted its authority over the states, and the chancellor could now bypass the president and the Reichstag and rule by decree.

Accompanying this drama was a brutal crackdown on the left by the SA. In a matter of weeks, the single largest political organization in the world—the Socialist Party of Germany—along with its extensive network of affiliated organizations and informal milieus, was dismantled and dispersed. Independent labor unions were outlawed. The Communist Party of Germany was destroyed, its leaders driven into exile, killed, or imprisoned in the first concentration camps. By the summer, all non-Nazi political parties were outlawed.

At the same time, the new regime initiated the "coordination" of German society, in which the civil service and its vast array of nonstate institutions, associations, and clubs was to be aligned with Hitler's leadership and the party's ideology. The civil service at all levels was purged of socialists, anti-Nazi liberals, and most Jews. Huge new party-sponsored organizations replaced unions, farmers' organizations, professional associations, and youth groups. Only the military and the churches remained untouched by the process, though they were both already fundamentally conservative institutions whose members were willing to support the new regime. Coordination could not have taken place without the willing, often enthusiastic participation of Germany's elite and millions of ordinary Germans. They were motivated by a complex mixture of conviction, opportunism, and fear. But the new regime also had to deliver the country from the economic crisis, and full employment was achieved by 1935, though not without warping the economy and causing all manner of unsustainable dislocations.

In the summer of 1934, a form of coordination extended to the SA. Having served its purpose in the 1920s and early 1930s, the 4-million-man-strong paramilitary had become a dangerous liability. Its leader, the brutally capable Ernst Röhm, was determined to make the SA Germany's new army and to pursue the "socialism" in national socialism to a far greater extent than Hitler knew most Germans, including its business and industrial elites, would accept. In June 1934, Hitler had Röhm murdered and the SA neutralized. A number of prominent conservatives and Catholic political activists were also killed, sending an unmistakable message that Hitler had no intention of sharing power with anyone.

During and long after the years of Nazi rule, political theorists and historians characterized the regime as totalitarian in intention and form. Hitler stood at the apex of a system in which a growing number of often bloated and corrupt party organizations existed uneasily along with the established institutions of the state. The result was a great deal of inefficiency and waste. It was Hitler who held the system together by applying the "leadership principle," which he defined in *Mein Kampf* as "authority of every leader downwards and responsibility upwards." Officials were expected to replicate the principle in their own domains. With a good deal of authority delegated, subordinates were expected to "work toward the Leader," as one midlevel party official put it in 1934. Also crucial was a divide-and-rule strategy that encouraged subordinates to compete with each other for resources and access to him while making concerted opposition next to impossible. Hitler was anything but a weak or detached dictator, and he would intervene decisively when he felt it necessary. One result of this arrangement was the propensity of regime officials to pursue increasingly radical policies, an inclination that reached its deadliest extent in the Holocaust.

Maintaining his position as the undisputed leader of the party, the army, and German society required the creation of a "myth of the leader": a quasi-mystical bond between Hitler and "racially pure" Germans, who put their faith in him as the savior who would return the nation to greatness. Creating and maintaining the myth involved the meticulous management of Hitler's public image, a task to which the other-wise notoriously dilettantish Hitler devoted intense and sustained attention. The single most important visual expression of the myth of a unified Germany standing before its savior is Leni Riefenstahl's film of the 1934 party rally in Nuremberg, *Triumph of the Will*. Behind the myth was a narcissistic individual, devoid of empathy and the ability to form close personal connections to anyone and valuing unwavering loyalty above all else.

Hitler could not rule by decree, coercion, and propaganda alone. In the second half of the 1920s, the most significant divide within the party was over just how "socialist" a national socialist Germany should be. Nor was it enough to restore full employment, particularly when it was his intention to prepare for a war of conquest that most Germans did not want. The regime and its ideology had to offer something positive to Germans, especially the young and idealistic. What amounted to Nazi socialism was not state ownership of factories and farms but mass mobilization through party organizations: the German Labor Front for laborers, the National Food Estate for farmers, an extensive welfare system that relied on the work of millions of volunteers, and the Hitler Youth and League of German Girls for young people. While membership could be obligatory and non-party-approved alternatives banned, there is no question that Nazi socialism held genuine appeal for many Germans and, not least, provided many material benefits.

INTRODUCTION

Many non-Jewish Germans recalled the years from 1933 to 1940 as the regime's "good years." Without a doubt, this recollection was colored by the nightmare that followed. But there is much evidence to suggest that there is a good deal of truth behind the sentiment. The republic was unstable, and society was polarized politically. It was born in humiliating defeat and bracketed by two traumatizing economic crises. Crime, disorder, and political violence seemed—and to some extent actually was—rampant. Hitler had promised to return the nation to greatness, and for many, he had done so. The radical Left was destroyed, full employment was restored, and Hitler embarked on a series of unbroken diplomatic victories that shredded the widely despised Versailles Treaty. And for six years, he did it without taking the country to war. Most Germans were not terrorized by the Gestapo and never saw the inside of a concentration camp.

For most Germans, these years were "good" for two reasons. One was because they were relatively normal. People went to school and work and church, attended the cinema and the theater, took holidays, fell in and out of love, and started families. The other was that national socialism was new and future oriented. It was particularly appealing—at least for a few years—to the young. After 1945, it was common to hear the party's organizations disparaged as intrusive and corrupt, at best a negligible presence in people's daily lives. There is some truth in this. But these organizations served an important integrative social— as well as political and economic—function. The party was not an alien presence in the lives of most ordinary Germans.

This is not to dismiss the reality of the regime's brutal coercive side. Effective organized opposition became all but impossible. Professional life and what had been a vibrant civil society were now pervaded by the party. The Gestapo was extremely effective at rooting out pockets of opposition, not least because the relatively small organization could rely on the willingness of ordinary Germans to watch and denounce their neighbors. Though the vast majority of non-Jewish Germans never had any contact with the Gestapo, everyone knew it existed, and the regime publicized the existence of concentration camps.

National socialism was also defined by who was to be excluded. Communists were the regime's very first target. Another were those belonging to a broad, regime-defined category known as asocials, or people deemed to be "unhealthy" to the German racial national community, or Volksgemeinschaft. Vagrants, habitual criminals, homosexual men, and the "work shy" were among its most prominent members. Removal of asocials would fall to the Schutzstaffel (SS). The elimination of the SA as a major power base in 1934 opened the door for the ascent of the SS and its leader, Heinrich Himmler. He would forge the organization as a state within a state. By 1936, the SS controlled all of Germany's police forces, including the Gestapo. It also ran the expanding system of concentration camps. Himmler began to use the camps as more than a prison for political enemies and regime opponents. By filling them with asocials, they would be a key instrument for "purifying" the Volksgemeinschaft.

Also to be excluded were those with hereditary mental and physical handicaps. With Hitler's explicit authorization, the regime and Germany's medical and public health communities undertook the forced sterilization of 400,000 Germans and then the mass murder of perhaps 275,000 mentally and physically handicapped Germans and non-Germans. Some of the personnel and methods developed for the latter operation, notably the gassing of victims in fixed installations, were deployed in the Holocaust.

Jews remained the object of Hitler's deepest hatred. As early as 1919, he had articulated a vision of their "uncompromising" removal from Germany. It was also at this point that he advocated replacing what he called "emotional anti-Semitism" with an "anti-Semitism of reason," meaning one involving laws based on the pseudoscience of "racial hygiene." But he realized that both would have to coexist, thus foreshadowing the monstrous hybrid of bureaucratic rationality and sadistic violence that characterized the regime's anti-Jewish policies and later the Holocaust. Hitler pursued multiple "final solutions" to the "Jewish question." In the peacetime years, the regime tried to force Jews to leave Germany, mainly by applying forms of economic pressure and social segregation. But relocation abroad was extremely difficult, given the economic depression, immigration restrictions, and anti-Semitism. Regardless, more than half of Germany's 1933 population of 522,000 Jews left the country between 1933 and 1939, an exodus that resulted in the widest geographic dispersal of any single group of people in modern history. Hitler was closely involved with the development of every major anti-Jewish measure, including the nationwide pogrom in November 1938. But as with "coordination," anti-Jewish policies required the willing participation of the country's elite and millions of ordinary Germans, who proved willing to abandon their neighbors, employees, customers, physicians, lawyers, teachers, and friends.

Hitler was an empire builder, and the Nazi Empire, as historian Shelly Baranowski puts it, began at home. The creation of a Volksgemeinschaft—the domestic imperium—began with the elimination of the Left and the targeting of asocials, the handicapped, and the Jews for removal from the otherwise "racially healthy" German national body. But Hitler always intended to extend the race-based empire far beyond Germany's borders. And he was in a hurry, perpetually afraid that he would die at a relatively young age and convinced that if he did not push the pace of rearmament, then the country's enemies would become too strong to overcome. His decision in March 1936 to send troops into the Rhineland in violation of the Versailles Treaty's terms was the turning point. The victory gave Hitler the initiative, both with the Wehrmacht's commanders and the British and French governments. Hitler's generals were right to be nervous about the risk the outnumbered Germans were taking, and had France and Great Britain acted decisively to enforce the treaty, Hitler would have suffered a humiliating setback and possibly have faced a coup by the military. Yet he estimated, correctly, that the Western Allies would not put up a fight, even one with relatively small risks for their own side.

Greatly emboldened, Hitler accelerated the diplomatic revolution that would lead directly to a general European war in 1939: a pact with Italy, the annexation of Austria, the dismemberment of Czechoslovakia, a nonaggression pact with the Soviet Union, and a brutal invasion of Poland. The main target was always the Soviet Union, but France and Great Britain would have to be taken out of the war first. With the defeat of the French army in just six weeks in 1940, Hitler achieved his single greatest military victory. He expected the British to submit, ideally without fighting, but here he failed. Undeterred by Winston Churchill's determination to fight to the end and by the increasing likelihood that the United States would soon enter the war on England's side, Hitler accelerated preparations for Operation Barbarossa, the single largest military operation of its kind in history. The Wehrmacht and the SS imported on a massive scale the brutality of modern colonial wars. For Hitler and Himmler, the objective was not only to destroy the Soviet system but also to clear out vast expanses of European Russia and Ukraine in preparation of the settlement of millions of German farmer-warriors. In the process, millions of non-Germans would be worked and starved to death.

The war in the East consumed Hitler in the last years of his life. Beginning in the summer of 1941, he lived mainly in his East Prussian headquarters—the Wolf's Lair—and largely disappeared from public view. Managing domestic affairs was left to Martin Bormann and Hans Lammers. The Führer myth began to lose its mystique and appeal among Germans, a process that only accelerated with the intensification of the Allies' strategic bombing campaign and the defeat at the battle for Stalingrad in the winter of 1942 and 1943. For all but the most deluded, it was not loyalty to Hitler that explains the tenacity of German soldiers and civilians alike in the war's last year but habits of obedience, hope for a miraculous turnaround, desperation, and not least the increasing willingness of the state to execute deserters on the spot and terrorize the populace.

It is easy to conclude that once Barbarossa failed and the United States entered the war, Allied victory was inevitable. But given the extent of German control over Europe through 1941, this victory would be hard fought; extremely costly; and achieved on multiple land, air, and sea fronts stretching from Moscow to the shores of the US Eastern Seaboard and from Norway to North Africa. The most important was the eastern front, where despite its initial losses, the extraordinary military-civilian mobilization in the Soviet Union produced the Grand Alliance's single greatest victory.

Given Hitler's disdain for his military commanders and the increasingly grim outlook for Germany's war effort, it can be difficult to understand why he was not removed by the only institution in a position to do so during the war: the army. But Hitler's generals shared his visceral anticommunism, his conception of Slavic peoples as subhuman, and to at least a certain degree his anti-Semitism. Its leadership had supported—albeit not without sporadic hesitancy—the drive to war and were responsible for the early victories. The Wehrmacht leadership, officer corps, and rank and file were deeply complicit in the vast crimes committed against combatants and civilians in the Soviet Union and the Balkans. Even the very few who eventually turned against Hitler did so only long after they had overseen the conquest of much of Europe and North Africa.

Devotion to duty and the oath they had taken to Hitler personally cannot be ruled out as explanations for their continued loyalty. One of the chief conspirators in the plot to assassinate Hitler in July 1944 predicted that whoever acted against him would be remembered in Germany as a traitor. For a long time after the war, he was right, as a significant number of Germans held negative views of the conspirators well into the 1950s. Bribery with gifts of money and property also played a role, as did fear for their lives and those of their families. In the war's desperate final year, when the Wehrmacht suffered most of its losses, the fight was less for Hitler and more for Germany's survival.

The war for "living space" involved a war against the Jews. The two were inseparable in Hitler's mind. That he ordered the November 1938 pogrom as war approached was no coincidence, and just over two months later, he proclaimed in public that if "international Jewry" was responsible for starting another world war, then the result would be the "extermination of the Jewish race." Far more than a single speech was involved in announcing and justifying a genocide to the German public, the Nazi Party, the military, and the SS. In an extensive verbal, textual, and visual propaganda campaign spanning the war's entire duration, the regime presented Jews as an active force in history—a force intent on destroying Germany—and not just a passive obstacle to the expansion of Germany's "living space."

In addition to ideology, geography and the unforeseen course of the war would be the two most significant factors shaping the course of the Holocaust. Nearly 10 million Jews lived in Europe in 1933, the vast majority in Poland and the Soviet Union—precisely where Hitler intended to establish "living space." The unexpected failure to defeat Britain and the Soviet Union in 1940 and 1941 meant European Jews could not be deported en masse to Madagascar or somewhere beyond the Ural Mountains. They would have to be killed in place, first by firing squads and then in purpose-built fixed installations. Much of the initiative for the deportations and killings came from officials on the ground in Eastern Europe and German-occupied Soviet Union. And it must be remembered that the Holocaust was a pan-European attack on a vulnerable minority. Without the extensive collaboration of millions of non-Germans, the genocide could not have been perpetrated the way it was. But Hitler was always the main driver in every major and many of the minor stages of the war against the Jews.

Hitler had threatened suicide at multiple crisis points in his life, dating back at least as early as the 1923 putsch attempt. In the last days of April 1945, he calmly and methodically made the decision to kill himself. For some time, he had accepted that total victory was out of reach. But he waited until the last minute to concede that the war was irretrievably lost. Consumed with self-pity as the Red Army closed in on his underground bunker complex in Berlin and as most of his highest-level officials deserted him, he ended his life believing all of Germany had failed him and was thus deserving of its fate.

The Dictionary

A

ADOLF HITLER, SEIN LEBEN, SEINE REDEN (ADOLF HITLER: HIS LIFE AND HIS SPEECHES). Hitler's first book was published in 1923 under the name of aristocrat and admirer Adolf Victor von Koerber. It was confirmed to have been written by Hitler in 2016. Intended to raise his visibility among and appeal to conservative nationalists, it contained a selection of Hitler's speeches and a short autobiographical sketch.

Hitler was moved to publish the book that year because of a dilemma. While he had become the leader of the **National Socialist German Workers' Party** (Nazi Party; Nationalsozialistische Deutsche Arbeiterpartei; NSDAP) and a popular speaker and was coming to see himself as a savior-like figure destined to lead Germany, he was still largely unknown, even in Bavaria. Part of the problem was that few people knew what he looked like. He had imposed a ban on photographs of himself, possibly to evade deportation to **Austria** or because he feared being assassinated or out of a desire to be able to drift about Bavaria unrecognized.

By the summer of 1923, he realized a radical change was necessary if he had any hope of achieving his ambitions. First, he hired photographer **Heinrich Hoffmann** to take a series of conventional headshots in which he dressed himself in civilian clothes and had postcards of his image distributed around Munich. Then he decided to publish some of his speeches in a book that would include a brief autobiography. His intended readers were not his existing supporters but conservative nationalists who knew little or nothing about him. Indeed, his desire to boost his visibility and acceptability among them led him to seek out an established conservative writer without connections to the Nazi Party. That person would have to agree to appear as the book's author.

Erich Ludendorff introduced Hitler to what seemed to be the perfect match. A near contemporary of Hitler's, Koerber was an aristocrat, a decorated **World War I** veteran, and a published author and journalist of some repute who was sympathetic to the idea of a rejuvenated conservative nationalism. His militant anti-Bolshevism and conspiratorial racialist anti-Semitism comported with that of Hitler (*see* JEWS).

The book was published by the Far-Right Deutscher Volksverlag (German People's Press) in Munich. Its cover featured a simple sketch of Hitler's face based on one of Hoffmann's photographs. As it was banned almost immediately, the book did not have its intended effect. But it is important for what it reveals about how Hitler perceived himself and his future at that moment. Using repeated references to the New Testament and comparing himself to Jesus, he presented himself as Germany's savior but not as its only possible leader. He knew he needed the support of the conservative nationalist establishment and that the far-better-known Ludendorff was at that moment the symbolic leader of the Far Right. Therefore, Hitler imagined leading Germany with Ludendorff. *See also* FÜHRER MYTH (FÜHRER MYTHOS); *MEIN KAMPF* (*MY STRUGGLE*); RELIGION.

AFRICA. When Hitler came to power, nearly the entire African continent was under the control of Great Britain, **France**, Belgium, **Italy**, Spain, and Portugal. Germany was among these states until the victors stripped it of all its colonies after **World War I**. Some **pan-German** and other right-wing ideologues demanded the restoration of lost colonies along with expansion into Eastern Europe and Russia. Though Hitler's vision of empire was directed mainly at the latter, he was attuned to Africa's **economic** and strategic value. In practice, however, his foreign policy and wartime actions there were largely reactive.

France's defeat in June 1940 proved to be the turning point. Hitler wanted **Francisco Franco** to declare war on Britain and needed his cooperation to construct airfields and naval bases in Spanish-controlled territories. But he refused to offer Franco control of French Morocco. Doing that would have endangered Hitler's position with France. His decisive military victory there notwithstanding, Hitler could not get the Vichy regime to commit to supporting an attack on Britain unless he offered the French more territory at the expense of Spain and Italy. And while France's North African colonies sided with Vichy, the French Camaroons and French Equitorial Africa (today Chad, the Central African Republic, part of the Republic of the Congo, and Gabon) allied with the Free French, thus denying Germany access to supplies of gold and other crucial raw materials. Belgian colonial officials made sure stores of similarly crucial riches in the Congo never fell into German hands.

Benito Mussolini's ambitions presented another problem. Through no actions of Hitler's own, Italy's invasion of Abyssinia in 1935 had worked to his advantage, as it helped sever Italy from the Western powers. But Mussolini was also determined to dominate the wider Mediterranean, also at the expense of French holdings. After Hitler excluded his ally from participating in the armistice-signing ceremony at Compiegne on 22 June 1940, Mussolini sent troops into Greece from Albania, a blunder that required a German military bailout. Italian incompetence also required Hitler's intervention in North Africa. In December 1940, a crack Anglo–Indian force managed, despite being vastly outnumbered, to halt an Italian invasion of Egypt from Libya. Meanwhile, the British navy inflicted severe damage on the Italian fleet in the Mediterranean. The end of Mussolini's imperial venture in Africa came in April and May 1941 after British-led African troops liberated Abyssinia, Eritrea, and Italian Somaliland in quick succession. *See also* AFRICA; BALKANS.

A deeply disappointed Hitler dispatched one of his most capable generals, **Erwin Rommel**, to Libya to regain control of North Africa. Rommel nearly succeeded until his **Afrika Korps** was defeated decisively at the second **Battle of El-Alamein** in November 1942. In the last days of this crucial engagement, Allied forces landed in Morocco and Algeria (**Operation Torch**), and by the following June, the Germans had been driven out of North Africa for good.

Hitler considered Africans to be subhuman and had no regard for or knowledge of African cultures. And he was hardly alone in viewing the presence of African soldiers in French uniform deployed on German soil after the First World War a particularly intolerable humiliation. In 1940, the murderous nature of Nazi ideology combined with the desire to avenge this perceived racial transgression led directly to the massacre by German forces of at least 1,500 African soldiers then serving in the French army.

Nazi Germany's greatest impact on the fate of Africa turned out to be an indirect one. By 1945, some 200,000 subjects of France's African colonies served in the Free French Army, making a contribution to Allied victory that remains largely unknown and unacknowledged in the West. But it was never forgotten in Africa. British, French, Dutch, and Belgian officials, by contrast, having no intention of abandoning their nations' colonies, very much wanted to forget their dependence on subjugated peoples of color. Grudging acknowledgment came in the form of half-hearted and unserious reform schemes that could never have salvaged the moral, human, and environmental wreckage of imperialism. Making matters worse for the colonizers was the fact that Allied victory had been ensured by the combined might of the Soviet Union and the **United States**, two states propounding their own versions of anti-imperialism. However flawed and hypocritical these were, Moscow and Washington were unwilling to see the status quo restored. From the perspective of colonial subjects, millions of whom had toiled, sacrificed, and fought to ensure Allied victory, rhetoric about a great contest between democracy and fascism was meaningless unless it also led to their liberation. The expectations and resistance of colonized peoples to the reimposition of foreign rule led to a great deal more bloodshed, making it difficult to pinpoint when the Second World War really ended.

AFRIKA KORPS (AFRICA CORPS). On 11 January 1941, Hitler ordered the creation of the Afrika Korps to serve as a kind of **Wehrmacht** fire brigade. Its mission was to prevent the loss of Axis control over North **Africa** to the British. The previous September, **Italian** forces launched an attack on British-controlled Egypt from Libya. Hitler had placed General **Erwin Rommel** in command of the nascent Afrika Korps, the nucleus of which landed in Tripoli in February 1941 as a light armored division. Joined by three Italian army corps and a German tank division, Rommel drove east toward Egypt, placing the Australian-controlled port city of Tobruk under siege. In January 1942, a British counterattack pushed him back into Libya, but Rommel, having received reinforcements from Germany, led a counterattack and drove the British back to Egypt. By June, German and Italian forces were less than 100 miles from the Nile Delta. That month, Hitler promoted Rommel to field marshal.

The tide turned again in September, when the British Eighth Army under General Bernard Montgomery stopped Rommel's advance and then forced him to retreat after the second **Battle of El-Alamein** ended in early November. Rommel and the Afrika Korps began the long retreat out of Egypt, across Libya, and into Tunisia, where it decimated inexperienced **United States** forces at Kasserine Pass. Along the way, German forces lashed out at **Jewish** communities in Libya and Tunisia, looting homes and dragooning men into forced labor.

Despite receiving some reinforcements from Egypt, the German presence in North Africa was coming to an end. Allied forces had landed in Morocco and Algeria (**Operation Torch**) just as El-Alamein ended. In May 1943, some 250,000 German and Italian troops surrendered to Allied forces in Tunisia. Rommel and his staff escaped. *See also* HOLOCAUST; SCHUTZSTAFFEL (PROTECTION SQUAD; SS).

AMANN, MAX (1891–1957). Born in Munich, Amann served as the staff sergeant at the headquarters of Hitler's regiment (*see* WORLD WAR I). After the war, Amann joined Aufbau (Reconstruction), a small right-wing group comprised of Russian émigrés and Germans. Immediately after Hitler achieved sole leadership of the **National Socialist German Workers Party** (Nazi Party; Nationalsozialistische Deutsche Arbeiterpartei; NSDAP) in July 1921, he asked Amann to manage the organization and its finances. A year later, he was put in charge of the party's publishing house, the Franz Eher Verlag. He became a member of Hitler's personal entourage, and they quickly developed a relationship of mutual respect and trust that lasted until Hitler's **suicide**.

Amann was arrested during the **Beer Hall Putsch**. He was supposed to have driven Hitler to **Austria** but could not reach **Ernst Hanfstaengl**'s home before Hitler was taken into custody. Though Hitler had put **Alfred Rosenberg** in charge of the party in his absence, he made Amann his deputy. He would help Hitler edit *Mein Kampf* and then have it published by Eher Verlag. Very importantly, he managed the book's royalties for Hitler, which would become substantial and make Hitler a wealthy man.

In the second half of the 1920s, Amann was focused on managing the party's business affairs. In November 1933, Hitler appointed him head of the Reich Association of German Newspaper Publishers and president of the Reich Press Chamber. In these positions, he played a central role in the dismantling of Germany's independent press and its consolidation under the total control of the Propaganda Ministry. By 1939, Amann had made Eher Verlag the world's single largest publishing concern. He enriched himself in the process. No other high-level official benefited more from the business dealings of the party and regime. This point was noted by the denazification tribunal that sentenced him to 10 years of hard labor and stripped him of his assets and pension rights. An impoverished Amann died in Munich in 1957. *See also* COORDINATION; DIETRICH, OTTO (1897–1952); GOEBBELS, JOSEPH PAUL (1897–1945).

ANGLO–GERMAN NAVAL AGREEMENT (1935). In March 1935, Hitler announced Germany's **rearmament** and the reintroduction of conscription. In response, British, **French**, and **Italian** officials convened in Stresa, Italy, a month later and confirmed their governments' joint commitment to upholding the provisions of the Pact of Locarno (1925). This treaty was supposed to guarantee the sanctity of Germany's western borders and the demilitarization of the **Rhineland**. The proclamation from Stresa did not seem to bother Hitler very much. But it was followed immediately by a **League of Nations** condemnation of his decision to reintroduce conscription and signs that the French and Soviets would soon conclude a Pact of Mutual Assistance, which they did on 2 May.

Within a few weeks, the much-trumpeted Stresa Front evaporated. Hitler had assessed it correctly as nothing more than a piece of paper. It was done in by the speedy conclusion of an agreement between London and Berlin on the relative size of the British and German navies. On 21 May, Hitler delivered his second "peace speech" to the Reichstag, in which he denied any intention of annexing **Austria**, criticized the new Franco–Soviet pact, and tried to assure British listeners that all Germany wanted was an air force of comparable size and a navy limited to only 35 percent of Britain's in terms of tonnage. The British admiralty had already taken to the idea of an agreement, and Hitler had expressed his interest to Lord Privy Seal Anthony Eden and Foreign Minister Sir John Simon in Berlin in March. **Joachim von Ribbentrop** was given a pompous special title and sent to London in early June to begin negotiations. Despite Ribbentrop's seemingly incompetent performance—he opened the negotiations by laying out Berlin's final position—the British agreed to Hitler's terms in two days' time and without consulting its allies. The admiralty's eagerness to seize the chance to limit the size of Germany's navy won over the cabinet.

The deal, concluded on 18 June, limited German naval construction to exactly what Hitler had demanded: 35 percent of Britain's, with an allowance for parity in the size of the submarine fleet. Ribbentrop, perhaps embellishing, wrote later that Hitler proclaimed it the happiest day of his life. Regardless, the pact was without question a major diplomatic victory for Hitler. It rendered both Stresa and Locarno meaningless and pounded a very large nail into the **Versailles Treaty**. Hitler had no intention of honoring the naval pact's terms and angrily abrogated it unilaterally on 28 April 1939 in response to the announcement of Britain's security guarantee to **Poland**. In retrospect, the pact marked the beginning of Hitler's diplomatic revolution in Europe. He would experience no more major diplomatic setbacks before the invasion of Poland. *See also* AUSTRIA; CZECHOSLOVAKIA CRISIS (1938–1939); NAZI–SOVIET NONAGGRESSION PACT (MOLOTOV–RIBBENTROP PACT; 1939); SPANISH CIVIL WAR (1936–1939).

ANTI-COMINTERN PACT (1936). The year 1936 was crucial in Hitler's diplomatic revolution. It began with the remilitarization of the **Rhineland** in March and accelerated with the decision to aid **Francisco Franco**'s rebellion in **Spain** in July and much improved relations between Germany and **Italy**, which **Benito Mussolini** declared represented an "Axis" in a speech in Milan on 1 November. On 25 November, Germany and **Japan** concluded a pact that publicly confirmed the two nations' mutual interest in opposing the Communist International (Comintern). Its most important element was contained in a secret protocol: Both pledged not to aid the Soviet Union should it attack either signatory. Italy joined the following year.

Negotiations between Germany and Japan had in fact begun in January 1935. **Joachim von Ribbentrop** dispatched a well-connected intermediary to Tokyo, where he found officials receptive to the idea of driving a wedge between Germany and China and possibly giving Japan a free hand in a war with the Soviet Union. Turbulence in Japanese politics delayed finalizing the pact until the fall of 1936. In August 1939, Tokyo renounced the pact in the wake of the **Nazi–Soviet Nonaggression Pact** but agreed to join a **Tripartite Pact** a year later.

Hitler's determination at that moment to connect with Japan—one that required him to declare the blood of the Japanese to be of similar quality to that of the Aryan—was not to the liking of Foreign Minister **Konstatin von Neurath** nor to Reichsminister of **Economics Hjalmar Schacht** nor to then **Luftwaffe** chief **Hermann Göring**, all of whom understood the importance to **rearmament** of raw materials from China. But Hitler was creating a parallel diplomatic establishment using the largely incompetent but toadying and ambitious Ribbentrop as a kind of shadow foreign minister.

While Germany, Italy, and Japan remained the pact's core members, it was expanded in late November 1941 to include **Bulgaria**, Croatia, Denmark, Finland, **Hungary**, **Romania**, Slovakia, and Spain.

APPEASEMENT. Hitler's dismemberment of **Czechoslovakia** in March 1939 followed by the nonaggression pact with the Soviet Union and the invasion of **Poland** fundamentally changed the meaning of the word *appeasement*. Prior to the crises of 1939 and the outbreak of a second general European war, appeasement was a tool of diplomacy wielded by British diplomats to resolve simmering conflicts before they boiled over into armed conflict. In Europe in the second half of the 1930s, it entailed a redress of German grievances arising out of the postwar settlement, grievances that most British officials viewed as legitimate. Though certainly not the only one, **Winston Churchill** was the most important and prescient critic of the policy.

What motivated Prime Minister Neville Chamberlain to pursue appeasement was its past successes in negotiations with other states and his understanding of the dilemma his country faced. Massive new expenditures on armaments were impossible, yet Great Britain's empire was under increasing threat from within (in the form of independence movements, especially in India) and from without (the growth of **Japanese**, **Italian**, and German power and imperial ambition). Making matters worse in 1937 and 1938 was a great deal of understandable uncertainty about allies, beginning with the nations of the British Commonwealth but more importantly **France**, the Soviet Union, and the **United States**. As for the latter three, France was deeply and dangerously divided, **Joseph Stalin** could not seem to execute his military commanders quickly enough, and had isolated itself in the Western Hemisphere.

Chamberlain inaugurated appeasement in mid-November 1937 by dispatching Edward Wood, Lord Halifax, a trusted member of his cabinet and an experienced diplomat, to Germany for an informal discussion of the international situation with Hitler. In a tense meeting at the **Berghof**, Halifax indicated that his country's government was open to satisfying Germany's demands regarding **Austria**, **Czechoslovakia**, and the **Polish** corridor if this could be done without generating crises that would lead to war. The British aristocrat, who met other military and party leaders during his visit, returned to London optimistic about the prospects of avoiding war over Eastern Europe. But Hitler sensed weakness and accelerated plans for an attack on Czechoslovakia (Case Green). Around the same time, Chamberlain's cabinet decided that should a war break out in Europe, Britain would not deploy an expeditionary force to France. Defense of the British Isles, the high seas, and the empire would be the priority.

The annexation of Austria in March 1938 elicited nothing more than verbal protests from London and Paris. It was, after all, a German-speaking nation in which the majority of its inhabitants seemed to have supported the move. Czechoslovakia was another matter. A successful attack on that country by Germany would alter the balance of power in

Europe. For France, it would be a test of its commitment to the independence of Eastern Europe's new states. For Stalin, it would bring Germany closer to the Soviet Union's borders and render Poland even more vulnerable than it already was. In May, intelligence reports suggested that Germany was preparing for an attack that month, leading the British ambassador in Berlin to warn German foreign minister **Joachim von Ribbentrop** that his country would be forced to respond. When an invasion did not take place, it appeared to Chamberlain that Hitler had backed down.

Infuriated, Hitler again accelerated plans for an invasion. He sensed correctly that Britain and France would not go to war over Czechoslovakia. Stalin's ability to act was constrained by the unwillingness of the Polish and **Romanian** governments to grant transit rights to Soviet forces. To Hitler's intense displeasure, war over his demands for the German-majority Sudetenland region in September 1938 and then the German occupation of Prague the following March was averted by diplomacy. Chamberlain traveled to Germany twice in September to meet with Hitler, and when it appeared that the limits of Britain's willingness to indulge Hitler had been reached, **Benito Mussolini** stepped in at the last minute to broker a peaceful resolution. Czechoslovak government officials were strong-armed by the British and French to abandon the Sudetenland and then sidelined in the September meetings, in which the fate of their country was sealed. Chamberlain returned to England to a hero's welcome.

Defenders of appeasement then and since have argued that it was Britain's only realistic option under the circumstances at the time. The costs of large-scale rearmament, the refusal of Commonwealth states to support military action, and no popular appetite for going to war to (as Chamberlain put it) defend a far-away country about which British citizens knew little all made negotiations appear to be the prudent, if not necessary, course of action.

But even allowing for these constraints and for the benefit of hindsight, it is difficult to avoid the conclusion that appeasement was a monumental failure. British officials had assumed that beneath the crude bluster and theatrics, Hitler was a normal statesman with whom one could reason. He was nothing of the sort. And there were in fact alternatives to negotiation. French forces could have taken action in western Germany, if not in Czechoslovakia itself, and Stalin might well have deployed the Soviet air force. The Czechs and Slovaks were hardly without weapons of their own. The September meetings also short-circuited a plot by **Wehrmacht** officers to overthrow Hitler. Whether limited military action and a coup attempt would have succeeded is, of course, unknowable.

ARDENNES OFFENSIVE (DECEMBER 1944–JANUARY 1945). In August and September 1944, Anglo–American armies drove the **Wehrmacht** out of northern **France** and the Low Countries. But in September, they failed to break through to the North German Plain. Here and in **Italy** and on the eastern front, German forces were putting up ferocious resistance, dashing hopes among Allied leaders of ending the war that year.

As early as July, Hitler was sensing an opportunity for an all-or-nothing counterattack in the West. The target would be Antwerp, which became the most important port supplying Allied armies in the West. Antwerp's capture would be accompanied by the deployment of new weapons—rocket-propelled bombs and jet-propulsion aircraft—that Hitler and **Joseph Goebbels** had been promising would work "miracles" (*see* WONDER WEAPONS). The counterattack would divide and starve American and British armies of supplies, forcing Washington and London to make a separate peace deal with Germany. Hitler would then be able to concentrate what was left of Germany's armed forces on holding off the Red Army.

The plan had no chance of success. The Wehrmacht and **Luftwaffe** did not have nearly enough resources to pull it off, and **Franklin D. Roosevelt** and **Winston Churchill** would not betray **Josef Stalin**. Regardless of the odds, planning for the operation—code-named Wacht am Rhein (Watch on the Rhine) and renamed Herbstnebel (Autumn Mist)—began after Hitler selected the heavily wooded and hilly Ardennes region of southern Belgium and northern

Luxembourg as its starting point. On 16 December, a half-million German troops crossed the weakly defended Belgian border. Four armored divisions of the Waffen SS (**Schutzstaffel** Protection Squad; SS) would spearhead the drive to the channel. Some of these troops would be responsible for murdering hundreds of American prisoners of war—most notoriously near the town of Malmedy on 17 December—and Belgian civilians [*see* RUNDSTEDT, GERD VON (1875–1953)].

Taken by complete surprise and with limited air support because of poor weather conditions, American forces contained the German advance to a bulge of territory, the westernmost point of which was nowhere near Antwerp. In terms of casualties, what became known in the **United States** as the Battle of the Bulge was the costliest single engagement ever fought by the US Army. The **Wehrmacht** and Waffen SS suffered around 80,000 casualties and lost irreplaceable equipment and weapons. Hitler's generals considered the operation a failure by the end of its first week, but Hitler persisted in believing that American forces would retreat in disarray to the Meuse River. On 7 January, he relented and ordered German forces to retreat to Germany, though fighting continued in Belgium to the end of the month. A hastily planned second counterattack in Alsace, code-named Nordwind (Northwind), was also repulsed quickly.

Autumn Mist would be the last major German offensive of the war. The diversion of troops and matériel from the eastern front to the Ardennes also facilitated the Red Army's advance westward from the Vistula to the Oder Rivers. Hitler departed his western headquarters for Berlin on 15 January, where he sunk into a deep and typically self-pitying depression. His **Luftwaffe** adjutant Captain Nicolaus von Below recalls him admitting that the war was lost, lashing out at the Luftwaffe and his senior officers for failing and betraying him, and musing about shooting himself—all before regaining his composure and pledging to never capitulate. *See also* MILITARY COMMANDER.

ARMENIAN GENOCIDE (1915). In April 1915, officials of the Turkish Committee of Union and Progress (part of the Young Turk movement) began the premeditated destruction of Armenian populations in Istanbul and parts of Anatolia. Between 600,000 and 1.5 million Armenians were killed or allowed to die. The genocide was part of a larger project of ethnic cleansing that also targeted Greeks, Assyrians, Kurds, and members of small Christian communities.

Imperial German officials in the Ottoman Empire—at that time allied with Germany—knew about the genocide as it was taking place, though they did not initiate nor facilitate it. After the war, the fate of the Armenians became a subject of considerable debate in Germany, with much of the press coverage devoted to demonstrating that the German government had played no role in the catastrophe. This debate reached a high point in 1921, when on 15 March a young Armenian assassinated one of the genocide's architects, Talat Pasha, in Berlin and the accused perpetrator was acquitted after a two-day trial.

The perception on Germany's Far Right, the members of which were active partisans in these debates, was that the Turks had solved the "problem" of minorities through the mass murder of Armenians and the 1923 population transfer agreement with Greece. This perception formed an important part of Hitler's and the **National Socialist German Workers' Party**'s (Nazi Party; Nationalsozialistische Deutsche Arbeiterpartei; NSDAP) positive conception of the new Turkish republic's modernizing project under the leadership of **Mustafa Kemal Atatürk**. But it is also telling that in 1923, when some on the radical Right in Munich were discussing in public what the fate of the Armenians might teach Germans about dealing with **Jews**, Hitler told a Spanish journalist that his preference would be mass executions. Because that did not seem possible at the time, he would opt for expulsions en masse.

Within the party after 1933, very little seems to have been written or spoken about the Armenian genocide specifically. A well-known comment attributed to Hitler in these years—"Who still talks nowadays of the extermination of the Armenians?"—is of questionable provenance.

Knowledge of and admiration for the Armenian genocide did not inspire the **Holocaust** nor provide a blueprint for it. By the time he came to power, Hitler had long accepted that exterminatory ethnic cleansing was necessary and right and could be undertaken without significant domestic consequences for the perpetrators or universal condemnation abroad.

ART. Hitler would always consider himself an artist. His failures to gain admission to the Academy of Fine Arts in **Vienna** in 1907 and 1908 may have dashed his hopes of becoming a professional artist, but they did nothing to dislodge aesthetics from occupying a central position in his **personality**. He had rudimentary skills as a draftsman, and the postcards he painted and sold in Vienna and Munich in the years he lived in those cities (1907–1913) provided something akin to a steady, if very modest, income. The scale of his self-regard and ambitions, however, far outweighed his willingness to apply the discipline necessary to cultivate a talent for painting, playing an instrument, composing music, or designing buildings.

His lifelong infatuation with the operas of **Richard Wagner** began when he was 12. In the visual arts, he preferred the aesthetic of ancient Greece and Rome and 19th-century German romanticism, particularly if the artist was not a product of the kind of academy that had rejected him. He was revolted by modernism in any form. The grandiose neoclassical architecture of Vienna's Ringstrasse seems to have left a lifelong impression on him. He would later infuse his admiration for this style with a dose of gigantism. The resulting monstrous hybrid is best exemplified by his fantastical plans for the reconstructions of Berlin and Linz (*see* NORWAY).

Once in power, Hitler's self-perception as an artist and his interests—narrow as they were—led him to devote considerable attention to culture, particularly architecture and the visual arts. He delivered an annual speech on culture and brought up cultural matters in his private monologues constantly. The moments in which Hitler appeared to be happy and contented was when he was in the company of artists. He could be indulgent toward a few who had taken political missteps on the grounds that as someone who understood the artistic temperament, he knew they could be harmless idiots when it came to politics. He did not, of course, believe he suffered from the same weakness. Rather, once in power he complained on multiple occasions of being burdened with domestic and party matters and mused about one day occupying himself completely with the arts. Unlike **Benito Mussolini**, who cared little about art and allowed the continued existence of some modernist currents in painting and design, Hitler made his aesthetic preferences the dominant ones in Germany. This meant establishing a Reich Chamber of Arts under **Joseph Goebbels**'s direction to sanction the production of art aligned with Hitler's tastes. It also entailed the disruption, destruction, and dispersal of one of the world's greatest cultures of artistic experimentation.

Beginning in 1933, works of literature by **Jewish**, leftist, and "anti-German" writers were burned and banned. The visual arts were targeted in 1937, when Hitler launched a "cultural offensive." The assault was connected to his racialist worldview and policies. If human beings could be "degenerate," Hitler believed, then so could the art they produced. To drive home the point to the public, he and Goebbels ordered an exhibit of "Entartete Kunst" (degenerate art) mounted in the summer. It displayed 650 paintings, drawings, prints, and sculptures by 112 artists, most of them German, accompanied by mocking and sarcastic commentary. The artwork had been confiscated from museums and looted from galleries and private homes and represented some of the greatest achievements of German and European modernism. This was only the opening salvo in the "cultural offensive": Around 21,000 works would be taken from collections in Germany and Austria between 1937 and 1939.

President of the Reich Chamber for the Visual Arts Adolf Ziegler, a painter favored by Hitler, had overseen the initial nationwide pillaging and curated the exhibit, which opened in Munich and traveled around the country. Hitler and Goebbels made well-publicized visits. It was a propaganda stunt without precedent, though one of uncertain impact on public opinion, as it could never really be determined how many of the 2 million Germans who visited the exhibition went to mock or to mourn.

"Entartete Kunst" was meant to be overshadowed by the opening of the House of German Art in Munich in 1937. The museum, designed by Paul Troost, is an important example of the kind of style Hitler favored in public buildings. It is one of the few significant Nazi-era buildings still being used for its original purpose. Hitler held Troost in high esteem and was pleased by its design. But he was appalled by the initial selection of works for the inaugural "Great German Art Exhibition," an exhibit intended to establish what was acceptable art in national socialist Germany. The jury reconsidered its selections, and the result was a mind-numbing display of some 1,200 unremarkable paintings of bucolic landscapes; portraits of blond Aryan archetypes; celebrations of Hitler and the Nazi movement; and neoclassical-style sculptures of nude, muscular warriors. It was not a popular success.

Hitler's hatred of artistic modernism did not prevent the regime from profiting from the sale of looted works. Around 5,000 pieces were destroyed in Berlin in 1939, but that year, the regime also had many works sold at auction in Switzerland or to private dealers.

The war provided an opportunity to expand state-sanctioned theft of all kinds of artwork from occupied Europe. In 1940, Hitler gave **Alfred Rosenberg**, one of the party's leading ideologues, sole authority to oversee the plunder of libraries, museums, and private collections in Europe. The property of Jews and Jewish institutions, such as rabbinical seminary libraries, were among the most important targets. By the fall of 1944, the task force had filled nearly 1.5 million railway cars with stolen books and artwork and transported around a half-million tons by ship.

Aware that the Nazi regime was engaging in the plunder of cultural treasures on a massive scale, the Western Allies established the Monuments, Fine Arts, and Archives Program (known informally as the Monuments Men) in 1943. Some 400 soldiers and civilians were deployed to locate and safeguard huge caches of art and artifacts as Europe was liberated and Germany occupied. Much was recovered then and since and in some cases returned to the families of the original owners or to the libraries and museums from which they had been taken. The complicated and often contentious efforts to establish the rightful ownership of Nazi-looted art continue to the present day. *See also* GÖRING, HERMANN (1893–1946); HOLOCAUST.

ASSASSINATION ATTEMPT (20 JULY 1944). Of multiple attempts on Hitler's life, the one that took place on 20 July 1944 came closest to succeeding [*see* ELSER, GEORG (1903–1945)]. This and a few previous attempts had resulted from a conspiracy among a handful of **Wehrmacht** officers, diplomats, and intelligence officers, many of them from aristocratic families. Their motivations varied, but predominant among them were revulsion at the brutal behavior of German forces in the East and the desire to avoid a catastrophic defeat, which seemed all but assured by the summer of 1943 (*see* OPPOSITION).

The obstacles facing the conspirators were daunting. They were small in number, had no base of popular support, and remained perilously close to being identified by the ruthlessly effective Gestapo. Hitler was well protected and prone to changing his plans at little or no notice. The plotters feared for their families' lives and were deeply conflicted about committing high treason in wartime. The timing of any move against Hitler was a complicated matter. Doing so between 1938 and 1940, the period of the regime's and the military's greatest victories, was inconceivable. But when Germany's advances stalled and then went into reverse, a significant problem remained: How could the conspirators act without undermining the increasingly desperate war effort? They had pinned their hopes on a separate peace, but the Western Allies did not take them seriously and had no intention of betraying **Joseph Stalin**, even if they should succeed in toppling the regime. And if the conspirators managed to kill Hitler, could a coup d'état really have taken place in a way that put the plotters securely in control? Resistance from die-hard regime loyalists was ensured, and given the fact that the plotters were largely isolated within the military, the state, and the party, they would have to seize the initiative in order to draw the far more numerous fence sitters to their side. Doing that required more than bravery and bluff; it needed meticulous planning for taking immediate control of key government ministries following Hitler's death.

The looming disaster at **Stalingrad** in the winter of 1942–1943 injected the conspirators—above all Colonel Henning von Tresckow, an army group center staff officer—with an even greater sense of urgency. The general plan was to assassinate Hitler, take control of Berlin and other cities, and establish a military dictatorship. An expected separate peace with the Western Allies would allow the Wehrmacht to focus on holding off the Red Army. A small team planned to shoot Hitler during one of his visits to the eastern front in March 1943. When this attempt failed to take place, Tresckow arranged for a package containing two bottles of cognac concealing a small British-made bomb supplied by Admiral **Wilhelm Canaris** to be placed on a plane carrying Hitler from army group center headquarters in Smolensk to Minsk. But the bomb failed to detonate, and the conspirators scrambled to retrieve the package before its contents were revealed.

The next took place just over a week later in Berlin. On 21 March, Heroes' Memorial Day, Hitler was scheduled to attend multiple ceremonies and inspect a collection of captured Soviet military equipment. An army group center intelligence officer volunteered to kill Hitler—and himself—with a bomb as Hitler inspected the display. But Hitler spent only a few minutes looking at the loot. The assassin had to sneak into a toilet and defuse the bomb.

In the fall of 1943, Major General Friedrich Olbricht approached Colonel Claus Shenk Graf von Stauffenberg, a young officer who had been badly wounded in North **Africa**, about joining the resistance. Stauffenberg, having already decided that Hitler had to be killed, took the lead in recruiting would-be assassins to make the attempt as soon as possible. No opportunities presented themselves until the following July, when he was assigned to serve as chief of staff to reserve army commander General Friedrich Fromm. This meant Stauffenberg would be in Hitler's presence at certain briefings. On 20 July, Stauffenberg and an accomplice, Major Ernst John von Freyand, joined a briefing with Hitler in a wooden hut in the **Wolf's Lair** compound. Freyand placed a briefcase containing one of two sets of explosives—the other could not be armed in time—in front of one of the legs of a heavy wooden table on which Hitler studied maps and photographs. Stauffenberg then excused himself and was preparing to leave the compound by car for a nearby airfield when he heard the explosion. Assuming Hitler was dead, he and another conspirator reached the airfield and took off for Berlin.

Hitler was, again, extremely lucky and suffered only minor injuries. Had both bombs been placed in the hut, he would have certainly been killed. Nor would he have likely survived had the briefing taken place in a concrete bunker rather than a flimsy wooden hut. The placement of the single bomb under a heavy table also protected him from the full force of the blast.

The plotters had based their plan for seizing power on an existing one, code-named Valkyrie, which involved mobilizing the reserve army in case of domestic unrest. In this case, they would claim to be deploying the force in response to a made-up attempt by the party and **Schutzstaffel** (Protection Squad; SS) to topple Hitler. The conspirators established their base at the headquarters of the Wehrmacht high command in a complex of buildings on the Bendlerstrasse in Berlin, also known as the Bendler Block.

The coup attempt began to fall apart almost immediately, mainly because the plotters had not planned for the possibility that Hitler might survive the explosion. Because his death could not be confirmed, General Fromm—very much a fence sitter—would not activate the reserve army. And because communications between the Wolf's Lair and Berlin were restored by the time Stauffenberg finally arrived at the Bendler Block, Field Marshal **Wilhelm Keitel** had been able to inform Fromm that Hitler was alive. When another conspirator announced to regional military commanders that Hitler was dead and Stauffenberg had placed Fromm under arrest, Hitler simply transferred control of the reserve army to **Heinrich Himmler**, and Keitel confirmed Hitler's survival with the regional commanders. On top of that, the plotters did not move to arrest key regime loyalists nor take control of radio stations nor even make a public statement. As a result of these lapses, **Joseph Goebbels** was able in the late afternoon to announce over the radio that Hitler was alive and even working again. The conspirators were now isolated in the Bendler Block. An unguarded Fromm placed the coup leaders under arrest and gave several of them the opportunity to shoot themselves before having Stauffenberg and three others unceremoniously executed in a courtyard, a decision that enraged Hitler and resulted in Fromm's own execution. Tresckow committed suicide in **Poland**.

Just after midnight, Hitler addressed Germans by radio, claiming repeatedly that "providence" had saved him so he could continue his mission, a statement that he seems to have believed. He also promised and then exacted a terrible revenge. Nearly all the other conspirators and many more connected to them—some 5,000 total—were arrested and around 200 executed within a few months of the attempt. Hitler's revenge extended to the conspirators' families: Their wives were sent to concentration camps, and their children were dispersed to orphanages.

The evidence, though fragmentary, suggests that reactions to the attempted assassination among German soldiers and civilians were mixed, ranging from despair to relief that it did not succeed. But Hitler's survival and Goebbels's subsequent efforts to blame the conspirators for Germany's military setbacks did not slow the accelerating decay of morale, despite whatever expressions of support that many felt obliged to continue proclaiming in public. The British and American governments thought little of the entire affair (*see* UNITED STATES OF AMERICA).

A few days before 20 July, Stauffenberg predicted that whoever acted against Hitler would be remembered in Germany as a traitor. For a long time after the war, he was right, as a significant number of Germans held negative views of the conspirators well into the 1950s. Leading West German politicians, however, made regular public statements honoring their memories. The plotters were moreover portrayed frequently and positively in West German stage, film, and television productions as men who sacrificed themselves to redeem Germany's honor. The elite resistance, its ranks filled with representatives of Germany's bourgeoisie, aristocracy, and Prussian-dominated officer corps, was of little interest to the communist regime in the communist German Democratic Republic (East Germany), where the priority was always to emphasize the struggle and sacrifices of German communists and the Soviet Union.

Thanks in large part to pressure from the plotters' surviving family members, a memorial was established in 1952 in the Bendler Block. West Berlin's city government approved an educational center at the site in 1967, and memorial and exhibition spaces were expanded over the following decades. During that time, the high profile of elite resistance was eclipsed by expanding popular awareness of the **Holocaust** and by the determination of a younger generation of Germans to acknowledge the socialist and communist resistance. A new permanent exhibition, opened in 2014, reflects this evolution in public perception by emphasizing the multiple forms that resistance took. But the memory of the professional officers who sacrificed their lives in July 1944, most notably Stauffenberg, maintains a prominent place in Germany. In a particularly appropriate tribute, recruits to the German army (Bundeswehr) take their oaths of allegiance on 20 July.

ATATÜRK, MUSTAFA KEMAL (1881–1938). The Republic of Turkey, established in 1923, and its leader until his death in 1938, Mustafa Kemal Atatürk, became objects of intense admiration for the postwar German Far Right in general and the **National Socialist German Workers' Party** (Nazi Party; Nationalsozialistische Deutsche Arbeiterpartei; NSDAP), the

Sturmabteilung (Stormtroopers; SA), and Hitler in particular. For the Far Right, which included numerous officers and diplomats who had recently served in Turkey, Atatürk and the "Ankara Turks" offered a more promising model for seizing power and staging a national revolution than **Benito Mussolini**, despite the latter's success in 1922.

World War I had resulted in the collapse of the Ottoman Empire and its replacement by what the Right saw as a "young" movement of national renewal led by a warrior-statesman who had kicked out foreign armies, dealt assertively with problematic minorities to consolidate an ethnostate, revised a hated postwar treaty from a position of strength, and set itself on a course of secular modernization. The republic's close relationship with the new Bolshevik regime in Russia was dismissed as nothing more than a shrewd tactical move devoid of any ideological significance.

Hitler imbibed and contributed to this discourse. He seemed well informed about Turkey, no doubt in part because his principal political adviser was Max Erwin Scheubner-Richter, who had served as a wartime vice counsel in eastern Anatolia and would be among those killed during the **Beer Hall Putsch**. Hitler was making favorable remarks about Atatürk and the Ankara government in speeches in 1922 and may have authored pro-Turkish articles for the main party newspaper, the *Völkisher Beobachter*. Hitler also made multiple references to Turkey during the post–Beer Hall Putsch trial. After his release from **Landsberg Prison** in December 1924, references to Atatürk and the new Turkey in the party press all but vanished, most likely because the party had decided on a "legal" path to power.

But Hitler had not forgotten him, and once in power, there was no need to be circumspect. In an interview with a Turkish newspaper in July 1933, he described Atatürk's movement as a "shining star" for the NSDAP in the 1920s. The comment was reproduced and repeated over the years in the German press. The year 1933 was also important because it marked the 10th anniversary of the Turkish Republic's founding, an occasion celebrated extensively in the Nazi press and by the SA. Effusive praise by Hitler continued over the following years, and Hitler sent Atatürk numerous congratulatory telegrams. In 1938, he described Atatürk as his teacher: Mussolini was the first pupil, and Hitler was the second. In April and September 1939, he stated outright that Turkey and Atatürk were "our model," a description that would be cited many times in the German press and repeated by Hitler. In late September 1939, Hitler told the Turkish ambassador that through his war in **Poland** and the final destruction of the **Versailles Treaty**, he was "copying Atatürk" in the way he destroyed the Treaty of Sevres. Just before the signing of the German–Turkish Friendship Treaty in 1941, Hitler repeated the role model comments in a rare speech to the **Reichstag** in April.

In the Nazi press, there was extensive and admiring coverage of Turkey after 1933, emphasizing Atatürk's unchallenged leadership, its modernization program, and the way in which the minority question had been handled. Nazi ideologues saw Kemalism, fascism, and national socialism as representing a new ideological vanguard for the world. And they considered non-**Jewish** Turks to be Aryans, thanks mainly to their demonstrated military prowess and desire to modernize along Western lines. Armenians, conversely, were denigrated as "Jews of the Orient" (*see* ARMENIAN GENOCIDE).

To the extent that any of the years-long outpouring of admiration presented developments in Turkey accurately was beside the point. For Hitler and party ideologues and propagandists, the new Turkey was less a blueprint to be copied and more a source of inspiration and an example to Germans and the world of how a leader who had adopted the principle of unchallenged leadership freed and modernized his new nation.

Hitler's admiration for Atatürk, which was not reciprocated, and the perceived ideological affinity between Germany and Turkey did not translate into a wartime alliance. Turkey provided refuge to German Jews and facilitated the transfer of some to Palestine. To be sure, Turkish neutrality in the Second World War in some ways helped Germany but only indirectly and temporarily. Ankara broke off diplomatic relations in August 1944 and declared war on 23 February 1945.

ATLANTIC CHARTER (1941). A joint statement of principles and broad objectives was issued on 14 August 1941 by **Franklin D. Roosevelt** and **Winston Churchill** at their first wartime meeting in Newfoundland's Placentia Bay. Reminiscent of Woodrow Wilson's 14 points, the charter called for a postwar world order based on self-determination, "freedom from fear and want," and a system of free trade. As it also called for the creation of an international body that would ensure global peace and security, it became a foundational document for the creation of the United Nations.

All of this was premised on what the charter described as the "final destruction of Nazi tyranny." Churchill and his entourage had hoped for a clearer commitment from Roosevelt that the **United States** would soon join the war on Great Britain's side. They had to settle for a symbolic step toward this goal, though more than symbolism resulted from the meeting, as Roosevelt promised to extend the US Navy's protection of British ships halfway across the Atlantic. Churchill also chafed at the reference to self-determination, which he understood—correctly—would be viewed as more than symbolic by anti-imperialists across what was left of the British Empire (see AFRICA).

Hitler allegedly flew into a rage when he first heard about the charter. Despite the fact that Churchill referred to it in public as merely "symbolic" and **Joseph Goebbels** dismissed it as a propaganda stunt, Hitler saw another nail being driven into the coffin of his strategy of forcing Britain out of the war. He also understood that it was only a matter of months before the Americans would enter the war. Everything for Hitler now depended on defeating the Soviet Union—which at that moment still seemed likely—and what **Japan** would do. The charter also accelerated the move toward the attempted total extermination of European **Jews**. For Hitler and Goebbels, it confirmed that "international Jewry" was provoking a new world war and that Hitler's "**prophecy**" from 30 January 1939 would be realized. It was not coincidental that in the late summer and fall of 1941, the mass murder of Jews in the East entered an even deadlier stage. *See also* BALTICS; BATTLE OF THE ATLANTIC (1939–1945); HOLOCAUST; OPERATION BARBAROSSA (1941); POLAND; TRIPARTITE PACT (1940).

ATOMIC BOMB. As it became clear by the end of 1941 that Germany would not win the war quickly, Hitler became entranced with the idea that new weapons could be developed and deployed to "miraculously" bring about victory (*see* WONDER WEAPONS). And there was plenty of interest in military and scientific circles in advancing two of the three most promising cutting-edge technologies: rocketry and jet propulsion. Hitler gave his support to the development of both, though rather belatedly. He was, however, reluctant to embrace a third: an atomic bomb.

German scientists had done the necessary theoretical work. The possibility of creating a weapon of unprecedented destructive power drew the interest of the **Wehrmacht**'s equipment chief, General Friedrich Fromm, who promoted the project aggressively despite knowing that building a working bomb would take years and a massive commitment of resources. Hitler, however, remained skeptical. He did not understand the science and remained influenced by the idea that theoretical physics was **Jewish** (*see* RACISM). But the main problem was that Germany needed a major victory in the East in 1942, one that would at least result in the capture of the Caucasus region and its oil [*see* BATTLE OF STALINGRAD (1942–1943)].

Even if Hitler had given a bomb project his early and enthusiastic support, one could not have been produced in time to have altered the course of the war. Scientists outside Germany, of course, also knew that an atomic bomb could be built. A bomb project was pursued briefly by **Japan**, and one was authorized in Great Britain in October 1941 and then in the **United States** in early December. A working bomb was only produced in the United States in July 1945. In the end, it was what one historian characterized as the "war of engines"—steady advances in airpower and tanks—by Allied militaries along with the ability to manufacture them in huge quantities that made the most difference. *See also* STRATEGIC BOMBING CAMPAIGN.

AUSTRIA. Austria was Hitler's birthplace and where he spent his formative years, yet he never identified as Austrian. During the period he lived in **Vienna** (1907–1913), he admired the architecture of the Ringsstrasse and certain musicians, but like any good **pan-German** chauvinist, he despised the city's multiethnic character and cosmopolitanism. And it was, after all, the place where he had experienced repeated personal setbacks and lived a precarious existence. While Hitler's fantasies of redeveloping Berlin are better known, he would become more obsessed with similarly fantastical plans for transforming Linz into a cultural and industrial megacity and the place where he would retire after the Second World War was won. But in his eyes, Linz was to be—as he put it—a great "German" Danubian city that would displace Vienna and all other European cities as a cultural capital.

Germany's annexation of Austria in March 1938 and Hitler's triumphant entry into Vienna was not an easily won victory. Like all pan-German ideologues, he embraced the cause of uniting ethnic Germans in a "greater Germany" and considered the post–**World War I** nation-state of Austria to be an artificial creation. Many Austrians felt the same in the months after the war's end and hoped their small, ethnically homogenous state would be annexed to Germany. Hitler departed from the pan-German consensus only in his willingness to abandon all claims on the South Tyrol, a predominantly German-speaking region that was transferred to **Italy** after the war.

Yet the terms of the **Versailles Treaty** prohibited unification, and attempts to create a customs union went nowhere. An even greater obstacle to unification, at least until the mid-1930s, was **Benito Mussolini**. The Italian dictator was intent on blocking the growth of German power and maintaining Italy's control of South Tyrol, one of its few postwar territorial prizes. And not all Austrians were in favor of annexation. Austrian nationalism would find a political home in what would become the country's largest party: the Christian Socials. It had its strongest base of support outside what the Right called "Red Vienna," in the deeply Catholic and conservative countryside, where paramilitaries mobilized to defend Austria's southern borders against Yugoslav irredentism.

Austrian politics had become deeply polarized before being hit by the Great Depression, which only widened the divisions. Following Hitler's appointment as **chancellor**, Austrian chancellor Engelbert Dollfuss created a dictatorship of the Right and banned the left-wing socialists. He and his quasi-fascist regime were committed to Austrian independence.

Hitler's long-standing resistance to forming ties with Far-Right parties in Austria did not prevent the emergence of an Austrian **National Socialist German Workers' Party** (Nazi Party; Nationalsozialistische Deutsche Arbeiterpartei; NSDAP), which managed to capture 16 percent of the vote in local **elections** in 1932. In the spring of 1933, Hitler, knowing that annexation at that moment was out of the question, tried applying **economic** pressure and fomenting domestic unrest to destabilize the Austrian government and bring local Nazis to power in much the same way he had become chancellor. But support for Austrian independence in Rome, London, and Paris was still too strong, and Hitler had to back down.

On 25 July 1934, Austrian Nazis assassinated Dollfuss and attempted a coup d'etat. They had been authorized to do so by Hitler, who had somehow gained the impression during his first state visit to Italy in June that Mussolini would not intervene. But forces loyal to the Austrian state led by Dollfuss's successor, Kurt von Schuschnigg, suppressed the putsch. Mussolini also sent troops to the border and threatened war with Germany if it attempted annexation. Having totally misread Mussolini's determination to maintain Austrian independence, Hitler was forced to back down again.

Four years later, the international situation had changed fundamentally. Far more securely ensconced in power, Hitler was intent on initiating his war of imperial conquest in Europe as soon as possible. Relations with Mussolini had also evolved into something like an alliance. In the meeting with his military chiefs in November 1937 that produced the **Hossbach Memorandum**, Hitler declared that the conquest of **Czechoslovakia** would be preceded by a military attack, if necessary, on Austria. Another campaign aimed at destabilizing the Austrian state commenced. On 12 February 1938 at the **Berghof**, Hitler badgered and threatened Schuschnigg, who had been trying his own version of **appeasement** by offering concessions to Germany that, of course, fell short of what Hitler wanted.

Schuschnigg's government was destabilized over the following month by proannexation agitation—including attacks on **Jews** and Jewish-owned property—by local Nazis. An increasingly desperate Schuschnigg made one final attempt to preserve his country's independence. On 9 March, he called for a plebiscite on the issue to be held four days later. Hitler ordered **Wehrmacht** corps to mobilize for an invasion and dispatched a special envoy to Rome to smooth things over with Mussolini. Schuschnigg backed down on 11 March, canceled the plebiscite, and appointed his pro-Nazi interior minister Arthur Seyss-Inquart as his replacement. Seyss-Inquart's chancellorship lasted two days. The intense pressure from Berlin was accompanied by an explosion of local violence against Social Democrats, anti-Nazis, and Jews orchestrated by the clandestine Austrian **Schutzstaffel** (Protection Squad; SS) officer Ernst Kaltenbrunner.

Seyss-Inquart used the manufactured disorder to request help from Germany. In a radio address on 12 March, **Joseph Goebbels** read Hitler's announcement that he had agreed to the "request," and German troops entered Austria. They were unopposed, but the claim that thousands of ecstatic Austrians hailed the invaders is pure propaganda. Hitler, then in Linz, signed the Law for the Reunification of Austria with the German Reich the next day, making it a state (the Ostmark) within the German Reich. After visiting his parents' gravesites, he entered Vienna in an open motorcade on 14 March, again to a manufactured rapturous reception.

The Anschluss (annexation) was a major victory for Hitler in every respect. His belief in the infallibility of his own instincts was further bolstered. The joyous reception upon his return to Berlin was not entirely orchestrated by Goebbels, though much of it was no doubt fueled by relief that war had been averted. Hitler ordered a plebiscite to be held on 10 April, and 99 percent of voters approved of the Anchluss. He had achieved a long-sought objective of pan-Germanism without a war—the Western powers did nothing more than issue words of protest—and set up Czechoslovakia as the next domino to fall. And there were, of course, many material benefits. Almost 7 million people were added to Germany's population, as were Austria's wealth, natural resources, and trade networks in southeastern Europe.

The new state's "coordination" took place with terrifying rapidity. Gestapo and SS Security Service (Sicherheitsdienst; SD) agents had accompanied the Wehrmacht's invasion and oversaw a wave of terror in which tens of thousands of Austrians—Schuschnigg among them—were arrested and imprisoned in Dachau and in a new camp, Mauthausen, near Linz (*see* CONCENTRATION CAMPS). Goebbels wasted no time in setting up a propaganda and press operation. The small Austrian army pledged allegiance to Hitler personally, as had members of the Wehrmacht. To Hitler's delight, the archbishop of Vienna obsequiously pledged the loyalty of Austria's Catholics.

For its 190,000 Jews, the Anschluss was an unmitigated disaster. The machinery of persecution, now finely tuned from years of experience in the "Old Reich," began operating alongside an explosion of outright banditry, assault, and public degradation. The disorder reached such an extent that even Gestapo chief **Reinhard Heydrich** threatened—to little immediate effect—local Nazis with arrest if they did not behave with some discipline. At the end of March, **Hermann Göring** decreed the orderly "redirecting" of the "Jewish economy," and by late summer, most assets owned by Jews were "Aryanized." The SD's leading "Jewish expert," SS second lieutenant Adolf Eichmann, was put in charge of facilitating Jewish emigration, an operation accompanied by less-well-known expulsions of thousands of Jews to **Hungary**, Czechoslovakia, and Switzerland. By the spring of 1939, around 100,000 Austrian Jews had emigrated or been expelled. *See also* HOLOCAUST.

Hitler being greeted by the Vienna Boys Choir, Vienna, 13 March 1938. The banner reads, "We sing for Adolf Hitler!" *Courtesy of the United States Holocaust Memorial Museum.*

B

BALKANS. When it came to the Balkans, Hitler's vision of a European Empire included **economic** dominance and an ideological bulwark against Bolshevism. His belief that Moscow's stated interest in the region posed a threat to Germany's southern flank and Axis unity was an important factor in his insistence that **Operation Barbarossa** be launched in the spring of 1941. But Hitler did not envision invasion and occupation for the Balkans. This only came about thanks to **Benito Mussolini**'s impulsive decision in October 1940 to invade Greece from Albania, which **Italy** had seized a year earlier, after Hitler occupied Prague without consulting the Italian dictator.

Unlike the easy victory in a tiny country already effectively controlled by Italy, however, Mussolini's inadequately numbered and unprepared forces met fierce resistance in Greece's mountainous terrain. Assisted by the British air force, Greek forces had driven the Italians back to Albania by December. The following April, after taking control of an unstable **Romania** and invading Yugoslavia, German forces struck Greece and occupied Athens by the end of the month. The country was divided into German, Italian, and **Bulgarian** occupation zones and governed in name only by a collaborationist regime. Like **Poland** and **Czechoslovakia**, Yugoslavia was dismembered and ceased to exist. Following the near-total destruction of Belgrade by the **Luftwaffe**, Serbia was subjected to a German military occupation, while the Independent State of Croatia was established as a satellite.

German victory in the Balkans in the spring of 1941 was swift and, as it turned out, Hitler's final successful campaign in Europe. But the operations and the ensuing occupations were costly, unwanted distractions. The German presence in the region was undone almost as quickly as it was established, after the collapse of Romania and Bulgaria in the summer of 1944 forced a retreat from Greece and the abandonment of the rest of the Balkans in early 1945. In the interim, partisan groups mobilized to fight the occupiers and each other (civil conflict was encouraged by the Germans), with implications that continue to be felt across the region to the present day.

The German occupation was also extraordinarily brutal, offering a preview of what was to come a few months later in Russia. Nearly 2 million citizens of the former Yugoslavia, the majority civilians, died in the war; 65,000 were **Jews**. The plunder of Greece by the **Wehrmacht** and greedy German companies may have led to the deaths of 300,000 Greeks by the war's end. Though Jews sought and received protection in the Italian occupation zone, after Italy's surrender on 8 September 1943, the Germans extended the "final solution" to the rest of the country. Around 60,000 Greek Jews—80 percent of its prewar population—were murdered. *See also* HOLOCAUST.

BALTICS. The three Baltic states (Lithuania, Latvia, and Estonia) gained their independence following the German collapse in November

1918. They became the target of Hitler and Nazi ideologues, particularly **Alfred Rosenberg**, a native of Estonia's ethnic German community. In sharp contrast to the way Hitler and other ideologues viewed Slavic peoples, they considered the Baltics historically Germanic. Its populations and landscapes would be made fully German again. But they were also coveted by **Joseph Stalin**, who intended to retake them along with other territories of the former Russian Empire lost in the Treaty of Brest-Litovsk in March 1918. A secret protocol of the **Nazi–Soviet Nonaggression Pact** made the latter possible, if only briefly. In 1940, the Soviets reoccupied the three states.

The short-lived occupation was a brutal one, so it was not entirely unreasonable for Hitler to expect the Germans to be greeted as liberators, as they in fact were, when the **Wehrmacht** swept through the region in the summer of 1941. The Baltic states, along with Belorussia, formed the Reichkommissariat Ostland (Reich Commissariat of the Eastern Lands). The Germans relied on locals to run the territory and allowed them unusually wide latitude relative to other parts of the East. They could marry Germans and serve in the **Wehrmacht**, Waffen SS [see SCHUTZSTAFFEL (PROTECTION SQUAD; SS)], and police units. They were even allowed to maintain their own police forces.

Collaboration was particularly useful and often enthusiastic when it came to the **Holocaust**. In some parts of Lithuania, mass murder by locals began before German forces arrived. Out of a population of 220,000 in June 1941, only around 12,000 Lithuanian **Jews** were alive in May 1945. Einsatzgruppen (SS mobile execution units) that followed the Wehrmacht into the Soviet Union murdered more than half of Latvia's preinvasion Jewish population of around 74,000 in less than four months; 25,000 more were killed in a single week in November and December 1941. Most of Latvia's much smaller Jewish community was destroyed, again with significant local collaboration, by the end of the year.

Despite all this, Hitler had no intention of supporting self-determination, and the regime embarked on a predictably unpopular program of "Germanization." But even this did not lead to the mobilization of partisan groups to anywhere near the extent seen in Belorussia, **Poland**, Russia, or **Ukraine**. In nearly every way, the Baltics represented a Nazi imperial hybrid, in which the non-Jewish population was treated far better than it was in other parts of the East while being subjected to Germanization in preparation for the wave of German settlers that never arrived.

BATTLE OF BERLIN (1945). The final major land battle in the European war began in mid–April 1945 on the banks of the Oder River, some 80 kilometers east of Berlin. After spending the previous four months overrunning pockets of fanatical German resistance from the Baltics to Budapest, Soviet forces advanced into Berlin as Hitler continued to hear situation reports and move nonexistent armies around on tabletop maps.

As surrender was unthinkable while Hitler was alive, the Red Army had to conquer much of the city street by street, even building by building. Historians have long speculated about why at this point German soldiers fought as ferociously as they did. Hitler no longer provided any meaningful inspiration. The effects of years of commitment, habits of obedience bolstered with threats of on-the-spot punishment for desertion or surrender, and sheer desperation were the main motivators. Older men and young boys were given crude antitank weapons and sent on suicide missions. Strikingly, among the city's most loyal defenders were non-German volunteers in the Waffen SS [see SCHUTZSTAFFEL (PROTECTION SQUAD; SS)]. Meanwhile, terrified civilians awaited the end in cellars, air raid shelters, subways, or any space that might provide some protection.

Stalin was willing to sacrifice huge numbers of Soviet soldiers to capture the city as quickly as possible. He also put his two ablest generals, Ivan Konev and Georgi Zhukov, in competition with each other. Certainly, Berlin had enormous symbolic significance. Stalin may also have hoped to scoop up scientists, equipment, and research related to the development of an atomic bomb, which the NKVD told him were all housed at the Kaiser Wilhelm Institute for Physics. What Stalin did not know is that everything of value had already been evacuated to the Black Forest region in Germany's Southwest. There was, however, no possibility Western Allied forces would arrive first, as Supreme Allied Commander Dwight Eisenhower had decided to focus on southeastern and southern Germany and leave Berlin to the Red Army. The British and American contribution to the battle was to have battered much of the city to rubble during the **strategic bombing campaign**.

The violence did not stop with the city's surrender on 2 May, as the Red Army continued its campaign of rape, a problem that would persist in Soviet-occupied Germany for the next several years. Around 75,000 Soviet soldiers were killed, with another 300,000 wounded. Some 275,000 Germans were killed, the majority civilians. The physical destruction rivaled that of most other major German cities, with the vast majority of buildings rendered uninhabitable. The Red Army established occupation headquarters southeast of the city center in Karlshorst, where Stalin demanded a second surrender ceremony take place on 9 May. *See also* JODL, ALFRED (1890–1946); KEITEL, WILHELM (1882–1946); SUICIDE (30 APRIL 1945).

BATTLE OF BRITAIN (1940). Following the rapid conquests of Denmark, **Norway**, the Low Countries, and **France** in the spring and summer of 1940, Hitler expected the British government to come to terms [*see* WESER EXERCISE (WESERÜBUNG)]. Though he had ordered the military to begin preparing for a cross-channel invasion, code-named Seelöwe (Sea Lion), he wanted to give London one last chance to negotiate a settlement without fighting. Concluding the war with Great Britain one way or another was becoming a matter of urgency as Hitler contemplated the possibility of the **United States** entering the war or of the Soviet Union abandoning the **Nazi–Soviet Nonaggression Pact**.

With his attention shifting in the summer to planning an invasion of Russia, he demanded that Britain come to terms in a long speech to the **Reichstag** on 19 July. The British government rejected it that day. After considering other ways to apply pressure, such as attacking British-held Gibraltar and reinforcing **Italian** forces in North **Africa**, he decided that Seelöwe should be ready to begin by mid-September but only if attacks on Britain by air and intensified submarine warfare did not force London to sue for peace. Given that the German navy did not have the capabilities to execute Seelöwe, and in any case Hitler did not really intend to attempt it, everything hinged on the **Luftwaffe**'s ability to demolish the Royal Air Force (RAF) and bomb Britain out of the war.

The Battle of Britain began as a duel between RAF and Luftwaffe fighter planes over southern England and the channel. By mid-September, German losses had become unsustainable. A crucial factor in Britain's favor was that British engineers had built the world's first integrated air defense system. A network of radar stations transmitted by telephone lines real-time information on the positions of enemy planes to control centers, which then relayed the information to pilots. Then there was the Spitfire, the new RAF fighter plane that German military officials admitted they had totally underestimated. German operations were also surprisingly scattershot.

Broadly, the Luftwaffe's targets were the RAF and its bases, ports not identified by the Germans as landing sites for Seelöwe, and stores of food. Poor weather delayed larger-scale attacks until the middle of August. The first bombing raids on residential areas of London on 24 August did not go unanswered: The RAF responded the next day with its first raid on Berlin (*see* STRATEGIC BOMBING CAMPAIGN). An enraged Hitler promised retaliation on a massive scale and ordered more attacks on London and other cities.

As the Battle of Britain wound down in mid-September, Hitler ordered Seelöwe postponed indefinitely. At the same time, what became known as the Blitz—the terror bombing of British cities—intensified. London was subjected to nightly attacks, 71 in total. Fifteen other British cities were targeted during the entire ordeal, which lasted for 267 days and killed around 42,000 people. Far more lives would have been lost had the British not mobilized an extraordinary array of successful civilian protection measures, including the relocation of 1.5 million citizens (most of them children) to the countryside.

The failure to subdue Britain in the fall of 1940, along with the decision not to expand military operations in the Mediterranean and North Africa, had major strategic repercussions around the world. Hitler accelerated his plans for an invasion of the Soviet Union. An added incentive was US president **Franklin D. Roosevelt**'s canny "destroyer for bases" deal with Britain in early September 1940, an arrangement that traded American access to British bases in the Atlantic and Caribbean for 50 obsolete destroyers. To Hitler, it was a warning signal that the United States might soon more fully enter the war. These developments led to the signing in Berlin on 27 September of a pact (the **Tripartite Pact**) between Germany, **Italy**, and **Japan**, the clear intention of which was to deter the United States from entering the war. *See also* BATTLE OF THE ATLANTIC (1939–1945).

BATTLE OF EL-ALAMEIN (1942). Two crucial engagements took place between German and British forces in June and November 1942, both at El-Alamein, a tiny Egyptian coastal town roughly 100 kilometers west of Alexandria. Both also involved each country's most talented generals, **Erwin Rommel** and Bernard Law Montgomery, and in both Montgomery prevailed.

The first battle, which began at the end of June and lasted through July, brought an end to Rommel's six-month-long advance east across North **Africa**. But Hitler retained his confidence in the bold and creative Rommel, whom he had just promoted to field marshal following his capture of the Libyan port city of Tobruk. But Rommel's overstretched forces could not break through to the ultimate prize: Cairo. On 23 October, Montgomery's forces, with strong air support, launched a counterattack at El-Alamein (sometimes referred to as the Second Battle of El-Alamein). After 10 days of brutal fighting, British forces broke through the German lines. A week later, Anglo–American forces landed in Morocco and Algeria [*see* OPERATION TORCH (1942)].

As usual, Hitler ordered Rommel to hold out, telling him that prevailing was only a matter of exercising enough will. But with his **Afrika Korps** (Africa Corps) outnumbered and low on fuel and ammunition, Rommel had already ordered a retreat. Hitler refrained from sacking one of Germany's greatest war heroes. He ordered the **Wehrmacht** to occupy the South of France, but otherwise the fight to capture **Stalingrad** consumed his attention.

Months of hard fighting remained as the Afrika Korps retreated to Tunisia, where the remains of one of the war's most effective forces would be captured and Rommel would be evacuated in May 1943. Of greatest significance was the fact that Cairo, and thus the Suez Canal, remained in Allied hands. But El-Alamein is less well known as a turning point in the history of the **Holocaust**. As had been the case in the invasion of **Poland** and in **Operation Barbarossa**, a **Schutzstaffel** (Protection Squad; SS) Einsatzgruppen (mobile execution unit) was assigned to follow the Afrika Korps into British-controlled Palestine, where it was to exterminate the **Jewish** population.

BATTLE OF KURSK (1943). A string of major setbacks in the first months of 1943 prompted Hitler and **Wehrmacht** leaders to plan for a major victory on the eastern front. First there was the disaster at **Stalingrad**. By May, it was clear that Germany had lost the **Battle of the Atlantic**, and General **Erwin Rommel**'s **Afrika Korps** had been driven out of North **Africa**. Around the same time, the British air force had begun a sustained bombing campaign on the Ruhr-Rhine industrial region (*see* STRATEGIC BOMBING CAMPAIGN). The **Schutzstaffel**'s (Protection Squad; SS) Sicherheitsdienst (Security Service; SD) was reporting a significant decline in civilian morale, worsened by a reduction in food rations. Large-scale propaganda campaigns seemed to be having little or no positive impact on the public's mood.

A tempting target for a major German counterattack presented itself in the form of a Soviet-controlled salient extending about 100 kilometers into the German line around the

Russian city of Kursk. Hitler approved a plan (Operation Citadel) for a surprise attack on the salient's flanks, with the objective of encircling Soviet forces. If successful, he did not expect it to turn to the tide of the entire war, but he believed it would boost morale in Germany and, not least, reassure nervous allies.

The plan set a target date of mid-May, but it had to be postponed several times, a situation that led Oberkommando der Wehrmacht (Armed Forces High Command; OKW) officers to recommend scrapping it altogether in favor of reinforcing German lines to repel the expected Red Army summer offensive. Another concern was whether a new generation of German tanks and their inexperienced crews would be ready for a major attack. But Hitler ordered Citadel to commence on 5 July (*see* MILITARY COMMANDER).

The operation was doomed from the start. Having been fed intelligence from British code breakers, the Red Army prepared for the German attack with formidable, multilayered lines of defense manned by 1.3 million soldiers backed by another half-million in reserve. The resulting battle for the Kursk salient became the single largest battle of the entire war. It is mainly remembered as the largest tank battle in history, though the extent of the Red Army's success in this aspect of engagement was overstated in Soviet propaganda and in much postwar writing. But overall, it was a magnificent victory for the Red Army, which halted the German advance in a week's time. The first counterattack began on 12 July and a second in early August. Hitler had already canceled Citadel on 13 July. The Allied invasion of Sicily (Operation Husky) had begun on 9 July, and Hitler knew he would need to redeploy some forces from Russia to the Mediterranean. There would be only one more major German offensive—this time against American forces in a quiet corner of Belgium in December 1944. *See also* ARDENNES OFFENSIVE (DECEMBER 1944–JANUARY 1945); UNITED STATES OF AMERICA.

BATTLE OF STALINGRAD (1942–1943). After the **Wehrmacht**'s advance on Moscow stalled in the fall of 1941, Hitler ordered an offensive against the South for the following summer. The main objective was to capture oil fields in the Caucasus region. This would require taking the gateway city of Stalingrad (now Volgograd), control of which would also allow Germany to cut off shipping to northern Russia via the Volga River.

The offensive (Operation Blue) began on 19 June 1942, and by mid-August the German Sixth Army, under the command of Colonel General Friedrich Paulus—along with elements of the Fourth Panzer (Tank) Army, augmented with **Italian** and **Romanian** divisions—had reached the city's outskirts. The rapid advance was due in part to the fact that **Joseph Stalin** had expected the Germans to resume their offensive on Moscow and concentrated Red Army defenses in the center and north.

The ensuing battle for the city from 19 August 1942 to 2 February 1943 produced one of the longest, deadliest, and most consequential single engagements of the entire war. Outnumbered and outgunned, Soviet forces defended the city with extraordinary tenacity and bravery. They made effective use of the destruction wrought by **Luftwaffe** bombing raids to dig in and attack German positions street by street and building by building.

The turning point came not in the rubble-strewn streets and bombed-out buildings but along the German flanks, which were not only long and exposed but also in some places weakly defended by Italian and Romanian units. Though skeptical, Stalin was willing to be convinced by his generals to a far greater degree than Hitler, and he agreed to the risky plan, which was executed brilliantly. By late November, Paulus's 330,000-strong army was encircled. Hitler's refusal to allow him to break out was one of the most disastrous military decisions he ever made (*see* MILITARY COMMANDER).

The worsening weather prevented an attempt, led by General **Erich von Manstein**, to relieve the trapped army. Defying Hitler, Paulus surrendered on 31 January, with remnants in the city giving up a few days later. Manstein's rescue force was also captured. Most of Paulus's men died en route to prison camps. Only about 6,000 of the nearly 100,000 taken prisoner returned to Germany.

The battle for Stalingrad was recognized at the time as a turning point in the war. The Soviet victory was accompanied by a cluster of other important developments that, taken together, put Germany almost entirely on the defensive. Four months after Stalingrad, German and Italian forces were driven out of North **Africa**. The **strategic bombing campaign** intensified throughout the year, and the tide turned against Germany in the **Battle of the Atlantic** [*see also* AFRIKA KORPS (AFRICA CORPS); BATTLE OF EL-ALAMEIN (1942); BATTLE OF KURSK (1943)].

Morale on the German home front sunk noticeably with the news of Paulus's capitulation. The **Führer myth** took a hit from which it never recovered, the damage compounded by the fact that Hitler had already largely withdrawn from the public's view. Adding insult to injury for Hitler, the Soviets convinced Paulus to broadcast antiregime and antiwar messages to Germany. As usual, Hitler blamed the incompetence and perfidy of senior Wehrmacht officers. He retreated even further from public view and left the real of work of managing what was left of the war effort and the battered home front to **Albert Speer**, **Heinrich Himmler**, **Martin Bormann**, and **Joseph Goebbels**.

BATTLE OF THE ATLANTIC (1939–1945). In the war's first years, the German navy proved terrifyingly effective in sending hundreds of British ships and millions of tons of shipping to the bottoms of the Mediterranean Sea and Atlantic Ocean. What **Winston Churchill** would call the Battle of the Atlantic—a titanic struggle for control of crucial shipping lanes—ultimately involved more than surface vessels and submarines; it also included new long-range aircraft and antisubmarine weapons, radar systems, and the ability to crack coded messages. As in other areas, the war in the Atlantic was one of dueling technologies in which the ability to adapt quickly to the enemy's innovations became the key determinant of victory.

The turning point came in the first half of 1943, when the Allies were able to deploy a range of new technologies alongside a more effective escort system. By May, German submarine losses had become so numerous that Admiral **Karl Dönitz** withdrew his remaining fleet for refitting and to figure out how to adapt to what had become an insurmountable material and technological advantage. But it would be to no avail.

Victory in the Atlantic was essential to the buildup for a cross-channel invasion of German-occupied **France** and not least the invasion itself [*see* FORTRESS EUROPE (FESTUNG EUROPAS); OPERATION OVERLORD (1944)]. German defeat in the Atlantic also coincided with catastrophic setbacks elsewhere—Stalingrad and North **Africa**—and the intensification of the Allies' **strategic bombing campaign**.

BAVARIAN SOVIET REPUBLIC (1919). In November 1918, Germany was convulsed in revolution. Following mutinies at two naval bases, two socialist parties toppled the Reich government in Berlin, formed the Council of People's Representatives, and established a democratic republic. In Munich, the revolution began on 7 November, when Kurt Eisner, the head of the city's Independent Social Democratic Party (USPD), led a bloodless revolt against the Bavarian monarchy and government. The next day, the USPD and the **Social Democratic Party of Germany** (Sozialdemokratische Partei Deutschlands; SPD) formed a new government and appointed Eisner as prime minister and foreign minister.

The coalition fractured, and in **elections** held on 12 January 1919, Eisner's party suffered a humiliating defeat by the SPD and the Bavarian Peoples' Party [*see* CENTER PARTY (ZENTRUM)]. A month later, a Far-Right Munich university student assassinated Eisner, and a member of a workers' council tried to kill his main rival in the SPD. Riots ensued, and on 22 February, representatives of the workers' and soldiers' councils that had sprung up around Germany declared the Central Soviet of the Bavarian Republic in Munich. In April, this body announced the establishment of the Bavarian Soviet Republic, and the leaders of the elected government decamped to Bamberg in northern Bavaria.

For its part, the **Communist Party of Germany** (Kommunistische Partei Deutschlands; KPD) refused to cooperate with the new regime because it was a creation of its bitter enemies, the socialists, and they tried to disband the Central Soviet and call a general strike. The Bamberg-based government-in-exile asked Berlin for military intervention, and the SPD chancellor Philipp Scheidemann dispatched Reichswehr troops and Far-Right paramilitary units to Munich. By the first week of May, the Soviet Republic had been overthrown. More than 600 people, more than half civilians, were killed in the ensuing "white terror."

When the revolution began, Hitler was in a military hospital in the North German town of Pasewalk, recuperating from the effects of a poison gas attack and possibly what physicians diagnosed as "war hysteria." In *Mein Kampf*, he wrote that the shock of learning of Germany's defeat and a successful revolution provoked such rage in him that he decided to go into politics. While it's no doubt true that the experience of those days was traumatic, the claim that it inspired him to become a politician is nonsense. It would in fact be his experiences over the next two years in the political hothouse of Munich that transformed the politically directionless war veteran into a Far-Right rabble-rouser and aspiring politician.

Hitler left the hospital on 19 November and arrived at the garrison in Munich two days later, where he faced demobilization and an uncertain future. In December, he was transferred to the town of Traunstein im Chiemgau in southern Bavaria and assigned to guard prisoners of war and imprisoned civilians. He returned to the Munich garrison in February; briefly served as a guard at the city's main train station; and was elected to serve as his company's liaison to the socialist-dominated government, a position that may have entailed him making statements in support of that government. Film footage, discovered recently, shows him in uniform attending Eisner's funeral procession and wearing a red-and-black armband, thus signifying his identification with the revolutionaries. He was then elected as a deputy battalion representative during the Bavarian Soviet Republic's brief reign.

What was the real nature of his relationship with the new communist republic? Contrary to his claims in *Mein Kampf*, he did not take an aggressive anticommunist stance. But neither did he join the exiled government in Bamberg or a paramilitary group, even secretly, as many soldiers did. What is clear is that Hitler had no coherent ideological orientation at that point beyond a hazy, resentment-fueled nationalism. He did what was necessary to remain in the army, and for a time that meant cooperation, however superficial and contingent, with socialist- and then communist-dominated governments. Nonetheless, his role during the Soviet Republic period was not anything he ever wanted publicized after he did become a politician and then dictator.

Given his determination to remain in uniform alongside the unformed nature of his political beliefs, his nomination—by a person whose identity has never been confirmed—to join a three-man team tasked with investigating the behavior of soldiers during the Soviet Republic turned out to be one of the most significant junctures of Hitler's life. Not only did this assignment keep him in the army, but it also provided a kind of protection against accusations that he had at one point been a committed communist. Had that been true, after all, he would not have been nominated to such a position. It was his work on this investigative body that brought him to the attention of **Karl Mayr**, who would be instrumental in cultivating Hitler as an anti-Bolshevist propagandist and then initiating his first contact with the **German Workers' Party** (Deutsche Arbeiterpartei; DAP). *See also* ECKART, DIETRICH (1863–1923); NATIONAL SOCIALIST GERMAN WORKERS' PARTY (NAZI PARTY; NATIONALSOZIALISTISCHE DEUTSCHE ARBEITERPARTEI; NSDAP); VERSAILLES TREATY (1919); WORLD WAR I.

BEER HALL PUTSCH (1923). On 8 November 1923, Hitler and an assortment of Far-Right militants attempted a coup d'etat, or putsch, against the Bavarian state, with the larger objective of toppling the Reich government in Berlin. Launched in one of Munich's largest beer halls, the Bürgerbräukeller, the attempt was a spectacular failure. But contrary to conventional wisdom at the time, it did not spell the end of Hitler's budding career as a politician.

In the fall of 1923, the republic seemed to be tottering on the edge of **economic** collapse, revolution, civil war, or some horrible combination of the three. In January, **French** and Belgian troops occupied the industrial Ruhr Valley region in response to Germany's failure to pay reparations. Chancellor Wilhelm Cuno called for passive resistance, but the resulting fall in production incited the government to print money to pay workers. A catastrophic bout with hyperinflation ensued.

Another source of instability resulted from Moscow's decision on 4 October to order the **Communist Party of Germany** (Kommunistische Partei Deutschlands; KPD) to start a revolution. On 20 October, the party's central committee ordered a general strike to be called the following day—the idea being that it would spark the revolution—but then immediately revoked the decision. The KPD was in fact nowhere near ready to stage a Bolshevik-style coup. Not having received the order to desist, however, local communists in Hamburg began occupying police stations and putting up barricades. Police and military units put down the revolt within three days. In late October, the Reich government deployed the Reichswehr to depose communist-socialist coalition governments in the neighboring states of Saxony and Thuringia.

These crisis-ridden months seemed to offer an opportunity for a seizure of power by the right. Certainly, Hitler and the **National Socialist German Workers' Party** (Nazi Party; Nationalsozialistische Deutsche Arbeiterpartei; NSDAP) benefited. Despite widespread support for passive resistance, Hitler continued to blame the "November criminals" for allowing Germany to be subjected to such humiliating measures in the first place [see "STAB IN THE BACK" MYTH (DOLCHSTOSSLEGENDE)]. He remained a popular speaker in Munich, and 35,000 Germans joined the NSDAP between February and November. The membership of the **Sturmabteilung** (Stormtroopers; SA) also expanded rapidly.

Such circumstances presented Hitler with a dilemma. On one hand, his supporters and the increasingly restless and well-armed SA expected action, and in his speeches, interviews, and the party press, he had been fashioning himself not only as its undisputed leader but also as Germany's future dictator and the nation's savior. On the other, Hitler was by no means the unchallenged leader of the entire Bavarian Far Right. Indeed, he was too little known in Bavaria. More important, he did not have the full support of state officials and the Reichswehr [see *ADOLF HITLER, SEIN LEBEN, SEINE REDEN* (*ADOLF HITLER: HIS LIFE AND HIS SPEECHES*)].

Certainly, Bavaria's conservative nationalist political and military establishment shared the Far Right's hatred of the republic and communism and very much wanted to break Berlin's control over the state. While Hitler, the NSDAP, and the SA had become too popular to ignore, this establishment believed they could be useful tools and kept under control. But there was no way its leaders would tolerate a coup attempt led by Hitler.

In September, former imperial army quartermaster General Erich Ludendorff, at that time the Far Right's symbolic leader, brokered the creation of the Deutscher Kampfbund (German Combat League), an alliance of paramilitary groups that included the SA. In response, the Bavarian government declared a state of emergency and appointed Gustav von Kahr, a former prime minister, as general state commissioner. Possessing virtually dictatorial powers, Kahr immediately took steps to ease the economic crisis. His success weakened the Kampfbund and led **Ernst Röhm** to create a new paramilitary group, the Reichskriegsflagge (Imperial War Flag), comprised of those elements from the Kampfbund who had refused to support Kahr, which included Ludendorff. The move set the stage for a showdown between Kahr and state officials on the one side and Röhm, Ludendorff, and Hitler and the other. Both camps wanted the same thing: the end of the republic. Inspired by **Benito Mussolini's** "March on Rome" and **Mustafa**

Kemal Atatürk's seizure of power the previous year, Hitler, Röhm, and Ludendorff demanded a takeover of the Bavarian state followed by a "march on Berlin." Kahr and his allies, conversely, wanted to rally Far-Right and conservative nationalist elements across Germany to pressure the Reich president to invoke emergency powers and install a dictatorship.

Despite the lack of support from the Reichswehr—on 3 November its chief, General Hans von Seekt, had ruled out any support for a coup in Berlin—Ludendorff, Hitler, and Röhm felt compelled to act. On the night of 8 November, Hitler and a handful of his closest associates charged into the Bürgerbräukeller, where Kahr and state military and police leaders were holding a meeting. Hitler fired his pistol at the ceiling and declared the beginning of the "nationalist revolution" and that the Bavarian and Berlin governments had already been overthrown. He had had the hall surrounded by paramilitaries, and SA men guarded the entrance. Under duress, Kahr and his associates acceded to Hitler's demands before slipping away to mobilize opposition to the plotters while Hitler was trying to learn why government ministries and army barracks had not yet been seized. It was clear that night that the Reichswehr and state police would oppose the putsch.

Undaunted, the following morning, Hitler led a march with around 2,000 supporters to link up with Röhm and Reichskriegsflagge men. State police confronted the marchers at the Feldherrnhalle, a monument to the Bavarian army in central Munich. An exchange of gunfire erupted—it is unclear who fired first—and 13 putschists, 4 policemen, and a bystander were killed (2 other putschists were killed elsewhere). Hitler suffered a dislocated shoulder when a mortally wounded comrade allegedly tried to pull him out of harm's way. The crowd dispersed, and most of the leading putschists were soon arrested or turned themselves in, including Ludendorff, **Hermann Göring** (who received a bullet wound), Julius Streicher, **Wilhelm Frick**, **Rudolf Hess**, and Röhm. Hitler fled the city in a car, intending to cross into **Austria**. A breakdown forced him to take refuge in the village of Uffing am Staffelsee at the home of two supporters, **Ernst Hanfstaengl** and his wife, Helene. On 11 November, a dramatic scene unfolded as Helene informed Hitler he was about to be arrested and then calmly talked him out of shooting himself.

That afternoon, after hastily leaving orders for the party's management with Helene, he was taken into custody and transferred to **Landsberg Prison**. Newspapers in Germany and abroad pronounced the end of his political career. The Nazi Party and SA were banned, and other paramilitary groups were dissolved. Kahr was ousted in early 1924, and parliamentary government returned to Bavaria. Hitler and nine others were charged with high treason and tried from 26 February to 27 March 1924 at the People's Court in Munich. Rather than evade responsibility for what was undeniably a fiasco, Hitler used the leeway granted him by a sympathetic judge to take full responsibility while insisting that he could not have committed treason against a government that was established by traitors in 1918 [*see* TRIAL (1924)].

He would continue over the following years to transform what should have been a career-ending stunt into a core element of the mythology surrounding him and, by extension, the Nazi Party. Those killed on 9 November were never forgotten—Hitler dedicated the first volume of ***Mein Kampf*** to their memories. After 1933, he turned 8 and 9 November into an annual commemoration, in which he would address "old fighters" in the Bürgerbräukeller and then lead a march to the Feldherrnhalle. In the closing scenes of **Leni Riefenstahl**'s ***Triumph of the Will***, Hitler uses the "blood flag"—a flag supposedly stained with the blood of comrades killed in Munich—to consecrate new party flags.

BERGHOF. Like other modern dictators, Hitler and his acolytes transformed a rural retreat into an important center of his regime's power. Unlike **Joseph Stalin** or **Benito Mussolini**, however, Hitler maintained only one: the Berghof complex outside the town of Berchtesgaden in the Bavarian Alps. In 1933, he purchased a modest house he had been renting since 1928 and had it expanded into the Berghof (literally, a "mountain court"). The purchase, arranged skillfully and discreetly by **Martin Bormann**, set in motion the years-long transformation of its once-idyllic surroundings into a barbed-wire-fence-enclosed complex that included two teahouses, a farm, a greenhouse, barracks for **Schutzstaffel** (Protection Squad; SS) personnel, and an annex of the **chancellery**. Bormann shrewdly bought up nearby properties and, more than any other high-level official, leveraged his work on the entire project to ingratiate himself with Hitler.

At the Berghof, Hitler wrote many of his most important speeches, conducted state business, supervised the war effort, and received foreign guests. He also used the house to recover from bouts of illness. It was here that any distinction between Hitler's private and political spheres was blurred or erased. The makeup of his inner circle only partly mirrored the regime's power structure. **Rudolf Hess** was excluded, as were **Heinrich Himmler** and **Joachim von Ribbentrop**, despite their importance to Hitler and the regime. Also absent was **Herrmann Göring**, even though he had purchased a home in the area. What mattered were Hitler's personal preferences and increasingly those of **Eva Braun**. **Joseph Goebbels** and his growing family were frequent visitors but not part of what became a stable core of regulars that included **Albert Speer** and his wife, Margarete; **Heinrich Hoffmann**; and a retinue of secretaries and assistants. It is evidence of Braun's importance to Hitler and the Berghof court that those who hoped to remain a part of his entourage cultivated her favor assiduously, as did Bormann and Speer.

For members of the inner circle, there was nothing spontaneous or particularly relaxing about life at the Berghof, as everything revolved around Hitler's schedule. As usual, he arose very late, conducted meetings before presiding over lunch, which was followed by more meetings and a short walk with his entourage to a teahouse. Dinner was also served

Hitler with Eva Braun and Heinrich Hoffmann at the Berghof, circa late 1930s. *Courtesy of Bridgeman Images.*

late, and afterward, Hitler held more meetings before films were screened. Then came the monologues, which could stretch long after midnight, in front of the fireplace.

Hitler departed the Berghof for the last time on 14 July 1944 for the **Wolf's Lair**. The house was badly damaged in a British air raid on 25 April 1945 and the SS set fire to the rest of it on 4 May. American and French troops occupied Berchtesgaden later that day. The Bavarian government destroyed all but one of the complex's remaining structures in 1952. *See also* PERSONALITY.

BISMARCK, OTTO VON (1815–1898). As one of the most important European statesmen of the 19th century and a German national hero, Bismarck and his legacy inspired Hitler. He read Bismarck's memoirs while in **Landsberg Prison**, and he would display busts and portraits of the great man in the **chancellery** and in his residences. Like millions of other Germans, Hitler revered Bismarck for his role in creating the German Empire in 1871 after defeating **France** in a short war. Also admirable was his creation of a social safety net that served as a national unifier while undercutting the socialists.

Hitler would come to see himself not as Bismarck's heir but as a statesman and military leader who had superseded him. Bismarck's decision to exclude **Austria** from the German Empire conflicted with Hitler's **pan-German** views, and Hitler remedied this perceived shortcoming in March 1938 by annexing the country. The memory of Bismarck's campaign against the Catholic Church in the 1870s (the Kulturkampf, or the cultural struggle) served a different purpose by discouraging Hitler from confronting the churches more aggressively. Bismarck, moreover, was not a conqueror but a peacemaker and alliance builder, and Hitler had no intention of being either.

He made clear his admiration for—but also his distance from—Bismarck in a speech on 14 February 1939 in Hamburg. The occasion was the launch of the battleship *Bismarck*. Hitler saluted his memory for unifying part of German-speaking Europe and pointed to his social welfare policies as the forerunner of national socialism. But he identified Bismarck's shortcomings in a way that boosted his own profile: namely, that he was too soft on Germany's enemies abroad and at home, failures that the new German Reich under Hitler's leadership were now overcoming. *See also* CENTER PARTY (ZENTRUM); RELIGION.

BLITZKRIEG (LIGHTNING WAR). The association of lightning and warfare can be traced back to antiquity. In the modern world, description of modes of warfare involving a combination of surprise, power, and speed can be found in writings by Italian, Russian, Polish, French, English, and German journalists and military professionals. This is particularly true for the post–**World War I** period, when military strategists were thinking about how to avoid another stalemate and how new technologies of warfare, above all the airplane and the tank, could be deployed in coordinated assaults to deliver rapid, conclusive victories.

As for the German word *Blitzkrieg*, one of the earliest known uses was by Soviet marshal Mikhail Tukhachevsky in a speech to the general staff academy in 1937. It also appeared repeatedly in reporting on the **Czechoslovakia crisis**, with the term meaning "a surprise attack that would quickly overpower the target." It also showed up frequently in the press over the following year. When Germany invaded **Poland** on 1 September 1939, a few reporters for American and British newspapers concluded that the attack made a blitzkrieg in the West impossible because now the Allies could prepare properly.

There is no evidence that Hitler or any German officer or writer invented the term, and it was never used formally to denote a tactical doctrine by any of Nazi Germany's military branches. In the meeting on 5 November 1937 with his military commanders that produced the **Hossbach Memorandum**, he did make a reference to "lightning" ("Blitzartig schnell," or "lightning quick") in the context of his desire for a quick takeover of Czechoslovakia but not to a blitzkrieg. Nor was it an invention of Anglo-American journalists writing about the invasion of Poland. It was only after the invasion of the

Low Countries and then **France** in the spring of 1940 that the term came to characterize a particularly effective and modern form of warfare pioneered by the Germans: fast-moving and closely coordinated air and ground assaults [*see* GUDERIAN, HEINZ (1888–1954); WESER EXERCISE (WESERÜBUNG)]. A version of blitzkrieg, of course, was attempted on a massive scale in **Operation Barbarossa**, but it had failed by the fall of 1941, and thereafter the term would be almost exclusively associated with German victories in Poland and Western Europe.

BLOMBERG–FRITSCH AFFAIR (1938). Twin near-scandals in early 1938 involving war minister General Field Marshal Werner von Blomberg and **Wehrmacht** commander in chief Colonel-General Werner von Fritsch that Hitler used to further consolidate his control over the military and foreign ministry. It produced one of the few high-level purges in the regime's history, albeit one less well known than the **Röhm purge** four years earlier or the aftermath of the failed **assassination attempt** of July 1944.

The affair began in January with the marriage of Blomberg to Margarethe Gruhn, a former prostitute who had posed for pornographic photos depicting sex with a **Jewish** man. Hitler knew next to nothing of Gruhn's past. Whatever he knew did not stop him from approving the union as a commendable example of social leveling in the new Germany and standing as a witness to the marriage. On 24 January, **Hermann Göring**—who coveted Blomberg's job—informed Hitler of the details of Gruhn's background. Multiple eyewitness accounts report that Hitler was wracked with anxiety at the consequences of the story becoming public knowledge. **Joseph Goebbels** considered the matter at that moment to be the regime's worst crisis since the Röhm purge and remarked that Hitler "looked like a corpse."

With possibly feigned regret, Hitler decided that Blomberg must be sacked. Göring urged Blomberg to nullify the marriage. But he refused, and a shocked Hitler hustled him out of the position with a 50,000 Mark gift and a full pension as a field marshal.

Fritsch was the obvious choice to succeed Blomberg. Yet just as the news of Blomberg's indiscretion was sinking in, Hitler recalled that in 1936, **Heinrich Himmler** showed him a police file suggesting that Fritsch had sex with a young male prostitute and that someone claiming to have witnessed the liaison had attempted to blackmail him. The accusations were false, and in any case, Hitler refused at that time to move against Fritsch and ordered the file destroyed (*see* HOMOSEXUALITY). But now that he faced the prospect of one scandal and the possibility of another erupting if he made Fritsch war minister, he ordered the file reassembled. It had in fact never been destroyed completely. Unbeknownst to Hitler, Göring and Gestapo officers were already moving against Fritsch by refabricating what they knew to be a false accusation. A new file was immediately given to Hitler, who decided that Fritsch, too, would have to be sacked.

An outraged Fritsch insisted the accusation was false. In a tense meeting with Hitler on 26 January, Fritsch continued to proclaim his innocence. In a bizarre scene, he was confronted in person by the blackmailer, who had been hurriedly fished out of a penal camp by the Gestapo. Hitler seems to have believed the accuser or at least simply no longer trusted Fritsch and ordered that he be interrogated by the Gestapo. He had already asked the justice minister, Franz Gürtner, for an opinion on the matter. The interrogation and Gürtner's report convinced Hitler of Fritsch's guilt, and on 27 January, he sacked Fritsch.

Two problems remained unresolved: How would the whole sordid mess be kept out of the public's eye, and who would replace the two men? In their final meeting on 27 January, Blomberg (and, later that day, Goebbels) suggested that Hitler take personal command of the Wehrmacht, an idea Hitler embraced immediately. On 31 January, he decided to embed Blomberg's and Fritsch's departures as part of a wider leadership overhaul in the War and Foreign Ministries. Hitler appointed himself supreme commander of the Wehrmacht (here meaning all of Germany's armed forces). The War Ministry was dissolved and replaced with the Oberkommando der Wehrmacht (Supreme

Command of the Armed Forces; OKW), led by Hitler loyalist General **Wilhelm Keitel**, who was subordinate only to Hitler [see JODL, ALFRED (1890–1946)]. Artillery general **Walther von Brauchitsch** succeeded Fritsch as Oberkommando des Heeres (Army High Command; OKH). At the same time, a dozen generals were forced to retire. Only the **Luftwaffe**'s and navy's leadership, under Göring and Admiral Erich Raeder, respectively, was unchanged. In the Foreign Ministry, **Konstantin von Neurath** was replaced by the incompetent but loyal **Joachim von Ribbentrop**, and a slew of ambassadorships changed hands. **Walther Funk** became **economics** minister, filling the position left vacant with **Hjalmar Schacht**'s departure in the fall of 1937.

Hitler's behavior in late January and early February suggests that he seized on the unexpected revelation of Gruhn's background and a simultaneous move by Göring and the **Schutzstaffel** (Protection Squad; SS) against Fritsch to further concentrate power in his own hands. He was determined to accelerate plans for a new war in Europe, plans he felt were being impeded by overly cautious officers like Blomberg and Fritsch. But sacking them outright after the crucial November 1937 meeting in the Reich chancellery that produced the **Hossbach Memorandum** would have risked a powerful backlash among army officers—unless the two men's credibility and honor could be besmirched.

On 5 February, Hitler told stunned military leaders about what he had done and why. None raised any objections, and certainly no one had any interest in the details becoming public knowledge. That night he announced the purge at what was to be the final meeting of his cabinet. He demanded that ministers remain silent about what had set the dramatic events of the previous week in motion.

In March 1938, a Reich war court acquitted Fritsch, but Hitler refused any public rehabilitation. Fritsch was instead given command of his former artillery regiment. He was killed in action during the invasion of **Poland**. Blomberg remained in retirement and married to Margarethe. He was arrested by Allied forces and died in prison in 1946.

BORMANN, MARTIN (1900–1945). As Hitler's personal secretary and chief of the **National Socialist German Workers' Party** (Nazi Party; Nationalsozialistische Deutsche Arbeiterpartei; NSDAP) **chancellery**, Bormann became the regime's second-most-powerful official. Born in 1900 in central Germany, he served in the army during **World War I** as an officer's batman at a garrison in Naumberg and afterward trained to be a farm manager in the northern state of Mecklenburg. He joined several obscure Far-Right-wing groups and a paramilitary unit, the Freikorps (Free Corps) Rossbach.

In 1923, he was involved in the brutal murder of a man he and his comrades believed to be a communist infiltrator and served a year in prison. He joined the NSDAP in 1925 and the Frontbann, the stand-in for the **Sturmabteilung** (Stormtroopers; SA) during the period of the party's post–**Beer Hall Putsch** ban. Within a year, he was working for the party full time. His talents lay not in brawling or speechifying but in managing seemingly mundane day-to-day party business. Like numerous other national socialists of his generation, he combined these skills with unwavering ideological commitment, ruthless ambition, and blind loyalty to Hitler.

In the wake of **Gregor Strasser**'s resignation in 1932 and the party's reorganization in 1933, Hitler appointed the loyal but inept **Rudolf Hess** as the "leader's deputy" and the equally loyal but highly competent Bormann as Hess's deputy. As Hitler became consumed with preparing for the war, it would be Bormann who became indispensible to Hitler in managing party and domestic affairs. Almost constantly in his presence (he was not included in military briefings), Bormann distilled complex matters for Hitler and translated his verbal orders, moods, facial expressions, and offhand remarks into directives for party offices. Bormann was also responsible for obtaining and developing the land that became Hitler's retreat in the Bavarian Alps, where he would also serve as his private secretary. (See BERGHOF.) Eventually, he would manage all of Hitler's private property and financial assets.

Following Hess's surprise flight to Scotland on 10 May 1941, Hitler appointed Bormann head of the party chancellery. On 12 April 1943, he became secretary to the leader. With these promotions and with Hitler consumed with the war, Bormann's position as the most important official on domestic affairs was solidified, not least because he now controlled access to Hitler for all but a small handful of other officials. He was envied and despised by **Hermann Göring**, **Joseph Goebbels**, **Albert Speer**, and **Wilhelm Keitel**, but none of them were ever able to marginalize or dislodge him.

It is tempting to conclude that Bormann became the "real power" behind Hitler. But doing so would be to misunderstand who Bormann was and the nature of his devotion to Hitler. He was ideologically compatible with Hitler in every way. The only significant divergence was his determination to take a more actively radical anti-Christian stance than Hitler was willing to tolerate, and even on that issue, Bormann never sought to undermine, manipulate, or bypass his boss (*see* RELIGION).

Nor was his devotion to Hitler contingent on his own greed and vanity. He was averse to the spotlight, did not use his position to enrich himself, and never needed to be bribed by Hitler with gifts of money or property. Nor did his loyalty hinge on a desire to build up an independent power base within the party or, not least, on Germany's military fortunes. Bormann craved Hitler's unshakable trust in him, and that trust could only be earned and maintained by his ruthless efficiency, skillfulness at dealing with his mercurial and distrustful boss, and ability to translate Hitler's intentions into directives.

Along with Goebbels, Bormann was alone among those officials closest to Hitler in never losing faith in him. In the war's final months, he mirrored Hitler's detachment from reality by issuing a pointless flood of directives to what was left of the party's regional offices. Even at the very end, he did not disobey or ignore orders or surreptitiously send out feelers to Allied governments.

The day before his **suicide** on 30 April, Bormann had Hitler's "political testament" [*see* PERSONAL WILL AND POLITICAL TESTAMENT (1945)] shipped to the **Berghof** compound. In it, he appointed Bormann party minister in the successor regime to be led by Grand Admiral **Karl Dönitz**. Among the last to leave the bunker, Bormann and a handful of others walked through a railway tunnel north toward the Friedrichstrasse train station on the night of 1–2 May. They emerged amid shelling and close-quarters fighting between German and Red Army soldiers. A few of the bunker's former denizens managed to escape the city, while others were captured by the Russians. Then Bormann disappeared.

Lacking definitive proof of his death or current whereabouts, the **International Military Tribunal** (IMT) charged and convicted him in absentia on counts 3 and 4 (war crimes and crimes against humanity) and sentenced him to death. Bormann's guilt was proven beyond any doubt by the documentary record, which was so extensive that his entire case was dispensed with in just over an hour. American prosecutor Telford Taylor recalled that no lawyer had ever been given a more thankless task than Bormann's defense attorney, who could hope only to have Bormann confirmed dead.

He had in fact committed suicide on 2 May 1945, near what is now Berlin's main train station. A construction crew discovered his remains in 1972. Though they were quickly identified as Bormann's by the director of the Institute for Forensic Medicine in West Berlin and by Bormann's former dentist, lingering uncertainty fueled decades of speculation that he had managed to escape to South America. DNA tests of the remains conducted in 1998 proved they were Bormann's. *See also* LEADERSHIP PRINCIPLE (FÜHRERPRINZIP).

BOXHEIM DOCUMENTS. By the spring of 1931, public disruptions and violent acts perpetrated by Far-Right and -Left paramilitaries were getting out of hand. The aggressiveness and radicalism of the **Sturmabteilung** (Storm-troopers; SA) was not only a problem for its victims and the republic's beleaguered domestic police forces but also for Hitler. The SA seemed increasingly out of control at the moment when the **National Socialist German Workers' Party** (Nazi Party; Nationalsozialistische Deutsche Arbeiterpartei; NSDAP) was on the verge of an even greater electoral breakthrough than had been achieved in **elections** the previous September. In April, Walther Stennes, a regional SA leader in Northeast Germany, occupied the party's main offices in Berlin and attacked its **Schutzstaffel** (Protection Squad; SS) guards. Hitler, concerned about reassuring military and **economic** elites that he would not pursue the kind of "national socialist" revolution dreamed of by SA radicals like Stennes, brought **Ernst Röhm** back from Bolivia to take charge of the essential but unruly organization. Hitler then had all SA men swear allegiance to him (Hitler) for good measure. Though the "Stennes revolt" had been suppressed, it would not be the end of the tensions between the paramilitaries, Hitler, and the party, culminating in the **Röhm purge** of June 1934.

Chancellor Heinrich Brüning had already decided to crack down on the disorder, whether instigated by Right or Left. In November 1931, police in the state of Hesse discovered a set of plans for the establishment of an SA-led military-style dictatorship in response to a communist seizure of power. They had been drawn up by Werner Best, a young lawyer and regional party official who would later become a Gestapo officer and **Reinhard Heydrich**'s deputy. Best had presented them to regional party officials at the Boxheim vineyard and then to national party figures in August 1930. There is evidence that **Joseph Goebbels** knew of the plan and discussed it with Hitler.

News of the documents' discovery embarrassed Hitler. He had, after all, promised to operate within the bounds of legality. He ordered **Hermann Göring** to reassure President **Paul von Hindenburg** that he had nothing to do with them and that he remained committed to a legal route to power. In early December 1931, Hitler gave held his first press conference with foreign reporters, in which he promised the party would obey the law. The scandal also damaged the possibility of a **Center Party** (Zentrum) and NSDAP majority coalition in Hesse, despite Brüning pressuring the public prosecutor to treat the matter as a minor incident rather than evidence of SA and Nazi Party ruthlessness. Conservative nationalists used the moment to try, without success, to draw voters away from the NSDAP, leading Hitler to lash out at his erstwhile allies.

Despite the blow to Hitler and plans for a regional Center-NSDAP coalition, Brüning was not in the mood to take chances with the SA and banned the wearing of uniforms by political groups. The ban did nothing to dissuade its members, who simply changed into civilian clothes. Brüning doubled down and, with the support of the **Social Democratic Party of Germany** (Sozialdemokratische Partei Deutschlands; SPD) and military officers, convinced Hindenburg to outlaw the SA in April 1932. The ban did little to restrain the paramilitaries.

As a public political scandal, the Boxheim affair blew over quickly. Charges of treason against Best were soon dropped for alleged lack of evidence, yet one more example of the leniency shown to the Far Right by the republic's conservative-dominated judiciary. The exposure of Best's plan, however, briefly opened a window on how the Nazis really intended to come to power: by seizing on a national emergency—such as an attempted Bolshevik-style coup d'etat—to establish a dictatorship. And Best wasn't really a lone actor, as police in Berlin discovered a similar set of plans in the spring of 1932.

But the main problem wasn't police raids and exposure. It was that the **Communist Party of Germany** (Kommunistische Partei Deutschlands; KPD) wasn't able to play its part. Despite its recent electoral successes, it was in no position to seize power in Germany, and in any case, **Joseph Stalin**, who controlled the KPD's leadership via the Communist International (Comintern), would not permit it to try. As it turned out, the moment for implementing a modified version of Best's plan came a month after Hitler was appointed **chancellor**, when a Dutch communist was arrested for allegedly starting the **Reichstag fire** on the night of 27–28 February. The fire, almost certainly a Gestapo-SA operation, greatly accelerated an existing wave of SA violence against the new regime's opponents and the emergency decree and **Enabling Act** that laid the legal foundations for Hitler's dictatorship.

BRAUCHITSCH, WALTHER VON (1881–1948). Brauchitsch was from a family steeped in the Prussian officer corps tradition. He served across the western front in **World War I**; received the Iron Cross, first class; and reached the rank of major. He remained in the army after the war and specialized in the development of artillery doctrine. When Hitler came to power, Brauchitsch was given command of the East Prussian military district and was appointed commanding general of the First Army Corps in 1935. The turning point came in February 1938, when Hitler sacked **Wehrmacht** commander in chief Werner von Blomberg and appointed Brauchitsch as his successor after promoting him to the rank of colonel-general [see BLOMBERG–FRITSCH AFFAIR (1938)]. Though some of the details remain unclear, Hitler loaned Brauchitsch a substantial sum of money and provided him with a monthly *Aufwandsentschädigung* (expense allowance).

Brauchitsch was competent but unable to stand up to Hitler effectively. While he was among those high-ranking officers who were extremely worried about the possibility of a general war breaking out over the **Czechoslovakia crisis**, he resisted being drawn into any attempt to overthrow Hitler. He was most closely involved in the invasion of **Poland**, **France**, the **Balkans**, and the Soviet Union [see OPERATION BARBAROSSA (1941)]. After the Wehrmacht failed to capture Moscow in 1941 and he suffered a heart attack in November, Hitler dismissed him and made himself commander in chief (*see* MILITARY COMMANDER). Allied soldiers arrested Brauchitsch at his estate in the Brdy Mountains outside Prague. He was called as a witness before the **International Military Tribunal** (IMT) but died in 1948 before he could be indicted by a British military court. *See also* JODL, ALFRED (1890–1946); KEITEL, WILHELM (1882–1946).

BRAUN, EVA (1912–1945). Hitler met Eva Braun sometime in the fall of 1929, when she was working as an assistant in **Heinrich Hoffmann**'s Munich studio. She was 18, and Hitler was 40. Over the following two years, he gave her small gifts and took her on occasional dates. They became closer after **Geli Raubal**'s suicide in September 1931. At that point, however, Hitler had already ruled out anything like a conventional private life, including marriage and children. The harsh press spotlight in the aftermath of Geli's suicide made him determined to keep the existence of his relationship with Braun out of the public eye. This level of discretion, along with the fact that by 1932 Hitler was thoroughly consumed with electioneering and holding the party together, may have prompted Braun to attempt suicide—or fake an attempt—toward the end of the year. She apparently made or staged a second attempt in May 1935. Yet Braun continued to tolerate being kept almost entirely out of the public eye.

In the fall of 1934, Hitler made it clear to those closest to him that he would not abide malicious gossip about her or attempts to poke around in his most private affairs. The relatively few party and military officials who were guests at Hitler's various residences and learned of Braun understood that they were not to speak of anything they witnessed. This regimen of secrecy was so effective that most Germans first learned of her existence and relationship with Hitler when the war ended and he and Braun were dead.

A lack of reliable sources—no personal correspondence between the two is known to have survived the war—make it difficult to assess the precise nature of their relationship. Eva seems to have grown out of the infatuation she apparently felt in their early years together and accepted her role as a mistress who was expected to maintain exceptionally stringent levels of discretion. Hitler purchased a villa for her in Munich, and when she wasn't residing there with her sister (and holding parties when Hitler was away), she was at the **Berghof**, where she became a central part of his inner circle. Multiple independent sources suggest that she and Hitler had a conventional sexual relationship (*see* PERSONALITY; WOMEN).

After the war, **Albert Speer** and others who belonged to the Berghof circle tried to portray her as a vacuous socialite with no interest in or knowledge of politics, the war, and genocide. She was in fact a shrewd political operative in her own sphere. Given her closeness to Hitler, this position was hardly unimportant, and she knew it. By feeding supposedly candid photos and home movies of Hitler and the members of the circle to Hoffmann, she was purposely contributing to the **Führer myth**, very much a political project.

The two seemed to grow increasingly close in the war years. Braun was the only person who could interrupt one of Hitler's monologues out of consideration for those being subjected to it. She became skilled in entertaining guests at the Berghof and occasionally lifting Hitler's spirits as Germany's war effort faltered. She remained completely loyal to him, the single most important reason he tolerated and even seemed to have valued her presence. This loyalty extended to the very end. In the fall of 1944, she decided she would share whatever fate awaited him and, as early as January 1945, planned to take her own life in the event of his death. She moved into the bunker complex on 7 March. It is not true that Hitler urged her to flee the city.

For years, she had been living in a kind of fantasy world. But it was one thing to keep the reality of the looming catastrophe at bay in the Berghof and quite another in the bunker as the Red Army battered Berlin to rubble and closed in on the **chancellery**. Yet even then, she tried to enjoy herself and entertain those around her. As late as 19 April, she wrote to a friend expressing confidence that all would soon turn around for Germany and that Hitler seemed full of hope. Ten days later, she and Hitler were married in a quiet ceremony in the bunker. The following day she killed herself while sitting next to him in his private study. *See also* SUICIDE (30 APRIL 1945).

BULGARIA. Like other states in the region, Bulgaria sought to maintain as much independence as possible while gaining long-sought-after territories at the expense of its neighbors. It managed to accomplish both to a greater extent than any other East European nation, at least for a few years. This was in large part because of its relatively marginal **economic** and strategic significance to Hitler. It was also due to the canniness of King Boris III, who once joked that as his army was pro-German, his subjects pro-Russian, and his wife Italian, he was the country's only pro-Bulgarian. Even Hitler and **Joseph Goebbels** would express grudging admiration for his ability to maneuver between two voracious great powers.

Despite its relative weakness, Bulgaria was not without some leverage. In 1940, as Hitler was trying to convince its government to join the **Tripartite Pact**, Boris deftly dangled the prospect of closer ties with Moscow to convince Hitler to force **Romania** to return southern Dobruja, which he did in September. Even then, the king resisted joining the pact until 1 March 1941. The moment at which his country mattered most to Hitler was in the run-up to the German invasion of Greece in early April, as Hitler needed the Bulgarian government to grant transit rights to German forces. The reward was the annexation of eastern Macedonia and western Thrace, two territories long coveted by Bulgarian nationalists.

In Thrace, the Bulgarians acted with extreme brutality, expelling thousands of Greeks, killing thousands more in response to local uprisings, and implementing a crude program of cultural "Bulgarianization" and the first stages of a settlement scheme. Bulgaria's role in the **Holocaust** was in some ways similar to other European states. Boris relented to German pressure to enact anti-Semitic laws in the fall of 1940, though they were never enforced with any rigor. In March and April 1943, the government rounded up and deported around 11,000 **Jews** in Macedonia and Thrace to Treblinka, where most were murdered. Yet attempts to deport Bulgarian Jews living in the "old kingdom" were met with powerful protests from opposition politicians and the Bulgarian Orthodox Church. Boris relented to the local pressure, and as a result, most of Bulgaria's prewar population of Jews (around 50,000) survived, though some 20,000 were forcibly expelled from Sofia to the countryside.

Of greater concern to Boris than Germany was the Soviet Union. While he would declare war on the **United States**, he would never do so on the Soviet Union. Nor did he contribute any forces to **Operation Barbarossa**. His only concession was to agree to police part of Serbia, which freed up some German forces for service in Russia. In the aftermath of the German debacle at Stalingrad, Boris concluded that Germany could not win the war and even quietly reached out to the Allies about a peace deal. He died on 28 August 1943, after a brief illness. The succeeding government continued to try to extricate the country from the war, an objective that took on considerable urgency when American planes began bombing raids in November. The following year, Bulgaria declared neutrality and then declared war on Germany, just as Soviet forces invaded on 8 September. Within a year, it would share the fate of most other Central and East European states occupied by the Red Army. While Dobruja remained part of Bulgaria, Macedonia and Thrace were returned to Yugoslavia and Greece, respectively. *See also* BALKANS.

CANARIS, WILHELM (1887–1945). Canaris was the chief of the Abwehr, the intelligence section of the Armed Forces High Command, from 1935 to 1944. He joined the German navy as an 18-year-old cadet in 1905. He served in **World War I** with considerable distinction, particularly as a submarine commander. It was also during the war that he developed intelligence-gathering skills. He remained in the navy through the 1920s and early 1930s, until he was chosen to head the Abwehr.

Canaris became a central figure in the elite **opposition** to Hitler. Like other members of this segment of opponents of Hitler and the regime, Canaris supported rearmament and German war aims, but they came to believe that Hitler would lead the country to catastrophe unless he was stopped or removed. Canaris's opposition began in earnest following the **Blomberg–Fritsch affair** and took concrete form during the **Czechoslovakia crisis**. In the case of the latter, Canaris was involved in a plot by high-ranking officers to overthrow Hitler should his attempt to grab Czechoslovakia provoke a war with Britain and **France**. He was also appalled at the brutality of the **Wehrmacht** and **Schutzstaffel** (Protection Squad; SS) in **Poland**, which he knew that Hitler had authorized.

Canaris and his deputy, Hans Oster, recruited to the Abwehr a network of regime opponents. They withheld intelligence from the military, mislead Hitler and high-ranking officers, and fed warnings and secrets to the Allies. It remains something of a mystery that Canaris was not removed sooner, not only for his repeated failures as an intelligence chief but also because he was never a Hitler sycophant.

SS Reich Security Main Office chief **Reinhard Heydrich** coveted Canaris's position, but Heydrich's assassination in 1942 gave Canaris something of a temporary reprieve. In January 1944, Hitler finally sacked him and placed him under house arrest. Responsibility for military intelligence was transferred to the Sicherheitsdienst (Security Service; SD) of the SS.

It was Canaris who supplied a bomb disguised as a gift of cognac that failed to detonate on a plane carrying Hitler in March 1943. It was something of a perverse irony that Canaris was arrested by the Gestapo in the sweep that followed the 20 July 1944 **assassination attempt**, as there was no convincing evidence that he was involved in that plot. He was imprisoned in the Flossenbürg **concentration camp** and hanged there on 9 April 1945, two weeks before its liberation by American forces.

CENTER PARTY (ZENTRUM). The Center Party formed in 1870 to represent the interests of most German Catholics, particularly in western Germany. Its sister party in heavily Catholic Bavaria was the more conservative Bavarian Peoples' Party. The Center Party was a crucial component of the Weimar coalition. The other two were the Marxist but anticommunist **Social Democratic Party of Germany** (Sozialdemokratische Partei Deutschlands; SPD) and the liberal German Democratic Party. Throughout the 1920s, the three were able to form a majority in the **Reichstag**

against the antirepublic Far Right and Left. In addition to representing Catholics against the Protestant-dominated Prussian political, military, and **economic** elites, the Center Party combined support for social welfare legislation with cultural conservatism.

Like the **Communist Party of Germany** (Kommunistische Partei Deutschlands; KPD), however, it was subject to strong political influence from abroad, in this case from the Vatican. Over the course of the decade, Pope Pius XI encouraged a turn to the antidemocratic Right in the Center Party as the most effective way to block liberalizing tendencies and to prevent the Left from dominating the Reichstag. His principal instrument was the Vatican's nuncio (an ecclesiastical ambassador to a state or international organization) to Germany and the next pope, Eugenio Pacelli, the man who would also succeed Pius XI as **Pius XII**. A turning point came in 1928, when Pacelli was instrumental in getting a close ally, the prelate and Reichstag deputy Ludwig Kaas, elected as head of the party.

The Vatican's support for right-wing authoritarian parties and regimes was hardly limited to Germany. It extended to its conclusion of a concordat with **Benito Mussolini**'s regime in 1929, its backing of Engelbert Dollfuss's dictatorship in **Austria**, and support for **Francisco Franco**'s forces in the **Spanish Civil War**. In 1931, Pacelli and Kaas already were planning for a concordat with a hoped-for antiliberal and antileft regime in Germany.

Thus, by the early 1930s, the Center Party had mutated from a pillar of German democracy to one of its principal gravediggers. The electoral earthquakes of September 1930 and July 1932 would mark another turning point. Though the SPD had lost support and an alliance between it and the KPD was out of the question, conservative nationalist parties could not assemble a majority coalition without the **National Socialist German Workers Party** (Nazi Party; Nationalsozialistische Deutsche Arbeiterpartei; NSDAP), and Hitler would not budge on his demand for the chancellorship or nothing. It would be the scheming between **Franz von Papen** of the Center Party, Hitler, and the circle around President **Paul von Hindenburg** in January 1933 that would end the impasse [*see* CHANCELLOR, APPOINTMENT AS (30 JANUARY 1933)].

Following the **Reichstag fire** on 27 February, Center Party delegates in the Reichstag voted in support of the **Enabling Act**. Over the following months, the **Sturmabteilung** (Stormtroopers; SA) and the Gestapo launched a sustained assault on the party, its members employed in the civil service, its newspapers, and its affiliated organizations. Meanwhile, Kaas continued to work with the Vatican on the concordat, as did Papen, who had been demanding publicly that the Center Party should dissolve itself, which it did on July 5 once the negotiations between Berlin and the Vatican were concluded. *See also* RELIGION.

CHANCELLOR, APPOINTMENT AS (30 JANUARY 1933). Hitler's and the party's prospects appeared dim at the end of 1932. Though the **National Socialist German Workers' Party** (Nazi Party; Nationalsozialistische Deutsche Arbeiterpartei; NSDAP) had become the single largest party in the **Reichstag**, it had lost seats the following November, and many observers suspected the party had reached the peak of its popularity. It was also running short on funds. That summer, Hitler lost the presidential **election** to **Paul von Hindenburg**, and while Hindenburg remained unwilling to appoint Hitler chancellor, Hitler remained just as stubbornly committed to accepting nothing less. Frustration was mounting among rank-and-file party members and the **Sturmabteilung** (Stormtroopers; SA). Despite the electoral gains, extensive grassroots mobilization, and violence, real power seemed persistently just out of reach. The news of **Gregor Strasser**'s resignation from the party in early December was another blow, leaving Hitler so badly shaken that he told **Joseph Goebbels** he was considering killing himself.

Given this state of affairs, Hitler's appointment as chancellor by Hindenburg on 30 January 1933 seems all the more remarkable. Three related factors made it possible. One was the inability of conservative nationalists to form a majority coalition in the Reichstag without the NSDAP. The second was Hitler's steadfast commitment to an all-or-nothing strategy. The third involved efforts among a small number of conservative nationalists with access to Hindenburg to resolve the first two problems.

A crucial first step to breaking the impasse was a meeting on 4 January between Hitler and **Franz von Papen** at the estate of banker Kurt von Schroeder outside Cologne. Papen believed an alliance with Hitler would allow him to undermine then chancellor Kurt von Schleicher, who had replaced Papen on 3 December. For his part, Hitler needed Papen's access to Hindenburg. The latter proposed a kind of dual chancellorship arrangement. Hitler was unmoved, though he agreed to include Papen allies in a new cabinet. Nothing was decided at the meeting, but it brought the two men closer together, if only in their determination to be rid of Schleicher.

On 9 January, Hindenburg encouraged Papen to continue talks with Hitler, though quietly. The press had sniffed out the supposedly secret 4 January meeting, and the following week, newspapers were filled with speculation about what Hitler and Papen were really up to. The two met again the night of 10–11 January and again made no progress. At that moment, Hitler and the party were pouring enormous resources into state parliament elections scheduled for 15 January in the rural region of Lippe-Detmold in northwestern Germany. The party received 39.5 percent of the vote, which was not a particularly impressive outcome. But party propaganda trumpeted it as a great victory.

The massive effort in a tiny rural area was clearly intended mainly to bolster the flagging energy and confidence of party members and supporters. By extension, a strong showing would presumably give Hitler more leverage with Papen by demonstrating that the party remained the key to a government dominated by the nationalist Right. Hitler then subjected regional party leaders to a three-hour speech in Weimar to denounce Gregor Strasser for secretly meeting with Schleicher in early December. Schleicher had tried to cleave Strasser and his followers away from Hitler. Though Strasser rebuffed the approach and resigned from the party, Hitler took the opportunity to end the career of the official most responsible for rebuilding the NSDAP after the **Beer Hall Putsch**. More generally, Hitler was reasserting his absolute authority over the party and justifying his all-or-nothing strategy.

At the same time, Schleicher's position was getting shakier. He was unable to divide the NSDAP. His promising job-creation proposals not only failed to win over the Left—the **Social Democratic Party of Germany** (Sozialdemokratische Partei Deutschlands; SPD) and trade unions remained unified in opposition—but also enraged the Right. **German National People's Party** (Deutschnationale Volkspartei; DNVP) delegates attacked him in the Reichstag as a Bolshevist, and a powerful organization representing Germany's wealthy landowners accused him of leading German agriculture to ruin. Then he and Oskar von Hindenburg, for reasons that remain unclear, had a falling out. But Schleicher's biggest problem was that he could not assemble a majority in parliament. By the third week of January, he had lost Hindenburg's confidence. But for Hindenburg, the ongoing, if still inconclusive, talks between Papen and Hitler pointed to the emerging possibility of a conservative nationalist–NSDAP coalition and hence a parliamentary majority. On 28 January, Hindenburg dismissed Schleicher. The following night, Papen got the president's approval for a new government with Hitler as chancellor. Papen used rumors of a coup to close a deal on a new cabinet quickly. He would serve as vice chancellor. Conservatives dominated the cabinet, with National Socialists occupying only two positions other than the chancellorship. Hindenburg remained in a powerful position as president. Though not blind to Hitler's and the NSDAP's radicalism, they were convinced that they could control him. This conviction led them to make the single most catastrophic political miscalculation in modern history.

Hitler was sworn in as chancellor shortly before noon on 30 January. He was 43 years old. Goebbels quickly put together a celebration involving hundreds of uniformed SA, **Schutzstaffel** (Protection Squad; SS), and Stahlhelm members who that night carried torches beneath the window of Hitler's new office in the **chancellery** as he stood on the balcony. Top party officials and ordinary Germans who supported Hitler were ecstatic, though very few outside Hitler's most devoted supporters saw the appointment as a turning point in modern history. If anything, many Germans assumed the government would soon fall as others had in rapid succession. Conservatives, along with many liberals and Social Democrats, assumed that Hitler would now be boxed in by the more experienced conservative elites, an opinion shared by foreign diplomats. The SPD committed itself to **opposition** within the limits of the law. Its leadership refused to support the **Communist Party of Germany**'s (Kommunistische Partei Deutchlands; KPD) call for a general strike.

The republic's many weaknesses, the **economic** crisis, the deeply divided Left, the apparent dynamism of Hitler and the NSDAP, Hitler's fixation on the chancellor's office, and the determination of a minority of conservative nationalists to undermine democracy did not make Hitler's appointment and everything that followed inevitable. Least of all did it spell the immediate end of democracy in Germany. But it was a political milestone, and having reached it, Hitler would waste no time in destroying the republic and creating his dictatorship. *See also* CENTER PARTY (ZENTRUM); COORDINATION (GLEICHSCHALTUNG); PIUS XII, POPE (EUGENIO PACELLI; 1876–1958); RÖHM PURGE (1934).

CHANCELLERY. In 1875, four years after the creation of the German Empire, a former

Hitler's first cabinet, Berlin, February 1933. From left to right: Walther Funk, Hans Heinrich Lammers, Walther Darré, Franz Seldte, Franz Gürtner, Joseph Goebbels, Paul von Eltz-Rübenach, Adolf Hitler, Hermann Göring, Kurt Schmitt, Werner von Blomberg, Wilhelm Frick, Konstantin Freiherr von Neurath, Hjalmar Schacht, Lutz Graf Schwerin von Krosigk, Johannes Popitz, Franz von Papen, and Otto Meissner. *Courtesy of the United States Holocaust Memorial Museum.*

palace on Wilhelmstrasse in central Berlin purchased by the Prussian state became the office of the Reich chancellor. A small modern annex was completed in 1930. It was in this annex that President **Paul von Hindenburg** appointed Hitler **chancellor**. Beginning in 1935, the annex was redesigned and expanded and became Hitler's Berlin residence. The renovation included the construction of the first of two underground bunkers, with a second added in 1943.

Hitler hated the annex but had no intention of moving into any existing palace. Planning for a grand new building, based in part on his sketches, began in 1934. In January 1938, Hitler gave **Albert Speer** the job of completing its design and building it in record time. Given an unlimited budget and answering to Hitler alone, Speer did it in 12 months, driving workers to exhaustion and injuries and deploying slave labor from **concentration camps**.

In contrast to its spare exterior, the new chancellery's interior was more ornate and decorated with different types of marble, wood paneling, tapestries, sculptures, mosaics, and large paintings. Hitler's office was enormous, 400 square meters, with impractically outsized desks and tables that he never used. The point was not to be practical but to overwhelm and intimidate visitors. Not least, the chancellery was to reflect Hitler's self-perception as a new kind of leader. It is revealing of his expanding megalomania that after a year in residence, he decided its living quarters were too small. Speer began working on what would have been an enormous palace, a nightmarish Nazi version of a palazzo of Renaissance Florence.

Hitler intended the complex to be part of Berlin's transformation into a gargantuan imperial capital to be renamed Germania. Along with the redesigned Templehof airport, the new chancellery was the only part of Hitler's grotesque architectural fantasy to be completed. It was heavily damaged in air raids in February 1945, and Hitler decamped for the newly built Führerbunker (leader's bunker), where he would spend the last weeks of his life. Largely reduced to a pile of rubble in the **Battle of Berlin**, it was completely demolished in 1949. *See also* SUICIDE.

CHURCHILL, WINSTON (1874–1965). As one of his many biographers observed, if it weren't for Hitler, Churchill's political career might have ended like his father's: in obscurity. Winston Churchill had long been wary of Hitler, and by 1938, he was Great Britain's best-known critic of **appeasement**. Refusing to believe statements by Hitler proclaiming his desire for peace, Churchill thought collective security should be pursued and the **League of Nations** supported but not without rearmament. Hence, he had little use for disarmament talks in **Geneva**. But Churchill's view was global in scope, his highest priority being the protection of Britain's increasingly restive empire. His strategic calculations and temperament precluded making a deal with Hitler, who for years had hoped for some kind of arrangement with Britain and probably never understood why Churchill chose to stay in the war.

That choice, of course, was totally dependent on American aid. The power imbalance between Britain and the **United States** was clear well before December 1941, despite the close relationship that had developed between London and Washington since 1940. Churchill understood the fact that Britain could not remain in the war without assistance from the United States, and that would entail accepting subordinate status in the alliance. Fortunately, Roosevelt saw Hitler as the greatest threat to American security and understood the necessity of keeping Britain in the war.

Like Roosevelt, Stalin, and Hitler, Churchill took charge of the entire war effort. Fortunately, the chiefs-of-staff committee and the war cabinet were staffed with competent men and functioned well. Their members and Britain's best generals held up against Churchill's constant meddling and flood of harebrained schemes. Most worrisome among the latter was his determination to open the second front in the Mediterranean, first in North **Africa**, then in what he called Nazi Germany's "soft underbelly"—the **Balkans**. Churchill got his way on the first part but not the second. The American preference for a cross-channel invasion of **France** prevailed.

Churchill was more concerned about the fate of postwar Eastern Europe than Roosevelt seemed to be. He even went so far as to meet one on one with Stalin in October 1944 to divide much of Eastern Europe and the Balkans into spheres of influence. But even if the American president had been more committed to the region's independence from Moscow, it is difficult to see how things would have turned out differently. The fact was that in the spring of 1945, the Red Army occupied nearly all of Eastern Europe, and **Japan** had not yet been defeated. In the short term, only a new war with the Soviet Union might have kept Eastern Europe independent, and that was unthinkable to all but a handful of deluded Nazis and fanatical American anticommunists.

Churchill's relative position in the alliance was greatly diminished by the end of 1943. The **Battle of the Atlantic** had been won, planning for **Operation Overlord** began in April, the tide of the war had turned definitively on the eastern front, the **strategic bombing campaign** was well underway, and Anglo-American forces had invaded **Italy**. The remainder of the war and the shaping of the postwar world would be determined by the Americans and the Soviets.

CINEMA AND TELEVISION, REPRESENTATIONS IN. No other modern dictator has been portrayed on film as frequently and as divergently as Hitler. Ironically, he authorized relatively few films of himself, with the three most important (*Victory of Faith*, ***Triumph of the Will***, and *Olympia*) directed by **Leni Riefenstahl**. Dramatic and documentary films about Hitler began appearing outside Germany as early as 1939. Up to the present day, most have fallen into one or more distinct categories: satires, incarnation of evil, the madman, counterfactual and fantastical, and humanizing. The most consistent form of Hitler portrayals has been the satire. Charlie Chaplin's *The Great Dictator* (1940) depicts a megalomaniacal Hitler-like character named Adenoid Hynkel, played by Chaplin. Hitler—or a Hitler impersonator—also appeared in several Three Stooges shorts; a 1943 Disney cartoon (*The Führer's Face*); a 1943 Warner Brothers cartoon, *Tokio Jokio*; and in Ernst Lubitsch's *To Be or Not to Be* (1942). These and others, such as the 1940 British film *Let George Do It!* (released in the **United States** as *To Hell with Hitler*), blend satire with fantastic scenarios involving unlikely characters impersonating, mocking, or even encountering Hitler.

After the war, the dominant trend in film and television productions became portrayals of Hitler at various stages of his life as evil personified, depictions that often reinforced the common misperception that he was a madman. Satires along the lines of *The Great Dictator* seemed inappropriate given the war's destructiveness and the growing awareness of the **Holocaust**. Chaplin points to this issue in his autobiography, in which he recalls being determined to mock Hitler's **racist** nonsense but confesses that he later regretted making the film, given what he had learned about Nazi genocide. To these would be added a growing number of television documentaries on Hitler—most notably a German series in the 1990s directed by Guido Knopp—that includes reenactments.

At the same time, Hitler (and ex-Nazis in general) became the subject of a spate of counterfactual and fantastical thrillers, the best known of which became the 1978 film adaptation of Ira Levin's novel *The Boys from Brazil*. The film imagines **Schutzstaffel** (Protection Squad; SS) physician Josef Mengele (a real-life SS officer who survived the war and escaped to South America) producing 95 clones of Hitler with the intention of raising the boys to lead a Fourth Reich. Others, like the cult classic *They Saved Hitler's Brain* (1963), blend satire (perhaps unintentional) and the conspiracy-counterfactual theme.

Since 2000, some of the most prominent productions have focused on Hitler's early life or on his last days. As one historian notes, these portrayals tend to humanize Hitler to a greater extent than ever before. The first two in this category, the 2002 feature film *Max* and the 2003 television series *Hitler—The Rise of Evil*, dramatize his early years. In *Max* (directed by the Dutch American Menno Meyjes), a young Hitler arrives in Munich after the war and befriends a fictional **Jewish** art dealer who tries to get him to develop his rudimentary talents so he can become a professional artist. The scenario also places *Max* squarely in the counterfactual category. The makers of *Hitler—The Rise of Evil* claimed to have based the series on the most reliable current scholarship, namely British historian Ian Kershaw's recently published two-volume biography, but the result not only presents a version of Hitler's early life derived more from *Mein Kampf* than Kershaw's books but also suggests that Hitler was born evil. Hence the series, while attempting to portray Hitler as a person, falls back on the older, more one-dimensional personification-of-evil trope.

The film that generated the most commentary—and controversy—related to humanizing Hitler was Oliver Hirschbiegel's *Der Untergang* (2004; released in English as *Downfall*). Unlike its immediate predecessors, the film was a huge hit in Germany and the United States. It depicts Hitler's final days in the **chancellery** bunker complex in Berlin. Hirschbiegel depicts Hitler as veering between bouts of morose self-pity and wild, delusional rants. The director and screenwriter aimed to make a historically accurate film, and it is shot in a spare, documentary style. Above all, the screenwriter, Bernd Eichinger, wanted to humanize Hitler. While the film attracted many favorable reviews from film critics and some historians, others questioned its detached presentation of Hitler and wondered what it was the filmmakers were trying to say.

Since *Der Untergang*, satires have dominated cinematic representations of Hitler. They had not really disappeared after 1945. Mel Brooks made *The Producers* in 1967 and remade Lubitsch's *To Be or Not to Be* in 1983, though Hitler is not a central character in either film. In 1970, British comedy group Monty Python released a sketch ("The North Minehead By-Election") for its series that features John Cleese as a Mr. Hilter campaigning as the leader of the National Bocialist Party in a local British election. In a famous 1975 episode of Cleese's series *Fawlty Towers*, the proprietor of a small inn (played by Cleese) suffers a head injury and terrorizes his well-behaved German guests with an unhinged imitation of Hitler, goose-stepping and screaming in German-sounding gibberish.

Comedies with Hitler as a central character have made a strong comeback in recent years, beginning with Swiss Jewish filmmaker Dany Levy's 2007 *Mein Führer*, a satirical account set in 1944 of a depressed Hitler being tutored by a Jewish acting coach who **Joseph Goebbels** hopes will rekindle his talent for crowd-rousing hate mongering. Levy's film was followed by Swiss director Urs Odermatt's *Mein Kampf*, which goes back to the years in **Vienna**, with a plotline that has a bumbling Hitler befriend two Jewish men with distinctly ominous consequences. American director Quentin Tarantino's 2009 *Inglourious Basterds* blends all themes. A loose remake of an eponymously named 1978 film, Tarantino's film blends the comedic, incarnation of pure evil, and counterfactual themes. Multiple story lines converge on the assassination of Hitler in a Paris theater by a group of Jewish American soldiers. German director David Wnendt's 2015 comedy hit *Er ist wieder da* (released in English as *Look Who's Back*) has Hitler waking up in Berlin in 2014 and becoming a celebrity. The 2019 film *JoJo Rabbit*, directed by Taiko Waititi, blends the fantastical and the comedic with a portrayal of a conflicted German boy who in the last years of the war conjures up an imaginary Hitler as a friend or perhaps a Satan-like figure.

Since the end of the war, historians, journalists, filmmakers, and actors have all debated the tensions between the different genres of Hitler representations, though satires no longer generate much controversy. Some lauded portraying Hitler as the incarnation of evil as appropriate and necessary, while others argued that doing so turned him into a one-dimensional caricature, a demon with strange powers rather than a human being. And while there have been many films about the regime's victims and opponents, there have been relatively fewer that deal with ordinary non-Jewish Germans whose support made the dictatorship and its crimes possible.

COMMUNIST PARTY OF GERMANY (KOMMUNISTISCHE PARTEI DEUTSCHLANDS; KPD). During **World War I**, the **Social Democratic Party of Germany** (Sozialdemokratische

Partei Deutschlands; SPD) split into two factions. The majority favored continued qualified support for the war effort, while a minority, the Independent Social Democrats, stood opposed. It was from within this minority faction that Karl Liebknecht and Rosa Luxemburg established the KPD in December 1918.

In early January 1919, the new party's most radical elements attempted to launch a Bolshevik-style coup d'etat in Berlin. With the support of the SPD, the army and right-wing paramilitaries (Freikorps, or Free Corps) suppressed the revolt with extreme violence, and Liebknecht and Luxemburg were murdered. More such attempted uprisings and violent responses followed over the next four years in Munich, the Ruhr industrial region, and the port city of Hamburg [see BAVARIAN SOVIET REPUBLIC (1919); KAPP PUTSCH (1920)]. The KPD had no mass support and faced the combined opposition of the SPD, centrist liberals, conservative nationalists, and the emerging Far Right. The violence of these years permanently split the Left.

But more than the poisonous legacy of the early 1920s produced this ultimately fatal division. Like the conservative nationalists and the Far Right, the KPD was determined to undermine the republic, which it viewed as nothing more than a vehicle to exploit the working class for the benefit of the bourgeoisie and the country's elites. Unlike the Right, however, the KPD's leadership was beholden to a foreign power. In the second half of the 1920s, as **Joseph Stalin** consolidated his power in the Soviet Union, non-Soviet communist parties worldwide came under his control via the Communist International (Comintern). Following Moscow's dictates meant labeling the SPD as "social fascists," in Stalin's eyes an enemy even more dangerous than the Far Right.

Despite the early defeats, the KPD became a mass party after the Independent Social Democrats dissolved in 1922. With the onset of the Great Depression, electoral support for the party jumped, reaching its high point of 16.9 percent of the vote in the November 1932 **Reichstag elections**. Like other parties, it maintained a paramilitary group, the Red Front Fighters' League, and attempted to mobilize support at the local level, almost exclusively in the working-class neighborhoods of large cities.

For Hitler and the **National Socialist German Workers' Party** (Nazi Party; Nationalsozialistische Deutsche Arbeiterpartei; NSDAP), the KPD was the principal political enemy. Violence between the **Sturmabteilung** (Stormtroopers; SA) and the Red Front escalated dramatically in the republic's last years. Yet Hitler's appointment as **chancellor** did not produce another attempted coup or even increased Red Front violence. Not only was there no authorization from Moscow to act, but also most German communists believed that the new regime represented capitalism's last gasp. The point was reinforced by the Comintern, which seemed to welcome the fascist dictatorship that its leaders believed would liberate the masses from the Social Democrats. In the meantime, the KPD, expecting a wave of persecution and a ban on its existence, prepared to go underground to await the expected revolution.

Instead, the new regime destroyed the party in a matter of months. The KPD's leadership, its rank and file, and its press were targeted in an extraordinarily violent nationwide assault led by the police and the SA, the latter deputized as police auxiliaries. The crackdown accelerated in the aftermath of the **Reichstag fire** in February 1933. Banned from the Reichstag, the regime outlawed the party on 6 March. By the summer, most local leaders had been imprisoned, and mass arrests of party members continued for years. Thousands were murdered in the early months of 1933 and executed over the following years, including party leader Ernst Thälmann, killed on Hitler's orders in Buchenwald in August 1944. Despite the years of hatred and violence leading up to 1933, the NSDAP welcomed former rank-and-file communists into its ranks. Surviving KPD leaders went into exile in Moscow, Mexico City, and elsewhere.

In Nazi Germany, a network of communists continued to operate underground. Some historians estimate that as much as half of the KPD's 300,000 members engaged in such oppositional activities as distributing antiregime leaflets and newspapers, though many of their efforts involved simply remaining intact and avoiding arrest, an extraordinarily difficult task given the effectiveness of the Gestapo. Complicating matters was that a significant number of communists were unwilling to subordinate themselves to the exiled leadership. A resistance group comprised of middle-class Germans of varying political views—including communists or communist sympathizers—formed what the Gestapo called the Rote Kapelle (Red Orchestra) in Berlin. Counted among its leading figures was **Luftwaffe** officer Harro Schulze-Boysen, who informed Soviet intelligence in March 1941 about the impending German invasion. The Gestapo broke up the group in August 1942, and many of its members were executed [see OPERATION BARBAROSSA (1941)].

At the war's end, many on the left saw in the example of the Red Orchestra or local communist groups that had operated independently of Moscow the possibility of overcoming the suicidal divisiveness of the prewar years. Their hopes were quickly dashed. Across occupied Germany, Allied forces quashed local antifa committees that had sprung up in the immediate aftermath of the regime's collapse. In the Soviet occupation zone, those German communists who took refuge in Moscow would become the leading figures of the revived KPD. In April 1946, Stalin forced a merger with the Social Democrats, creating the Socialist Unity Party, the party that would rule the German Democratic Republic (East Germany) until 1990. A communist party was reestablished in what would become the Federal Republic of Germany (West Germany), but the SPD's fiery anticommunist leader, Kurt Schumacher, resisted all attempts at unifying the two. In 1956, the Federal Constitutional Court of West Germany banned the KPD as a subversive organization. The fear the radical Left generated among West Germans remained disproportionate to its negligible size and highly splintered existence.

CONCENTRATION CAMPS. Modern concentration camps were developed in such late-19th-century colonial settings as Spanish-ruled Cuba and British South **Africa** to imprison insurgents or separate civilians from them. Imperial Germany also constructed them to particularly deadly effect in German South West Africa (today Namibia). During the 1904–1907 war against insurgents, imperial forces imprisoned some 14,000 Hereros in several camps. Conditions were so atrocious that the death rate reached 45 percent. The concept of a system of camps to hold civilians outside the established penal system and to use them as a source of forced labor was pioneered by the Bolsheviks when Vladimir Lenin created what would become the gulag.

Hitler did not want to replicate that system, though something akin to it was eventually constructed in Germany and German-controlled Europe. In 1921, he mused about placing **Jews** in concentration camps as punishment for allegedly undermining the nation. In the constitution the **National Socialist German Workers' Party** (Nazi Party; Nationalsozialistische Deutsche Arbeiterpartei; NSDAP) had planned for Germany should the **Beer Hall Putsch** be successful included a provision for "security risks and useless eaters" to be placed in camps. Five months before Hitler was appointed **chancellor**, the party's press announced that should the NSDAP come to power, it would immediately place **Social Democratic Party of Germany** (Sozialdemokratische Partei Deutschlands; SPD) and **Communist Party of Germany** (Kommunistische Partei Deutschlands; KPD) officials and other unspecified enemies in concentration camps. Interior Minister **Wilhelm Frick** promised the same on 10 March 1933, right before the opening of the first official camp at Dachau near Munich.

Dachau had been preceded by a profusion of "wild" camps—Berlin alone had 170—which were makeshift holding centers and torture chambers used by the **Sturmabteilung** (Stromtroopers; SA), local police, and the **Schutzstaffel** (Protection Squad; SS) in the spring of 1933. As many as 100,000 people may have been held in these facilities in 1933, with around 600 killed, though the actual number is probably higher. Most of the victims were KPD and SPD members or trade union activists. Parallel to this wave of terror and score settling was the construction of the camp at Dachau, which would become the model for all future camps. The SS was given responsibility for overseeing what would become a massive network of camps, satellite camps and sub-camps, ghettos for Jews, and a much smaller number of death camps (see HOLOCAUST). By the end of the war, around 44,000 facilities inside and outside Germany had been built or appropriated from existing structures.

In Germany, the first camps were used to hold political opponents, and most of those who survived the experience were soon released. But the camp system continued to expand, as it was given a new purpose by **Heinrich Himmler** and other SS officials: to protect the "health" of the German national "body" by removing harmful elements from contact with the public (see RACISM). These elements included a dwindling number of political opponents and a growing number designated as "asocials," a flexible category that included "vagrants" and "work-shy" Germans. The SS, which assumed control of all police forces in Germany in 1936, also targeted gay men (see HOMOSEXUALITY), Jehovah's Witnesses, and a small number of recalcitrant clergy (see RELIGION). As the main enemy, Jews in peacetime Germany were expected to leave the country and not be held in camps, and it was only in the aftermath of the Kristallnacht pogrom in November 1938 [see NIGHT OF BROKEN GLASS (REICHSKRISTALLNACHT; 9–10 NOVEMBER 1938)] and then late in the war that they would constitute the majority of camp inmates. During the war, most were either confined to ghettos, shot in mass executions, deployed as slave labor, or murdered in the death camps.

Despite what many Germans claimed after the war, the existence of the camps was not kept secret from the public, though regime propagandists lied about conditions inside them. Publicizing the camps was meant to both reassure the public that the regime was protecting it from its enemies and to warn it about the dangers of **opposition**.

COORDINATION (GLEICHSCHALTUNG). Hitler's appointment as **chancellor**, the ensuing wave of terror directed mainly at communists, the decrees and laws following the **Reichstag fire**, and the outlawing of non-Nazi political parties and labor unions formed the political and legal bases of Hitler's dictatorship. Yet this left the country's vast array of institutions, associations, clubs, societies, and other organized manifestations of civil society largely untouched. So in the spring and summer of 1933, the regime initiated what its officials would call "Gleichschaltung," usually translated as "coordination."

The German term was borrowed from engineering and denotes the synchronization of electrical circuits. Applied to society, it meant aligning political and institutional life with Hitler's leadership and the regime's ideology and policies. It began with the assertion of the central government's power over Germany's states and purges of the civil service at all levels, from state ministries down to the mayors of towns and villages. Much of this was accomplished by brute force, though on 7 April, the regime promulgated the Law for the Restoration of a Professional Civil Service, which systematized the purge of **Jews** and politically unacceptable officials (though mainly to appease President **Paul von Hindenburg**, Jewish **World War I** veterans were exempted temporarily).

One result was a massive increase in applications to join the **National Socialist German Workers' Party** (Nazi Party; Nationalsozialistische Deutsche Arbeiterpartei; NSDAP). Nearly all independent professional associations were disbanded and incorporated into new party-controlled organizations, like a Reich corporation for industry, the **Hitler Youth** and League of German Girls, students' and teachers' leagues, and associations for lawyers and physicians. Only two major institutions stood outside the process: the churches and the military (see RELIGION).

By reducing and controlling the forms of communal life individual Germans could join, Gleichschaltung extended the party's authority as deeply into German life as possible. The possibilities for organized resistance were reduced to nearly nothing. It is evidence of the success of Gleichschaltung that the Gestapo, the secret political police, remained a relatively small organization, with the vast majority of non-Jewish Germans never coming into contact with it nor its agents.

Gleichschaltung was not simply imposed from above. It worked like a pincer. The party; its proliferating organizations; and the **Sturmabteilung** (Stormtroopers; SA), **Schutzstaffel** (Protection Squad; SS), and police represented one arm. The willingness of millions of Germans to voluntarily—and in many cases enthusiastically—conform to the new regime and its ideology represented the other. The latter form is sometimes characterized as *Selbstgleichschaltung* ("self-coordination") and was driven by a complex mixture of fear, opportunism, and ideological conviction. Whatever motivated the millions of Germans who conformed, the result was the astonishingly rapid consolidation of Hitler's dictatorship.

CZECHOSLOVAKIA CRISIS (1938–1939). In the 1920s and 1930s, Czechoslovakia had a stable parliamentary democracy and a relatively well-developed **economy**. Its security was guaranteed by **France**, and in 1935, the Czechoslovak and Soviet governments signed a mutual assistance pact. Yet fatal vulnerabilities to German aggression were exposed after Hitler set his sights on dismembering the country.

Like all the states of Central and Eastern Europe created in the aftermath of **World War I**, Czechoslovakia was a multiethnic entity and contained a German-speaking minority. Most of the country's 3 million ethnic Germans resided in the Sudetenland, a strategically and economically significant strip of territory bordering Silesia, Saxony, and Bavaria in Germany and (until March 1938) Upper and Lower Danube in **Austria**. There was an active local Nazi organization that capitalized on the rather poor treatment of ethnic Germans by Czechs and demanded full autonomy. By the fall of 1938, the Czechoslovak government had agreed to almost of all of the Sudeten Nazis' demands but not, of course, to full autonomy.

For Hitler, the desire to annex the territory was more than an expression of his **pan-German** ethnonationalism. The region also contained a significant number of industries. But he wanted control of the entire country, especially its western Czech lands. There was more industrial infrastructure, such as Skoda, a major manufacturer of arms, and raw materials needed for Germany's **rearmament**, the breakneck pace of which was racking up serious domestic economic problems. At the meeting with his military chiefs in Berlin in November 1937 that produced the **Hossbach Memorandum**, Hitler impressed upon those present that time was not on his side—he believed he might die of cancer at a relatively young age. Germany's enemies were, moreover, gaining in strength. His unnerved officers feared Hitler was courting disaster by risking war with Great Britain and France before rearmament was sufficiently advanced. They also believed that Czechoslovakia's defenses were stronger than Hitler assumed. But he was certain that France and Britain would not fight to defend Czechoslovakia, and he turned out to be right.

France's security guarantee existed on paper only. In the spring of 1938, French military officials had concluded that no direct assistance to Czechoslovakia could be provided in the case of a German invasion. As for the Soviet Union, the extent of Moscow's ability to protect the country was constrained by the unwillingness of the **Polish** and **Romanian** governments to grant land transit rights to the Red Army. Nor could Poland be counted upon to offer any support, particularly because it coveted the small territory of Teschen, which Czechoslovakia received in the post–World War I territorial reorganization of Eastern Europe. Crucially, British officials made it clear to French diplomats that Britain would not fight to defend the country. London would instead continue to pursue **appeasement**, which at that time simply meant a willingness to make reasonable concessions to the Germans to avoid war.

In September 1938, British prime minister Neville Chamberlain made two trips to Germany to meet with Hitler. In the first, he seemed to defuse the crisis by securing a verbal pledge that in exchange for the Sudetenland, Hitler would make no more territorial demands in Europe. No Czechoslovak officials were in attendance. French and British diplomats had strong-armed the Czechoslovak government into agreeing to surrender the troublesome but valuable territory. In their second meeting, Hitler demanded the Czechs submit to the Sudetenland's occupation by 1 October, or German forces would invade. At that point, members of Chamberlain's cabinet insisted the ultimatum be rejected, and the British, French, and Soviet militaries began to mobilize for war.

The crisis was defused when **Benito Mussolini** hastily arranged a meeting in Munich on 29–30 September between the German, British, French, and Italian governments. Representatives of the Soviet Union were not invited. Given Italy's relative military weakness, Mussolini was keen to avoid a general European war at that moment. The resulting agreement formally ceded the Sudetenland to Germany in exchange for a pledge from Hitler that he would cease demanding territory in Europe. Again, no Czechoslovak officials were present, as the country's fate was sealed by others, including those who had pledged to protect it. Abandoned by its allies, the Czechoslovak government had no choice but to submit. Chamberlain returned to England to a rapturous reception, and opinion polls showed widespread support for the agreement there and in France and the **United States**, which had played no role in the crisis.

In March 1939, German forces entered Prague unopposed. Hitler turned the Czech half of the country into the Protectorate of Bohemia and Moravia and placed it under the control of "Reichsprotekor" **Konstantin von Neurath**. Slovakia became the collaborationist Slovak state ruled by the quasi-fascist Slovak People's Party. Poland seized Teschen, and **Hungary** gained two small slices of territory along the Slovak-Hungarian border. Czechoslovakia had ceased to exist. The former president of the legitimately elected government, Edvard Beneš, formed a government in exile in London. After wavering, Chamberlain extended a security guarantee to Poland on 31 March, and the British and French militaries began discussing a coordinated response against Germany. Chamberlain also authorized the deployment of an expeditionary force to France and the first peacetime draft in the country's history.

The dismemberment of Czechoslovakia represented a major victory for Germany. For the second time in a single year, Hitler had obtained a crucial territorial component of his envisaged empire in the East without a war. Not least, Germany gained control of the country's considerable industrial and financial resources and a huge cache of armaments. Hitler completed the diplomatic revolution in Europe with the negotiation of a **Nazi–Soviet Nonaggression Pact** five months later.

Yet he was angered at not getting the war he wanted. The series of meetings in September led him to proclaim that he would never participate in another international conference. The behavior of the British and French governments did, however, reinforce his belief in the fundamental weakness of democratic systems and the infallibility of his own instincts. With the stakes much higher than they had been in the remilitarization of the **Rhineland** and the annexation of Austria, he had again prevailed over his domestic doubters and foreign opponents. *See also* HEYDRICH, REINHARD (1904–1942); HOLOCAUST.

D

DARRÉ, RICHARD WALTHER (1895–1953). Born in Argentina in 1895 to German parents, Darré served in **World War I** and then studied agriculture and animal breeding. He embraced "scientific" **racism** and explained his central idea in two popular books published in 1928 and 1929: Farmers formed the "racial" foundation of the German people. He believed capitalism and industrialized, heavily urbanized societies and the "rootless" **Jews** who preyed on the peasantry would all be replaced by a healthy "race" of farmer families. Though Darré was obsessed with Germany's mythic past, he did not advocate a return to the Middle Ages but racial regeneration among the peasantry as the key to a modern future.

Darré had met Hitler in May 1930 and joined the party in July. He convinced Hitler to create an agricultural division, and Darré's publisher paid his salary. Darré's racialist utopianism was complemented by a talent for organization and practical political advocacy. Since the late 1920s, his followers had been influencing local farmers' unions to the benefit of the **National Socialist German Workers' Party** (Nazi Party; Nationalsozialistische Deutsche Arbeiterpartei; NSDAP), especially in northern and eastern Germany, which became party strongholds by the spring of 1933. This dramatic and rapid change in the party's popular support in regions where it had heretofore failed to make significant inroads gave Darré a good deal of political influence in the regime's first years. This influence extended to the **Schutzstaffel** (Protection Squad; SS). He inspired **Heinrich Himmler**, who shared Darré's interests in farming, animal husbandry, and racialism, to transform the organization from a small, elite bodyguard into a community of "racially pure" families. It was Darré who was made responsible for certifying that recruits and their prospective spouses were racially suitable.

In June 1933, Darré replaced **Alfred Hugenberg** as agriculture minister and was also named peasant leader. His first major achievement was the promulgation of the *Reichserbhofgesetz* (hereditary farm law). Some 700,000 farms of sustainable size would be maintained through a single, hereditary-based transfer, the goal being to prevent them from being sold off or broken up into less productive units. The law also provided farmers with state protection from excessive debt. Hitler announced the new law on 1 October at the first annual fall harvest festival in the north-central German town of Bückeberg. Darré had identified this region—Lower Saxony—as the geographic center of his envisioned future farmer-based national community. He shared Hitler's sense for the importance of political theater, and the annual festival—which had deep roots in German history—was transformed into a propaganda spectacle that soon attracted more attendees than the **Nuremberg party rallies**.

More controversially, Darré also oversaw the establishment of the Reichsnäherstand (National Food Estate; RNS), which set prices for agricultural goods and food products. It became a huge operation, with agents in every German village. The RNS did more than control prices. Darré understood how backward farming was in Germany and was determined to modernize it. So the RNS established a peasant university and two agricultural *Gymnasia* (high schools) in Goslar in Lower Saxony. The agency developed an extensive outreach program to farmers in a massive effort to get them to modernize.

Given the importance of farming to the nation's **economy** and the size of the agricultural workforce (comprising about one-third in 1933), the RNS became one of the most powerful entities in Nazi Germany. At the local level, the intrusiveness of the RNS quickly generated considerable resentment. In Berlin, Darré's advocacy of subordinating the production of agricultural machinery to the RNS along with proposals by his acolytes to replicate the RNS model for all of German industry encountered fierce resistance from Finance Minister **Hjalmar Schacht** and industrial interest groups.

Darré was also an imperialist. In early 1936, he articulated his vision of Germany's expansion to RNS officials: Germany's "living space" would encompass the territory between its eastern borders and the Ural Mountains and that between the **Baltics** and the Caucasus. This was only "natural" because it was the right of the superior races to displace the inferior. By then he had already reached the limits of his personal influence though the RNS would have a longer-term impact on farming and food production.

His downfall came in 1942. He had become critical of Himmler's grandiose resettlement scheme, fearing it would leech away his prized "racially pure" stock of peasants from Germany and thus doom the nation. Increasingly sidelined and thoroughly corrupt—he had used the RNS to enrich himself—Hitler replaced him with his deputy, Herbert Backe. Like Darré, Backe was a committed ideologue devoted to Himmler's expansionist vision and far more ruthless, especially when it came to increasing shipments of grain to Germany.

Arrested by the Americans in 1945, Darré was 1 of 21 defendants in the ministries trial, 1 of the 12 Subsequent Nuremberg Trials [*see* NUREMBERG MILITARY TRIBUNAL (NMT)]. Convicted on three counts (atrocities against civilian populations, plunder and spoliation, and membership in criminal organizations) and sentenced to seven years' imprisonment, he was released in 1950 and died in Germany three years later.

DIARY HOAX (1983). In April 1945, Hitler ordered a cache of his personal papers flown out of Berlin. But the plane crashed, and its cargo was destroyed. In 1983, Gerd Heidemann, a reporter for the German mass-circulation news magazine *Stern* and a collector of Nazi memorabilia (he had an affair with **Hermann Göring**'s daughter Edda while negotiating the purchase of Göring's yacht), claimed to have come into possession of diaries supposedly kept by Hitler. He refused at first to name his source.

The plane crash in 1945 was real. The diaries were fabricated by Konrad Kujau, a compulsive forger. Kujau later claimed to have spent years teaching himself to copy Hitler's handwriting and signature. It is mystifying that anyone took the documents seriously. Kujau embossed their covers with the letters *FH* instead of *AH*; and such entries as "Have to go to the post office, to send a few telegrams"; "Eva tells me I have bad breath"; and "Must do something about the way Göring is throwing his weight around" were glaring signs of forgery.

It was the temptation of publishing what promised to be one of journalism's greatest scoops that prevented a thorough vetting. *Stern*'s publisher paid more than 9 million Deutsche Marks for 62 volumes but agreed that only Heidemann and one editor would be permitted to authenticate them. Heidemann claimed the secrecy was necessary to protect the identity of the diaries' source in East Germany. The 22 April 1983 edition of *Stern* finally broke the story, its cover blaring, "Hitler's diaries discovered."

The British newspaper *The Sunday Times* had secured publishing rights in the United Kingdom and the Commonwealth for $200,000. The editors asked Hugh Trevor-Roper, Lord Dacre of Glanton, one of Britain's most prominent historians and the author of several books about Hitler, to confirm their authenticity [*see TABLE TALK* AND *THE TESTAMENT OF ADOLF HITLER* (1941–1944; 1945)].

He did so but quickly had second thoughts. On 24 April, as the edition of the *Sunday Times* with the headline "Hitler's Secret Diaries" was rolling off the presses, Trevor-Roper told its editor that he was reversing his initial assessment. In response, Rupert Murdoch, the paper's owner, told the editors, "Fuck Dacre. Publish."

Trevor-Roper made his concerns public at a press conference held by *Stern* on 25 April. A few days later, representatives of the German federal archives informed the magazine's editors that the diaries were forgeries. Tests proved the ink to have been around two years old. *Stern*'s top editors were fired, as was the chief editor of the *Sunday Times*. Heidemann and Kujau were convicted of fraud and each sentenced to four years and eight months' imprisonment. After his release, Kujau opened a gallery of forgeries and ran a license forging business on the side. Murdoch, who allegedly proclaimed that as the owner of a newspaper he was in the entertainment business, was pleased with the resulting increase in the *Times*' circulation. Trevor-Roper's reputation was damaged irreparably.

DIETRICH, OTTO (1897–1952). Other than **Joseph Goebbels**, no other **National Socialist German Workers' Party** (Nazi Party; Nationalsozialistische Deutsche Arbeiterpartei; NSDAP) propagandist was as important to Hitler and the regime, above all in its anti-**Jewish** policies. Following his service in **World War I**, Dietrich earned a doctorate in political science in 1921. After working as a journalist, he joined the party in 1929 as a press specialist, served as Hitler's press adviser, and was appointed party press chief in 1931. Since he had been a business reporter in the industrial city of Essen, he was also an important conduit for Hitler to the Ruhr's industrial elites. In 1934, Hitler made him the party's press chief for all of Germany and, four years later, press chief for the German government and a state secretary in the Propaganda Ministry. Dietrich had also joined the **Schutzstaffel** (Protection Squad; SS) in 1932.

His position gave him daily direct access to Hitler (though he was never a member of the **Berghof** inner circle) and power over the press and the party's publications. He was instrumental in shaping Hitler's public image and constructing the **Führer myth**. Another important responsibility was selecting foreign press clippings to present to Hitler each day. Dietrich and his staff also ran a daily press conference at the Propaganda Ministry, in which highly secret directives were issued—over 75,000 to more than 3,000 newspapers between 1933 and 1945. These directives determined what the press could publish, and Dietrich also issued rules for what it could not report. Criticism of Hitler, the party, and war was prohibited, and newspapers could not report freely on events abroad or reprint speeches or declarations by Allied leaders.

Dietrich's job involved more than censorship. He was instrumental in conveying Hitler's interpretation of the war to the public, and that interpretation centered on Hitler's conspiratorial anti-Semitism. For Hitler, "international Jewry" was responsible for Germany's humiliation in 1918 and the 1920s and was now responsible for starting another world war. And as he had pronounced in his 30 January 1939 **prophecy speech**, the result this time would not be Germany's defeat but the "annihilation" of the "Jewish race." Thus, if war came, it would be a war of both revenge and self-defense. The latter became increasingly important in the regime's propaganda output after the **Battle of Stalingrad**, when "international Jewry" was blamed for every setback and the public was warned that if Germany did not prevail, it would be destroyed.

Not surprisingly, Dietrich's influence earned him Goebbels's enmity, and their relationship became so acrimonious that Hitler was forced to order the two men to cooperate. More than anything else, the power and trust invested in Dietrich revealed the importance Hitler attached to the press and its role in shaping his image and explaining the war to the public.

Dietrich retained Hitler's confidence until March 1945, when Hitler accused him of defeatism and put him on leave. He was arrested by the British and was one of 21 defendants in the ministries' trial (also known as the Wilhelmstrasse trial), 1 of the 12 Subsequent

Nuremberg Trials [see NUREMBERG MILITARY TRIBUNAL (NMT)]. He was indicted and convicted on five of seven counts, including crimes against peace, war crimes, and crimes against humanity. His trial and conviction marked a watershed moment in international law. Dietrich was the only representative of the party propaganda and press apparatus tried in this case and the very first high-level political official to be prosecuted for inciting war crimes and crimes against humanity via the press. Sentenced to seven years, he was released in 1950. While serving his sentence in **Landsberg Prison**, Dietrich wrote his memoirs in which he criticized Hitler and denounced the crimes he had spent years helping to instigate and justify. *See also* HOLOCAUST.

DÖNITZ, KARL (1891–1980). A former submarine commander in **World War I**, Dönitz remained the most influential champion of developing the navy's submarine warfare capacities. The terrifying early effectiveness of Germany's fleet in the **Battle of the Atlantic** seemed to vindicate his vision over that of navy chief Admiral Erich Raeder, who had remained wedded to surface fleet warfare. In January 1943, Hitler replaced Raeder with Dönitz, and the initial results were highly promising, as his submarines continued to sink dozens of Allied ships while suffering hardly any losses. Dönitz combined a high level of competence with unwavering devotion to Hitler. And though the Allies soon prevailed in the Atlantic, Hitler retained enough confidence in him to name him Reich president in his political testament [see PERSONAL WILL AND POLITICAL TESTAMENT (1945)].

Dönitz was based in Plön in northern Germany when he was informed on 1 May of Hitler's death. The new regime would be located in the port city of Flensburg, near the border with Denmark. Dönitz assumed the title of Führer and appointed a cabinet of his choosing. He bypassed **Heinrich Himmler** and **Joachim von Ribbentrop**. **Albert Speer** was the only high-level civilian figure from Hitler's retinue chosen by Dönitz. He left the high command of the **Wehrmacht** under the control of **Alfred Jodl** and **Wilhelm Keitel**.

Dönitz hoped to arrange a partial surrender to the Western Allies in the vain hope of

Albert Speer, Grand Admiral Karl Dönitz, and General Alfred Jodl on the day of their arrest by British forces in Flensburg, 23 May 1945. *Courtesy of Bridgeman Images.*

forming a new alliance against the Soviets. He also wanted to buy time to allow as much of the Wehrmacht as possible to make it to American-controlled territory. Dönitz dispatched two delegations to Supreme Allied Commander Dwight D. Eisenhower's headquarters in **France** to propose a conditional surrender, which Eisenhower rejected out of hand. He gave members of the second delegation, led by Jodl, 30 minutes to agree to unconditional surrender, or he would order the resumption of air attacks on German cities (*see* STRATEGIC BOMBING CAMPAIGN). Representatives of all four Allied powers were present when the surrender was signed in the early hours of 7 May. They went into effect two days later, when the full document was signed at Marshal Georgi Zhukov's headquarters outside Berlin [*see* BATTLE OF BERLIN (1945)].

Dönitz and other members of his government were arrested by British soldiers on 23 May. He was among the 24 defendants at the **International Military Tribunal** (IMT) and was charged on three of the four counts and convicted on two (planning a war of aggression and crimes against the laws of war). After serving his entire 10-year sentence, he retired to northern Germany. During and after his imprisonment, he maintained that he was still Germany's legal and legitimate head of state. His many supporters in the Federal Republic of Germany's Far-Right scene thought so, too. In the first of two memoirs, Dönitz was unrepentant though now critical of the regime he had supported without reservation. Despite all the freely available evidence of his slavish devotion to Hitler and the war, Dönitz's grossly distorted version of his past has long been embraced by gullible armchair admirals inside and outside Germany.

DRUG USE. Hitler was a hypochondriac, an impulse fueled by his obsessive fear of dying at a young age, the intense stresses of ruling Germany in peace and wartime, and his reliance on his ambitious principal personal physician, Theodor Morell. In 1936, he began taking an expanding cocktail of substances provided and administered by Morell, in part to treat specific ailments, in part to boost his energy levels, and possibly in part to keep him dependent on Morell, who leveraged his close association with Hitler to enrich himself.

During the war, Hitler was taking around 80 varieties of substances, a bizarre combination of vitamins, glucose, steroids, and hormonal preparations derived from animal organs. They could not, however, prevent his **health** from deteriorating steadily. Yet Hitler trusted Morell until the very end, even after being presented with evidence by other physicians that some of the substances Morell was providing were harmful or at least exacerbating preexisting problems.

After the disastrous **Battle of Kursk** in July and August 1943 and ahead of a meeting of Axis states, Morell began administering Eudokal, or oxycodone, a powerful synthesized form of opium, to Hitler. Following the failed **assassination attempt** in July 1944, another physician administered small doses of cocaine 50 times over 75 days—to Hitler's considerable satisfaction—until Morell intervened and resumed the Eukodal regimen.

It is not certain that Hitler was addicted to drugs in the conventional sense. Morell administered Eukodal sporadically. Certainly, Hitler's medications and the drugs he took were not responsible for his total lack of empathy, his manic activity, his ability to speak for hours on end, and his paranoia, as these traits were all evident before he began his association with Morell. *See also* PERSONALITY.

DUNKIRK (26 MAY–4 JUNE 1940). By 20 May, only 10 days after German forces invaded the Low Countries, around 400,000 British and **French** forces were surrounded in northern France, their backs against the English Channel. It was Hitler who prevented the situation from becoming a catastrophe for the British army. On the morning of 24 May, he learned that Colonel-General **Gerd von Rundstedt** had ordered tanks to halt their advance to the coast to allow the infantry to catch up. Hitler confirmed the order and allowed Rundstedt to determine when to resume the attack, which he did two days later. By that time, however, a bold British evacuation plan—Operation Dynamo—had mobilized hundreds of military and civilian vessels to cross the channel and pick up as many soldiers as possible at Dunkirk. Some 860 boats evacuated around 340,000 soldiers to Britain (200,000 were British, most of the rest were French) before German forces captured the city on 4 June. Between 30,000 and 40,000 French troops were taken prisoner.

Hitler quickly came up with an excuse for the colossal blunder by claiming the order was an act of mercy meant to motivate the British to make a deal with him. More likely, he agreed with Rundstedt that German forces were stretched dangerously thin across northern France. Besides, he did not want to delay the drive to Paris. **Hermann Göring**, moreover, had ensured Hitler that the **Luftwaffe** was capable of decimating the trapped Allied forces [*see* KESSELRING, ALBERT (1885–1960)]. German planes strafed and bombed the beach and some of the ships, but the attacks were not enough to prevent Dynamo's success.

Hitler's intervention at this level of the chain of command should also be understood as a move to assert his authority over **Walther von Brauchitsch** and **Franz Halder**, who were baffled by the decision to delay the attack on such a vulnerable and valuable target. More such interventions by Hitler would follow with even more deleterious consequences for Germany's military fortunes (*see* MILITARY COMMANDER).

Dynamo put a great deal more strain on the already fraying Franco–British relationship. British officials' perceptions of French officers and ordinary soldiers as inept, dithering, and cowardly were enhanced, while their French counterparts believed their allies were abandoning them. Particularly galling to French officers, and not least to the terrified soldiers awaiting evacuation on the exposed stretch of beach, was the lack of British air support. But on this point, **Winston Churchill** was prioritizing the defense of the British Isles. Dynamo's success produced a brief surge of patriotic euphoria in Great Britain, a surge no doubt intensified by one of Churchill's most famous speeches to Parliament on 4 June, in which he pledged that Britain would fight the expected German invasion everywhere and to the end. Less well remembered was his reminder that evacuations do not win wars.

E

ECKART, DIETRICH (1863–1923). Eckart was a Bavarian right-wing journalist and political activist who became one of Hitler's earliest—and hence most important—mentors. After failing as a playwright, Eckart moved to Munich during **World War I** and became active in the city's burgeoning Far-Right scene. His prominence was due mainly to his editorship of the outspokenly anti-Semitic magazine *Auf gut deutsch* (*In Plain German*) and the lectures he gave, including to the **German Workers' Party** (Deutsche Arbeiterpartei; DAP).

He met Hitler in the winter of 1919–1920 and recognized his talents as a speaker and political rabble-rouser. Eckart's anti-Semitism undoubtedly rubbed off on Hitler, as did his tendency to encourage Hitler to perceive himself as a true genius [*see* FÜHRER MYTH (FÜHRER MYTHOS); JEWS]. In more practical terms, Eckart provided financial support and coached him in the writing of articles. He also became a conduit to sympathetic members of Munich's elite (including a small subculture of right-wing artists) and exiles from the **Baltics**, notably **Alfred Rosenberg**. Eckart may also have introduced Hitler to photographer **Heinrich Hoffmann**. He had even better connections to wealthy sympathizers in Berlin, connections he and Hitler would use productively. The fact that Eckart was, like Hitler, a failed professional artist who nonetheless considered himself an artist most likely bonded the two men.

As with **Karl Mayr**, however, the tutor-mentor relationship would not last. Hitler soon dispensed with Eckart, whom he rightly suspected of lacking administrative capabilities. But he did not forget him after Eckart suffered a fatal heart attack in December 1923. The second volume of *Mein Kampf* is dedicated to his memory, and Hitler later repeatedly stressed to confidants Eckart's importance to his early years. *See also* NATIONAL SOCIALIST GERMAN WORKERS' PARTY (NAZI PARTY; NATIONALISOZIALISTISCHE DEUTSCHE ARBEITERPARTEI; NSDAP).

ECONOMY. During and long after the period of Nazi rule, journalists, economists, political theorists, Marxists, and historians debated the nature of the regime's economic structure. Marxists considered it nothing more than an expression of monopoly capitalism. Others have denied any significant connection to capitalism. Still others propose that Nazi Germany's economy was a hybrid that combined heavy doses of state direction; the maintenance of private property relations; and pervasive inefficiencies, waste, corruption, and unsustainable distortions that pushed the pace toward a calamitous war. Categorizations aside, the question of the regime's economic policies is closely bound up with every major aspect of its history: the consolidation of power, daily life for ordinary Germans, the persecution of German and European **Jews**, **rearmament**, foreign policy, and eventually territorial conquest.

Hitler knew next to nothing about how an industrialized economy worked. His and the party's early thinking on the matter were influenced strongly by the ideas of the crank anti-Semitic economist **Gottfried Feder**. The **Nazi Party program** reflected his influence and called for nationalizing industries and redistributing land, an agenda that dissuaded the bulk of Germany's business elite from supporting the **National Socialist German Workers' Party** (Nazi Party; Nationalsozialistische Deutsche Arbeiterpartei; NSDAP) in the 1920s.

But it would be Hitler's obsession with expanding Germany's "living space" that played the most important role in shaping his economic ideas. He believed that a war of conquest in the East would do more than provide living space and eliminate Germany's deadliest enemies. It would also transform Germany into a global economic superpower capable of challenging the power of the **United States** in particular. It's also clear that Hitler was determined to prevent a repeat of the situation during **World War I**, when Great Britain's naval blockade caused serious deprivations on the home front and thus, in his mind, severely undercut the war effort.

Enmeshing Germany in the world economy was out of the question. That meant autarky based on the possession of a continental empire. Once in power, party officials would draw on a strand of thinking that emerged in the late 19th century emphasizing the development of markets and networks of exchange within Europe, with Germany acting as the regional hegemon. But Hitler knew this would never be enough to achieve full self-sufficiency along with superpower status. The ideal—as well as the envisioned future enemy—was the United States. In Hitler's mind, the Americans had conquered a continent. They displaced and killed off supposedly inferior native peoples and settled a vast, practically self-sufficient, and secure empire containing boundless arable land and natural resources. The lesson for Hitler as he looked to the East could not have been clearer.

The most pressing priority for the new regime in 1933, however, was the unemployment crisis. More than a third of the workforce was jobless. The economy was already beginning to recover beginning in the summer of 1932, and the regime's first work creation programs—notably the construction of the Autobahn (a national highway system)—was an important step toward recovery, though such projects were short-lived and did not restore full employment. That objective was reached by 1935, thanks to rearmament. Yet the priority Hitler placed on massive and rapid rearmament could not be squared with two fundamental related problems: Germany's need for ever larger quantities of imports and the limited reserves of foreign currencies required to pay for them. This dilemma posed a mounting threat to rearmament and to the regime's popularity, as consumers were forced to deal with shortages, rationing, poor-quality substitutes, and frozen wages. Hitler's solution was to accelerate the timetable for the war he was convinced would resolve all the country's economic problems.

While the Nazi Party's program contained strongly anticapitalist elements, its principal advocates were sidelined or driven out of the party. Private property and businesses ranging from giants like IG Farben all the way down to the smallest producers were mostly left intact. Business leaders wary of the party taking the *socialism* in *national socialism* seriously were certainly relieved to see its "left" wing quashed, the **Communist Party of Germany** (Kommunistische Partei Deutschlands; KPD) completely destroyed, and independent labor eliminated [*see* GERMAN LABOR FRONT (DEUTSCHE ARBEITSFRONT; DAF); LEY, ROBERT (1890–1945)]. But the drive to rearm, and especially the promulgation of the **Four-Year Plan** and establishment of a massive organization under **Hermann Göring**'s control, renewed the doubts of some as the regime became more intrusive.

The most prominent critic was Fritz Thyssen, one of the very few major industrialists to support the NSDAP before 1933. By 1939, he was denouncing the regime's economic policies, likening the situation in Germany to that in the Soviet Union. While private property did remain largely intact—some significant concerns, like the country's largest aircraft manufacturer and its most important source of iron ore, were seized outright by the state—it was subordinated to the needs of the regime. And while the regime had eliminated the independent labor movement and froze wages in 1933, it also froze prices three years later.

The proliferation of state agencies competing for products along with a variety of incentives and loopholes encouraged investment, competition, and innovation. But it is possible to overstate the distinction between the public and private sectors. In reality, the Nazi economy operated as a public-private symbiosis, in which both sides fed off each other for mutual benefit. This held true even in 1942, when **Albert Speer** was given effective control of much of the economy as the tide of the war turned against Germany.

The regime also committed robbery on a massive scale before and during the war, mainly through Aryanization—meaning theft— of property and assets owned by German and other European **Jews** and outright plunder carried out by ordinary soldiers, greedy businessmen, the **Schutzstaffel** (Protection Squad; SS), and various party satraps. Just as the line between the state and private enterprise was blurry at best, theft became so pervasive and systematized that one historian concluded it had in fact become "business as usual." By one recent estimate, plunder and eventually the requisitioning of forced labor from Western and Eastern Europe ended up accounting for more than one-third of Germany's expenses related to the war.

Anyone perusing images of Germany in May 1945 will quickly get the impression that the entire country was a pile of rubble. But this was actually far from the case, and the highly uneven destruction accounts to a considerable extent for Germany's relatively rapid reconstruction, especially in its western half. While there is a consensus among historians that 1945 was not a *Stunde Null* (zero hour) for Germany, there is considerable debate over the extent to which the public-private symbiosis of the Nazi period shaped the West German economy. What is not in dispute is that most of Germany's business elite went unpunished after the war. *See also* DARRÉ, RICHARD WALTHER (1895–1953); NUREMBERG MILITARY TRIBUNAL (NMT); SCHACHT, HORACE GREELEY HJALMAR (1877–1970).

ELECTIONS. The revolution that began in November 1918 produced a liberal democratic republic—the Weimar Republic—with a constitution that was in many ways the world's most progressive for its time. It provided for a parliamentary system based on proportional representation, and the franchise was expanded to include **women**, thus more than doubling the electorate. Citizens' basic rights were guaranteed, as was the right to state-funded social welfare provisions.

In practice, the most important feature of Weimar's electoral politics was its fragmentation (as many as 29 parties held at least one seat in the **Reichstag** between 1919 and 1933), a condition that only worsened in the republic's final years. With the exceptions of the **National Socialist German Workers' Party** (Nazi Party; Nationalsozialistische Deutsche Arbeiterpartei; NSDAP) and the **Communist Party of Germany** (Kommunistische Partei Deutschlands; KPD), all the main parties had their origins in Imperial Germany (1871–1918). In the republic's early years, the most important was the **Social Democratic Party of Germany** (Sozialdemokratische Partei Deutschlands; SPD), which, along with the liberal German Democratic Party (Deutsche Demokratische Partei, DDP) and the **Center Party** (Zentrum), formed the center–moderate left Weimar coalition in the Reichstag.

Beginning in 1923, a series of crises pushed electoral politics to the right. In January, **French** and Belgian forces occupied the Ruhr industrial region in response to German resistance to paying reparations. In response, the German government called for passive resistance while printing money to pay idled workers. A disastrous bout with hyperinflation was the result. That awful year also witnessed an attempt by communists to ignite a Bolshevik-style revolution and Hitler's **Beer Hall Putsch**. Both were suppressed, and the **economic** crisis passed [*see also* TRIAL (1924)].

A shift back to the center and moderate left in the 1928 elections reflected the political and economic stabilization of the mid-1920s, the Weimar Republic's golden years. Though the parties of the Weimar coalition had bled some voters to the Far Left and Right, the ensuing brief period of relative stability kept the NSDAP and KPD on the political margins. But the economic crisis that began with the crash of the stock market in the United States in October 1929 hit Germany quickly and with particular ferocity. By 1932, about one-third of the workforce was unemployed. The fragmentation of Germany's political landscape prevented parties in the Reichstag from agreeing on a response to the disaster, with the main issue being the funding of unemployment benefits. In response, President **Paul von Hindenburg** invoked an article in the constitution (article 48) that granted the chancellor the power to rule by decree. While elections continued to be held and citizens' rights remained protected by the constitution, the political system had become a presidential dictatorship.

In the meantime, the NSDAP had staged its two electoral breakthroughs. The first came in the 14 September 1930 Reichstag elections, in which the party increased its share of the vote from 2.4 percent to 18.5 percent. The second came in July 1932 elections, when the NSDAP became the single largest party in the Reichstag with 37.8 percent of the vote and 230 seats. Yet Hitler's insistence on accepting nothing less than the chancellorship prevented the formation of a conservative-Nazi coalition until Hindenburg relented in late January 1933 [see CHANCELLOR, APPOINTMENT AS (30 JANUARY 1933)].

Much of the party's success can be attributed to the effects of the worsening economic crisis. But this factor alone cannot explain its meteoric rise. Nor was there anything particularly original about the party's platform, which was comprised of stock Far-Right elements alongside somewhat vague appeals to socialism [see NAZI PARTY PROGRAM (25-POINT PROGRAM)]. That the NSDAP emerged as the only party able to reach a relatively wide base of support just as the Depression hit Germany is mainly attributable to three other factors. One was Hitler's abilities as a speaker. Another was his success at suppressing challengers to his leadership from within the party. Third was an extensive grassroots mobilization effort that succeeded in presenting the NSDAP to voters as an anti-Marxist, nationalist, and socialist party with no equivalent among Germany's parties. *See also* BOXHEIM DOCUMENTS; FEDER, GOTTFRIED (1883–1941); GERMAN NATIONAL PEOPLE'S PARTY (DEUTSCHNATIONALE VOLKSPARTEI; DNVP); GERMAN PEOPLE'S PARTY (DEUTSCHE VOLKSPARTEI; DVP); GOEBBELS, JOSEPH PAUL (1897–1945); HARZBURG FRONT; HUGENBERG, ALFRED (1865–1951); LEADERSHIP PRINCIPLE (FÜHRERPRINZIP); PAPEN, FRANZ VON (1879–1969); STRASSER, GREGOR (1892–1934); YOUNG PLAN REFERENDUM (1929).

Presidential election poster, most likely spring 1932. "Workers of the head and the hand: Vote for the front soldier Hitler!" *Courtesy of the German Propaganda Archive; Randall Bytwerk.*

ELSER, GEORG (1903–1945). While there were more than 40 plots to assassinate Hitler, only a few came close to succeeding. The first took place on 8 November 1939. Elser, a 36-year-old Swabian joiner planted a bomb in the Bürgerbräukeller in Munich, where Hitler launched the ill-fated **Beer Hall Putsch** in 1923 and where he subsequently presided over an annual ceremony commemorating the event.

Elser had flirted briefly with the communists but was not otherwise politically engaged. Though angered by Germany's ongoing **economic** problems, he was motivated mainly by a desire to avert another war. He decided to act in 1938. Elser obtained explosives and detonators from his factory and construction jobs. After scouting the beer hall's layout and moving to Munich, he spent weeks taking a late meal and hiding in a storeroom. He then worked through the night, hollowing out a small space in a pillar near the speaker's dais, timing the noisiest stages of his work to coincide with the automatic flushing of the hall's toilets. The bomb was equipped with a fail-safe timer and was encased in a purpose-built wooden box. Elser lined the space in the pillar with cork to muffle the sound of the timer's ticking.

Sheer luck saved Hitler's life. He began his speech 30 minutes earlier than usual and cut it short to catch a train to Berlin. Elser had missed the announcement in the local press of the earlier start time. The bomb detonated 13 minutes after Hitler left the podium. Eight people were killed and 63 wounded. As Elser had predicted, a portion of the ceiling came down above where Hitler had been standing.

Elser was detained while attempting to cross into Switzerland. Customs officers found evidence of his handiwork on his person and turned him over to the police. He was interrogated for several days before confessing. Regime officials were convinced Elser was a British agent, and the transcripts of his interrogations reveal that he went to great lengths to convince them that his was a conspiracy of one. He was imprisoned in Sachsenhausen and then Dachau. Hitler may have kept him alive in the belief that he could have some future propaganda value. Elser was executed on **Heinrich Himmler**'s orders on 9 April 1945. *See also* ASSASSINATION ATTEMPT (20 JULY 1944); CONCENTRATION CAMPS; OPPOSITION.

ENABLING ACT (1933). Following Hitler's appointment as **chancellor**, he, **Joseph Goebbels**, and the **Sturmabteilung** (Stormtroopers; SA) wasted no time in moving to create a dictatorship. Parallel to a propaganda campaign and a wave of SA violence aimed mainly at communists, Hitler sought a legal basis for one-man, one-party rule. In the negotiations with **Franz von Papen** in January 1933, he made it clear that he wanted a new law passed that would allow him to circumvent both the **Reichstag** and the president. Such a law—an "enabling act"—would require an amendment to the republic's constitution, which would require a two-thirds majority vote in the Reichstag with at least two-thirds of its delegates present. The moment arrived in the aftermath of the **Reichstag fire** on the night of 27–28 February.

As the ongoing crackdown on communists intensified, President **Paul von Hindenburg** needed little convincing to sign an emergency decree on 28 February that suspended basic rights guaranteed by the constitution. The **election** scheduled for 5 March was not delayed, but the decree allowed the SA to engage in rampant voter intimidation and the suppression of campaign activities by the **Social Democratic Party of Germany** (Sozialdemokratische Partei Deutschlands; SPD) and the **Communist Party of Germany** (Kommunistische Partei Deutschlands; KPD).

Between the election and the vote on the act, Hitler and Goebbels courted the favor of Hindenburg, who, despite having agreed to appoint Hitler chancellor, remained suspicious of his ambitions to concentrate total political power in his hands. Goebbels staged an elaborate ceremony in Potsdam on 21 March, the occasion of the new Reichstag's inauguration. Potsdam, located just outside Berlin, was a small city with great symbolic significance for Germany's conservative nationalist tradition. The summer residence of the Prussian kings, Sanssouci, is located in the town, as are the tombs of Friedrich Wilhelm I and his successor, Friedrich II ("the Great"). The event was choreographed to showcase the supposed unity between conservative nationalists, Hitler, and national socialism. It certainly was no celebration of national unity, which did not exist. No SPD deputies, let alone representatives of the KPD, attended.

In the Potsdam garrison's church, Hindenburg gave the opening speech and saluted the son of exiled emperor Wilhelm II (*see* HOHENZOLLERNS). Hitler, looking noticeably uncomfortable in formal civilian attire, gave a speech in which he heaped praise on Hindenburg. The spectacle had the intended effect on the president, who had already been signaling that he was coming around on Hitler. And while some conservatives remained uneasy about the Nazis, there is evidence that the ceremony had a positive impact on the wider public.

Two days later, the new Reichstag convened in Berlin's Kroll Opera House to vote on the Enabling Act. Formally the Law to Remedy the Distress of the People and Reich, it was drafted by Reich interior minister **Wilhelm Frick**. Not only would it permit the Reich government to make laws and treaties with other nations without the Reichstag or the president for four years, but also those laws could violate the constitution. Debate on the act, such as it was, did not take place under anything like normal circumstances. Hitler had hundreds of armed SA and **Schutzstaffel** (Protection Squad; SS) men stationed in front of and inside the opera house, where they lined up behind the delegates, blocked the exits, and shouted abuse at SPD and **Center Party** (Zentrum) delegates.

Hitler, having exchanged formal attire for his brownshirt uniform, gave a two-and-a-half-hour speech, most of which was devoted to vague promises that the new government would restore the **economy** and seek peace abroad. At the end, he demanded passage of the Enabling Act to allow his government to do only what was necessary for the nation without having to bring every single matter before the Reichstag. That body would continue to exist, as would Germany's states, and he pledged not to take any actions against the churches, the latter promise clearly directed at wavering Zentrum delegates. But in case anyone missed the point, he concluded by threatening civil war if the act was not passed (*see* RELIGION).

Despite the blatant intimidation, its passage was not assured. Hitler was disappointed that the **National Socialist German Workers' Party** or (Nazi Party; Nationalsozialistische Deutsche Arbeiterpartei; NSDAP) won 43.9 percent of the vote in the quasi-free election. Even with the support of a coalition of Far-Right parties, he still didn't have the supermajority needed to pass the act. The key became the Zentrum. During a recess following Hitler's speech, its members decided to support it. In the end, 441 Reichstag delegates voted in favor and 94 opposed. Those 94 belonged to the SPD, making it the only party to have voted against it, with its chairman, Otto Wels, courageously proclaiming his party's steadfast opposition. No KPD delegates were present, as they had either been arrested or fled the country and in any case would have risked their lives had they tried to enter the building.

It should not be surprising that conservatives voted in favor. While the threat of violence should not be discounted as a motivating factor, the act represented the achievement of their long-sought objective of destroying the republic and the Left. The Zentrum, which was not unified in its support, had already taken a hard turn to the Right, and negotiations between party leaders and the Vatican on a concordat had been underway for several years [*see* PIUS XII, POPE (EUGENIO PACELLI; 1876–1958)].

The passing of the act was the single most important legal step taken in the creation of Hitler's dictatorship. The law took effect the next day and was renewed three times, making it the legal foundation for the dictatorship until May 1945. Any possibility that conservatives might control or moderate Hitler had all but vanished. With formal political power at the top secured, what followed was the Gleichschaltung (**coordination**) of the rest of the political system and Germany's vast array of institutions, ranging from the professions to organized labor and to even the smallest local clubs and associations. And it was no coincidence that a week after the act's passing, the first major anti-**Jewish** policy was implemented: a call for a national boycott of Jewish-owned businesses and Jewish professionals.

EUTHANASIA PROGRAM (AKTION T4). With Hitler's explicit authorization, the regime and Germany's medical and public health communities undertook the forced sterilization of some 400,000 Germans and then the mass murder of perhaps 275,000 mentally and physically handicapped Germans and non-Germans. Some of the personnel and methods developed for the latter operation, notably the gassing of victims in fixed installations, were deployed in the **Holocaust**.

By the beginning of the 20th century, a significant stratum of medical scientists, social workers, jurists, and criminologists in the Western world had concluded that social welfare programs and improvements in medical care were actually weakening the health of national communities and contributing to increased crime rates and general cultural degradation. It was urgent, so this argument went, to use state power to separate those considered to be degenerate—a broad category that included children and adults with hereditary mental and physical disabilities but could also include the homeless, alcoholics, habitual criminals, and the poor—from populations considered to be healthy and thus presumably productive and law abiding. In post–**World War I** Germany in particular, debates over laws and social policies related to real or imagined disabilities were influenced strongly by successive **economic** crises, prompting some to argue the costs of maintaining asylums could not be justified in humanitarian or utilitarian terms.

In addition to incarceration in prisons or asylums, several other countries had enacted forced sterilization laws. A minority in the eugenics (or racial hygiene) community advocated medical murder, or "euthanasia," also referred to frequently at the time as "mercy killing." Such views by no means went uncontested in democratic states, including Germany before 1933, and for **religious** reasons, many Christians and **Jews** opposed medical murder and hindering procreation. But Hitler's views on creating a healthy racial community mostly comported with the agendas of racial hygienists, though his views on euthanasia remain unclear well into the 1930s (*see* RACISM). Yet his appointment as **chancellor** meant that beginning in 1933, the most radical racial hygienists would have the upper hand in pursuing actions forbidden during the Weimar Republic, and they could do so without **opposition** from dissenting or more moderate colleagues, who would be either purged or cowed into silence.

On 14 July 1933, the regime promulgated the Law for the Prevention of Genetically Diseased Offspring, which required sterilization for men and **women** judged by hereditary health courts to be afflicted with one or more of nine supposedly hereditary disorders. Around 400,000 Germans were sterilized, with complications from tubal ligations resulting in the deaths of thousands of women. In 1935, the law was extended to the children of relationships between **African** soldiers and German women (the "Rhineland bastards"), and around 600 to 800 children were sterilized, more than half the total in Germany. The operation was a highly secret one—it even bypassed the hereditary health courts—because it could not be proven that hereditary disabilities were the direct result of African parentage.

The mass murder of German citizens was another matter, and even after 1933, medical and state officials debated the merits of taking such a drastic step. Crucial was the lack of a clear directive from Hitler. There is next to no surviving evidence of his views on euthanasia before 1938. That year, he received a letter from a man begging him to approve the killing of his severely physically disabled son. Hitler authorized his attending physician, Karl Brandt, to arrange for the child's murder and then ordered Brandt and the head of the Führer's chancellery, Philipp Bouhler, to formalize a way of dealing with such cases in secret. Bouhler, Brandt, and a small group of officials initiated the first stage of the Euthanasia Program, aimed at children. By the end of the war, around 5,000 would be killed by lethal injections or starvation.

In the summer of 1939, Hitler verbally approved the extension of the program to adults and put his orders in writing in October. A secret headquarters to run the expanded operation was established in a townhouse on Berlin's Tiergarten park, the abbreviated version of its address, T4, becoming the informal name for the action. Between January 1940 and August 1941, 70,273 disabled Germans were murdered with poison gas in what were disguised as showers at six facilities in Germany and **Austria**. Fictitious causes of death were sent to family members. The **Schutzstaffel** (Protection Squad; SS) initiated a version of the program in **Poland**, where around 4,000 inmates of asylums were executed, mainly to free up space for use by the German military. Beginning in the summer of 1940, some 4,000 to 5,000 Jews housed in asylums—regardless of their mental and physical states—were slated to be murdered.

One obstacle to continuing the operation in Germany proved insurmountable: public opposition to medical murder from influential Catholic clergy. There was no way to keep the operation entirely secret, and in December 1940, Pope **Pius XII** issued a statement condemning the killing of the handicapped. The following August, the popular Bishop of Münster, August Count Clemens von Galen, who was otherwise pro-Nazi and anti-Semitic, denounced the program in a sermon. The arch anticlerical **Martin Bormann** advocated his execution, but Hitler refused to take any action after being warned by **Joseph Goebbels** that persecuting the bishop would cost the regime popular support in a city that was being subjected to repeated British bombing raids (*see* STRATEGIC BOMBING CAMPAIGN). Protestant clergy never protested the killings in public. By the end of the year, Hitler ordered T4's operations partly suspended. The murder of children continued, and that of adults resumed in August 1942 in conditions of stricter secrecy.

Given the scope of the Euthanasia Program, a postwar judicial reckoning with its many perpetrators was quite limited. At the **Nuremberg Military Tribunal** (NMT), 23 German physicians and administrators were tried for their involvement in the Euthanasia Program and for conducting medical experiments on **concentration camp** prisoners. Sixteen were convicted, and seven were sentenced to death. Only four of the defendants were involved with T4. A few other trials of physicians, nurses, and other officials took place in occupied Germany, but the vast majority of those responsible at all levels for one of the regime's most heinous crimes were never prosecuted.

F

FAMILY. Hitler's ancestry can be traced back reliably to the Waldviertel region of northeastern **Austria**. There is no evidence that any of his ancestors were **Jewish**. Nor has it ever been proven that Hitler had a son out of wedlock with a **French** woman during his **World War I** service. For reasons that remain unclear, his father, Alois Schicklgruber (1837–1903) changed his last name to Hitler in 1876. Alois worked as a customs official in the town of Braunau am Inn in Upper Austria. With his mistress and then second wife, Franziska Matzelsberger (1861–1884), he had a son, also named Alois (1882–1956), and a daughter, Angela (1883–1949). While Franziska was dying of tuberculosis, Alois Sr. began an affair with Klara Pölzl [see HITLER, KLARA (NÉE PÖLZL; 1860–1907)], the nanny to Angela and Alois Jr. and possibly either Alois Sr.'s second cousin or half-niece. Five months after Franziska's death in August 1884, Alois and Klara were married. Their first two children, born in 1885 and 1886, died young. On 20 April 1889, their third was born in Braunau and named Adolf. Two brothers followed, but they also died young. In 1896, Paula (d. 1960) was born.

In 1892, Alois moved the family to nearby Passau, Bavaria. Adolf spent his early years living with Paula, Alois Jr., Angela, and Klara's unmarried sister Johanna Pölzl. Alois Sr., with whom Adolf was never close, died suddenly in 1903. Klara, who doted on Adolf, died of breast cancer in 1907, an event that affected her son deeply.

Alois Jr. had left home in 1896, moved to Ireland, and in 1910 married Brigid Elizabeth Dowling. Their son, William Patrick Hitler, was born in 1911. Alois Jr. then left them, moved to Hamburg and remarried; as he was still legally married to Brigid, he was soon charged with bigamy. William would spend years in Great Britain, Germany, and the **United States** trying, without much success, to capitalize on his connection to his increasingly famous uncle. During the war, he served with some distinction in the US Navy. Afterward, he worked as a hospital administrator. He married; had four children; and moved to Long Island, New York, where he lived until his death in 1987.

Angela had three children with her husband, Leo Raubal, one of whom was **Angela "Geli" Raubal**, with whom Hitler had a short, intense, but probably nonsexual relationship from 1928 to 1931 (*see* WOMEN). A son, also named Leo, became Hitler's favorite nephew. Following his capture by the Red Army at Stalingrad, Hitler offered to exchange him for **Joseph Stalin**'s son Yasha, then a prisoner of the Germans. Stalin refused. Leo survived the ordeal and in the 1960s would be among several of Adolf Hitler's relatives who schemed, unsuccessfully, to obtain royalties from the sale of *Mein Kampf.*

Hitler took little interest in the lives of his own extended family, the members of which are barely mentioned in *Mein Kampf*. At one point during the war, he boasted that he had no sense of family history and that he belonged only to "my ethnic community." Hitler kept his sister and other relatives—Geli Raubal was the exception—at arm's length, and none ever became regular fixtures in his private circle at the **Berghof**, his Bavarian retreat in Obersalzburg, though Angela worked there as a housekeeper.

After the war, his relatives shared the hardships of millions of other Germans and Austrians, a fact Paula Hitler believed her brother would have found fitting. Several died in Russian captivity. Paula spent most of the war living in **Vienna**, until near the war's end, when she was relocated to Berchtesgaden, probably on **Martin Bormann**'s orders, near the Berghof, presumably to await the arrival of her brother. She lived there under a pseudonym until her death in 1960. Hitler's increasingly distant surviving relatives live in the Waldviertel and New York State.

FEDER, GOTTFRIED (1883–1941). A civil engineer by profession, Feder professed to be an expert on **economics**. He became a prominent member of the Far-Right scene in Munich late in **World War I** and immediately after, though he had attempted, without success, to get officials in the short-lived **Bavarian Soviet Republic** to pay attention to his crackpot economic theories. Feder's most influential idea, first proposed in a pamphlet he published in 1919, was that **Jews** controlled financial markets in a way that ensnared ordinary Germans in what he called "interest slavery." Freeing people from this form of bondage meant outlawing and promoting something he termed "creative capital." His fusion of anti-Semitism and selective anticapitalism would

Adolf Hitler (top row, center) as a 10-year-old schoolboy, Leonding (near Linz), Austria, 1899. *Courtesy of Bildarchiv Preussicher Kulturbesitz.*

exert a powerful early influence on Hitler and the ideology of the **German Workers' Party** (Deutsche Volkspartei; DAP) and the **National Socialist German Workers' Party** (Nazi Party; Nationalsozialistische Deutsche Arbeiterpartei; NSDAP).

Hitler first encountered Feder in a course organized by **Karl Mayr** at Munich University in the summer of 1919. Feder also happened to be the featured speaker at the 12 September meeting of the DAP, which Hitler attended. He defended Feder's **pan-Germanism** with such vigor that cofounder Anton Drexler encouraged him to become active with the party. Feder's influence is most clearly seen in points 11 and 12 of the **Nazi Party Program** (25-Point Program), which demanded the outlawing of "work-free, effortless income" and the confiscation of all wartime profits. These were implicitly anti-Semitic parts of the party's platform. Hitler also incorporated Feder's ideas in his early speeches, and Feder was part of a circle of mentors and admirers of Hitler who met to discuss politics in Munich cafés. He participated in the **Beer Hall Putsch** though was not prosecuted and served as a **Reichstag** delegate from 1924 to 1936.

Feder's influence on Hitler and in the NSDAP outlasted that of two of Hitler's other early mentors: Mayr and **Dietrich Eckart**. Feder was appointed to lead the party's economic council in 1931 but lost influence when he aligned himself with **Gregor Strasser** in 1932. More damaging to his status was the opposition to him by a handful of pro-Nazi industrialists whose support Hitler needed. Accordingly, Hitler shunted Feder off to a minor post in the Economics Ministry in 1933. A year later, another one of Feder's opponents, Economics Minister **Hjalmar Schacht**, sacked him. Feder took a post at the Technische Hochschule in Berlin and died in obscurity in 1941.

FORTRESS EUROPE (FESTUNG EUROPAS). Hitler, the Propaganda Ministry, and the military applied the term *Festung* (fortress) to characterize the defense of wartime Europe. For Germans and other Europeans, *fortress* conjured images of walled medieval cities and castles (the remnants of which were a common sight in many parts of Germany) designed to withstand long sieges and keep out the diseased and the unwanted.

In the Second World War, the term was often applied metaphorically and not just by the Nazi regime. The **Luftwaffe** and ground-based antiaircraft installations were supposed to turn the skies above Germany into a kind of impenetrable fortress. Both sides hoped the heavy bombers they had been developing since the 1930s would be capable of defending themselves from enemy fighters—the US Army Air Force even named its most effective heavy bomber, the Boeing B-17, the "flying fortress." Both sides learned the hard way that this would not be case. In November 1943, as the Red Army surrounded German forces at Stalingrad, Hitler ordered General Friedrich Paulus to turn the city into a fortress (*hedgehog* was a related metaphor) rather than try to break out (*see* MILITARY COMMANDER).

But *fortress* was more than a metaphor. World War I, interwar, and World War II Europe was laced with border and field fortifications of unprecedented size (e.g., Hindenburg Line, Maginot Line). For Hitler, it was both the possibility of a relatively quick victory in the East and then the failure to achieve it that led him to order and expand the construction of a whole series of concrete fortifications, the most extensive of which was the Atlantic Wall. In late 1941, Hitler suspected that the success of **Operation Barbarossa** might provoke an Anglo-American invasion in **France** or **Norway**. So he ordered installations built along French, Belgian, and Dutch coastlines. These were bolstered and expanded beginning in the summer of 1942 and the first half of 1944. As was the case in other mammoth Nazi construction projects, coerced labor was deployed extensively [*see* TODT, FRITZ (1891–1942)]. In 1943, 200,000 to 250,000 slave laborers in France worked on the Atlantic Wall. In addition to a heavy naval presence in the North Sea, Narvik and Bergen in Norway were defended by 114 artillery batteries and more fortifications were constructed on stretches of France's Mediterranean Sea coastline. The acceleration of construction in the first half of

1944 produced more than 5,000 installations along the Atlantic and Mediterranean.

The Atlantic Wall was indeed a formidable barrier, but in the end, it could not withstand overwhelming Allied air and naval superiority, the boldness of Operation Bodyguard and **Operation Overlord**, and a good deal of luck (especially with the weather) leading up to and on 6 June 1944. Bickering between German generals and Hitler's bungling behind the fortifications also undermined their effectiveness. The Allies, moreover, never intended to invade Norway, and the landings in southern France that began on 15 August 1944 (Operation Dragoon) met little effective resistance.

In the wake of its multiple invasions of the supposedly impenetrable Festung Europas, notably Sicily (Operation Husky) in July 1943 and Overlord, the Western Allies applied the term in a mostly derogatory and triumphalist way, thus using the Nazis' own propaganda against the regime. Since the war and especially in recent decades, "Fortress Europe" has become a rallying cry for those Europeans (mainly on the left) who support easing restrictions on migrants and asylum seekers or those (mainly on the far right) who want to keep them out.

FOUR-YEAR PLAN. Following the 1936 summer **Olympics**, an exhausted and irritable Hitler retreated to the **Berghof** to recuperate, though he was not idle. In August and September, he wrote a long memorandum on accelerating **rearmament** and preparing the nation's entire **economy** for war within the next four years. As he saw it, Economics Minister **Hjalmar Schacht** was not doing enough in either category. Hitler's plan was to push the pace of rearmament and make Germany as self-sufficient as possible in foodstuffs and crucial raw materials, including the development of new substitute synthetics, particularly fuel and rubber. It extended and intensified the older objective of achieving autarky through territorial conquest rather than participation in globalized networks of trade and finance. It also portended a dramatic increase in the regime's role in the economy, which did in fact take place.

As always, the specter of Germany's economic strangulation during **World War I** haunted Hitler's imagination. And, again, he identified the stakes for the nation now as life or death. The remarkable document began with a long exposition of Hitler's worldview, the core idea being that the growing power of the Soviet Union had to be countered, or the "international Jewry" that stood behind Bolshevism would annihilate the German people (*see* JEWS). His murderous animosity notwithstanding, he also expressed a kind of admiration for **Joseph Stalin**'s state-directed five-year plans.

The circulation of the full text was restricted to **Hermann Göring** and war minister General Field Marshal Werner von Blomberg. Schacht was excluded and soon placed on leave. On 4 September, Göring gave a preview of its main point at a secret meeting of Prussian state government officials: "All" economic activity had to be geared toward preparing for the forthcoming war with Russia. Then Hitler announced the plan at the annual **Nuremberg party rally**, but he left out any mention of war, focusing instead on restoring and maintaining a strong domestic economy.

Hitler put Göring in charge of implementing the plan on 18 October, greatly expanding his authority over the economy and cementing his status as the regime's second-most-powerful official. Like Hitler, he made admiring references to Stalin's five-year plan. Göring then created a new agency to administer his expanded economic empire, staffing it with party officials, military officers, and specialists to deal with raw materials, food production, allocating labor, price controls, and foreign currencies. The four-year plan organization would oversee investments of huge sums of money in developing the ability to produce crucial raw materials domestically, synthetic rubber and iron ore being the two highest priorities, thus reducing or eliminating reliance on imports.

Typical for the regime, Göring's bloated bureaucracy duplicated or competed with the responsibilities of other ministries, despite maintaining a "general council" as a coordinating body. There were successes, notably in the increased production of coal, lignite, aluminum, and synthetic rubber and fibers up to 1939. But Germany was nowhere near self-sufficiency when the war began. Exports fell, and an increase in imports only further drained the country's reserves of foreign currencies. Ordinary Germans would soon feel the effects of the regime's voracious appetite for raw materials and were burdened with shortages, black markets, rationing, shoddy-quality consumer goods, and squads of **Sturmabteilung** (Stormtroopers; SA) and **Hitler Youth** tearing out iron fences and rooting in people's cellars for scrap metals.

Industrial conglomerate IG Farben would be the most significant producer and beneficiary of the organization's investments. But the entire endeavor also revealed to leaders of Germany's major industrial concerns that the regime posed a serious threat to their interests, mainly through its accelerating intrusion into the hitherto mostly private sector. Nowhere was this more evident than in the creation of the massive Hermann Göring Works in July 1937. The entirely state-run enterprise nationalized privately owned sources of iron ore, took over steelworks, and produced iron and steel at prices subsidized by the state, thus putting private concerns at a competitive disadvantage.

Implementing the plan, finally, produced significant strategic consequences. Hitler had ordered a crash program in making Germany self-sufficient and prepared for a long war beginning in the early 1940s. But the demands the plan placed on the economy and German society would mean the war would have to come sooner than Hitler anticipated, and when it came, it would have to be won quickly. It also mattered that Hitler believed he had very little time left to rule effectively as a dictator. His solution to the dilemmas, as he lay out to senior military officers in early November 1937, would incite him to accelerate the diplomatic revolution he was leading by targeting **Austria** and **Czechoslovakia**. *See also* HOSSBACH MEMORANDUM (1937).

FRANCE. In his first years as a political agitator, Hitler directed much of his ire at the "Western powers"—Great Britain, France, and the **United States**. Point 2 of the **Nazi Party Program** (25-Point Program) demanded the abrogation of the **Versailles** and St. Germain Treaties, a demand directed substantially though not exclusively at France. As for Germany's future as a great power, there were several competing ideas in the early 1920s within Munich's Far-Right scene and among those close to Hitler. One imagined a German-Russian alliance once Bolshevism had been vanquished. Another advocated Franco–German rapprochement. By the time Hitler wrote *Mein Kampf*, however, he had embraced the goal of conquering Lebensraum (**living space**) in the East and making Germany the dominant power in Europe. Doing this would require isolating and subduing France, and that would involve an alliance with **Italy** and some kind of arrangement with Britain.

Hitler began pursuing this scenario almost immediately after becoming **chancellor**. The first steps involved withdrawing from the **League of Nations** and from an international disarmament conference and ordering **rearmament**, the reintroduction of conscription, and the construction of a new air force (**Luftwaffe**). At the same time, he worked to isolate France through an **Anglo–German naval agreement** and by pursuing closer ties with **Benito Mussolini**. Destabilizing France was a major motivation behind his decision to aid **Francisco Franco**'s rebellion in Spain [*see* SPANISH CIVIL WAR (1936–1939)]. France was also a crucial factor as Hitler eyed **Czechoslovakia** in late 1937. He was well aware that the French possessed a formidable army, and his top military advisers were extremely nervous about provoking a war before Germany was adequately prepared. And as much as most Germans despised the Versailles Treaty and fantasized about taking revenge, there was no popular enthusiasm for war.

Yet Hitler was convinced that divisions between London and Paris over disarmament and security in Europe, along with France's severe internal divisions and labor unrest, would allow him to seize Czechoslovakia without risking general European war. A war between France and Italy would give him the same opportunity. And once Czechoslovakia and then **Austria** were taken, he expected **Poland** would be cowed into neutrality in any conflict between Germany and France.

For its part, the French government increased spending on armaments and built a massive fortification (the Maginot Line) along its border with Germany, though only with Germany and not Belgium. In April 1935, France joined England and Italy in the Stresa Front, which involved a pledge to guarantee the terms of the 1925 Pact of Locarno. Another seeming victory was the conclusion in early May 1935 of a Treaty of Mutual Assistance with Moscow with the clear aim of deterring Germany. But the pact was largely symbolic, and the Stresa Front dissolved when London and Berlin concluded the Anglo–German Naval Pact in June and Italy invaded Abyssinia (later Ethiopia) in October. The weak Anglo–French response to the brutal Italian campaign effectively killed off what was left of the League of Nations; brought Mussolini and Hitler closer together; and weakened the confidence of the Polish, **Romanian**, and Yugoslav governments in France as a guarantor of their nations' security.

Then in March 1936, Hitler won a major victory by dispatching a small force into the **Rhineland** in open violation of the Versailles Treaty. The French government did nothing in response. Mobilizing for an offensive operation, even a small one, would have been time consuming, expensive, and deeply unpopular, and it was clear that the British would not support an armed response to the remilitarization of the territory. The parlous state of France's finances led to a cutback in defense spending just as another European war loomed on the horizon.

As the British took the lead in attempting to **appease** Hitler over Czechoslovakia, the French followed along, aware that the defense of that country's sovereignty was impossible. Following the German occupation of Prague in March 1939, the French again followed Britain in promising to defend **Poland** against the German attack that everyone assumed was now inevitable. The only thing that might have staved it off was an Anglo–French–Soviet alliance. But **Joseph Stalin** instead chose to conclude a **Nazi–Soviet Nonaggression Pact** with Germany, the only country in a position to allow him to retake territories lost to the Bolsheviks in 1918. Two days after the German invasion of Poland, Britain declared war on Germany. The French declaration followed six hours later. Both amounted to nothing more than words, as Poland was dismembered by the **Wehrmacht** and then the Red Army.

The war in Western Europe began eight months later when Germany attacked Denmark, **Norway**, the Low Countries, and then France [see WESER EXERCISE (WESERÜBUNG)]. To most people's astonishment, the French army collapsed in six weeks. Hitler had ordered a daring attack through the densely wooded Ardennes region of southern Belgium that succeeded in cutting off the British Expeditionary Force in northern France before turning south. French resistance crumbled, and German troops entered Paris on 14 June. Three days later, Hitler—then at his headquarters in Brûly-de-Pesche in southern Belgium—was informed that the new French prime minister, Philippe Petain, had requested an armistice. Hitler ordered the French railway car in which German generals signed the armistice in November 1918 to be hauled out of the museum where it was being displayed and brought to the very same site in the forest of Compiègne. In that car on 22 June, Hitler sat in silence as **Wilhelm Keitel** dictated Germany's terms to the French delegation. He spent the next several days touring the **World War I** battlefields where he had served, before taking an early-morning tour of Paris lasting just three hours. Hitler had achieved his greatest military victory and reached the high point of his popularity and power in Germany.

France was divided into a northern (including Paris) and Atlantic coastal zone occupied by Germany. The Center and South were administered by a collaborationist regime based in the spa town of Vichy. Hitler's treatment of France was at first surprisingly lenient. He treaded with care after having bungled the installation of a pro-German government in Norway that the majority of Norwegians would never accept as legitimate. It was essential that Petain remain in France and not decamp to London or North **Africa** and that the empire remain loyal to the Vichy regime.

Hitler envisioned an economically weakened and politically decentralized state subservient to Germany. While Alsace-Lorraine was annexed, he desisted from more extensive changes and rejected Mussolini's and Franco's requests for territorial and material spoils. And the Vichy regime was a willing collaborator, particularly when it came to rounding up and deporting **Jews** (see HOLOCAUST). But its legitimacy in France suffered a fatal blow when the Germans announced labor conscription in August 1942, a move that provoked strikes, work stoppages, and riots and swelled the ranks of what had been a tiny resistance. The Allied invasion of North Africa (**Operation Torch**) in November 1942 led to the German occupation of the rest of France and a further hollowing out of Vichy's authority and legitimacy. Three months after the Allied invasion of France at Normandy (**Operation Overlord**), the regime's leadership fled to southwestern Germany and formed a short-lived government in exile. By that time, Allied forces had broken out of Normandy, invaded southern France (Operation Dragoon), and liberated Paris.

FRANCO, FRANCISCO (1892–1975). Spain did not figure prominently in Hitler's increasingly fervid strategic calculations after he became **chancellor**. When the Spanish military revolt began in July 1936, he was attending the annual Wagner festival in Bayreuth and had to ask **Richard Wagner**'s grandson Wolfgang to fetch his school atlas, as he had no idea where the capital of Spanish Morocco was. Within a week, however, Hitler had ordered German transport and fighter aircraft sent to the colony, which Franco, a Spanish army general, used to fly 13,500 soldiers to Seville. More assistance was forthcoming, as Hitler realized a nationalist victory in the **Spanish Civil War** would redound to Germany's benefit. He was right in the short term but wrong when it came to longer-term strategic prospects.

While German assistance to the nationalists was not as extensive as **Italy**'s, it was no doubt of value to Franco, especially at the beginning of the Spanish army's rebellion. As Hitler hoped, the long civil war that followed brought Germany and Italy closer together. The opportunity to test new weapons and train personnel was an added benefit [see BLITZKRIEG (LIGHTNING WAR); LUFTWAFFE (AIR FORCE)].

Conversely, Franco's right-wing dictatorship ultimately proved to be of no help to Hitler in resolving a major strategic dilemma in the fall of 1940. The Luftwaffe's failure to deliver a fatal blow to the Royal Air Force in the **Battle of Britain** inspired Hitler to look to the Mediterranean, where it might be possible to cripple British naval power. That could only be done with the assistance of Vichy **France**, Italy, and Spain.

In October 1940, Hitler traveled to the Franco–Spanish border to convince Franco to enter the war on Germany's side. Franco's agreement was essential to staging Operation Felix, a land-based attack on British-held Gibraltar, which, if successful, could have closed off the Mediterranean to the British navy.

Hitler with Albert Speer (left) and the sculptor Arno Breker (right) in Paris, 28 June 1940. *Courtesy of the United States National Archives and Records Administration.*

Hitler also hoped to use Spanish Morocco and Spanish-controlled islands off the northwest coast of **Africa**, from which he could launch a campaign against the **United States** once Britain and the Soviet Union were finally finished off.

But Hitler's arrogance and unwillingness to acknowledge the concerns of his existing and hoped-for allies prevented all of this. This was because he offered nothing in exchange. Franco, who was under some pressure from Spanish fascists energized by victory in the civil war and eager for Spain to become a major player in a "new Europe" mobilized against Bolshevism, expected to be compensated with parts of French Morocco. But Hitler refused to force Vichy France to hand over any territory for fear that such a move would only incite French forces there to side with the British and Free French. Nor was Hitler responsive to Franco's pleas for desperately needed supplies of wheat.

Infuriated by Hitler's and Foreign Minister **Joachim von Ribbentrop**'s maladroit diplomacy and possibly informed by one of Admiral **Wilhelm Canaris**'s agents that Germany could not force Spain to act, Franco held firm and refused to commit to entering the war. The distaste was mutual—Hitler soon told **Benito Mussolini** that he would rather have his own teeth extracted than deal with the Spanish dictator. In the end, Franco repaid Hitler by agreeing to the dispatch of 45,000 Spanish volunteers to fight around **Leningrad** in 1941. He would outlive Hitler as a dictator by 30 years.

FRICK, WILHELM (1877–1946). Trained as a lawyer and deemed unfit for military service in **World War I**, Frick served as a midlevel bureaucrat in Munich's police department until he was appointed head of the criminal police in 1923. Already an admirer of Hitler, he helped the party obtain permissions to hold marches and demonstrations. He was arrested after he attempted to block the city's police from intervening in the **Beer Hall Putsch** and was one of the 10 defendants in the 1924 **trial** of the conspirators. Convicted but given a suspended sentence, Frick lost his position in the police department and got a job with the city's social welfare office. At the same time, he obtained a **Reichstag** seat in the May 1924 **elections** representing the National Socialist Freedom Movement, the stand-in for the banned **National Socialist German Workers' Party** (Nazi Party; Nationalsozialistische Deutsche Arbeiterpartei; NSDAP).

After the party was refounded in 1925, he was among the first 12 members to gain Reichstag seats in the May 1928 elections. When the NSDAP became part of the governing coalition in the state of Thuringia in 1929, Frick was appointed minster of the interior and education, making him the first Nazi Party member to serve in a ministerial position. His attempts to purge leftists from the government; ban newspapers, plays, and films that displeased him; and promote Nazi **racism** in the state's schools got him removed a year later following a **Social Democratic Party of Germany** (Sozialdemokratische Partei Deutschlands; SPD) motion of no confidence.

It may well have been because of this inauspicious performance in Thuringia that **Franz von Papen** agreed to Frick's appointment as Reich minister of the interior in January 1933 [*see* CHANCELLOR, APPOINTMENT AS (30 JANUARY 1933)]. At that time, the ministry did not have authority over the police. But Frick became one of the principal architects of Hitler's dictatorship. He acted quickly to concentrate power in his ministry following the **Reichstag fire** by preparing the Reichstag Fire Decree, centralizing political authority in the Reich at the expense of the states, and drafting laws that **coordinated** much of German society with the new regime. He also played an important role in the development and promulgation of the Law for the Prevention of Genetically Diseased Offspring and the **Nuremberg Race Laws** [*see* EUTHANASIA PROGRAM (AKTION T4)].

Frick lost most of his power and influence after Hitler appointed **Heinrich Himmler** chief of police for all of Germany in June 1936. Hitler finally dispensed with Frick in August 1943, having decided that he was too old and not radical enough to do what was necessary to maintain the home front after Anglo–American bombing raids destroyed much of Hamburg (*see* STRATEGIC BOMBING CAMPAIGN). He replaced him as interior minister with Himmler. Frick spent the rest of the war as protector of Bohemia and Moravia. He was among the major war criminals tried by the **International Military Tribunal** (IMT). Convicted on three of the four counts (crimes against peace, crimes against humanity, and war crimes), he was sentenced to death and hanged.

FÜHRER MYTH (FÜHRER MYTHOS). The Führer Mythos was the manufactured image of Hitler as a heroic figure chosen by destiny to save Germany and the German "race." Nationalists there, as elsewhere, had long celebrated male leaders who had led or supposedly saved their peoples: The first century CE Cherusci leader and Roman citizen Armenius (renamed Hermann by 19th-century nationalists), Frederick Barbarossa, Frederick the Great, **Otto von Bismarck**, **Paul von Hindenburg**, and Kaiser Wilhelm II were important examples (see HOHENZOLLERNS). The impulse to seek a savior was greatly intensified by the aftermath of **World War I**. Humiliation and occupation by foreign powers, a revolution that produced what was for many a decidedly unheroic liberal democratic republic, and the specter of communism prepared the political ground for the embrace of a strong leader capable of uniting the nation and returning it to greatness.

This is not to suggest that Hitler's ascent to power was a foregone conclusion. For one thing, it took several years from the time he became active in politics for him to believe he would be Germany's savior by becoming its unchallenged leader. For another, the Führer Mythos had to be constructed and maintained, a project to which Hitler and **Joseph Goebbels** devoted an enormous amount of time and energy.

The myth was to serve several purposes. One was to hold a party with strong fissiparous tendencies together. A second was to legitimize Hitler's claim to total and unchallengeable political authority over Germany. Yet another was to conceal the unexceptional realities of his past.

Mein Kampf was foundational to its formation, particularly the putatively "autobiographical" first half. But this turgid, almost unreadable book was only the beginning: Visual imagery and sound were ultimately more important building blocks. The myth was maintained mainly by Hitler's in-person performances, whether monologues delivered to subordinates or in carefully prepared speeches given at the annual **Nuremberg party rallies** to the party faithful every November 9 or to the **Reichstag** [see BEER HALL PUTSCH (1923)]. The presence of an audience was crucial. His speeches recorded into a studio microphone were rather lackluster and explain why Goebbels resorted to recording and broadcasting his live speeches. The mass production and distribution of inexpensive radios became an essential component of Goebbels's strategy. Cinemas became another vital tool, with the myth's single most influential visual presentation being **Leni Riefenstahl's** *Triumph of the Will*.

Hitler did not wish to be worshipped like a deity. Yet there was an unmistakable **religious** dimension to the myth and how he wanted, indeed needed, people to respond to it. And it is clear that despite its highly manufactured nature, performing it influenced how Hitler perceived himself. In short, Hitler was also performing for Hitler, and he came to believe his own mythology.

At the same time, there was also a significant amount of distancing built into the myth-making machinery. Though Hitler occasionally had himself filmed or photographed smiling with children or accepting gifts and flowers from adoring admirers, he strove to make himself personally distant and unknowable to most party officials and ordinary Germans alike. To be sure, since he was a young man, secretiveness was a prominent feature of his **personality**. But Hitler's furtiveness carried over into his career as a politician for practical reasons. There were aspects of his early life that did not comport with the image presented in *Mein Kampf* of an unrecognized artistic genius whose destiny as a leader was revealed to him in the fevered days of November 1918. And after the scandal of his half-niece **Geli Raubal**'s suicide in September 1931, he kept his increasingly close relationship with **Eva Braun** away from the public and most party officials (see WOMEN).

Moreover, Hitler eschewed some of the visual antics and trappings of modern "strongmen" dictators. Unlike **Benito Mussolini** (and rather more like **Joseph Stalin**), he never allowed himself to be photographed or seen partly clothed or engaged in anything like manual labor or driving a vehicle. He dressed simply and did not adorn himself with real or fake medals and similar kinds of regalia [*See* GÖRING, HERMANN (1893–1946)]. But the most important purpose of such distancing was to enhance the aura of the man supposedly chosen by destiny to lead Germany. Such a man could not really be known by others, and he certainly could not be presented to his followers as attending to anything like an ordinary life.

Assessing the impact of the myth on the functioning of the regime and Hitler's popularity among ordinary Germans is difficult. On one hand, there is evidence that many Germans embraced him as a savior figure, particularly in the prewar years and following the military victories of 1939 and 1940. Criticism was often directed not at Hitler but at party officials perceived to be incompetent or corrupt. Yet the legacies of the First World War and the turmoil of the republic had made many Germans receptive to a form of nationalist authoritarianism. Some of Hitler's top military leaders seem to have been taken in by the myth, yet there was also a significant degree of ideological compatibility, and Hitler lavished his generals with gifts of money and property. To a great extent, Hitler's divide-and-rule style required that subordinates accept his authority in more than name only. **Schutzstaffel** (Protection Squad; SS) leader **Heinrich Himmler** was steadfastly loyal to Hitler until the very end of the war. But Himmler and other SS officials created an organization and distinct culture, the existence of which was not entirely dependent on its members blindly accepting the myth. Among the most powerful officials, the myth seems to have had its firmest grip on one of its principal architects: Goebbels.

It was inevitable that the myth's power would lose its grip once the tide of the war turned against Germany in 1943. Hitler retreated from public view, and no propaganda, no matter how skillfully crafted and delivered, could convince a growing number of Germans that he was in fact the opposite of their savior. *See also* AUSTRIA; BLITZKRIEG (LIGHTNING WAR); ECONOMY; FRANCE; RHINELAND, REMILITARIZATION OF THE (1936); WESER EXERCISE (WESERÜBUNG).

FUNK, WALTHER (1890–1960). Born in East Prussia and educated in Berlin and Leipzig, Funk became a financial journalist in the 1920s. He met Hitler in 1931, joined the **National Socialist German Workers' Party** (Nazi Party; Nationalsozialistische Deutsche Arbeiterpartei; NSDAP), and became Hitler's **economic** adviser. Working for the party's press service, he was mainly useful because he had contacts with industrialists. In 1933, he began working in the Propaganda Ministry's Reich Chamber of Culture. The turning point in his career came after Hitler dismissed minister of economics and Reichsbank president **Hjalmar Schacht** in November 1937 and replaced him with Funk, first as economics minister, then as Reichsbank chief a year later. The appointment had nothing to do with Funk's qualifications, which were minimal, but because he was competent enough and would be easily steamrolled by **Hermann Göring** and his **Four-Year Plan** organization. Though possessing little real power, Funk was actively complicit in the Aryanization of the economy—the expropriation of **Jewish**-owned property and assets. He was also complicit in the storing of valuables taken from murdered Jews by the **Schutzstaffel** (Protection Squad; SS), such as jewels, gold jewelry, gold eyeglass rims, and gold teeth, in Reichsbank vaults.

Among the defendants tried by the **International Military Tribunal** (IMT) in Nuremberg, Funk was convicted of and sentenced to life imprisonment. He seemed not to fully understand why he was in the dock and succumbed to bouts of uncontrollable weeping on the stand. American prosecutor Telford Taylor later speculated that this pathetic performance by the physically unimpressive Funk may have spared him the death penalty. In poor health, he was released in 1957 and died three years later.

G

GENERAL PLAN FOR THE EAST (GENERALPLAN OST). When Hitler thought of **living space** (Lebensraum) for the German people, he imagined the vast territories of the European Soviet Union, above all **Poland**, Russia, Belarus, and **Ukraine**. Once conquered, the East would be transformed into a "Garden of Eden," where millions of healthy German farmers would live in bucolic towns, farming with the most modern machinery, their communities connected by superhighways and high-speed rail networks. It was a vision that illustrated the combination of the modern and the reactionary in Nazi ideology.

As for the millions of Russians, Ukrainians, and other ethnic groups already populating the region, they would be enslaved and allowed to die off. The industrial cities built by **Joseph Stalin** would be depopulated by deportation and starvation. Hitler even envisioned a version of contemporary antivaccination campaigns: Russians and Ukrainians would be told that vaccinations would harm rather than protect their children, thus increasing the death rate. The harvests of Russian and Ukrainian farmland would feed German soldiers and settlers and, of course, the German home front. This element of the plan was known as the "hunger plan," the details of which were developed by officials in the Agriculture Ministry and the **Wehrmacht**.

This mad scheme was formalized as the Generalplan Ost. Its most enthusiastic proponent was **Heinrich Himmler**. Two days after the launch of **Operation Barbarossa**, he set a group of talented young academics in the **Schutzstaffel** (Protection Squad; SS) to work on drawing up the plans. Hitler approved a revised version of it a year later. Some 30 million people were to be uprooted—**Jews** were included in the estimates—with the objective of Germanizing much of Eastern Europe in a single generation's life span. The remaining population would be enslaved in some fashion, murdered, or Germanized if their physical appearances bore a close enough match to the Aryan ideal. Himmler and his officials blended grandiose fantasizing with an obsessive attention to detail. Yet other officials—even within the SS and loyal to Himmler—could not help pointing out flaws in the plan's demographic projections, the almost unimaginable estimated cost of the entire enterprise, and serious logistical problems.

Any chance of realizing the plan, of course, depended above all on German victory in Russia, and that never came. Not that the impatient Himmler intended to wait to begin experimenting with smaller-scale test projects in Poland and then in Ukraine. But local Nazi rulers behaved so brutally that despite the intense dangers, armed resistance groups mobilized where before there had been none. In Hegewald, the pilot settlement in Ukraine, partisan forces soon drove out the few German settlers. Moreover, Himmler was able to send far fewer settlers than he anticipated, and many of them were hardly the type of strapping blond farmer-warriors who populated his grotesque fantasies.

GENEVA DISARMAMENT CONFERENCE (1932). In response to the destructiveness of **World War I**, international disarmament became an elite and popular cause in much of the Western world. US president Woodrow Wilson included it among his agenda for world peace, presented in the form of 14 points in a speech to the US Congress in January 1918. The architects of the **League of Nations** envisioned disarmament as one of the new organization's priorities throughout the 1920s, and calls for disarmament proliferated among millions of liberals and leftists around the world. This wave of antiwar idealism—inspired by the very real carnage of the First World War—crested on 27 August 1928, when representatives of 15 nations (later joined by 47 more) signed a pact pledging not to resort to war to resolve disputes. The German government was among the original signatories of Kellogg-Briand Pact, also known as the Pact of Paris.

Internationalism in general and disarmament in particular were, of course, anathema to conservative nationalists and the Far Right in Germany. Immediately after he was appointed **chancellor**, Hitler cannily used the rhetoric of "international" disarmament to oppose German participation in any multilateral disarmament agreement. He insisted that Germany wanted peace and expected to be treated with respect as an equal among the world's great powers. If other states were unwilling to disarm, then no one could reasonably expect Germany to remain in a state of relative weakness. Hitler's position was strengthened by the fact that the British and **French** governments were divided over the issue, with the latter far less inclined to disarm than the former. There were other enormous challenges facing proponents of disarmament, such as securing the compliance of individual states and regulating a massive international trade in arms. Then there was the problem that the world was becoming increasingly divided into nations seeking to maintain the international status quo (Great Britain, France, and the **United States**) and those determined to revise it (**Japan**, **Italy**, the Soviet Union, and Germany).

In the 1920s, Reichswehr officers in Germany attempted to subvert the restrictions imposed by the **Versailles Treaty**, though they had to do so clandestinely to prevent an international backlash and because of the strength of antiwar sentiment in Germany. But by the early 1930s, officers, diplomats, and political leaders were determined to increase spending on defense-related infrastructure, with the goal of unilateral **rearmament**. No one was more determined to take this course than Hitler.

In February 1932, an international disarmament conference convened in Geneva. Germany sent a delegation but withdrew it in the fall over the question of equality of status with Great Britain and France. The dispute was resolved in Germany's favor, and the conference resumed with German participation but not for long. Hitler withdrew from the conference and the league in October 1933. He called a plebiscite in which 95 percent of voters supported the regime's position. The conference limped on pointlessly until June 1934. The moment accelerated the momentum for rearmament in Germany and laid some of the groundwork for the diplomatic revolution in the second half of the decade.

GERMAN AMERICAN BUND (AMERIKA-DEUTSCHER VOLKSBUND). The German American Bund was an organization of US-based adherents of national socialism inspired but not supported by the Nazi regime. It was founded in Buffalo, New York, in 1936 by Fritz Kuhn, a German-born veteran of the German army in **World War I** who became a naturalized US citizen in 1934. The bund was the successor to the disbanded pro-Nazi Friends of New Germany, which had been authorized to form by **Rudolf Hess** in 1933 as part of an effort to mobilize support for the new regime abroad by German citizens or people of non-**Jewish** German descent.

Though it mimicked the style, appearance, and some aspects of the **National Socialist German Workers' Party** (Nazi Party; Nationalsozialistische Deutsche Arbeiterpartei; NSDAP) organization and the **Sturmabteilung** (Stormtroopers; SA), the bund was not a puppet of Berlin. Though its stated purpose was to increase support in the **United States** for the Nazi regime, it also professed to be opposed to importing the Nazi model to America. In this sense, the bund was a product of increasingly strong domestic currents of antiliberal **racist** nativism, mainly among Anglo-Saxon-descended White Protestants. The post–Reconstruction Era American South had established racial segregation by law, informal customs, and extreme violence. Around the turn of the century, an influx of immigrants, many of them Asians or Catholics or Jews from poorer parts of Europe, provoked even greater fears among White Protestants that their dominant position in society was being challenged by "others."

The establishment of the first communist dictatorship in the former Russian Empire, labor unrest, and bombings by anarchists further eroded what was already a deeply compromised democratic political system by provoking a postwar red scare in which thousands were arrested and deported. Nativist sentiments were intensified by the widespread belief that the United States had been tricked into entering the First World War. Though well on the way to achieving global superpower status and not really isolated in the 1920s, isolationism became a powerful political force even before the onset of the Great Depression.

If isolationists were determined to keep the United States out of the world's affairs, then they also wanted to keep much of the world out of the United States. In 1924, Congress passed a law (the National Origins Act, or Johnson-Reed Act) severely restricting immigration through a system of quotas designed to keep out supposedly undesirable people. At the same time, the Ku Klux Klan had been experiencing a rebirth, expanding out of the South and into an organization with a national presence. Similar groups emerged in the wake of the Depression, along with charismatic populists like Louisiana politician Huey Long and Detroit-based priest Charles Coughlin, whose radio show attracted millions of listeners. The influence of European-style fascism made itself felt in the United States, and small militant groups formed around the country.

While sharing a bundle of hatred and fears, fascist groups in America were nonetheless disunited, as they were elsewhere in the world. One of the numerous fascist or overtly pro-Nazi groups was the German American Bund. It eventually counted perhaps 25,000 members. It sponsored 70 divisions around the country and built around 20 training camps. The high point of its visibility was reached on 20 February 1939 with a rally in New York City's Madison Square Garden. Standing before a huge banner of George Washington, Kuhn and other speakers denounced the Jews and communists, who they claimed controlled the US government, and referred to President **Franklin D. Roosevelt** as "Rosenfeld." The bund's claim that it did not want to simply import German Nazism to the US notwithstanding, the speakers advocated a boycott of non-Aryan businesses and the application of Nazi race laws to the US. The rally drew 20,000 members and supporters. It also attracted a crowd of thousands of antifascists (estimates vary from 10,000 to 100,000) and some 1,700 police officers to keep the two groups separated.

Though the bund was in part an expression of intensifying nativism and racism, it was too closely associated with a foreign regime to become anything more than a political sideshow. Hitler rather unenthusiastically greeted a delegation of bund officials in Berlin during the 1936 **Olympic Games**. But he was in fact wary of the attention-seeking Kuhn and the opposition the bund was generating in the United States. As Hitler pushed the pace of **rearmament** and planned his war of territorial conquest, he was counting on American neutrality, and the bund's stunts and dustups with antifascists were not helpful. In February 1938, the regime prohibited German citizens residing in the United States from joining the organization, a decision that so outraged Kuhn that he traveled to Germany and sought a meeting with Hitler. The request was denied, and in a truly bizarre scene, Kuhn was lectured by a midlevel Nazi official on the necessity of respecting the rule of **law**.

In the end, the group disintegrated after the beginning of the war in Europe. It had drawn the attention of investigative reporters, the FBI, and the US House of Representatives'

Committee on Un-American Activities. The bund also inspired the production in 1939 of the first overtly anti-Nazi Hollywood film: Warner Brothers' satirical *Confessions of a Nazi Spy* (see CINEMA AND TELEVISION, REPRESENTATIONS IN). Kuhn proved to be typical of numerous Nazi party officials in Germany: He was **corrupt**. After the spectacle of the Madison Square Garden rally and the fights that broke out in the hall, New York City mayor Fiorello La Guardia ordered the group's headquarters raided and its finances investigated. Kuhn was convicted of embezzlement and replaced as bund leader in December 1939. Bund chapters disbanded or were banned in a few states. Kuhn's citizenship was revoked in 1943, and he was deported to Germany in September 1945. Two years later, he was detained in the former **concentration camp** at Dachau pending denazification proceedings. Tried and convicted in April 1948, he was sentenced to 10 years' imprisonment and released shortly before dying in obscurity in 1951.

GERMAN LABOR FRONT (DEUTSCHE ARBEITSFRONT; DAF). Drawing the large and growing number of German workers—the industrial working class represented nearly half of the country's working population—away from the Left was the main reason the **German Workers' Party** (Deutsche Arbeiterpartei; DAP) and then the **National Socialist German Workers' Party** (Nazi Party; Nationalsozialistische Deutsche Arbeiterpartei; NSDAP) were created. During the Weimar Republic, Hitler campaigned on a message of national unity over class conflict. Once appointed **chancellor**, he had to follow through on his promise to unite the country while remedying the unemployment crisis as quickly as possible. One of the biggest potential obstacles was that while the party had attracted a significant number of workers to its side in **Reichstag** and local **elections**—25 percent by 1932—a majority still voted for the **Social Democratic Party of Germany** (Sozialdemokratische Partei Deutschlands; SPD) or the **Communist Party of Germany** (Kommunistische Partei Deutschlands; KPD). Moreover, most belonged to independent trade unions and hundreds of affiliated clubs and associations. The party's own trade union, the National Socialist Factory Cell Organization, counted only 300,000 members in 1933.

Socialism of the Nazi variety did not entail abolishing private property. But it did mean subordinating the individual to the Volksgemeinschaft (people's community). So when it came to business and labor, a middle ground had to be found. Business owners would have to have enough freedom of action to compete and adapt, but they could not be permitted to exploit their employees. Conversely, workers would need to be protected but not be coddled and certainly could not be allowed to set themselves as a class against the rest of the country. They also had to believe that they were valued and respected and were contributing to the building of a new Germany and, later, victory over the nation's enemies.

Hitler's approach to workers involved a combination of repression, mobilization, and ongoing surveillance. Repression was fast and comprehensive. In just a few months, from March to July 1933, the regime dismantled one of the industrialized world's greatest organized labor movements. The SPD and KPD were suppressed and outlawed. Many of its leaders and activists were driven into exile, imprisoned, or killed. To be sure, Hitler was helped by the fact that the Left was fatally divided. It also helped that the SPD stuck rigidly to legalism and was unprepared for such a comprehensive crackdown. In addition, the KPD's leadership was controlled by Moscow and blinded by the belief that the Nazis were nothing more than harbingers of the workers' revolution. Independent unions and other forms of organized working-class life were disbanded and banned. As in other areas of German life, organized resistance by working-class men and women became and remained extremely difficult and dangerous [see COORDINATION (GLEICHSCHALTUNG); OPPOSITION].

The job of mobilizing workers fell to the DAF. Established on 2 May 1933, it became one of the party's largest organizations, counting 25 million members by 1942. Hitler declared its main political purpose to be replacing the old ideal and institutions of working-class solidarity with the social cohesion he believed held the nation together through **World War I**. It was no accident that military references and terminology were pervasive in the organization. The DAF's leader, **Robert Ley**, was a veteran who had been badly wounded at the front. Though he possessed virtually no relevant professional experience, he was an early Nazi party member and, most important of all, an unwavering Hitler loyalist.

Eliminating the SPD, KPD, and independent labor unions may have pleased business owners and industrialists, but there was also potential that the DAF and the Labor Ministry would become excessively interventionist. Though the new regime quickly proved to be business friendly, mainly because of the priority Hitler placed on suppressing the Left, reducing unemployment, and initiating **rearmament**, the state did become increasingly intrusive and controlling [see DARRÉ, RICHARD WALTHER (1895–1953)]. Making matters worse was the rampant corruption in the huge organization and Hitler's willingness to tolerate the erratic behavior of the alcoholic and brain-damaged Ley.

The task of mobilizing workers was made easier by the return of full employment by 1936. Another important factor was the increase of younger workers with weaker attachments to the pre-Nazi working-class parties and organizations and a greater willingness to accept the new order. The DAF's best-known initiative was the Kraft durch Freude (Strength through Joy; KdF) organization, which provided myriad leisure activities for workers. These included inexpensive vacations, including cruises on new ships the *Wilhelm Gustlof* and the *Robert Ley*. Hitler also authorized Ley to oversee the production of a cheap, reliable **Volkswagen** (people's car) that workers would pay for in advance in small installments. Ferdinand Porsche designed the prototype, though the war prevented it from being put into production.

To address a shortage of residential housing all over Germany, the DAF also constructed the first of what were planned to be hundreds of thousands of stand-alone homes and apartment buildings, though the entire effort had to be shelved by 1942. Also partly constructed was a massive resort complex, Prora, that stretched for 4.5 kilometers along the Baltic Sea beachfront on the island of Rügen. Dismissed by exiled Social Democrats as unimportant, at least some of the DAF's programs did succeed in making the ideal of a Volksgemeinschaft more than propaganda. For many workers, the DAF made it a lived experience, at least for a few years.

The DAF declined in significance, if not size and ambition, beginning in 1939. Within a few years, the war took priority over everything. And Ley was no match for the rapacious and predatory party officials and groups competing for power, resources, and bounty in the East, notably **Hermann Göring** and his **Four-Year Plan** organization, **Heinrich Himmler** and the **Schutzstaffel** (Protection Squad; SS), the **Wehrmacht**, and industrial giants like IG Farben. Nor did Ley and the DAF have any say in managing the nearly 8 million non-Germans brought to Germany as slave laborers.

GERMAN NATIONAL PEOPLE'S PARTY (DEUTSCHNATIONALE VOLKSPARTEI; DNVP). Also known as the German Nationals or Nationalist Party, the DNVP was the most important nonfascist Far-Right party and one of the Weimar Republic's principal gravediggers. It was formed in 1918 as a combination of the old conservative party and smaller nationalist groups. As the party of the conservative nationalist establishment, its base was narrow but influential: aristocratic landowners, the Prussian-dominated military elite, and some industrialists. It was opposed to the republic and sought the restoration of the **Hohenzollern** monarchy. Like other parties, it sponsored paramilitary "fighting leagues" and did not hide its approval of political terrorism directed at democrats and leftists. It did well in **elections** in the first half of the 1920s. By the end of 1924, it was the second-largest party in the **Reichstag**, after the **Social Democratic Party of Germany** (Sozialdemokratische Partei Deutschlands; SPD).

The DNVP's opposition to the republic, however, made it a rather unreliable coalition partner. In the October 1928 elections, it lost almost a quarter of its Reichstag seats. As a result, the party took a more radically right-wing turn by appointing a new leader, **Alfred Hugenberg**, a press and film baron and industrialist long identified with the **pan-German** movement. The party's new program remained aggressively nationalist but adopted a pan-German agenda; demanded the Reichstag be transformed into an administrative body; and embraced a crude, conspiratorial anti-Semitism. Hugenberg's dictatorial leadership style drove some members to other parties, and his efforts to broaden the base of the DNVP's support failed [*see* HARZBURG FRONT; YOUNG PLAN REFERENDUM (1929)]. One result of these efforts was to bring Hitler out of his post–**Landsberg Prison** public obscurity.

The DNVP continued to lose voters to the **National Socialist German Workers' Party** (Nazi Party; Nationalsozialistische Deutsche Arbeiterpartei; NSDAP) in the 1930 and 1932 elections, and the two became bitter rivals. But it remained just strong and well connected enough to be a necessary component of any conservative nationalist coalition. In the tense negotiations leading up to Hitler's appointment as **chancellor**, Hugenberg secured control of the Economics Ministry and the Ministry of Food. But as with all other parties, over the following months, it would be undermined, harassed, and marginalized by the far more aggressive, skilled, and radical Nazis. In May 1933, it took a major step toward dissolution by renaming itself the German National Front (GNF)—less an independent political party and more an appendage of the NSDAP. When at the end of the month a few GNF members dared to complain to Hitler about their party's fate, he exploded and threatened to allow the **Sturmabteilung** (Stormtroopers; SA) to kill all of them. He then increased the harassment and arrests of GNF groups and members.

When Hugenberg's position in the cabinet became untenable, he tendered his resignation to President **Paul von Hindenburg** on 26 June. As Hindenburg did nothing, Hugenberg made the mistake of appealing to Hitler directly, who only increased the pressure by demanding he resign and the GNF agree to disband. In a twist to the legend of the god Saturn devouring his own children, Hitler and the political revolution he was leading had consumed their enablers.

GERMAN PEOPLES' PARTY (DEUTSCHE VOLKSPARTEI; DVP). At the end of **World War I**, the prewar National Liberal Party split into the centrist, prorepublic German Democratic Party (Deutsche Demokratische Partei; DDP; after 1930 the Staatspartei, or State Party), and the right-of-center DVP. The DVP opposed the republic and socialism and espoused a classical liberal **economic** agenda alongside a roster of culturally conservative positions. Ironically, given its basic hostility to the republic, the DVP produced its greatest statesman, Gustav Stresemann, who served as chancellor in 1923 and as foreign minister from 1923 to 1929. His sudden death in October 1929 removed an important moderate figure from the DVP and the republic's political landscape more generally, and the party took a rightward turn.

The DVP had reached the high point of its popularity early in the Weimar Republic, receiving just over 13 percent of the vote in June 1920 **Reichstag elections**. Its support fell steadily thereafter, and it won just under 2 percent in the November 1932 elections. Like all other parties, except the **Social Democratic Party of Germany** (Sozialdemokratische Partei Deutschlands; SPD), its deputies voted in favor of the **Enabling Act** (*see* REICHSTAG FIRE). And just like every other non–**National Socialist German Workers' Party** (Nazi Party; Nationalsozialistische Deutsche Arbeiterpartei; NSDAP) in the spring and summer of 1933, it was subjected to an increasing campaign of intimidation and harassment by the Nazis. Its leader dissolved the party on 4 July.

GERMAN WORKERS' PARTY (DEUTSCHE ARBEITERPARTEI; DAP). The political turbulence of the last year of **World War I** and its immediate aftermath spawned an array of Far-Right groups, parties, and paramilitary units, especially in Munich. One of them was the Thule Society, a kind of Far-Right secret society of middle-class businessmen, journalists, and students that grew out of the much larger **Pan-German** League and whose members included a number of future prominent **National Socialist German Workers' Party** (Nazi Party; Nationalsozialistische Deutsche Arbeiterpartei; NSDAP) officials, notably **Alfred Rosenberg** and **Rudolf Hess**. As the society hoped to draw working-class Germans away from Marxist socialism, one of its founders, journalist Karl Harrer, contacted Anton Drexler, a Munich locksmith working for the Bavarian railways. Drexler had joined the Far-Right German Fatherland Party during the war and in 1918 established the Free Workers' Committee for a Just Peace and cofounded an informal political workers' group. The latter became the nucleus of the DAP, established by Drexler and Harrer in Munich on 5 January 1919.

Drexler and the party's first members belonged to what was then a fringe political current that sought to combine nationalism and socialism, though not of the Marxist variety. They also drew inspiration from the pan-German movement and were among those anti-Semites who saw **Jews** as the creators of Bolshevism. Most of its earliest membership was comprised of lower- and middle-class veterans and Freikorps (Free Corps) members from southern Germany and a few ethnic German émigrés from the **Baltics** and Russia. By the end of the year, the DAP, though small in terms of membership, had become an important part of Munich's Far-Right political landscape, and it drew the attention and support of talented and well-connected right-wing political operatives and army officers. The story that it was nothing more than a motley collection of disgruntled oddballs until Hitler showed up and transformed it through his skills as a speaker and organizer is nothing more than a product of Hitler's self-mythologizing [see FÜHRER MYTH (FÜHRER MYTHOS)].

It would be one of the city's well-connected and ambitious right-wing military officers, **Karl Mayr**, who would be responsible for Hitler's first contact with the DAP. Mayr ordered Hitler and seven others to attend a meeting, held in a Munich beer hall, on 12 September 1919. Because Hitler had already demonstrated an ability to make attention-grabbing speeches, Mayr may have thought it would be useful to have one of his better public speakers join a party he wanted to influence. Sure enough, Hitler launched a diatribe that got Drexler's attention, and he urged Hitler to join, which he did soon after. At that point, the DAP was not issuing membership numbers or cards. When it began doing so in January 1920, members were listed in alphabetical order, with the count beginning at 501 to give the impression the party was much larger than it was. Hence Hitler was listed as member number 555. He claimed in *Mein Kampf* to have been the party's seventh member, but this was his ranking on its central committee.

Drexler's approach was well timed, as Hitler was looking to join a political group, having just been rejected as a writer for the German Socialist Party's newspaper. Hitler quickly became one of the DAP's most popular public speakers. He made anti-Semitism a prominent theme and thus played an important role in situating hatred of Jews at the center of Munich's Far-Right political scene.

But Hitler's ambitions were beginning to extend beyond ranting in beer halls. He wanted to exert a controlling influence over the party and prevent it from being co-opted by one of the larger and, at that moment, more influential Far-Right parties, notably the **German National Peoples' Party** (Deutschnationale Volkspartei; DNVP). His maneuvering resulted in Harrer quitting the party, which put Drexler in charge, though not for long.

At a meeting on 24 February 1920, Hitler read out the new **Nazi Party Program** (25-Point Program). It was also at this meeting that the DAP was formally renamed the National Socialist German Workers' Party. *See also* ECKART, DIETRICH (1863–1923); FEDER, GOTTFRIED (1883–1941); RÖHM, ERNST (1887–1934).

GODWIN'S LAW. In 1991, an American lawyer, Mike Godwin, proposed, "As an online discussion continues, the probability of a comparison to Hitler or to Nazis approaches one." It became widely understood as an attempt to take the moral high ground as a way of avoiding intellectual surrender. A kind of corollary to Godwin's Law asserted that a person making such a comparison automatically becomes the argument's clear loser. Godwin later insisted that his intention was to criticize lazy thinking. Referring to the Nazis or Hitler in an online debate, Godwin believed, signaled that one was unwilling to make thoughtful, relevant comparisons to either and thus unable to conclude an argument with intellectual and moral integrity.

The impetus to use references to Nazis and Hitler to win an argument or assert one's superior moral sensibilities is based on an assumption that both represent a kind of ultimate, timeless evil. *Nazi* and *Hitler* are held in reserve as a kind of talisman so potent that once it is produced, the recipient will be shamed into conceding defeat.

The durability of Godwin's Law goes against the longer-running trend of normalization, defined as situating Nazis and Hitler within, rather than outside of, history's vast pantheon of evildoers. Invoking or falling victim to Godwin's Law, in other words, confirms the status of Nazis and Hitler as representing an evil that is historically abnormal to the point of incomparability. *See also* CINEMA AND TELEVISION, REPRESENTATIONS IN.

GOEBBELS, JOSEPH PAUL (1897–1945). Goebbels was the Nazi regime's most important propagandist and one of its most influential ideologues. His copious diaries are the single most important source on much of the regime's history at its highest level. Among the highest-ranking Nazi Party officials, he became the most devoted to Hitler personally. Goebbels was born and raised in a staunchly observant Catholic family in the Rhineland. Alone among leading party officials, Goebbels possessed a doctorate (in literature).

Intelligent, vain, deeply cynical, and intensely ambitious, he was also beset by insecurities related to his physical appearance. He was short in stature and, like nearly every other party leader, bore no resemblance to the Aryan ideal. A physical disability resulting from a childhood bout with polio left him with a clubfoot and rendered him unfit for military service in **World War I**. By contrast, Hitler and nearly every other party leader had either served or joined one or more paramilitary units. Goebbels's resentments were also fed by the fact that he was a highly educated man, with pretensions to become a novelist, playwright, and poet, who had joined a party in which intellectuals and intellectualism were despised. He compensated for these perceived inadequacies with a ferociously puritanical embrace of anti-**Jewish racist** nationalism and slavish devotion to Hitler.

Like other leading party figures, Goebbels was deeply immersed in Far-Right politics before he met Hitler. He joined the **National Socialist German Workers' Party** (Nazi Party; Nationalsozialistische Deutsche Arbeiterpartei; NSDAP) in 1922 and was appointed its business manager in the Ruhr region three years later. At first, he was **Gregor Strasser**'s right-hand man and an influential figure on the party's "left" wing, going so far as to demand Hitler's resignation in 1926 on the grounds of his supposed bourgeois orientation. But Goebbels switched sides, and Hitler rewarded him with an appointment as the party's leader in Berlin-Brandenburg. Berlin was then a **Social Democratic Party of Germany** (Sozialdemokratische Partei Deutschlands; SPD) and **Communist Party of Germany** (Kommunistische Partei Deutschlands; KPD) stronghold, and Goebbels became the Left's bête noire through his ceaseless agitation. At the same time, he built the foundations for the vast propaganda apparatus he would eventually control, mainly by founding a new party newspaper, *Der Angriff* (*The Attack*), and through staging rallies, marches, protests, and otherwise provoking the Left at every turn. His efforts also had the effect of further marginalizing the party's "left" wing, which up to that point had been dominant in northern Germany.

For his success in Berlin, Hitler rewarded him with another promotion in 1929: Reich propaganda leader. Goebbels's devotion to Hitler had in the meantime become complete, and he was instrumental in perpetuating the **Führer myth**. And, like Hitler, he came to believe in it. The next promotion came in March 1933, when Hitler appointed him Reich minister for public enlightenment and propaganda, a position of enormous power, as it gave Goebbels control over the press and the other two most important modes of mass communication: radio and film. His ministry also controlled the performing and visual arts. Long a radical anti-Semite, his hatred of Jews had become boundless.

His successes in purging the press and the arts of Jews and the anti-Semitic propaganda that poured out of his ministry notwithstanding, his desire for a more radical approach to the entire "Jewish question" had to be held in check until 1938 [see NUREMBERG RACE LAWS; OLYMPIC GAMES (1936)]. Along with Hitler, he was the chief instigator of the **Night of Broken Glass** on 9–10 November 1938. During the war, Goebbels became an ideological instigator and architect of the **Holocaust**, mainly through his unflagging devotion to fulfilling Hitler's prophecy and by providing the public with an ongoing account of the war as a life-or-death struggle between Judeo-Bolshevism and the German "race" [see PROPHECY SPEECH (30 JANUARY 1939). It was due to Goebbels's (and Press Chief **Otto Dietrich**'s) propagandizing that the existence of a war of annihilation against the Jews—if not its operational details—was not kept secret from the public.

There were limits to Goebbels's power and influence. While he and Magda provided a kind of surrogate family for Hitler, they were not a regular part of the inner circle at the **Berghof**. And Goebbels actually had little influence on domestic or foreign policy making. Nor was his control of propaganda really total, as Dietrich, party publishing magnate **Max Amann**, and **Alfred Rosenberg** all had extensive authority in this area. He had no role in the making of a singularly important piece of propaganda: **Leni Riefenstahl**'s *Triumph of the Will*. Moreover, the **Wehrmacht** and Foreign Ministry maintained in-house propaganda operations. Yet Goebbels's power increased as Germany went on the defensive following the **Battle of Stalingrad**. He shared and bolstered Hitler's conviction that greater willpower and sacrifice—with the help of **"wonder weapons"**—would produce victory.

It was Goebbels who seized the moment immediately after Stalingrad to rally the party and German citizens to an unprecedented level of commitment and sacrifice. In a three-hour-long speech broadcast live on 18 February 1943 and heard by millions of Germans, he called for "total war," though it was not clear what that meant in practical terms. Goebbels could shout into a microphone all he wanted, but it would not in any way reverse Germany's military fortunes in Russia or over the skies of its cities or in the Atlantic [see BATTLE OF THE ATLANTIC (1939–1945); STRATEGIC BOMBING CAMPAIGN].

Another demonstration of steely devotion came in the tense hours after the failed **assassination attempt** on Hitler on 20 July 1944, when Goebbels played a crucial role in confining the conspirators to the War Ministry in Berlin, thus derailing the coup attempt. Hitler's faith in his propaganda chief increased, and he appointed Goebbels plenipotentiary for total war in July, a position that gave him extensive powers to keep the home front mobilized. By that point, however, Goebbels's orders could only make matters worse.

There were no limits to Goebbels's slavish loyalty to Hitler. With the exception of **Martin Bormann**, Goebbels was the only highest-level party official to remain completely loyal to Hitler to the very end. This loyalty extended even beyond Hitler's **suicide**, though it did involve a single and highly uncharacteristic act of disobedience. In his **personal will and political testament**, Hitler had selected Goebbels to be the new Reich chancellor. Instead, following Hitler's suicide on 30 April 1945, Goebbels and Magda had their six children murdered in the bunker complex below the **chancellery** and then instructed a member of **Schutzstaffel** (Protection Squad; SS) to kill the two of them.

GÖRING, HERMANN (1893–1946). From the late 1920s to 1940, no party official was as important to Hitler and the **National Socialist German Workers' Party**'s (Nazi Party; Nationalsozialistische Deutsche Arbeiterpartei; NSDAP) entire political project as Göring. Born in Bavaria in 1893, Göring was raised in an upper-middle-class home. His father had been an important official in German South West Africa (today Namibia), and Hermann attended a military academy before serving with considerable distinction as a pilot in **World War I**. At the war's end, he commanded the squadron named for Manfred von Richthofen and had been decorated with the Pour le Mérite, then Germany's highest military honor. Now something of a celebrity, he burnished his reputation by marrying into Swedish nobility. A fervent nationalist and antirepublican, he joined the Nazi Party in 1922 and quickly became devoted to Hitler.

Göring was a major catch. Multilingual, handsome, and charismatic, he was well known beyond Far-Right circles and well connected to the conservative nationalist establishment. He was also intelligent, shrewd, and utterly ruthless. The first of his many important appointments, head of the **Sturmabteilung** (Stormtroopers; SA), came quickly. He participated in the **Beer Hall Putsch** but managed to evade capture and prosecution by fleeing the country for four years. He picked up where he left off when he returned in 1927 by becoming a **Reichstag** delegate. In July 1932, he was elected president of the Reichstag. Following his appointment as **chancellor**, Hitler appointed Göring to three important posts: interior minister for the state of Prussia, head of the Prussian police and the Gestapo, and aviation minister. In the first two positions, he played a central role in the wave of political terror against the Left in the spring of 1933 and in constructing the legal foundations for Hitler's dictatorship in the wake of the **Reichstag fire**.

With the announcement of **rearmament** in 1935, Hitler put him in charge of the new **Luftwaffe**. A year later came the appointment to head the **Four-Year Plan**. Göring leveraged this position to create what became one of the largest—if not the largest—industrial conglomerate in world at that point: the massive Hermann Göring Works. Though many party officials used their positions to enrich themselves, none did so to a greater or more ostentatious extent than Göring [see LEY, ROBERT (1890–1945)]. He made a point of showing off his huge residences, a massive wardrobe, medals, jewels, and an **art** collection amassed largely by plunder.

Göring was completely in line with Hitler's expansionist aims, even if he counted among those who preferred a diplomatic solution to the **Czechoslovakia crisis**. Though he eschewed the biological **racism** that underpinned **Heinrich Himmler's** anti-Semitism, Göring nonetheless pushed the pace of anti-**Jewish** measures. It was Göring who oversaw the accelerated **economic** disenfranchisement of Germany's Jewish population following the **Night of Broken Glass** on 9–10 November 1938. He warned of a "final reckoning" with the Jews should another world war begin some three months before Hitler issued the same threat in his **Prophecy Speech** to the Reichstag. And it was Göring who on 31 July 1941 transmitted Hitler's order to **Schutzstaffel** (Protection Squad; SS) Reich Security Main Office chief **Reinhard Heydrich** for a "comprehensive solution" to the "Jewish question" in German-occupied Europe. *See also* HOLOCAUST.

In scheming against war minister General Field Marshal Werner von Blomberg and **Wehrmacht** commander in chief Colonel-General Werner Freiherr von Fritsch in late 1938 and early 1939, Göring hoped to take over Blomberg's post [see BLOMBERG–FRITSCH AFFAIR (1938)]. But he had nearly reached the extent of his influence. Hitler did, however, name Göring his successor. And while the Luftwaffe's operations in **Poland** and **France** were successful and earned him promotion to Reich marshal, Göring's influence went into steep decline following his monumental failure in 1940 to subdue Great Britain by air attacks [see BATTLE OF BRITAIN (1940)]. With Hitler having lost faith in him and increasingly pushed aside by **Martin Bormann**, Himmler, **Joseph Goebbels**, and **Albert Speer**, he became a bloated caricature of his former self. On 23 April 1945, having decamped to Bavaria, he cabled Hitler to inform him he intended to initiate their succession agreement. Hitler responded by threatening to have him executed for high treason unless he resigned his posts, which Göring did immediately. Hitler or perhaps Bormann then had Göring placed under house arrest. Following Hitler's **suicide**, Göring surrendered to US forces on 6 May.

Hermann Göring under arrest by American soldiers, Nuremberg, 9 May 1945. Standing in the center is Rolf Wartenberg, a German Jewish refugee who joined the US Army. *Courtesy of the United States Holocaust Memorial Museum.*

Though he was technically the second-highest-ranking party official in captivity (Bormann was dead, but this had not been confirmed, and former grand admiral **Karl Dönitz** had served briefly as Reich president after Hitler's death), Göring was without question the star defendant at the **Nuremberg Military Tribunal** (IMT). He was unrepentant and cagey under cross-examination. Charged and convicted on all four counts with nothing entered into the record in mitigation, he managed to commit suicide—possibly with the assistance of a US Army guard—on 15 October 1946, just hours before he was to be hanged.

GUDERIAN, HEINZ (1888–1954). The son of a Prussian general, Guderian became one of Hitler's more talented officers, though his importance as an innovator in the development of armored warfare has been overstated. He was attending general staff training in Berlin when **World War I** began. He served as a radio section commander on the western front, supply officer, and then in the intelligence division before being promoted to the general staff in early 1918. In the war's aftermath, he served with army and paramilitary forces on the frontiers of the new state of **Poland** and in the **Baltics**. Like a handful of other visionaries in Great Britain and **France** (among them Charles de Gaulle in the latter case), he became devoted to developing motorized and armored forces capabilities. His ideas and the zeal with which he promoted them in extensive writings earned him more than a few enemies among hidebound fellow officers, notably cavalrymen. But they found a champion in Hitler and became foundational to developing the fast-moving and closely coordinated air and ground assaults that became known informally as **blitzkrieg** (lightning war). In 1935, Guderian was given command of one of the first three new tank divisions. Three years later, he was put in charge of the Panzer Troops Command. Following service in the annexation of **Austria** and the invasion of Poland, Guderian led 7 of the 10 tank divisions in the invasion of France.

Though he was involved in some of the **Wehrmacht**'s greatest victories in the first months of **Operation Barbarossa**, Hitler removed him in December 1941 for disobeying what Guderian believed were Hitler's pointlessly self-destructive orders (*see* MILITARY COMMANDER). Despite this demotion, Hitler ordered that Guderian be given a 2,300-acre estate with no tax liability in occupied Poland, one of many gifts Hitler showered on the military's leadership. The debacle at the **Battle of Stalingrad** moved Hitler to appoint him inspector general of armored forces. Hitler hoped that he would restore the fighting capacities of tank armies and maximize the effectiveness of a new tank, the Mark VI Tiger, which Hitler viewed as a kind of **wonder weapon**.

Though Gudarian remained loyal to Hitler as Germany's leader and played an important role in suppressing the would-be coup resulting from the **assassination attempt** in July 1944, he never regained the trust Hitler once had in him. His continued willingness to defy Hitler's orders led to his final dismissal on 28 March 1945. Guderian was arrested by American forces in May 1945 and spent the next three years as a POW. He avoided prosecution by the **International Military Tribunal** (IMT) and the **Nuremberg Military Tribunal** (NMT) and extradition to the Soviet Union, in part because of a lack of documentary evidence and in part because he cooperated with Allied prosecutors as they built cases against his former comrades. He remained an apologist for Hitler and became an influential propagator of the myth of the "clean Wehrmacht" in his work for the US Army's Historical Division. Three years before his death in 1954, he published his memoirs, translated into English as *Panzer Leader*. Full of lies and omissions—like others of its kind—it is of value as an influential document of postwar mythmaking rather than as a reliable firsthand account of the Wehrmacht's wartime record.

H

HALDER, FRANZ (1884–1972). A career staff officer from Würzburg, Halder served as chief of staff of the Oberkommando des Heeres (**Wehrmacht** high command; OKH) from 1938 to 1942. He was thus at the center of every one of Germany's major military operations, from the bloodless occupation of Prague in March 1939 to **Operation Barbarossa** [*see* HOSSBACH MEMORANDUM (1937)]. His diaries from the period were used as evidence by **International Military Tribunal** (IMT) and **Nuremberg Military Tribunal** (NMT) prosecutors and rank among the more important such documents for histories of the war's first half.

Motivated by a desire to avoid a wider European war in the fall of 1938, Halder was part of a coup plot during the **Czechoslovakia crisis**. Like other high-ranking officers, however, he was not ideologically opposed to Hitler's vision of a race war in the East. And like others, he received substantial gifts of money from Hitler. Halder was fully aware of what the **Schutzstaffel** (Protection Squad; SS) planned to do in **Poland** and oversaw the writing of the Commissar Order and the Barbarossa Decree, thus sealing the fates of millions of prisoners of war and noncombatants. Beginning with Operation Barbarossa, Hitler and Halder quarreled constantly over strategy. Hitler sacked him in September 1942 when he realized that victory in Russia could not be achieved that year.

Halder was arrested in the aftermath of the 20 July 1944 **assassination attempt**, though he was not involved in that particular conspiracy. But the Gestapo learned of his involvement in earlier plots, and he was imprisoned in the Flossenbürg and Dachau **concentration camps**. Formally dismissed from the army on 31 January 1945, he was evacuated to the South Tyrol, where he was arrested by American troops on 5 May.

Despite his complicity in war crimes and crimes against humanity, Halder evaded prosecution by both the IMT and NMT by cooperating with the prosecution. During and after the trials, he became perhaps the single most influential promoter of the myth of the "clean Wehrmacht"—the myth that the army had fought a conventional war in Russia and that the SS was responsible for any crimes that may have been committed. He was able to do this mainly through his assistance to prosecutors in both tribunals and because the US Army hired him to oversee the production of historical case studies of the war written by hundreds of ex-Nazi officers. Halder used both opportunities to sanitize the history of the war in the East.

At the same time, he was providing the Americans with intelligence about the Soviet Union. He was also strikingly successful at distancing himself and other high-level officers from their mistakes by deflecting all the blame for the failure of Barbarossa to Hitler's incompetence as a **military commander**. Halder's final contribution to postwar mythmaking was to make himself accessible to journalists and gullible historians, a strategy also deployed with great success by **Albert Speer**. After receiving a Meritorious Civilian Service Award from US President John F. Kennedy in 1961,

Halder enjoyed a comfortable retirement in Bavaria until his death in 1972.

HANFSTAENGL, ERNST (PUTZI; 1887–1976). A significant challenge for Hitler when he entered politics in the early 1920s was that he was completely cut off from Munich's elite. Hanfstaengl would be an early and important conduit to this reservoir of money and influence.

Born in Munich, Hanfstaengl's father was a successful publisher, and his mother an American. After graduating from Harvard in 1909, he moved to New York City and worked for a branch of his father's business. He was well connected socially, having gotten to know Theodore and Franklin Roosevelt, Charlie Chaplin, and William Randolph Hearst. At one point, he was engaged to the writer Djuna Barnes. He instead married Helene Niemeyer, an American, in 1920, and the couple moved to Germany a year later. In November 1922, he attended one of Hitler's speeches and was deeply impressed, though seemingly more by the performance than the substance. The two met on several other occasions, and in 1923 Hitler became a regular visitor to the Hanfstaengls' Munich apartment, visits that served a personal as much as a political purpose for the otherwise socially isolated Hitler. Soon, Hitler was bringing along some of his closest party associates and their spouses.

Despite vast differences in their social backgrounds, the good-natured Hanfstaengl was capable of putting the prickly, insecure Hitler at ease with his sense of humor, admiration for **Richard Wagner**, and skill at playing the piano. Hitler also seems to have formed a strong connection with Helene, though there is no evidence the two were romantically involved (*see* WOMEN). To Ernst and Helene, Hitler was something of an amusing curiosity, with his clumsy but charming provincial **Austrian** manners and shabby, mismatched clothes. It was at the Hanfstaengls' summer home in the Bavarian Alps that Hitler sought refuge in the wake of the **Beer Hall Putsch**, and it was Helene who allegedly talked him out of shooting himself before he could be arrested.

Ernst made himself useful in other ways. He invested in the party's newspaper, the *Völkischer Beobachter*, and convinced Hitler to have it printed in a larger-scale, American-style format. Hitler appointed him head of the party's foreign press division, and he got Hitler's 1924 **trial** covered in a number of important American newspapers. He would also help edit *Mein Kampf*'s turgid and bloated prose.

Hanfstaengl served briefly in the Propaganda Ministry in 1933, where he quickly ran afoul of **Joseph Goebbels** and lost his position. He remained in contact with Hitler until 1937, when he left the country, first for Switzerland, then the **United States**. There may have been several attempts by regime officials, probably worried about what he might divulge, to lure him back to Germany. Regardless, Hanfstaengl remained in the United States and cooperated with the wartime intelligence agency, the Office of Strategic Services, in analyzing Hitler's **personality**. He returned to Germany after the war, where he—predictably—wrote a memoir about his years with Hitler.

HARZBURG FRONT. By the fall of 1931, Hitler had maneuvered himself into the position of having to forge stronger connections to conservative nationalists. The previous summer, he had moved against the "left" wing of the **National Socialist German Workers' Party** (Nazi Party; Nationalsozialistische Deutsche Arbeiterpartei; NSDAP) and its leading figure, Otto Strasser. As political polarization and the **economic** crisis deepened, he also felt compelled to reassure Germany's most influential business leaders—most of whom did not support the NSDAP—that the party was not in fact their enemy. He was not particularly successful in either endeavor, at least in the short term.

In the summer of 1931, **Alfred Hugenberg**, Stahlhelm (**Steel Helmets**) chief Franz Seldte, and Hitler revived their alliance from the anti–**Young Plan Referendum** campaign to form the "national opposition" to the government of Chancellor Heinrich Brüning (**Center Party**; Zentrum). A rally of nationalist parties and groups held in Bad Harzburg in north-central Germany, where an NSDAP–**German National Peoples' Party** (Deutschnationale Volkspartei; DNVP) coalition governed locally, took place on 11 October. There were marches, speeches, a manifesto, and a demand for new **Reichstag elections**.

But Hitler was obstinate and undiplomatic, showing up late and refusing to observe a march of Stahlhelm members. Having achieved its first major electoral breakthrough in Reichstag elections in September 1930, the Nazi Party had become too large to ignore but not strong enough to dominate the Right. Hitler needed the support of conservative nationalists, and they needed him, but he was temperamentally unsuited to the kind of unheroic compromises required to build and maintain a coalition.

The front, then, existed on paper only. It wasn't strong enough to achieve one of its principal objectives—the toppling of Brüning's government, which withstood an NSDAP-DNVP motion of no confidence less than a week after the rally. The front fell apart in the fractious 1932 presidential election campaign, in which the Nazi Party and the DNVP put up their own candidates—Hitler and the Stahlhelm's second-in-command, Theodor Duesterberg—against sitting president **Paul von Hindenburg**. One more version of the front would appear in the cabinet agreed to in the negotiations over Hitler's appointment as **chancellor**. For a different set of reasons, it, too, would not last longer than a few months. *See also* ENABLING ACT (1933); REICHSTAG FIRE (27–28 FEBRUARY 1933).

HEALTH. For most of his adult life, Hitler was reasonably healthy. If anything, his vegetarian diet and avoidance of tobacco and alcohol probably made him healthier than many other men of his time, though he never took to any remotely strenuous exercise routine. A minor war wound in his left leg, irritable bowel syndrome, and recurring benign polyps on his overexerted vocal cords were relatively minor matters. The **Landsberg Prison** doctor who examined him in 1924 noted an undescended testicle, or cryptorchidism [*see* BEER HALL PUTSCH (1923)]. It is unclear what, if any, psychological impact that condition had on Hitler. In August 1941, he endured a fairly serious bout of dysentery. His penchant for sweet pastries most likely contributed to a longer-running problem: the awful state of his teeth, most of which eventually had to be removed [*see* SUICIDE (30 APRIL 1945)]. There is no evidence that he had syphilis.

While the wounds he received in the 20 July 1944 **assassination attempt**—perforated eardrums, splinters and scrapes, minor burns and singed hair, a swollen right arm—healed, some of those closest to him recalled that he never really seemed to have physically recovered from the event. Indeed, his health seemed to be deteriorating for months before the explosion, and he spent the spring and most of the summer of 1944 attempting to recuperate at the **Berghof**. He had in fact been diagnosed with high blood pressure and arteriosclerosis. He had some difficulty walking; his posture deteriorated; and he developed a tremor in his left arm that disappeared briefly after the attack, only to soon reappear.

It seems clear that Hitler was exhibiting symptoms of idiopathic Parkinson's disease. Indeed, there is some evidence of symptoms appearing in the early 1930s. He may have contracted measles encephalitis from his younger brother Edmund, who died of the disease, and encephalitis at a young age can in later life lead to Parkinson's. In any case, Parkinson's was never diagnosed in Hitler while he was alive. It is also possible that his consumption of methamphetamines made him more susceptible to the disease or at least had a neurodegenerative effect that worsened preexisting Parkinson's.

His condition became enough of an impediment to his ability to function as a head of state and supreme military commander that he cut back on his public appearances and radio broadcast speeches. **Martin Bormann**, **Joseph Goebbels**, **Albert Speer**, and **Heinrich Himmler** became even more important to the war effort and managing the home front, though Hitler never became some kind of puppet in 1943 and 1944. But it cannot be ruled out that if he did have Parkinson's, then it would have affected his motor skills and could have impaired his judgment and ability to make decisions.

Madman or *insane* are still common terms used in popular descriptions of Hitler as a person or of his state of mind. But he was not insane in a clinical sense. No one in that condition could have lived and acted as Hitler did. And the informal use of these terms conflates irrational, criminal, and immoral acts with insanity. It also suggests that Hitler was not responsible for his actions. Moreover, the kinds of physical examinations that might have informed psychiatric evaluations were also never performed on him.

While he was clearly a hypochondriac, he was never addicted to **drugs**. There's no evidence that the exotic cocktail of medicines and vitamins provided to him by his principal physician, Theodor Morell, degraded his faculties to the point where he did not know what he was doing or saying. *See also* PERSONALITY.

HESS, RUDOLF (1894–1987). Hess was born in Alexandria, Egypt, into a merchant family with Bavarian roots. In **World War I**, he served in the infantry on the western and eastern fronts and as a pilot. He did not serve with Hitler, as is often claimed. In 1920, he joined the **National Socialist German Workers' Party** (Nazi Party; Nationalsozialistische Deutsche Arbeiterpartei; NSDAP), became Hitler's most devoted early follower, and worked effectively to build up the party and bring it out of obscurity. A participant in the **Beer Hall Putsch**, he was not among Hitler's codefendants in the 1924 **trial**, but after turning himself into the police, he was reunited with Hitler in **Landsberg Prison**, where he served as a kind of secretary until his release in January 1925. Hess resumed this position throughout the remainder of the decade and was given the title deputy to the leader (Stellvertreter des Führers) in April 1933. He became increasingly influential on domestic affairs and even to some extent in the early stages of Germany's territorial expansion in Eastern Europe, as he and his far more ruthlessly effective deputy **Martin Bormann** concentrated political power in the party's hands. That Hitler's confidence in Hess remained seemingly rock solid is evinced by the fact that he named Hess second in line—after **Hermann Göring**—to succeed him.

Like Bormann, Hess was not an empty vessel when he met Hitler but a committed and fanatical ideologue whose worldview was influenced strongly by Far-Right historian Karl Haushofer, with whom Hess had studied after the war. Hess's devotion to Hitler personally and to fulfilling his vision of a Germanic racial empire makes his decision—known only to himself and perhaps a few others—to fly solo to Scotland on 10 May 1941 with a peace offer to the British government all the more difficult to understand.

There has been a great deal of speculation, then and since, about Hess's mental state, with an enraged Hitler being among the first to conclude that his deputy had quite clearly lost his mind. But Hess was not insane. When he made the flight, Britain had not surrendered, and the invasion of the Soviet Union (**Operation Barbarossa**) would soon be launched. Most likely, Hess was motivated by a desire to save Hitler from what he expected—correctly, it turned out—to be a calamitous two-front war. He also believed in the existence of an influential bloc in Britain that would be receptive to a peace offer delivered by one of the most powerful officials in Germany in the interests of confronting a common enemy. But this is evidence of ignorance about political realities in Britain at that moment, not insanity.

Immediately after parachuting into the countryside outside Glasgow, Hess was detained and questioned at length before being dispatched to Wales, where he spent the rest of the war in relatively comfortable conditions. Suspicions that British officials somehow lured him to Britain in an effort to undermine Hitler are baseless. But **Joseph Stalin** believed that Hess and British intelligence were cooperating to realize the objectives of Hess's mission. Stalin demanded that he be tried by an international tribunal, and Hess was transferred to Nuremberg in early October 1945. Like the other defendants, he was questioned multiple times but, unlike them, claimed to suffer repeated bouts of amnesia, a practice he had taken up during his wartime confinement and one he continued even after admitting on the stand that he had been faking all along [*see* INTERNATIONAL MILITARY TRIBUNAL (NUREMBERG TRIALS; IMT)].

Even had his behavior in the courtroom not been utterly bizarre and his defense lawyer competent, the documentary evidence alone was enough to convict him on at least the conspiracy and crimes against peace charges, though including war crimes and crimes against humanity would have been entirely justified. He was sentenced to life imprisonment in Spandau Prison in West Berlin. When he committed suicide in August 1987, the nearly 93-year-old Hess was its sole prisoner.

HEYDRICH, REINHARD (1904–1942). In the relatively short period of his involvement with the **Schutzstaffel** (Protection Squad; SS) and Nazi regime, Heydrich played a decisive role in creating the police state in Germany and abroad and in the **Holocaust**. Born in Halle, Saxony, and raised in a cultured middle-class family (his parents were musicians, and Reinhard would become a skilled violinist) he joined the navy in 1922. He was forced to resign in 1931 following the revelation of his relationship with a woman who claimed to be his fiancée at time when Heydrich was already engaged to another woman. He managed to get a meeting with **Heinrich Himmler**, in which he impressed the SS chief with what sounded like extensive knowledge of intelligence operations.

That the tall, blond, athletic Heydrich very much fit Himmler's Aryan archetype and undoubtedly played a role in the SS chief's decision to hire him. More important, of course, was Heydrich's loyalty to Himmler, his administrative competence, and the intensity of his ideological commitment. This was a combination typical of the many young men belonging to Heydrich's generational cohort who would staff the middle and upper echelons of the SS. Working closely with Himmler, Heydrich played a key role in creating an intelligence operation, the Security Service (Sicherheitsdienst; SD), and consolidating SS control over all police services in Germany. He also created the Security Police (Sicherheitspolizei; SIPO), which combined the Gestapo, criminal, and border police forces into a fearsomely effective instrument of domestic repression. Further consolidation took place in 1939, when he formed the Reich Security Main Office (Reichsicherheitshauptamt; RSHA), which merged the SD, SIPO, and other units for duty in German-occupied Europe.

At the same time, Heydrich was a major driver of the regime's increasingly radical anti-**Jewish** policies, first through the relentless push for accelerated emigration and then mass deportation and murder [*see* WANNSEE CONFERENCE (1942)]. Contrary to allegations during his life and long after his death, he did not have any Jewish ancestry.

In September 1941, Heydrich was reassigned to the post of deputy Reich protector of Bohemia and Moravia. His main responsibility was to suppress **opposition** in the increasingly restive "protectorate." Believing he had succeeded in this task to a greater extent than he actually had and unwilling to appear fearful in public, he rode around Prague in an open car. On 27 May 1942, British-trained Czech commandos attacked his motorcade with machine guns and a bomb (Operation Anthropoid). An explosion injured Heydrich, but he was treated quickly and seemed to be recovering when his condition suddenly worsened. He died on 4 June. The full autopsy report, discovered in 2004, fails to make clear the exact cause of his death, though it seems to have been the result of a postsurgery infection. Predictably, the regime responded with extraordinary savagery. Most notoriously, Hitler ordered the town of Lidice razed and its male inhabitants murdered. The Czech anti-Nazi resistance was destroyed, with significant implications for the country's postwar takeover by Soviet-backed communists.

Heydrich was the only high-level regime official targeted for assassination by the Allies. The operation was supported by the leader of the Czech government in exile, Edvard Beneš, who had been promised a free hand to expel ethnic Germans from the country after the war. Then and since, the strategic value, legality, and morality of Anthropoid have been matters of intense debate.

HIMMLER, HEINRICH (1900–1945). Other than Hitler, no other Nazi regime official did as much as Himmler to build a "racial state" in Germany and an empire in Eastern Europe and the Soviet Union. Born in Munich and raised in a devout middle-class Catholic home, Himmler was intelligent, pompous, fastidious, and lacking in natural athletic ability. He wanted to be a military officer and in December 1917 enlisted in a Bavarian reserve battalion. But the war ended when he was still in training, and like many other German men of his generation, he believed that he had missed out on a life-defining experience. After the war, he gravitated to the Far-Right paramilitary scene while studying agriculture at what is today the Technical University in Munich. His diaries from the period also reveal a turn to a radical form of **racist** anti-Semitism.

In 1923, he joined the **National Socialist German Workers' Party** (Nazi Party; Nationalsozialistische Deutsche Arbeiterpartei; NSDAP) and distinguished himself as a highly capable organizer, propagandist, and election campaigner. It was also at this time that he broke with the Catholicism that had been a central feature of his upbringing. An obsession with ancient Germanic culture, rituals, and symbols filled the resulting void, and he would eventually become openly hostile toward Christianity (see RELIGION).

Himmler was not among Hitler's earliest acolytes, but he would soon become one, his loyalty remaining steadfast until the war's final months. In 1925, he joined the **Schutzstaffel** (Protection Squad; SS), which was at that time a largely ceremonial bodyguard unit consisting of a few hundred men and subordinate to the much larger **Sturmabteilung** (Stormtroopers; SA). Himmler persuaded Hitler to entrust him with transforming it into an elite unit comprised of "racially pure" personnel. In 1929, Hitler appointed him to lead the entire organization, the first of several high-level party titles Himmler would amass.

Himmler built up the SS into a powerful tool of domestic repression and then genocidal imperialism. In March 1933, he authorized the construction of the first **concentration camp** at Dachau near Munich, which would become the model for future camps inside and outside Germany. The SS would oversee what would become a massive system of thousands of camps in Germany and German-controlled Europe.

Until the summer of 1934, however, a major obstacle remained to the further expansion of the SS: the SA. In June, Hitler had Himmler and the SS oversee the **Röhm purge**. With the SA neutralized, Himmler henceforth answered to Hitler directly. By 1936, Himmler had subordinated all of Germany's police forces—which had traditionally been under the control of individual states—to the SS. These included the secret domestic political police force, the Gestapo. The SS had become the dictatorship's single most powerful coercive tool.

Himmler would not stop at monitoring the population (including the Nazi Party itself) and suppressing domestic **opposition**. He would deploy the SS as a tool of social engineering by using the expanding network of camps to imprison those Germans he and Hitler considered a threat to the political and "biological" health of the nation: communists and other leftists; a small number of dissident clergymen; and "asocials," a broad category encompassing habitual criminals, "workshy" individuals, pacifists, and vagrants. Gay men (see HOMOSEXUALITY)—Himmler was deeply homophobic—were also targeted for incarceration in the camps and in many cases killed, mutilated, or subjected to medical experiments.

Another significant step was taken with the creation of an armed forces division, the Waffen SS, to serve at Hitler's disposal. Himmler would expand the Waffen SS, which would serve under the operational command of the **Wehrmacht** during the war, into a million-man-strong force of 38 divisions, some of them comprised of non-German volunteers and conscripts.

As for its personnel, Himmler envisioned the SS as the basis a new kind of Aryan aristocracy, a human seedbed for a new Germanic "master race." The members of this "race"—which Himmler fantasized would eventually number in the hundreds of millions—would populate the kinds of farming communities that he believed had once shaped Nordic peoples into a superior type of human being. Potential recruits and their prospective spouses had to go through a rigorous application process involving a genealogy test to certify genuine "Aryan heritage" [see DARRÉ, RICHARD WALTHER (1895–1953)]. The ideal recruit would also conform to the Aryan ideal: tall and blond. Himmler also sought to distinguish the SS with custom-made black uniforms, a silver skull and crossed bones symbol, and the letters *SS* fashioned as twin lightning-shaped bolts.

In building up its administration, Himmler revealed a talent for personnel recruitment. His single most important appointment was **Reinhard Heydrich** as head of the SS's security service, the Sicherheitsdienst (SD), and later the Reich Main Security Office (Reichsicherheitshauptamt; RSHA). Himmler; Heydrich; and another talented recruiter, Gottlob Berger, also cultivated a cohort of relatively young men, often possessing doctoral degrees from German universities, into its middle and upper ranks. Like Himmler and Heydrich, these recruits had been too young to serve in World War I and combined ruthless ideological conviction with administrative competence. No micromanager, Himmler encouraged SS personnel to take initiatives that he presumed would be guided by their allegedly racially superior instincts and abilities.

Himmler's imperial vision centered on constructing farming communities populated by "racially pure" Germans, mainly in the vast spaces of **Poland**, the **Baltics**, Russia, and **Ukraine**. The SS would remove, kill, or enslave local populations of Slavic peoples, **Jews**, and **Romani** ("Gypsies") to make room for the arrival of thousands of German settlers and what he expected to be their many offspring. Though Hitler mocked Himmler's obsession with ancient Germanic cultures, he was convinced that SS families really could rejuvenate the health of any community whose resident population had shown signs of genetic and cultural "degeneration." In July 1942, Hitler approved Himmler's colonization scheme as part of the **General Plan for the East**.

In the end, there was very little colonization by ethnic Germans. The most important role Himmler and the SS played in the war was in the policing of the occupied territories and the related mass murder of Jews. While Himmler envisioned the Nazi Empire in the East as cleared of all "biologically inferior" elements, he followed Hitler in singling out the Jews as Germany's most dangerous racial enemy. In regular and close consultation with Hitler, the SS under Himmler and Heydrich (until the latter's assassination in Prague in May 1942) oversaw the deployment of Einsatzgruppen (special task forces, mobile execution squads) that operated behind the Wehrmacht following the invasion of the Soviet Union (**Operation Barbarossa**) in June 1941. Einsatzgruppen operations were ultimately responsible for the murder of around 2 million Jews, a phase of the genocide historians now refer to as the "**Holocaust** by bullets." The SS also organized the mass deportations of European Jews to ghettos in the occupied East. In late 1941 and early 1942, Himmler engineered the transition to the use of poison gas in hybrid camps like Auschwitz and Majdanek and in the death camps, purpose-built fixed installations in Poland that were dismantled in 1943. In the Holocaust's final phase, Himmler ordered the evacuation of surviving Jews from the concentration camps. They were to be marched away from advancing Allied armies and into Germany. Thousands were killed during the evacuation process or died en route.

Hitler's trust in Himmler was damaged severely by his disastrous stint as an army group commander on the eastern front in January 1945. By then, the limits of Himmler's loyalty to Hitler had finally been reached. With Germany's total defeat and occupation looming, Himmler made contact with the Swedish Red Cross in the vain hope of negotiating surrender in the West only. At the same time, he met with a Swedish representative of the World Jewish Congress and agreed to the release of a small number of concentration camp prisoners to facilitate negotiations for a separate peace. He last saw Hitler in the bunker complex in Berlin on 20 April and fled the city that day. A week later, a shocked Hitler learned of Himmler's attempt to reach out to the Americans (*see* UNITED STATES OF AMERICA) and British via Swedish intermediaries and ordered him arrested. In his **personal will and political**

Heinrich Himmler at SS headquarters in Hegewald in German-occupied northeastern Ukraine, 7 October 1942. *Courtesy of the United States Holocaust Memorial Museum.*

testament, Hitler stripped Himmler of his titles and expelled him from the party.

Himmler nonetheless expected the SS under his leadership to play a role in the new government led by Grand Admiral **Karl Dönitz**, but Dönitz refused to have anything do with him. On 21 May, he was detained at an Allied checkpoint around Neuhaus in Germany's Far North. He had been carrying false identification papers but soon revealed his identity to a British interrogator. On 23 May, he managed to commit suicide using a cyanide capsule hidden in his teeth. His remains were buried in an unmarked grave.

HINDENBURG, PAUL VON (1847–1934). A Prussian aristocrat and officer, Hindenburg served as chief of the general staff of the Imperial German Army during **World War I** and as Germany's president from 1925 until his death on 2 August 1934. He personified the conservative nationalist establishment and was its leading symbolic figure. He was held in high esteem across most of the political spectrum, and even long after his death, many Germans perceived him as a national hero who was at best an effective, if short-lived, bulwark against the Nazis and at worst a senile old man manipulated by conservatives desperate to contain Hitler and the **National Socialist German Workers' Party** (Nazi Party; Nationalsozialistische Deutsche Arbeiterpartei; NSDAP).

Why this was so has to do with a myth of Hindenburg—fostered by his supporters and believed fervently across Germany—as a man perpetually capable of rescuing Germany. A hero of the war with **France** in 1870 that resulted in the creation of the German Empire, he came out of retirement to command a dramatic victory over Russian forces at Tannenberg in August 1914. He again emerged from retirement to run for the presidency in 1925 following the sudden death of Friedrich Ebert. The timing was significant: Germany had just endured years of severe turmoil, and many Germans viewed Hindenburg as the only person who could keep the country from disintegrating. And while he was a monarchist, Hindenburg supported the democratic republic in the second half of the 1920s, support that contributed to its relative stability in those years. He again appeared as a kind of savior when he ran against Hitler—who astutely avoided personal attacks on his opponent during the campaign—in the 1932 presidential **election**, this time amid a severe **economic** crisis and the skyrocketing popularity of the NSDAP.

Yet Hindenburg became a principal gravedigger of German democracy and one of the most important single enablers of Hitler's dictatorship. He was one of the originators of the **"stab in the back" myth**, and like all conservative nationalist and Far-Right politicians, he helped keep it alive, thus undermining the republic's legitimacy. When unemployment jumped in the winter of 1929–1930, he began to subvert parliamentary government by appointing **Center Party** leader Heinrich Brüning as chancellor following the collapse of the governing coalition in March. Because Brüning had no majority in parliament, Hindenburg invoked an article in the constitution that allowed the president to govern by emergency decree. His intention was to neutralize the **Social Democratic Party of Germany** (Sozialdemokratische Partei Deutschlands; SPD)—which then held the most seats in the **Reichstag**—and parliament more generally and to pave the way for an authoritarian regime.

But the main source of his infamy is his decision on 30 January 1933 to appoint Hitler **chancellor**. Though Hindenburg disliked and distrusted Hitler, by the beginning of 1933, it had become clear that the conservative nationalists could not hope to assemble a governing majority without him and the NSDAP. At the end of January, a small circle of his advisers convinced him that a new coalition with Hitler as chancellor was the only alternative to declaring a state of emergency, something Hindenburg wished to avoid. Hitler, he was assured, could be controlled by the more

Hitler genuflects to President Paul von Hindenburg on the Day of Potsdam, 21 March 1933. *Courtesy of the United States Holocaust Memorial Museum.*

experienced and better-connected conservative nationalists. Besides, crucial ministries—notably Foreign and War—would be occupied by men Hindenburg trusted. Hindenburg was not senile, as has long been alleged. Like other conservatives, he misunderstood and underestimated Hitler.

Hindenburg's role in enabling Hitler's consolidation of power continued until his death. In the aftermath of the **Reichstag fire** on 27–28 February 1933, he signed a supposedly temporary emergency decree and then legislation that suspended the basic rights guaranteed by the constitution, thus neutralizing the Reichstag's powers while greatly enhancing those of the chancellor. And while Hindenburg insisted on protections for long-serving **Jewish** civil servants, veterans, and those whose fathers or sons had been killed in the First World War, he raised no objections to other anti-Jewish measures. In November, he gave a speech, broadcast across the country, in which he backed Germany's withdrawal from the **League of Nations**. In June 1934, he made it clear to vice chancellor **Franz von Papen** that he would not support a conservative nationalist move against Hitler that von Papen hoped to incite with an incendiary anti-Nazi speech he had just given at the University of Marburg. Indeed, it was fears that von Papen would continue to seek Hindenburg's support for such a move that provoked Hitler to initiate the purge of the **Sturmabteilung** [Stormtroopers; SA; *see* RÖHM PURGE (1934)].

For his part, Hitler understood the depth of Germany's reverence for Hindenburg and deferred to him skillfully in the 20 months from his appointment as chancellor to Hindenburg's death. On 21 March 1933, Hitler bowed ostentatiously to Hindenburg during an elaborate ceremony held at the garrison church in Potsdam to inaugurate the newly elected Reichstag. Following Hindenburg's death, regime propaganda continued to celebrate his memory. In his political will, published in part by the regime two weeks after his death, Hindenburg praised Hitler and the national socialist movement. Hitler chose not to publish the portion expressing support for the restoration of the monarchy. *See also* HOHENZOLLERNS.

HITLER, KLARA (NÉE PÖLZL; 1860–1907). Klara Pölzl began working as a maid for Alois Hitler in 1876. He hired her eight years later to help him with his two children when his wife, Franziska, became ill with tuberculosis. Klara was Alois's niece (twice removed), so a papal dispensation was required before they could marry following Franziska's death in August 1884. Their first three children died in quick succession in 1887 and 1888. On 20 April 1889, she gave birth to a son they named Adolf.

While it is clear that Adolf never had a close relationship with his father, a paucity of reliable sources has led to much speculation about the relationship between him and Klara. A modest and pious person (though not as passive as once thought), she endured Alois's mercurial, tyrannical temperament and doted on Adolf and his younger sister, Paula. Very much unlike Alois, who expected his son to follow his example and become a low-level civil servant, Klara indulged her son's disinterest in formal education and propensity to spend his time painting and attending the theater. And there seems little question that Adolf loved his mother deeply, a word he used in *Mein Kampf* to describe his feelings toward her. He was profoundly distraught by her death from breast cancer in 1907. During the Second World War, he saved the life of Eduard Bloch, the **Jewish** physician who did his best to ease her suffering, by protecting him from the **Schutzstaffel** (Protection Squad; SS) in Linz. Portraits of Klara were displayed prominently in all of Hitler's multiple residences, including the bunker in Berlin, and he kept a small photograph of her on his person. *See also* FAMILY.

HITLER YOUTH (HITLERJUGEND; HJ). The Nazi Party created a youth division in 1922, the Youth League of the **National Socialist German Workers' Party** (Nazi Party; Nationalsozialistiche Deutsche Arbeiterpartei; NSDAP). Four years later, it was renamed Hitlerjugend (Hitler Youth; HJ) and placed under **Sturmabteilung** (Stormtroopers; SA) control. It was not the only party-sponsored organization for young people created in those years—there were leagues for young **women** and students. Membership in the HJ and other groups remained small, as they had to compete with myriad other groups.

After Hitler's appointment as **chancellor**, HJ leader (until 1940) Baldur von Schirach consolidated all other youth groups except those sponsored by the Catholic Church. In 1936, all nonparty sponsored youth organizations were banned, and membership was made compulsory. Boys between 15 and 18 joined the HJ, and girls joined the Bund Deutscher Mädel (League of German Girls; BDM) at 14. Both groups sponsored a wide range of activities, including labor service. Preparation for military service was, of course, a particularly high priority for HJ members. The organization was also deployed as a propaganda tool, and HJ detachments paraded at the annual **Nuremberg party rallies** and were featured prominently in **Leni Riefenstahl**'s *Triumph of the Will*.

The HJ's overarching purpose was to ensure ideological conformity and prepare young people for war. Membership was also supposed to serve the party's goals of national unification and socially leveling, though in the case of the latter, the sons and daughters of the educated middle class came to play dominant roles. While historians have identified a distinct Hitler Youth generation comprised mainly of Germans born between 1925 and 1933, the extent to which ideology made its mark on HJ members depended to a large extent on when they experienced their formative years. Those who grew up with memories of the Weimar Republic's turbulent years were more inclined to embrace the mission of creating a Volksgemeinschaft (people's community) than those with little or no memory of the pre-Nazi period. Moreover, as the early idealism dissipated, dissent and **opposition** became more common, especially in Catholic areas of Germany (*see* RELIGION).

During the war, both boys and girls were dragooned into various forms of military service, notably in the defense of cities from Allied air attacks and into the 12th **Schutzstaffel** (Protection Squad; SS) Panzer Division commanded by General Kurt Meyer. In the last desperate months of the war, HJ members armed with crude weapons were sent on what were suicide missions against Soviet tanks [*see* BATTLE OF BERLIN (1945); LUFTWAFFE (AIR FORCE); STRATEGIC BOMBING CAMPAIGN].

Like all party organizations, the HJ was disbanded by Allied occupation authorities. Schirach was tried by the **International Military Tribunal** (IMT), though he was acquitted on the charge of crimes against peace and sentenced to 20 years for his later role in the deportation of **Austrian Jews**. Schirach's successor, Artur Axmann, evaded capture by the Red Army by changing his identity, though he was soon arrested by American counterintelligence agents. A German denazification court sentenced him to three years in prison as a "major offender," though he was not charged with committing war crimes. In West Germany, most former HJ members focused on rebuilding their lives and supported the new liberal democratic system, with many recalling the prewar years as the "good years" of the Nazi regime. In the communist German Democratic Republic (East Germany), former HJ members were absorbed seamlessly into a new mass youth organization, the Freie Deutsche Jugend (Free German Youth; FDJ).

HOFFMANN, HEINRICH (1885–1957). As Hitler's official photographer for 20 years, Hoffmann did more than any other individual, save for filmmaker **Leni Riefenstahl**, to create the image of Hitler for public consumption [*see TRIUMPH OF THE WILL* (1935)]. To this day, his photographs shape popular perceptions of Hitler. Hoffmann served as an army photographer in **World War I** and then gravitated to Munich's Far-Right scene. He chronicled the Munich Soviet Republic in photographs and published them as a book in 1919. Ironically, his collection from that period includes images of Hitler serving the republic, a fact Hitler would soon go to considerable lengths to obscure. It was most likely **Dietrich Eckart** who introduced the two men in the early 1920s, and from around 1923 to 1943, Hoffmann served as Hitler's devoted image maker.

In stark contrast to his dilettantism and slapdash work habits, Hitler devoted an enormous amount of time and attention to shaping and controlling his public profile [see FÜHRER MYTH (FÜHRER MYTHOS)]. It was in this area that Hoffmann became indispensible. Hitler trusted his aesthetic judgment and discretion, and Hoffmann proved to be a loyal servant—and shrewd, as he became wealthy from royalties paid for the use of his Hitler images.

Hoffmann published several books displaying Hitler as a statesman and military leader and two that attempted to show his devotion to children and that he could relax in traditional Bavarian garb and make small talk with ordinary Germans. All of it amounted to a highly contrived act of image making. In 1929, Hoffmann introduced Hitler to **Eva Braun**, who was then working as an assistant in his studio (*see* WOMEN). It was also in 1929 that Hoffmann claimed to have discovered Hitler in a photograph he took of a massive crowd gathered in Munich's Odeonsplatz on 2 August 1914 to cheer the outbreak of the war. The photo was almost certainly faked in Hoffmann's studio.

Given his responsibilities, Hoffmann spent a good deal of time with Hitler in his private residences and favorite restaurant while electioneering before 1933 and on his state visit to **Italy** in 1938. The two remained on relatively friendly terms until around 1941. Two years later, Hitler imposed a ban on new photographs of him being circulated in public. Hoffmann also participated in and benefited from the confiscation and destruction of **art** deemed degenerate by Hitler and **Joseph Goebbels** and—like other regime officials and military officers—in amassing works from Dutch dealers following Germany's occupation of the Netherlands in

The Odeonsplatz in Munich, 2 August 1914. The photo, taken by Heinrich Hoffmann, was almost certainly altered to include what appears to be Hitler's face (circled and in enlargement). *Courtesy of the United States Holocaust Memorial Museum.*

the spring of 1940. His appetites made him a target of the American (see UNITED STATES OF AMERICA) wartime intelligence agency (OSS) as a prominent looter of art. He was arrested by American soldiers on 10 May 1945 and convicted of war profiteering. Released from prison in 1950, he published his memoirs in 1955 and died two years later. The bulk of his collection of photographs was seized by the US Army during the occupation and is currently held by the US National Archives. Hoffmann's grandson sold an additional batch to the State Library of Bavaria in 1993.

HOHENZOLLERNS. The Hohenzollern dynasty originated in the 11th century in what is today the German state of Baden-Württemberg. By the 14th century, it had come to rule the principality of Brandenburg, which surrounded Berlin. It expanded its rule eastward over the following centuries to form the largest and most powerful of the German-speaking territories: Prussia. In the mid-19th century, its leaders, above all **Otto von Bismarck**, led the drive to create the German Empire in 1871. A member of the Hohenzollern royal house would serve as emperor until the revolution of 1918, when Wilhelm II abdicated and fled the country for the Netherlands. There, he embraced the **"stab in the back" myth**, nursed a deep hatred of the Weimar Republic, and brooded about the restoration of the monarchy, believing the fascist regime in **Italy**, which coexisted with the country's monarchy, could be a model for Germany. He despised **Jews** in particular and in 1927 advocated their mass murder by poison gas. Though he did not return to Germany after Hitler took power, he was ecstatic about German victories in **Poland** and Western Europe [see WESER EXERCISE (WESERÜBUNG)]. Wilhelm died in 1941.

Wilhelm II's son, the crown prince and also named Wilhelm, remained in Germany, where he sought the monarchy's restoration and opposed the republic. His younger brother was an even more fanatical Nazi and joined the **Sturmabteilung** (Stormtroopers; SA). To Hitler's considerable satisfaction, he received the junior Wilhelm's backing in the 1932 presidential **election** against sitting president **Paul von Hindenburg** and became an outspoken advocate of the SA and the **Schutzstaffel** (Protection Squad; SS). Like his father, he was deeply anti-Semitic. He and other members of his family became committed supporters of Hitler's regime. Collectively, with their name, connections to the nation's elite, and resources, they formed an important source of conservative nationalist support for Hitler at an early, crucial stage in the regime's history. This orientation was typical of other aristocratic families.

It proved to be a one-way infatuation, as Hitler had no intention of sharing power with the conservatives any more than was absolutely necessary to **rearm** and prepare for war or to maintain internal control. By 1934, Hitler was ready to dispense entirely with the detritus of Germany's monarchies, including the Hohenzollerns, and banned their organizations in 1934. After his friend former chancellor Kurt von Schleicher and his wife were brutally murdered in their home during the **Röhm purge**, Wilhelm backed away from active political engagement with the regime. Yet he rebuffed approaches from members of the elite **opposition**. At the end of the Second World War, he was arrested by **French** troops in **Austria** and spent the last six years of his life in Baden-Württemberg, the dynasty's birthplace.

Following Germany's reunification in 1990, a law permitted former citizens of the German Democratic Republic (East Germany) to claim restitution for properties seized by the communist regime. The catch was that the claimants and their descendants could not have supported either the Nazi or communist dictatorships. In recent years, living descendants of both Wilhelms hired distinguished historians to assert that their ancestors had not been committed Nazis. At the same time, they have deployed batteries of lawyers and used their connections to multiple political parties to silence those who call attention to the overwhelming evidence that proves otherwise.

HOLOCAUST. What became known after the Second World War as the Holocaust was a German-led pan-European assault on a vulnerable minority population. Hitler bears primary responsibility as its instigator and driving force. His belief that **Jews** were members of a "race" who conspired to exterminate the German people and take over the world formed the core of his worldview. As early as September 1919, he was articulating a vision of what he called the "uncompromising removal" of Jews from Germany [*see* PERSONAL WILL AND POLITICAL TESTAMENT (1945); RACISM; SUICIDE (30 APRIL 1945)].

From 1933 to 1939, the regime's policies emphasized stripping Germany's relatively small Jewish population of its civil and **economic** rights in hopes they would leave voluntarily. Immigration restrictions around the world, combined with the fact that the regime attempted to rob Jews of most of their property and assets as a condition of emigration, put this objective out of reach [*see* NIGHT OF BROKEN GLASS (REICHSKRISTALLNACHT; 9–10 NOVEMBER 1938); NUREMBERG RACE LAWS].

Hitler's goal of "uncompromising removal" never changed. But what determined the course of the Holocaust was the unforeseen course of the war. And while in his **Prophecy Speech** to the **Reichstag** on 30 January 1939 Hitler announced to the world his intention to "annihilate" the Jews of Europe in the case of a second world war, he almost certainly never issued a single written or verbal order for genocide. There was, in short, no detailed "blueprint" for the genocide. In the end, several "final solution(s) to the Jewish question in Europe"—a euphemism deployed by the regime—were attempted.

Everything hinged first on whether Great Britain would come to terms in 1940. In 1938, Hitler enthusiastically embraced a plan to deport Europe's Jews to the island of Madagascar. Carrying it out, however, depended on eliminating the British navy as a factor in the war following the defeat of **France**. But when Britain remained in the war, the **Madagascar Plan** had to be shelved in the late summer of 1940. Now everything depended on the planned war in the East. Eastern Europe from **Poland** to European Russia and the **Baltics** to **Hungary** would become the epicenter of the genocide of the Jews for two reasons: Hitler had targeted most of this territory as Lebensraum (**living space**) for German settlement and because this is where the overwhelming majority of Europe's roughly 10 million Jews lived.

In late July 1941, Hitler had **Hermann Göring** charge **Schutzstaffel** (Protection Squad; SS) Reich Security Main Office chief **Reinhard Heydrich** with coming up with the next "solution": deporting Europe's Jews to someplace deep inside the Soviet Union. He also ordered the deportation of Jews (and Poles) from territory annexed from Poland and **Austria** to the "General Government," an order that met strenuous objections from its administrator, Hans Frank. To placate Frank, Hitler promised that the Jews sent to the territory would soon be cleared out. He gave Heydrich the job of figuring out how all Jews in spaces conquered by Germany—which Hitler then assumed would soon include the rest of Poland, the Baltics, Belarus, **Ukraine**, and all European Russia—were to be deported. Thus a new "final solution" had been formulated, with the logistics to be determined following the presumed success of **Operation Barbarossa**.

Hitler did not wait for victory to order the deportation of some 60,000 German Jews. A number of simultaneous developments seem to have been behind his seeming urgency of this order, issued some time in early September 1941. One was what historians now routinely describe as a kind of euphoric state induced by the expectation of immanent victory in Russia that seized Hitler and the regime's leadership. Another was the growing likelihood that the **United States** would soon enter the war. Hitler seems to have believed that the deportation of German Jews in full view of the foreign press would deter President **Franklin D. Roosevelt** from declaring war on Germany. Hitler was also enraged by news of the deportation of ethnic Germans in the Volga region of the Soviet Union to Siberia. Just as he believed Jews controlled the White House, he believed they controlled the Kremlin. In the case of the ethnic Germans in Russia, Hitler's deportation order was a form of revenge for a "Jewish" attack on a German minority. Jews were also being targeted as revenge for the intensification of the British Royal Air Force's bombing campaign against German cities (*see* STRATEGIC BOMBING CAMPAIGN).

Around the same time, armed resistance had increased in Eastern and Western Europe. Hitler again held Jews collectively responsible because communists were a strong presence in partisan groups, and for Hitler, communism was a Jewish conspiracy. So he ordered the intensification of local reprisals by the SS and **Wehrmacht**, which soon gave way to wider deportation plans. In January 1942, Heydrich presided over a meeting of regime officials—the **Wannsee Conference**—to assert his office's authority over the entire project and to coordinate what would be continent-wide transports to the East.

The deportation of German and other European Jews—Łódź and the Lublin district in Poland, Riga, and Minsk were the target destinations—led the SS to plan for extending the mass murder already being carried out by four Einsatzgruppen (SS mobile execution units) that followed the Wehrmacht into the Soviet Union to specific locations. To make "space" for the expected arrival of tens of thousands of Jews, local Jewish populations would be killed. Though shooting operations continued, the principal method (and most of the key personnel) were transferred from the **Euthanasia Program** to construct and oversee the operation of poison gas chambers in fixed installations. The first such installation—that is, the first death camp—was built in the fall of 1941 at Belzec on Himmler's orders. Others soon followed: Sobibor, Treblinka, and Birkenau (part of the larger Auschwitz conglomerate). Majdanek would also serve temporarily as a killing center. The operation, code-named Reinhard in honor of Heydrich's memory following his assassination in Prague, concluded in the summer of 1943. Belzec, Treblinka, and Sobibor were dismantled. Birkenau was captured largely intact by the Red Army in January 1945. The vast majority of Reinhard's 1.7 million victims were Polish Jews.

Hitler may have been the driving force in the Holocaust, but the infrastructure of genocide was necessarily vast, with much of the initiative coming from the local level in the East. It was the single deadliest expression of the **leadership principle**: the authority of every leader downward and responsibility upward. It mattered greatly that the principal high-ranking party figures—**Joseph Goebbels**, **Heinrich Himmler**, **Martin Bormann**, **Rudolf Hess**, and **Alfred Rosenberg**—were all **racist** anti-Semites, as were legions of lower-level officials in state ministries, the Wehrmacht, and especially the SS. And the Holocaust could not take place the way it did without the active and passive collaboration of millions of non-Germans.

The "uncompromising removal" of the Jews from Hitler's envisioned Lebensraum was an integral part of what was to be a wider war of genocidal conquest in the East. Hitler intended to wage a race war in the fullest sense of that term, and the leadership of the Wehrmacht was fully prepared to fulfill his orders, as was the SS. Regarding the former, the army's leadership and an untold number of noncommissioned officers (NCOs) and enlisted men did not dissent from planning and waging a race war against Slavs and Jews. As for the latter, the army and the SS coordinated their operations closely, indeed symbiotically. The four SS Einsatzgruppen comprising around 3,000 men were assisted by the Waffen SS, special police battalions (Order Police), and local collaborators. Together, they perpetrated what is now often referred to as the "Holocaust by bullets."

In the space of nine months in 1941 and 1942, these operations may have killed around 2 million Jewish men, women, and children, possibly about one-third of all Holocaust victims, though historians continue to debate the number of victims. In an effort to ease the logistical and psychological burdens (on the perpetrators) of close-quarter killing, the SS turned to using poison gas pumped into trucks.

The final stage of the genocide came with the evacuations of **concentration camps** (including Auschwitz) beginning in the summer of 1944, as the Red Army closed in from the East, and the British and American armies, from the West. Inmates were first taken by train or ship and then marched on foot toward the center of Germany. Part of the idea was to conceal evidence of mass murder. Another was to use them as slave laborers, mainly in what was left of Germany's armaments industry. Finally, Himmler believed that those who survived the ordeal of evacuations and marches could be used as hostages in hoped-for separate peace negotiations with the Western Allies. Regardless, thousands died en route. It is a particularly perverse irony of history that on VE Day, most Holocaust survivors found themselves in Germany. At that point, somewhere around 6 million—more than 60 percent of Europe's 1933 Jewish population—had been killed or allowed to die.

There has been much debate about how much the rest of the world knew about the Holocaust as it was taking place and what might have been done to slow or at least disrupt the killing. A good deal of detailed information about mass killings made its way—members of the Polish underground played a crucial role here—to Western Allied governments. The British had also intercepted and decrypted coded German messages about Order Police killing operations in Poland as early as 1939. The Vatican was receiving accurate information about mass murder earlier than once thought. What remains unknown is the extent to which Soviet intelligence services knew about the genocide. As for the question of what Allied governments might have done during the war: By the time British and American forces were close enough to have taken any military action, the vast majority of the genocide's victims were dead. Again, what Soviet forces might have been able to do is unclear. Roosevelt was certainly correct in believing that the quickest way to end the mass murder was to defeat Nazi Germany as soon as possible.

HOMOSEXUALITY. In the imperial period (1871–1918), Berlin was the birthplace of the modern gay rights movement. In the years of the Weimar Republic, that city and a few others became important international centers of gay and transgendered life. But these facts should not obscure the reality that Germany, like other societies, was deeply homophobic. Paragraph 175 of the Reich criminal code— dating back to 1871—outlawed homosexual acts among men but not **women**.

The radical Right in Germany, including the **National Socialist German Workers' Party** (Nazi Party; Nationalsozialistische Deutsche Arbeiterpartei; NSDAP), had long counted in its ranks numerous men who were bisexual or engaged in same-sex relationships. Beginning in 1933, the party and the regime persecuted gay men with particular intensity. On 6 May, the pioneering Institute for Sexual Research (Institute für Sexualwissenschaft), whose head, physician Magnus Hirschfeld, was an outspoken advocate for the rights of sexual minorities, was raided and destroyed by Nazi university students and the **Sturmabteilung** (Stormtroopers; SA). The main nodes of the country's rich gay and transgender cultures— its bars, nightclubs, and publications—were shut down, though some continued to exist despite the extraordinary risks. A series of police raids in December 1934 led to the arrests of some 2,000 alleged gay men.

There is no credible evidence that Hitler was gay or had same-sex encounters as young man. As a politician, he tolerated the presence of comrades he knew to be same-sex oriented, most notably **Ernst Röhm**, as long as they were loyal and effective. He would, however, readily use homophobia to justify actions against them if it suited his purposes. The regime also deployed accusations of homosexuality and pedophilia to harass the Catholic Church [see BLOMBERG–FRITSCH AFFAIR (1938); FUNK, WALTHER (1890–1960); RELIGION; RÖHM PURGE (1934)].

In general, committed national socialists embraced the standard litany of homophobic stereotypes, mainly that gay men were effeminate, weak, and prone to criminal behavior. There was also the "problem" that gay men would produce few or no children. As was the case in the pre-Nazi period, attitudes toward lesbians were far more ambivalent. Among Nazi ideologues, opinion differed on the sources of homosexuality and what to do about it. In line with pre-Nazi-period psychology, eugenics, and criminology, some continued to accept the false belief that homosexuality was a mental disorder of which one could be cured.

The most dangerous bastion of homophobia was the **Schutzstaffel** (Protection Squad; SS). **Heinrich Himmler** possessed a pathological fear and hatred of gay men and believed they needed to be exterminated to preserve the health of the "race." In the later 1930s, it was the SS and Gestapo that drove intensifying persecution of gay men and alleged gay men, both outside and within the party. Paragraph 175 had been amended in 1935 in a way that defined homosexual acts more broadly and authorized much harsher punishments, thus giving the police a freer hand to conduct raids and arrests. In the meantime, the Gestapo created an index of gay men (including and especially those in the party), and gay men became particularly vulnerable to denunciations.

Imperial, Weimar, and Nazi Germany were hardly alone in criminalizing homosexuality. What did make the Nazi regime distinctive was the incarceration of gay men in **concentration camps**. Estimates of the number imprisoned from 1933 to 1945 range from 5,000 to 15,000. As a group, gay men were not targeted for systematic extermination. But the extreme brutality to which they were subjected (their status was indicated by a pink triangle sown onto their uniforms) led to a high mortality rate relative to other non-**Jewish** groups of prisoners. Many were also forced to undergo castration as a form of punishment and "cure" and in some cases were subjected to medical experiments.

The fact that paragraph 175 long predated 1933 made it possible for occupation authorities and the three postwar German states to continue the legal persecution of gay men. Indeed, legalized homophobia is one of the strongest through lines connecting imperial, Weimar, Nazi, and the postwar Germanys. Paragraph 175 was struck from the Federal Republic of Germany's legal code in 1994.

HOSSBACH MEMORANDUM (1937). A document based on notes taken by Hitler's **Wehrmacht** adjutant, Colonel Friedrich Hossbach, of a meeting in the Reich **chancellery** on 5 November 1937 between Hitler, War Minister Werner von Blomberg, Foreign Minister **Konstantin von Neurath**, and the commanders in chief of the armed forces. It provides a snapshot of how Hitler at that moment envisioned taking the first steps toward conquering Lebensraum (**living space**) for Germany.

Hitler had not desired the meeting, but Blomberg convinced him that it was necessary to resolve a dispute between the armed forces chiefs over the allocation of raw materials. Rather than settle the matter on the spot, however, Hitler expounded for two hours on the need to move against **Austria** and **Czechoslovakia** in the very near future. His reading of the international situation suggested that these conquests could be undertaken at minimal risk.

Despite the lack of a stenographer, Hitler asserted that the matters under discussion were so important that his words were to be taken as his last will and testament. Hossbach realized that some record of Hitler's remarks should be taken down, so he took copious notes of Hitler's monologue, though not of most of the ensuing discussion. A professional officer and no Hitler sycophant, Hossbach also wanted to keep other high-ranking officers informed of Hitler's thinking, especially General Ludwig Beck, chief of the general staff. Beck, among other officers, was particularly concerned that a move against Czechoslovakia would produce a general European war, for which Germany was nowhere near prepared.

Hitler began by repeating his well-known claim that Germany's survival depended on the enlargement of living space and the resources—especially food—it would provide. As anything other than limited autarky or participation in an international **economic** trading system, including the acquisition of overseas colonies, would not solve the problems of space and food, living space would have to be taken by force within Europe. The conquests of Austria and Czechoslovakia would provide at least some foodstuffs, but more important, they would secure Germany's southeastern flank, free up forces for deployment in the West, and allow the Wehrmacht to draft enough soldiers to create 12 new divisions.

Hitler was aware of the unsustainable pressures on the German economy brought about by the ongoing implementation of the **Four-Year Plan**. But he believed that a short victorious war would solve all the country's economic problems. His fears of an early death also intensified his interest in precipitous military action. Finally, if Germany did not act by 1943–1945 at the latest, then the regime's radical momentum at home would have atrophied, and foreign enemies would have become too strong.

He believed that the country's growing power would inevitably provoke its two most powerful enemies, Great Britain and **France**, but insisted that both were not as strong as they seemed. He then speculated that two cases would necessitate a German offensive before 1943. One involved a domestic political crisis in France that would prevent it from moving against Germany. In this case, Germany would attack Czechoslovakia immediately. The second envisioned France becoming involved in a war with **Italy** in the Mediterranean, which in his mind would also rule out a simultaneous war with Germany. Regardless, Hitler was convinced Britain had no desire to defend Czechoslovakia, and he believed France would not do so without British support.

As to the reactions of other states, he thought a lightning-quick move against Czechoslovakia would deter the Poles from any action against Germany [see BLITZKRIEG (LIGHTNING WAR)]. Italy remained a question mark, in that **Benito Mussolini** had given Hitler no clear indication that he was willing to acquiesce to a German takeover of Austria. Hitler said little about Russia, and it is likely he thought **Joseph Stalin**'s purges and **Japan**'s successes in its war with China had made the Soviet Union particularly vulnerable and unlikely to come to Czechoslovakia's assistance.

Hossbach reported that Fritsch, Blomberg, and Neurath all challenged Hitler's assumptions about France's supposed inability to attack Germany even if it found itself at war with Italy and on the strength of Czech fortifications. The rest of the meeting was taken up with a discussion of **rearmament**, the details of which Hossbach did not record.

Hitler had been thinking for months along the lines he laid out in the meeting. Having given up on reaching a strategic understanding with Britain, he had become much more enthusiastic about an alliance with Italy. He also remained confident in the rearmament program, despite its slackening pace and Reich economics minister **Hjalmar Schacht**'s warnings about the pressures to which the economy was being subjected. At the beginning of 1937, Hitler told **Joseph Goebbels** that Germany would be fully prepared for war by 1942–1943 but that he would act sooner if the right opportunity arose. By mid-March, he was musing to him about the necessity of annexing Austria and Czechoslovakia.

Someone like Goebbels needed no convincing, though he was worried about the public's lack of enthusiasm for war. Hitler did need to persuade the influential and fundamentally conservative military and Foreign Ministry officials of the need to prepare for a war much sooner than they thought possible. Blomberg's demand for a meeting on resource allocation presented him with the opportunity. Hitler did not, however, succeed in persuading those gathered in the chancellery on 5 November. Even **Hermann Göring** did not support going to war in 1938. The issue was not Hitler's larger strategic vision, which was well known to them. Rather, it was the proposed timing that was so unnerving, particularly the possibility of having to fight Britain and France before Germany was adequately rearmed and with the economy in a precarious state.

Instead of backing down, Hitler moved decisively to clear away what he considered roadblocks to accelerated rearmament and low-risk moves against Austria and Czechoslovakia. The cautious Schacht, whom Hitler had already decided to remove, was replaced by **Walther Funk**, a close ally of Goebbels, who would also take control of the Reichsbank in early 1939. The influence of Göring's Four-Year Plan administration over the economy became predominant, and expenditures on rearmament exploded in 1938. Whatever problems this caused the economy would, Hitler believed, be resolved only by a war of territorial conquest.

As for the principal military leaders, Hitler did not ignore their concerns completely. Yet a month after the meeting, the Wehrmacht's operations staff altered a plan for an attack on Czechoslovakia even if the military was not yet adequately prepared for war, the underlying assumption being that France and Britain would not intervene. It would be the unexpected **Blomberg–Fritsch affair** in early 1938 that gave him cover for pushing both men out and replacing them with more compliant officers while making himself commander in chief of the Wehrmacht. On 4 February 1938, he replaced Neurath with the far less capable but more obsequious **Joachim von Ribbentrop**. Thus the period from late 1937 to the first months of 1938 mark a major step in Hitler's consolidation of power. But it did not produce the war he wanted. As it turned out, the annexation of Austria and the dismemberment of Czechoslovakia took place without igniting a wider war, much to Hitler's chagrin in the case of the latter.

At the end of the war, British and American officials obtained a copy of Hossbach's notes, and it became an important piece of the prosecution's evidence at the Nuremberg **International Military Tribunal** (IMT), especially when it came to count 1 of the indictment: the "common plan or conspiracy" to wage aggressive war. There is no credible evidence that the document was a forgery or doctored by IMT prosecutors.

HUGENBERG, ALFRED (1865–1951). Along with **Paul von Hindenburg** and **Franz von Papen**, Hugenberg was a principal conservative gravedigger of the Weimar Republic. He was to the German media landscape of the 1920s and early 1930s what Rupert Murdoch was to global media in the 1990s and 2000s. Born in Hanover, Hugenberg was a cofounder of the **Pan-German** League in 1890 and directed the Krupp industrial conglomerate during **World War I**. He then turned to the newspaper and film industries, buying up local papers and press agencies and gaining control over Germany's largest film production company, UFA (Universum Film AG).

At the same time, he joined the **German National People's Party** (Deutschnational Volkspartei; DNVP), served as a **Reichstag** delegate, and became the party's leader in 1929. Hugenberg used his wealth and media acquisitions to undermine public support for the republic. Like other members of the conservative elite facing dwindling electoral support, he believed Hitler and the Nazi Party could be co-opted and controlled. In the negotiations leading up to Hitler's appointment as **chancellor**, Hugenberg received the **Economics** and Agricultural Ministries but was immediately pilloried in the Nazi press and bypassed by Hitler. By June, he had been hounded out of his own party, at that point renamed the German National Front; its members then dissolved it under extraordinary pressure from Hitler and the **Sturmabteilung** (Stormtroopers; SA). He wisely retreated from politics, though he remained in the newspaper and publishing business and even managed to drive a hard bargain when the Nazi Party's press sought to acquire one of his publishing houses. He escaped any kind of legal reckoning for his role in Hitler's ascent to power, with a local denazification tribunal judging him as a mere "fellow traveler" three years before his death in 1951.

HUNGARY. As Hitler accelerated the pace toward war in 1937, southeastern Europe presented opportunities and perils. On one hand, Hitler could count on powerful currents of authoritarianism, anticommunism, and anti-Semitism and on the attractions of close **economic** and strategic ties to Germany. On the other, Hungary, **Bulgaria**, and Yugoslavia were unstable, militarily vulnerable states with multiethnic populations and in a constant state of near conflict with each other over territorial claims (*see* BALKANS). And should Germany award territory in exchange for joining a regional bloc of anti-Soviet states, doing so would alienate other potential partners. Hence his wariness about ties to these countries and continued hope for an arrangement with Great Britain.

Hungary's leaders wanted parts of Slovakia and all of Carpatho-**Ukraine**. In early November 1938, Germany and **Italy** arbitrated the transfer of these territories to Hungary. Authoritarian leader Admiral Miklos Horthy led Hungary into the **Anti-Comintern Pact** in 1939 and the

Tripartite Pact a year later. Further territorial gains were made at **Romania**'s and Yugoslavia's expense in 1940 and 1941, respectively. Hungarian forces also fought in the Soviet Union, suffering particularly high casualties—around 100,000—at the **Battle of Stalingrad**.

Concerned about his ally's reliability and vulnerability, Hitler had German forces occupy Hungary in March 1944 with Horthy's consent (Operation Margarethe). By the fall, as the Red Army prepared to advance into Hungary, Horthy abandoned his country's alliance with Germany on 15 October. Hitler knew this was coming and arranged for Horthy's resignation and replacement by the viciously anti-Semitic fascist Arrow Cross, led by Ferenc Szálasi. Massacres of thousands of **Jews** by Arrow Cross militants and Catholic priests began immediately. **Schutzstaffel** (Protection Squad; SS) lieutenant colonel Adolf Eichmann and hundreds of SS officers had already been dispatched to Budapest to oversee what would become the roundup and deportation of around 440,000 Jews—the last large intact Jewish population in Europe—to Auschwitz, where most were murdered in a matter of weeks (*see* HOLOCAUST).

The Red Army, supported by Romanian and Bulgarian troops, occupied Budapest by the end of January 1945 and the entire country by April. In 1949, the Hungarian government was taken over by a Soviet-style dictatorship and had become part of the Soviet security bloc in Eastern Europe. As early as December 1944, Soviet officials had ordered the expulsions of ethnic Germans. Of the roughly half-million ethnic Germans, some 213,000 were forced out of Hungary.

I

INTERNATIONAL MILITARY TRIBUNAL (NUREMBERG TRIALS; IMT). As early as January 1942, officials of nine governments in exile debated the question of what was to happen to those responsible for war crimes. They expressed a clear preference for a judicial process over summary executions and other acts of violence (Declaration of St. James). A United Nations (UN) War Crimes Commission was created, though it could do no more than gather evidence. The proposal for an international tribunal came from the Soviet ambassador to Great Britain in November 1942. Another turning point came a year later, during an Allied foreign ministers conference held in Moscow. The ministers declared their respective governments' intentions to send Germans accused of war crimes to the countries in which the crimes had been committed while reserving for themselves the authority to prosecute those who committed offenses in no "particular location."

Even then, they conceded that summary executions would take place. **Winston Churchill** and other British officials, who all recalled the farcical post–**World War I** trials in Germany, were particularly keen on approving on-the-spot executions. In May and June 1944, the war cabinet was producing lists of top Nazi officials who would be expected to take their own lives or be killed by other Germans. Failing these outcomes, they would be summarily executed, as the scale of their crimes put them outside the boundaries of the law. For Hitler, Churchill wanted an electric chair, which he thought the Americans could supply via Lend-Lease. British officials continued to advocate summary executions as late as April 1945. **Franklin D. Roosevelt** was initially receptive to the idea but then backed away.

Roosevelt's successor, Harry Truman, and Soviet and **French** officials all favored trials for the major war criminals. It would be lawyers in the US War Department—strong proponents of trials—who would formulate the legal framework for an international military tribunal. The idea of an international court was not new. But an important American innovation was to propose charging the Nazi regime's "organizations" with conspiracy to commit war crimes. This meant that an individual could be charged and found guilty on the basis of membership in a criminal organization with the extent of his or her knowledge of or participation in its crimes determining the severity of the sentence. The architects of this idea had the **Schutzstaffel** (Protection Squad; SS) principally in mind and won skeptics over after a Waffen SS unit murdered nearly 100 American prisoners of war during the Battle of the Bulge and the Red Army liberated Auschwitz two weeks later (*see* HOLOCAUST).

Negotiations among the Allied states accelerated in the first half of 1945. Soviet officials suggested the designation "international military tribunal" and recommended that a charter of its principles be drawn up. The Allies approved the charter on 8 August 1945. They agreed to establish an international tribunal to try those whose alleged crimes "have no particular geographic location" before judges representing the four Allied states. Significantly, the charter made clear that being given orders could not absolve a defendant of responsibility, though it could be taken into account as a mitigating factor in sentencing. The accused would be charged on one or more of four counts: conspiracy or common plan, crimes against peace (an important Soviet contribution), war crimes, and crimes against humanity.

Robert Jackson, the chief justice of the US Supreme Court, was appointed chief prosecutor. Defendants had the right to be informed of the full text of the indictment and to defense counsel of their choosing. There would be no reviews of verdicts or system of appeals. The trial would be held in Nuremberg, in part because of the city's symbolic significance to the party and in part because its hall of justice (and its attached jail) was undamaged [see NUREMBERG PARTY RALLIES (1923–1938); NUREMBERG RACE LAWS].

There was general agreement among the Allies over the selection of most defendants, though the British delegation wanted a small roster for the purposes of a short, uncomplicated trial, while the other three insisted on including surviving high-ranking military and economic officials. Despite **Joseph Stalin**'s claims to the contrary, Hitler was dead, though his name was on an early list [see SUICIDE (30 APRIL 1945)]. **Joseph Goebbels** and **Heinrich Himmler** were also dead, as was **Martin Bormann**, though because this could not be confirmed at the time, he would be tried in absentia. There were 24 defendants in total, including Bormann, representing the highest-ranking surviving leadership of the **National Socialist German Workers' Party** (Nazi Party; Nationalsozialistische Deutsche Arbeiterpartei; NSDAP), the SS, and the German military, plus Hitler's early conservative nationalist enabler, **Franz von Papen**, and the first economics minister, **Haljmar Schacht**. The inclusion of the ailing and senile 75-year-old Gustav Krupp was an embarrassing error, as it was his son Alfried whom the tribunal really wanted. The senior Krupp was deemed medically unfit to stand trial, while **Robert Ley**, the former chief of the **German Labor Front** (Deutsche Arbeitsfront; DAF), killed himself a month before the proceedings began. The inclusion of Hans Fritzsche, a relatively minor Propaganda Ministry official, was a sop to the Soviets, who had none of the living highest-level officials in custody. In addition to the individual defendants, the Reich government, the NSDAP's leadership, the SS and its security service (Sicherheitsdienst; SD), the Gestapo, and the **Wehrmacht**'s general staff and high command were indicted as criminal organizations.

The IMT convened from 20 November 1945 to 1 October 1946. All the defendants pleaded innocent, and none, with the exception of the composed and crafty **Albert Speer** and the emotionally debilitated **Walther Funk**, showed anything like remorse on the stand. Of the 22 tried, 19 were convicted, with 12 sentenced to death and 7 to terms in Spandau Prison in Berlin. Fritzsche, Schacht, and Papen were acquitted. The highest-visibility defendant, **Hermann Göring**, committed suicide in his cell shortly before his execution.

The trial was not without its critics, then and since. For them, it was nothing more than the imposition of victor's justice. Some questioned the legal legitimacy of the IMT and denounced the imposition of ex post facto law. Even the IMT's defenders would concede that Allied forces had violated some of the laws their governments were preparing to prosecute others for committing. Many critics also found the presence of Soviet representatives an outrage against the ideals of a liberal democratic jurisprudence and memory. It was, after all, the **Nazi–Soviet Nonagression Pact** that gave Hitler a free hand to invade **Poland** and then Western Europe, a fact the defendants and their lawyers were intent on calling attention to, along with conclusive evidence of Soviet responsibility for the 1940 Katyn massacre.

Yet the proceedings were a legal watershed. For the first time in history, an international court held officials of a state accountable for violations of international law. The IMT's architects also hoped it would deter states in the future from launching wars of conquest. It marked the introduction of the term *genocide* into international law and informed the UN's 1948 Genocide Convention and Universal Declaration of Human Rights. It would also inspire the establishment of the International

Criminal Court in 2002. Of enormous importance was the amount of evidence amassed by the prosecution, making the IMT one of the most important sources for documenting the history of the regime and its crimes. First and foremost, the IMT would demonstrate to the German public that vast crimes had been committed in its name. And it would leave no doubt, as was the case after World War I, which state bore responsibility for starting the war.

The IMT also represented the tip of the iceberg in terms of postwar trials in Europe alone. The Allies agreed that Germans accused of war crimes could be tried in their respective occupation zones. From 1946 to 1949, the **United States** would preside over 12 "successor trials" (**Nuremberg Military Tribunal**; NMT), which prosecuted 177 high-ranking regime, military, medical, and business leaders. Thousands of trials involving Germans and those accused of collaboration took place in other states on both sides of the iron curtain.

ITALIAN SOCIAL REPUBLIC (REPUBLIC OF SALÓ). As Allied armies prepared to invade the **Italian** Peninsula from Sicily, **Benito Mussolini** met with Hitler in northern Italy in July 1943. When Mussolini returned to Rome, he was deposed by the Grand Council of Fascism and arrested. The king appointed General Pietro Bagdolio to lead a new nonfascist government. Its attempt to extricate Italy from the war provoked a German invasion and months of fighting between the **Wehrmacht**, Allied forces, and rapidly proliferating Italian partisan groups [see KESSELRING, ALBERT (1885–1960)].

Remaining loyal to his ally but more concerned about the impact the collapse of the first fascist regime would have on Germany's other increasingly unsteady allies, Hitler had Mussolini sprung from prison on 12 September in a dramatic operation led by **Schutzstaffel** (Protection Squad; SS) major Otto Skorzeny. Whether Mussolini wished to be rescued is unclear. Hitler installed him as the leader of a puppet state, the Italian Social Republic, with its capital in the small north-central town of Saló. There was no question that Wehrmacht, SS, and German Foreign Ministry officials were really in charge. Northern Italy's significance increased going into 1944 as the eastern front drew nearer and the region—comprising the country's industrial heartland—was rocked with strikes and an emerging civil war between antifascist partisans and the remnants of Mussolini's regime. On 27 April 1945, with German forces having been almost entirely driven out, partisans captured Mussolini and his mistress and executed them the following day. *See also* BULGARIA; HUNGARY; ROMANIA; SUICIDE (30 APRIL 1945).

J

JAPAN. The signing of the **Anti-Comintern Pact** in 1936, the **Tripartite Pact** in 1940, and the idea of an "axis" connecting Germany, **Italy**, and Japan suggests a closer relationship between Germany and Japan than actually existed. As the possibility of an alliance with Great Britain faded in 1936, Hitler sought closer ties with Japan. The approach was championed most aggressively by then ambassador to Britain **Joachim von Ribbentrop**, who dismissed concerns among Foreign and War Ministry officials that China, an important supplier of raw materials, would be alienated.

Over the next two years, Hitler became convinced that Japan's ambitions in Asia would deter the British and **French** from confronting him over his planned annexation of **Austria** and attack on **Czechoslovakia**. Though Japan left the Anti-Comintern Pact in 1939 after Germany signed the **Nazi–Soviet Nonaggression Pact**, it was lured back following Germany's conquest of Western Europe in the spring and summer of 1940 and signed on to the Tripartite Pact [see NORWAY; WESER EXERCISE (WESERÜBUNG)]. Tokyo's main objectives at that point, however, were to avoid antagonizing the Soviets and discouraging the **United States** from entering the war. When **Operation Barbarossa** faltered, Hitler urged Japan to attack the Soviet Union, but by then, Tokyo had set its sights on Southeast Asia and war with the United States. Germany and Japan went their separate ways for the remainder of the war.

In February 1942, as Japanese forces marched down the Malayan Peninsula on their way to capture Singapore, British writer George Orwell described a terrifying scenario in a radio broadcast: He predicted that the center of the world might soon become India. There was, he claimed, a "general plan" for the Germans to break through to the Persian Gulf while Japan took control of the Indian Ocean, potentially making India the world's new geostrategic center. While German and Japanese breakthroughs were possible at that point, there never was any German–Japanese "general plan." The two regimes never coordinated their respective war efforts, making the Axis more ideal than reality.

JEWS. Hitler did not form a coherent anti-Jewish ideology until after **World War I**. There are all kinds of rumors and falsehoods surrounding the preceding years: It is not true that Hitler's anti-Semitism was the result of his anger at Jewish physician Eduard Bloch, who treated his dying mother [see HITLER, KLARA (NÉE PÖLZL; 1860–1907). Hitler was in fact deeply grateful to Bloch for doing his best to ease her suffering and then saved his life during the **Holocaust**. Also untrue is the rumor that Hitler was cheated by Jewish **art** dealers when he lived in **Vienna**. He conducted normal business transactions with several Jewish art dealers. And there is no evidence to support Hitler's own claim in *Mein Kampf* that during his years in Vienna, he learned about the supposed true nature of Jews. Nor is there evidence that he adopted or expressed anti-Semitic views during his wartime service.

There is, by contrast, convincing evidence that Hitler was exposed to and embraced powerful currents of anti-Semitism in postwar Munich, right at the time he became active in Far-Right politics. He made them the foundation of his worldview, a foundation that would remain unchanged for the rest of his life. Some of their features had deep roots in Germany, indeed in Western Christendom more generally. Others were of much more recent origin. Three were of particular importance. First, there was the belief that Jews were members of a race rather than members of a faith who defined themselves as Jews by rabbinical law, by familial ties, or by participation in individual and communal practices and rituals (*see* RACISM). Second, Hitler believed that Jews everywhere were part of a conspiracy to eliminate the "German race" and take over the world (*see* PROTOCOLS OF THE ELDERS OF ZION). Jews, in this paranoid conspiratorial mindset, had power and acted. Hitler and Nazi ideologues updated older conspiracy theories and associated Jews with Bolshevism, hence the Nazis frequent use of the term *Judeo-Bolshevism*. The fervent belief in Judeo-Bolshevism and a racist mindset that also considered all ethnic Slavic peoples to be subhuman goes a long way in explaining the extraordinary violence with which the Germans conducted the war in the East, beginning with the invasion of **Poland** in 1939.

Hitler and the Nazis saw conspiratorial Jewish power not just emanating from Russia but also at work all over the world. He believed that Jews controlled international finance—in those years meaning the City of London and Wall Street. He also believed that they controlled the governments of the world's Western powers, especially Great Britain and the **United States**, the media, and Hollywood. The belief in the globalized nature of supposed Jewish power was based on some very old prejudices about Jews: namely, that they were a people without roots and without a culture of their own. Rather, Hitler accepted that they were highly adaptable parasites who stole the ideas of others and enriched themselves in the process.

The third major element involved social Darwinism. It was a perversion of the theories of British naturalist Charles Darwin, who had nothing to do with social Darwinism. A handful of writers in England came up with and popularized the idea in the 1800s. Humans, like other species, compete with each other for survival and dominance. This competition is natural and good because it ensures that only the strongest and fittest survive. It was used to justify repressive domestic laws, social policies, and imperialism. A version of it was also applied to rationalize a form of capitalism that supposedly worked best when it was least constrained by regulations or interference by the state.

As Hitler articulated as early as 1919, the solution to the so-called Jewish problem was what he called the "uncompromising removal" of Jews from Germany. This would begin with denaturalization, hence point 4 in the **Nazi Party Program**: No Jew could be a citizen of Germany [*see* NATIONAL SOCIALIST GERMAN WORKERS' PARTY (NAZI PARTY; NATIONALSOZIALISTISCHE DEUTSCHE ARBEITERPARTEI; NSDAP)]. In a letter written in September, Hitler wrote about the forms that anti-Jewish measures needed to take in the future. At that moment, he believed that overt violence would have to be replaced with what he called "anti-Semitism of the head": rational, law and science based, and bureaucratic. But he soon revised this view and concluded that the two forms of anti-Semitism—bureaucratic and violent—would have to coexist. Here, intentionally or not, he foreshadowed the lethal mixture of raw sadism and technical efficiency that characterized the genocide of Europe's Jews during World War II.

Hitler also made references to mass murder as part of a solution to the "Jewish problem." In the aftermath of the **Armenian genocide** in 1923, Hitler told a Spanish journalist that his preference in dealing with Germany's Jews would be mass executions. And there is a passage in *Mein Kampf* in which he muses about murdering some Jews with poison gas. These comments should not be understood as a prediction, as if Hitler was some kind of oracle who could see into the future. They do, however, indicate that mass murder was present in his thinking at an early point in his political career.

Throughout the 1920s, Hitler made many references to Jews in his speeches, and anti-Semitic themes were prominent in party propaganda, but anti-Jewish messages were not a big vote getter. This does not mean that there was little or no anti-Semitism in Germany. Rather, anti-Jewish prejudice was a diffuse phenomenon, as one historian put it recently. It was there in various forms and degrees of intensity. It was only when Hitler and the party came to power and destroyed the republic that they could pursue "uncompromising removal" with fewer and fewer restrictions on their actions. For ordinary Germans, the new regime and its ideology focused and channeled this diffuse culture of anti-Jewish sentiment [see CHANCELLOR, APPOINTMENT AS (30 JANUARY 1933); COORDINATION (GLEICHSCHALTUNG)]. The regime also, of course, had the tools of coercion at its disposal. But for the most part, among non-Jewish Germans, there was little to no public or private resistance to accelerating persecution of their fellow citizens.

Throughout the 1920s and after 1933, Jews were vulnerable to violent attacks by members of the radical Right, including the **Sturmabteilung** (Stormtroopers; SA). But such violence was relatively rare and sporadic. Hitler understood that most Germans would not tolerate mobs of SA men attacking anyone on the streets, including Jews. Hitler was also highly sensitive to foreign opinion. The press in Europe and the United States reported regularly on developments in Germany, including anti-Jewish policies, and was often harshly critical. Jewish and non-Jewish antifascists mobilized in public demonstrations against the Nazi regime and fought with pro-Nazis and homegrown fascists [see GERMAN AMERICAN BUND (AMERIKADEUTSCHER VOLKSBUND); NIGHT OF BROKEN GLASS (REICHSKRISTALLNACHT; 9–10 NOVEMBER 1938)].

From 1933 to 1939, the regime's policies emphasized not violence but stripping Germany's relatively small Jewish population of its civil and **economic** rights in hopes they would all leave voluntarily. Immigration restrictions around the world combined with the fact that the regime robbed Jews of most of their property and assets made reaching the goal of total emigration impossible. Yet by the end of 1938, nearly a quarter of German Jews (by then including **Austria**'s Jews) had left the country. Most would never return, and most of those who remained would be murdered.

There were several milestones of anti-Jewish policy in the prewar years: The first involved the attempted nationwide boycott of Jewish-owned businesses that began in April 1933. It was not particularly successful. But the first purge of the civil service, which began around the same time, was successful. Meanwhile, party radicals and SA men humiliated, assaulted, and sometimes killed Jews, and **Joseph Goebbels** was eager to whip up as much anti-Jewish resentment in the press as possible. But the boycott and the violence were damaging Germany's reputation abroad and hindering diplomacy for the still-isolated country. In early May 1935, economics minister and Reichsbank president **Hjalmar Schacht** warned him that anti-Jewish violence and the negative publicity it generated abroad were damaging the economy.

It was at this juncture that Hitler acted to restrain "emotional anti-Semitism" and promoted an "anti-Semitism of reason." In August 1935, he ordered an end to unsanctioned acts of violence and promulgated the **Nuremberg race laws** a month later. For German Jews, the laws formed a juncture rather than a turning point or rupture. Radical grassroots anti-Semitism had to be further suppressed before and during the 1936 **Olympic Games**. But after the games, pent-up frustrations coincided with Hitler's determination to accelerate emigration and prepare the public for war. This combustible situation produced the third major turning point: a nationwide pogrom in November 1938, which did accelerate emigration.

What role did ordinary non-Jewish Germans play in the accelerating persecution? A minority formed what we could call activists from the grassroots level all the way up to Hitler. Matters are more complicated when it comes to the majority. Nazi ideology and propaganda built on preexisting prejudices, and most Germans went along. Certainly, some coercion was involved—there's no question that protesting anything the regime did when it came to the Jews was very dangerous.

Opportunism was also a factor, especially when it came to property and other assets that Jewish families often sold to finance emigration. In this category, however, it was the state that was the biggest beneficiary. Persecution of the Jews and later the Holocaust involved theft on a massive scale. And there was a considerable amount of passivity: a lack of individual or collective protest. Many Germans simply looked the other way.

In 1933, Germany's Jewish population was around 67 million. In January of that year, official figures list 523,000 Jews, or less than 1 percent of the population and 0.5 percent of Europe's Jews. In Germany, about 80 percent, or around 400,000 out of the 523,000, were German citizens. The rest were Polish citizens who were legal residents of Germany. Seventy percent of German Jews lived in urban areas, with 50 percent living in the 10 biggest cities, above all Berlin. The vast majority of German Jews were working class or middle class and thoroughly assimilated, considering themselves Germans first and Jews second and increasingly not Jewish at all, as conversions and intermarriage were becoming more common. Most voted for the Social Democrats or the liberal or conservative nationalist parties. Very few were attracted to Zionism.

In the face of accelerating persecution and a great deal of indifference and even hostility to their plight abroad, German Jews responded with extraordinary courage and resourcefulness. Jewish communities across Germany mobilized. They formed their own organizations and took steps to prepare their children for life abroad. And German Jews sought refuge all over the world. Refugees went all over Europe; to the United Kingdom; to Australia and New Zealand; to Shanghai, Palestine, Kenya, and South Africa; to the Caribbean and South America; and to the United States and Canada. The German Jewish diaspora produced the widest geographical dispersal of any single group of people in human history. In the process, many developed a sense of Jewish identity where there had been little or none before.

Hitler did everything in his power to realize his "prophecy" of January 1939. When the possibilities of deporting Jews to **Madagascar** and then somewhere beyond the Ural Mountains evaporated, mass murder in Europe—mainly the **Baltics**, Poland, Belarus, western Russia, and **Ukraine**—became the last "final solution." The determination with which the regime pursued genocide, even very late in the war, highlights the extent to which Hitler and hundreds of thousands of officials, soldiers, and civilians embraced racialist, conspiratorial anti-Semitism.

JODL, ALFRED (1890–1946). Born into a distinguished military family from Würzburg, Jodl served with considerable distinction on the western and eastern fronts in **World War I**. He became a fervent supporter of Hitler in 1937 and 1938. After serving as a staff officer in the Reichswehr and then the **Wehrmacht** in the 1920s and 1930s, Hitler appointed him chief of the operations staff of the Oberkommando der Wehrmacht (Supreme Command of the Armed Forces; OKW) in April 1938. Jodl became one of his most important military advisers, delivering the daily briefing on the military situation throughout the war.

Yet Hitler's concentration of supreme authority over the military in his hands along with the way he divided up the organization of the armed forces put limits on any single high-ranking officer's influence. A division of responsibility obtained during the war in which the OKW had responsibility for operations in the West while the Oberkommando des Heeres (Supreme Command of the Army; OKH) dominated in the Soviet Union. The commanders in chief of the OKH (**Walther von Brauchitsch** until December 1941), navy (Erich Raeder), and **Luftwaffe** (**Hermann Göring**) operated independently from and in competition with the OKW [see KEITEL, WILHELM (1882–1946)]. Jodl attempted to navigate between the various centers of authority, nearly always taking Hitler's side. When he sided with other officers in 1942 over strategy on the eastern front, Hitler decided to replace him with General Friedrich Paulus until Paulus's surrender at the **Battle of Stalingrad**. Jodl remained in his position, having become indispensible to Hitler.

Following Hitler's suicide, Admiral **Karl Dönitz** ordered Jodl to sign the Instrument of Surrender at the Supreme Allied Command headquarters in Rheims, **France**, on 7 May 1945. He was arrested two weeks later and indicted on all four counts by the **International Military Tribunal** (IMT). In addition to extensive documentation, his diary revealed the extent to which he supported Hitler and Germany's war aims. Like other former officers sitting in the dock, he insisted he was only doing his duty and following orders and even added that he held great respect for international law as the basis of the "humane conduct of war." He also claimed total ignorance of the **Holocaust** and that he knew of the existence of only two **concentration camps**. In short, he lied straight through the presentation of his defense. Given that many Germans and non-Germans were also convinced that Jodl was in fact an honorable officer who did his duty and obeyed orders, his death sentence was highly controversial. In February 1953, a West German denazification court attempted to exonerate him posthumously.

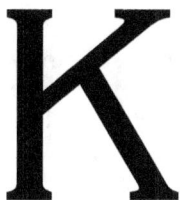

KAPP PUTSCH (1920). In March 1920, Wolfgang Kapp and a small group of other right-wing nationalists, paramilitaries, and a few army officers initiated a coup attempt against the young Reich government. The putschists managed to take control in Berlin for a few days before a general strike and the lack of support from the army and the conservative political establishment restored the democratically elected government. Kapp fled to Sweden and died in 1922 shortly after his return to Germany.

Hitler played a marginal, almost farcical, role in the attempt. **Karl Mayr**, a supporter of Kapp, ordered another Kapp ally, **Dietrich Eckart**, to fly to Berlin and establish a line of communication between the putschists in the capital and those in Munich. Eckart brought Hitler with him. They went in disguise, with Hitler wearing a false beard and posing as an accountant. Terrified, he spent the first flight of his life violently ill and would not board another airplane for years. The pair was delayed when their plane ran out of fuel and had to land outside Berlin, where they were allegedly surrounded by angry leftists and had to talk their way back on the plane for the short last leg of the journey. It was a wasted trip, as the coup attempt was already collapsing when they landed. They returned to Munich two days later.

The aftermath of the putsch led to the fall of the **Social Democratic Party of Germany** (Sozialdemokratische Partei Deutschlands, SPD)–led government in Bavaria and its replacement by a right-wing cabinet and prime minister. Some of the putschists decamped from Berlin to Bavaria, injecting the Far-Right scene in that state with new energy. An important result of these shake-ups was that establishment conservatives and radicals formed closer institutional and personal ties, with the putsch attempt in Berlin providing the Bavarian Far Right a kind of lesson in how not to go about establishing an authoritarian nationalist regime. Though Hitler's own involvement in the attempt was negligible, the fallout altered the right-wing context in Bavaria in a way that would redound to the benefit of the **German Workers' Party** (Deutsche Arbeiterpartei; DAP) and **National Socialist German Workers' Party** (Nazi Party; Nationalsozialistische Deutsche Arbeiterpartei; NSDAP) and him personally.

KEITEL, WILHELM (1882–1946). Keitel was born in the Duchy of Brunswick (Braunschweig), and though a Hanoverian, for much of his adult life he would be mistaken for a Prussian. A professional military officer, he served as an artillery officer on the western front in **World War I** and then on the general staff. In 1919, he organized paramilitary units (Freikorps, or Free Corps) on the border with the new **Polish** state. He continued to serve in the Reichswehr and then War Ministry until the fall of minister Werner von Blomberg in 1938 [see BLOMBERG–FRITSCH AFFAIR (1938)]. In the shake-up that followed, Hitler took direct control of the armed forces and appointed Keitel as chief of the Oberkommando der **Wehrmacht** (Armed Forces High Command; OKW).

Among all high-ranking military officers, none was more slavishly devoted to Hitler than Keitel. His servility earned him the contempt of his fellow officers and the nickname Lakeitel, a take on *Lakai*, or *lackey*. Keitel's intellectual shortcomings were also acknowledged widely, even by Hitler, who allegedly told Field Marshal **Gerd von Rundstedt** that Keitel had the brains of a movie usher. Hitler bribed and rewarded Keitel with enormous tax-free lump-sum payments on the occasion of his 60th birthday and when Keitel was looking to expand the size of his family's estate.

Keitel was a crucial figure in ensuring Hitler's desire for a brutal war of conquest in Poland and the Soviet Union was realized by the Wehrmacht. He also made sure that the **Schutzstaffel** (Protection Squad; SS) would be able to operate behind the front lines as **Heinrich Himmler** wished [see NIGHT AND FOG DECREE (NACHT UND NABEL; 1941)]. Keitel participated in the bloody purge that followed the 20 July 1944 **assassination attempt** and remained loyal to Hitler to the very end. He retained his position in the short-lived government led by Grand Admiral **Karl Dönitz**. When **Joseph Stalin** demanded a second surrender ceremony be held on 9 May 1945 at Soviet occupation headquarters in Berlin, it was Keitel who signed the terms of surrender.

Keitel was arrested with the rest of the Dönitz government and charged on all four counts by the **International Military Tribunal** (IMT). On the stand and in his final statement to the court, Keitel for once demonstrated a capacity for independent thought and admitted that he bore personal responsibility for the orders and directives he had signed. He nonetheless insisted that he was duty bound to follow orders. Keitel was convicted on all four counts, sentenced to death, and hanged on 16 October 1946.

KESSELRING, ALBERT (1885–1960). The son of a local school official, Kesselring joined the Bavarian army as a cadet in 1904. He served on the western and eastern fronts in **World War I**, received two Iron Crosses, and ended the war as an officer on the general staff. He remained in the Reichswehr through the 1920s but in 1933 was discharged and appointed to an administrative position in the new Reich Commissariat for Aviation, which would soon become the Reich Air Ministry. The ostensible purpose of the commissariat was to oversee Germany's civilian aviation industry, but its real purpose was to begin developing a new air force (**Luftwaffe**). Following the Luftwaffe's formal creation in 1935, he was soon promoted to general lieutenant and then chief of staff and played an important role in the new force's rapid expansion. He also received training as a pilot.

Kesselring commanded air fleets during the invasions of **Poland** and the Netherlands. In the latter, he ordered the bombing of Rotterdam. He also oversaw the Luftwaffe's unsuccessful attempt to disrupt the evacuation of much of the British expeditionary force from Dunkirk (*see* FRANCE). He then led air fleets in the **Battle of Britain** and the ensuing Blitz and in **Operation Barbarossa**. In November 1941, he was appointed commander in chief of military operations in the Mediterranean, where for a time he was successful in increasing the flow of supplies to **Erwin Rommel's Afrika Korps** (Africa Corps). Beginning in 1943, he commanded German forces in **Italy**, where he proved extremely effective in slowing the Allies' advance. He also approved a subordinate's decision to execute 15 uniformed Office of Strategic Services commandos from the **United States** who had been taken prisoner. Around the same time, he ordered the reprisal executions of 335 Italian civilians in what became known as the Ardeatine Massacre (or Fosse Ardeatine Massacre). Hitler transferred him to northwestern Europe in March 1945 in the vain hope that he could repeat his performance in Italy and slow the Allied march eastward [see RUNDSTEDT, GERD VON (1875–1953)].

Kesselring remained loyal to Hitler; did not join the **opposition**; and, like other high-ranking officers, received a regular bribe. He surrendered to an American officer in **Austria** on 9 May 1945 and was transferred to British custody the following year. He was tried by a British military court in Venice from February to May 1947, primarily for his well-documented role in the Ardeatine Massacre. Kesselring considered his actions legal. Convicted, he was sentenced to death but became the beneficiary of a powerful Anglo–German campaign for clemency. His British champions included **Winston Churchill** and a number of British officers who had fought Kesselring and considered him an honorable soldier and the victim of mindless victor's justice. His death sentence was commuted, and he was released in October 1952 on the (questionable) grounds of poor health. His release provoked a major public outcry in Italy, to which Kesselring responded by claiming he saved untold Italian lives and proposing a monument be constructed in his honor.

Even before he was released from prison, he became the honorary president of three West German veterans' groups. He contributed to the myth of the "clean Wehrmacht" by contributing to the US Army's Historical Division's massive project of military case studies written by hundreds of ex–Nazi officers [see HALDER, FRANZ (1884–1972)] and in his memoirs, published in 1953 as *Soldat bis zum letzten Tag* (*A Soldier to the Last Day*, published in English as *A Soldier's Record*). His funeral in 1960 was attended by a rogues' gallery of former comrades (some of them serving as newly minted West German Bundeswehr officers), ex-**Schutzstaffel** (Protection Squad; SS) officers, **Karl Dönitz**, and **Franz von Papen**.

KUBIZEK, AUGUST FRIEDRICH (GUSTL; 1888–1956). The only son of an upholsterer in Linz and an aspiring musician, Kubizek was a friend of Hitler's during his years in Linz (1905–1907) and **Vienna** (1907–1913). He shared Hitler's intense interest in opera, and the two met at a local performance in 1905. At that time, Hitler was living with his mother and spending his time painting, reading, wandering around the city, and attending the theater [see HITLER, KLARA (NÉE PÖLZL; 1860–1907)]. Shortly after Hitler returned to Vienna in February 1908 following his mother's death the previous December, Kubizek joined him, as he had been accepted to the conservatory of music, and they shared a room in a boardinghouse. Most of their time together involved attending the opera and Hitler subjecting Kubizek to lengthy monologues. In November, Hitler moved to another apartment and cut off contact with his friend. They did not have a falling-out. Rather, Hitler was most likely trying to avoid being contacted by his sister and other relatives in Linz whose patience for his unwillingness to find steady work and support himself was running out.

After **World War I**, Kubizek settled in Eferding, **Austria**, where he became a civil servant. He resumed contact with Hitler in 1933 and met him again in person in Linz in April 1938, shortly after Germany annexed Austria, and twice more in 1939 and 1940. In 1938, a party journalist approached him about recording his recollections of his friendship with Hitler for the party's archives, and he agreed. Nothing came of this until **Martin Bormann** hired him to finally write the memoir. Unable to complete the project before the war's end, Kubizek nonetheless saved what he had written, along with copies of letters from Hitler and postcards painted by him. In 1953, Leopold Stocker Verlag published *Adolf Hitler—Mein Jugendfreund* (*Adolf Hitler—My Boyhood Friend*). The book attracted a good deal of attention and sold well. An incomplete translation was published in Great Britain in 1954, and a complete version appeared in English in 2011.

Kubizek's memoir is an essential but problematic source: essential because it is the only substantial account we have of a young Hitler written by a personal friend. The memoir offers a largely sympathetic and even admiring portrait of Hitler as a very young man. In a series of short, themed chapters, Kubizek provides many anecdotes and observations about Hitler's habits and **personality**: his intense grief over his mother's death, a brief infatuation with a young **woman** in Linz but otherwise disinterest in women and sex, his obsession with the operas of Richard **Wagner** and Vienna's grandiose architecture, his aversion to socializing with other people, and his resentful **pan-Germanism** (*see* ART). Overall, Kubizek leaves the reader with the impression that Hitler dwelled in a fantasy world, a world in which the pure artistic genius Hitler was convinced he possessed could make anything possible. Kubizek rarely seems to have challenged these delusions of grandeur.

Yet *Adolf Hitler—My Boyhood Friend* is problematic for several reasons. One involves the contexts in which the manuscript was written. Kubizek had completed about 150 pages when the war ended, but only a portion survived. That portion is highly adulatory, which should not be surprising given that it was commissioned by one of the most powerful figures in the party. Kubizek had to rely heavily on memory to fill out the much longer version published in 1953. He also drew material from **Mein Kampf**, allowing some of its passages to influence his own recollections. Historians have noted multiple factual errors, embellishments (such as quoting Hitler at length from memory), and exaggerations, some of which have appeared repeatedly in secondary accounts of Hitler's life and the regime's history.

The two most significant distortions involve Hitler's supposed premonition of becoming a political leader after attending a performance of one of Wagner's operas in Linz and his attitudes—or lack of them—toward **Jews**. Regarding the latter, Kubizek portrays Hitler as an increasingly radical anti-Semite. Taken together, these stories played an important role in perpetrating the myth—now thoroughly discredited by historians—that Hitler's anti-Semitism was formed in Linz and Vienna and that even at this very young age, it was clear to him that he was destined to be a political leader.

Complicating matters was an attempt by a jealous competitor, Franz Jetzinger, to discredit Kubizek. Jetzinger, a Linz librarian, was planning to write a study of Hitler's youth based in part on materials provided to him by Kubizek when Kubizek surprised him by publishing *Adolf Hitler—My Boyhood Friend* first. A chagrined Jetzinger then produced his own book three years later in which he claimed Kubizek had gotten several significant moments in Hitler's youth completely wrong, notably Hitler's presence at his mother's death in 1907 and the fact that he had very little money. Jetzinger's shoddy research and his animosity toward Kubizek had a deleterious long-term effect on scholarly and popular perceptions of Hitler's youth and the formation of his personality.

L

LAMMERS, HANS HEINRICH (1879–1962). A figure largely unknown outside historians of the regime, Lammers was nonetheless a figure of considerable importance to Hitler. Born in Upper Silesia (now part of **Poland**), Lammers earned a doctorate in law and served as a district court judge. After his wartime service, during which he was twice decorated, he served in the Reich Interior Ministry. Initially a **German National Peoples' Party** (Deutschnationale Volkspartei; DNVP) member, Lammers joined the **National Socialist German Workers' Party** (Nazi Party; Nationalsozialistische Deutsche Arbeiterpartei; NSDAP) in 1932. In 1933, Hitler appointed him head of the **chancellery**, a position he would retain until late April 1945, making him one of the regime's longest continually serving high-level officials.

It was something of an ideal choice. In Lammers, Hitler had an intelligent, capable, and loyal servant who nonetheless did not have the ambitions, temperaments, and sheer greed of bureaucratic empire builders like **Hermann Göring**, **Joseph Goebbels**, and **Albert Speer**. Officials like Lammers were essential to the functioning of a dictatorship in which the dictator behaved like Hitler, with his irregular working habits; sporadic attention to detail; and propensity to allow subordinates to compete with each other for turf, resources, and access to him. Like **Martin Bormann**, Lammers's power was based on Hitler's trust in him, his control over access, and his ability to translate Hitler's wishes into concrete directives. These abilities became particularly important after Hitler became consumed with managing the war.

Lammers would, however, be edged out by Bormann. The end for one of Hitler's most loyal servants came, somewhat ironically, with Lammers's involvement with Göring's attempt on 23 April 1945 to take control of the country. Hitler had Göring and Lammers put under house arrest. Lammers served as a witness for the defense before the **International Military Tribunal** (IMT) in Nuremberg. He also provided Allied investigators with a good deal of information about the Nazi regime's inner workings and its corruption. He was a defendant in the ministries trial, one of the 12 successor Nuremberg trials. Indicted on all counts, he was convicted of four, including war crimes and crimes against humanity, and given a 20-year sentence. The US high commissioner for West Germany John J. McCloy halved his sentence, and Lammers was released in December 1951. He died in Germany in 1962.

LANDSBERG PRISON. Completed in 1908 on the outskirts of Landsberg am Lech in Bavaria, Landsberg Prison is a medium-security facility where Hitler was imprisoned for just over nine months in 1924 following his conviction for high treason [see BEER HALL PUTSCH (1923)]. The terms of Hitler's imprisonment were those of Festungshaft (fortress imprisonment) a form of incarceration that afforded inmates extensive privileges, including exemption from performing manual labor. It also mattered that the warden and some of the guards were self-proclaimed national socialists or at least admirers of Hitler. He later claimed they wept on the day of his release.

Hitler's cell was on the prison's second floor, his wing nicknamed Feldherrenhügel (General's Hill). It was spacious, airy, appointed with comfortable furniture and a large personal library, and afforded him a view of the surrounding countryside. He received an abundance of packages and flowers from well wishers, and visitors noted his cell looked like a delicatessen and smelled like a greenhouse. One admirer brought him a gramophone.

Members of his inner circle—**Rudolf Hess**; Hermann Kriebel; and his driver, Emil Maurice—also shared the wing. Among inmates in the relatively small facility, Hitler was the unquestioned leader. New arrivals were ordered to present themselves to him, and he presided over communal meals and gave atypically short speeches at weekly social events. A model prisoner, he ordered his subordinates to obey all prison regulations.

Hitler spent much of his time reading, corresponding, writing what would become the first volume of *Mein Kampf*, and thinking about the party's future. A good deal of time also had to be devoted to receiving a steady stream of visitors—up to five every day in the first two months of his imprisonment alone and 330 in total—which included his lawyers, members of the **National Socialist German Workers' Party** (Nazi Party; Nationalsozialistische Deutsche Arbeiterpartei; NSDAP) inner circle, wealthy benefactors, and curious well wishers from a strikingly diverse array of backgrounds.

Beyond Landsberg's walls, the party and the German Far Right more generally seemed to be disintegrating. The NSDAP, paramilitary groups involved in the putsch, and the *Völkischer Beobachter* had all been banned and party property confiscated. Hitler had ordered that during his incarceration, **Alfred Rosenberg** was to be put in charge of the party, which Rosenberg renamed the Grossdeutsche Volksgemeinschaft (Greater German People's Community), but he was toppled in June by jealous rivals, and the party splintered into rival blocs. More successful was **Ernst Röhm**, who reorganized the **Sturmabteilung** (Stormtroopers; SA) and created a new umbrella paramilitary group, the Frontbann.

Rather than try to manage the disorder from his prison cell, Hitler announced his withdrawal from political activity on 7 July. It was an adroit move, given the fractious nature of the now dissolved and effectively leaderless NSDAP. Meddling in the endless squabbling would, he believed, not be conducive to maintaining his status as the sole leader of an ethnonationalist movement. Besides, the disunity in Hitler's functional absence could be read as a sign of his singular importance as a leader. If necessary, he would rebuild the party from the ground up once he was released. Finally, he probably feared such meddling might jeopardize his chances for early release. It would certainly take time away from writing his book. He restricted the number of visitors he would see and set himself to laboriously typing most of the first volume in his remaining months as a prisoner.

Given his record of good behavior, Hitler hoped to be released on 1 October 1924, exactly six months after his sentencing. But Bavarian state prosecutors, unconvinced that he and his followers would abandon their efforts to overthrow the state, fought to keep him in Landsberg. The Bavarian Supreme Court, possibly swayed by the extremely weak showing by Far-Right parties in national **elections** held 7 December, overruled the prosecutors' office. He was released 20 December 1924.

Once he was in power, Hitler's cell became a pilgrimage site for **Hitler Youth** (Hitlerjugend; HJ) detachments. It was also used to hold political prisoners. The prison was liberated by American (*see* UNITED STATES OF AMERICA) forces on 30 April 1945. Beginning in December, the US Army used it to hold prisoners convicted in its own postwar trials and in the Subsequent Nuremberg Trials [*see* NUREMBERG MILITARY TRIBUNAL (NMT)]. The army designated the facility War Criminal Prison No. 1. It remains a functioning Bavarian state correctional institution.

LAW. The **program** of the **National Socialist German Workers' Party** (Nazi Party; Nationalsozialistische Deutsche Arbeiterpartei;

NSDAP) called for the replacement of Roman law with "German common law." By the time the program was being written, the Far Right in Germany had rejected legal positivism and the standard of judges acting as impartial interpreters of an extensive body of legal codes. Rather, the Right embraced what its most influential legal thinker, Carl Schmitt, would call "decisionism." The idea was that the law and the judicial system was not beholden to a constitution and criminal and civil codes but to what the sovereign decided was in the best interests of protecting the people.

When Hitler was appointed **chancellor**, Schmitt had already spent several years advising the previous two chancellors on expanding executive power based on articles in the republic's constitution (42 and 48) that granted the president extensive powers in cases of national emergencies. The constitution's liberal architects, of course, had intended these to be invoked rarely and temporarily. For Schmitt, they were to serve as the basis for a new political and legal order.

Schmitt's ideal was quickly realized by the new regime. Hitler used the **Reichstag fire** to lay the legal foundations for his dictatorship. For Hitler, the law was no more than a tool of what he would call "ethnic self-preservation." In practice, the regime created what German **Jewish** lawyer and political scientist Ernst Fraenkel would call the "dual state," comprised of the "normative state" and the "prerogative state." The former included the constitution, codified law, and the judicial system. The latter was the arbitrary powers exercised by the regime. This mainly meant Hitler and the **Schutzstaffel** (Protection Squad; SS), which assumed all police powers in 1936.

In practice, there was little distinction between the two "states." The apparatus of the normative state was purged of Jewish and liberal lawyers and judges and filled with Nazi or at least compliant servants [*see* COORDINATION (GLEICHSCHALTUNG)]. It became the source of the regime's most notorious laws, such as the **Nuremberg race laws**. Outside the preexisting but increasingly nazified judicial system, Hitler ordered the creation of the Volksgerichtshof (People's Court) to prosecute a wide range of political offenses. The proceedings bore virtually no resemblance to a fair trial and sentenced nearly 11,000 people to prison terms and 5,179 others to death. The court's most notorious judge-president was Roland Freisler, who presided from 1942 to 1945. A Hitler sycophant who wore traditional judge's robes and screamed abuse at defendants in his courtroom, Freisler personified the regime's perversion of the rule of law. Parallel to the Volksgerichtshof was a network of Sondergerichte (Special Courts) across Germany and in a few German-occupied territories.

Freisler's appointment to the Volksgerichtshof was part of a wider shake-up of the judiciary initiated by Hitler. His new justice minister, Otto Georg Thierack, had served as Freisler's predecessor, and Hitler ordered him to create a new, expressly "national socialist" legal system, one that he fully expected to violate established law. Hitler's intention was clear: to replace the "normative" state with the "prerogative" state.

Freisler was killed in an air raid on 3 February 1945. At the **Nuremberg Military Tribunal** (NMT), 16 former Justice Ministry, Volksgerichtshof, and Sondergerichts officials were prosecuted in the Justice Case, mainly on charges of crimes against humanity. The most common defense of the accused was similar to that proffered by military officers: They were obeying the sovereign. As one historian of the trial put it, they implemented the Führerprinzip (**leadership principle**) in the legal sphere.

LEADERSHIP PRINCIPLE (FÜHRERPRINZIP). Hitler had already become the leader of the **National Socialist German Workers' Party** (Nazi Party; Nationalsozialistische Deutsche Arbeiterpartei; NSDAP) when he defined what would become a crucial component of his continued dominance over the party and his dictatorship: the leadership principle. He described it in *Mein Kampf* as "authority of every leader downwards and responsibility upwards." It had four essential components. One was a charismatic leader of genius and vision unconstrained by democratic processes or institutional constraints and capable of making bold decisions. Much of the leader's ability to wield power in this way depended on the creation and maintenance of a cult of personality, also known in Hitler's case as the **Führer myth** (Führer mythos). The second was a divide-and-rule approach to leadership based on the social Darwinist premise that conflict and struggle were keys to survival and mastery. Third was the absolute loyalty of subordinates. Fourth was the willingness of subordinates to replicate the "leadership principle" in their own domains.

This combination made it possible for Hitler to delegate responsibility downward and intervene at decisive moments. Beginning in 1933, the Führerprinzip drove the creation of new agencies and new, important-sounding titles that duplicated and bypassed existing bureaucracies with their long-standing institutional structures, written rules, and hierarchies. In the first three years of the dictatorship alone, Hitler created 10 new "Supreme Reich Authorities" without abolishing existing ministries (an important exception was the merger of the **chancellor**'s and president's offices in 1934). Administrative boundaries were not defined clearly, resulting in what one Nazi-era Foreign Ministry official called "national socialist administrative anarchy." Given this and the fact that Reich ministers answered directly to Hitler, there was ferocious ongoing competition for access to him, resources, and expanded realms of authority.

Given the duplication, administrative bloat, waste, corruption, and difficulties in allocating resources in a rational manner that this system of rule produced, it is striking that the regime functioned as well and as long as it did, especially in the war's final year. Though Hitler's popularity declined in the war's later years, the system of "authority downwards and responsibility upwards" seems to have outlasted the vanishing myth of the charismatic genius and no doubt helps explain why the Germans fought to the very end. See also HIMMLER, HEINRICH (1900–1945); HOLOCAUST; LAW; SCHUTZ-STAFFEL (PROTECTION SQUAD; SS).

LEAGUE OF NATIONS. For Hitler, the League of Nations had three major strikes against it. For one thing, it exemplified the kind of pacifist internationalism that he detested. For another, Germany's admission to the league in 1925 following the signing of the Pact of Locarno represented the high point of the Weimar Republic's diplomacy. The republic's most important statesman, Gustav Stresemann, and his **French** counterpart, Aristide Briand, would share the Nobel Peace Prize in 1926 for their work on the pact. But for Hitler and the conservative nationalists, league membership with its attendant entanglements was not the way to restore Germany's great-power status. Finally, Hitler was hardly alone among Germans in seeing the league as a tool of the wartime allies to enforce the terms of the **Versailles Treaty**. Germany's colonies became league mandates, as did the coal-rich Saar region, which was administered (and exploited) by France. Danzig (now Gdańsk in **Poland**) and its environs became a "free city" under league protection.

As a condition of Hitler's appointment as **chancellor**, the Foreign and War Ministries were headed by conservative nationalists. While they shared his broad goals of **rearmament** and territorial revisions (especially with Poland), their initial approach to all major foreign policy and security matters was highly restrained. That meant remaining in the league for the time being so as to avoid diplomatic isolation and **economic** sanctions.

But once he had full dictatorial control by the summer of 1933, Hitler turned his attention to foreign policy. On 14 October, he took Germany out of the league-sponsored disarmament conference, and the league, the following day. The ostensible reason was that as a full member, Germany was being denied equal status over the issue of armaments. The move was genuinely popular in Germany—**Reichstag elections** and a plebiscite on the regime's policy were held for good measure—and Hitler made a point of stressing in public his country's commitment to peace. He had guessed, correctly, that international outrage at the decisions would quickly abate. Having delivered collective security in Europe a major blow, Hitler pressed on with rearmament and began pursuing bilateral agreements, notably a nonaggression pact with Poland in 1934 and the **Anglo–German Naval Agreement** in 1935.

Hitler's withdrawal accelerated the league's slide into irrelevance. The disarmament conference collapsed in June 1934, and the league did nothing more than issue a verbal protest when Hitler announced German rearmament nine months later. Nor could it do anything in response to Italy's invasion of Ethiopia in 1935 or Japan's war in China or the Spanish Civil War.

LENINGRAD. Of the three armies—Army Groups North, Center, and South—attacking the Soviet Union in Operation Barbarossa, Army Group North's main objective was Leningrad (now Saint Petersburg). Along with Ukraine, the capture of the Baltic Sea port city was a higher priority for Hitler than Moscow, as it would ensure the uninterrupted flow of Swedish iron ore through the Baltics. As with Moscow, Hitler wanted the city surrounded and its population of 5 million starved. Though he admired Leningrad's beauty, he intended for it to share the fate of all Soviet cities: total demolition. The fact that in Leningrad's case, doing so would eliminate its port facilities and industry is evidence of the priority Hitler placed on the war's ideological objectives. And Saint Petersburg—as he stubbornly called it—held special symbolic significance, as he considered it the birthplace of Bolshevism and the gateway through which its poison had spread west.

As in the Center and South, Army Group North made rapid initial progress. But by December, the advance had stalled, and in some places, German forces had to retreat. Leningrad remained surrounded, though Army Group North had failed to link up with Finnish forces advancing down the Karelian Isthmus. Regardless, the city's capitulation became Hitler's second-highest priority (after the Caucasus) for the spring and summer of 1942. Tenacious Soviet resistance and successful counterattacks made it clear by August of that year that the city would not be taken before the winter. As usual, Hitler blamed the failure here on the incompetence and timidity of his generals (see MILITARY COMMANDER).

From early September 1941 to the end of January 1944—872 days—Leningrad was subjected to a siege by a relatively small German force. As Hitler's attention was increasingly consumed by the need to capture the Caucasus, Leningrad became a relatively lower strategic priority but one that still occupied great symbolic importance in his mind.

The mobilization of the city's defense was one of the Allies' signal achievements, though it came at the cost of around 1 million military and civilian lives, with the latter enduring the worst hardships and losses. And it is often overlooked that the siege was one of the greatest of the Wehrmacht's many crimes. *See also* BATTLE OF STALINGRAD.

LEY, ROBERT (1890–1945). A Catholic Rhinelander who studied chemistry before serving as a pilot in World War I, Ley joined the National Socialist German Workers' Party (Nazi Party; Nationalsozialistische Deutsche Arbeiterpartei; NSDAP) in 1924 and quickly rose in the ranks while also serving as a Reichstag delegate. He was a brutish, temperamental man who augmented his party work and Reichstag duties with street brawling and vicious anti-Semitic attacks in the party press. Though he had no experience in either business management or with organized labor, Hitler put him charge of the new German Labor Front (Deutsche Arbeitsfront; DAF) in May 1933. Ley led the DAF, which became the regime's single largest mass civilian organization, until the end of the war.

He was able to consolidate and expand his power after the head of the party's labor brigade, the Factory Cell Organization, was gunned down in a bar fight and its "leftist" and socialist-oriented officials were pushed out after the Röhm purge. Ley proved to be a ruthless and highly ambitious administrator. Most important, he was an ideological fanatic whose loyalty to Hitler was absolute. Though he parroted Hitler's belief that workers were soldiers all serving the same "army"—the German nation—in practice, Ley ensured the DAF was business friendly. And thoroughly corrupt. With the possible exception of Hermann Göring, Ley was the single most corrupt official in the regime, and he and his minions enriched themselves at the expense of both

German business interests and especially ordinary workers.

Ley's portfolio also came to include creating a network of "Adolf Hitler schools." These were to be secondary schools run by and for **Hitler Youth** (Hitlerjugend; HJ) members and were to serve as a kind of feeder academy to party leadership positions, which would in turn send their graduates to Ordensburgen (Order Castles). Beginning in 1934, three Ordensburgen were created in Pomerania, the Rhineland, and Bavaria. Lacking in academic rigor, they emphasized physical exercise and ideological instruction. The demands of the war limited their further expansion.

The effects of severe head injuries he received in the First World War were greatly exacerbated by his alcoholism. Ley's increasingly bizarre and embarrassing behavior, which included drunkenly driving a car carrying the Duke and Duchess of Windsor through a factory gate, earned him only a warning from Hitler, which in any case Ley ignored. He held on to his post, though during the war, his power was siphoned away by Göring, **Heinrich Himmler**, and later **Albert Speer**. He had no influence on managing the **new order** in the West nor the imperial project in the East nor over the growing army of slave laborers brought to Germany.

Ley was arrested by American troops in the Bavarian Alps on 16 May 1945. He was indicted on three counts by the **International Military Tribunal** (IMT) but managed to hang himself in his jail cell before standing trial.

LINDBERGH, CHARLES (1902–1974). Lindbergh became a global celebrity after piloting the first nonstop solo trans-Atlantic flight in May 1927. An anti-Semite and isolationist, he moved with his family to England in 1935 and then to **France**. In 1936, the American military attaché in Berlin asked Lindbergh to evaluate the state of the new **Luftwaffe**, and **Hermann Göring** was perfectly happy to show off his new air force to the famous American. Lindbergh fawned over Göring's achievements, pronounced the Luftwaffe unbeatable, and advocated Anglo–French **appeasement**. Lindbergh and his wife, Anne, also attended the summer **Olympic Games** as Göring's guests and made two more trips to Germany before the war began. In October 1938, Göring presented Lindbergh with the Service Cross of the German Eagle on Hitler's behalf. Charles and Anne were planning to move to Berlin, though the **Night of Broken Glass** (Reichskristallnacht; 9–10 November 1938) seems to have changed their minds.

Upon his return to the **United States** in 1939, Lindbergh was still famous enough to get an in-person meeting with President **Franklin D. Roosevelt** but far too compromised to be reinstated as an active-duty Army Air Forces officer. Following the outbreak of the war in Europe, Lindbergh became the star speaker of the isolationist America First Committee and in a speech on 11 September 1941 blamed Great Britain, **Jews**, and Roosevelt for driving the United States into the war.

Though Roosevelt had blocked Lindbergh from service, Lindbergh's fellow Jew hater and isolationist Henry Ford had no such qualms about hiring him as a consultant, and Lindbergh spent much of the war improving the design of various fighter planes. With the support of admirers in the military, he slipped quietly into the Pacific theater in 1944 and flew more than 50 combat missions. Almost immediately after Roosevelt's death, Lindbergh was appointed to a US Navy commission charged with learning about new German aircraft technologies, and he continued to serve as a consultant to the US military into the 1950s.

He remained an unrepentant isolationist and never apologized for his pro-Nazi and anti-Semitic stances in the prewar years, in his memoirs going so far as to equate the **Holocaust** with the behavior of some American soldiers toward Japanese prisoners of war.

LIVING SPACE (LEBENSRAUM). In the early 1920s, Hitler was hardly alone among Europeans in believing—and hoping—the Bolshevik regime would not survive. He was encouraged in this belief by monarchist (White) Russian and **Baltic** German émigrés from the revolution, notably Erwin von Scheubner-Richter and **Alfred Rosenberg**. Following the collapse of the Bolshevik regime, Hitler thought the restored monarchy (with its Germanic roots) would make a powerful anti-Western Russo-German alliance possible. But when the Bolsheviks prevailed in the Russian Civil War and the regime seemed to stabilize, he abandoned this fantasy and in *Mein Kampf* took a radically different position, one that drew on a longer-standing ultranationalist fantasy of expanding Germany's territory in the East to create living space.

In the late 19th century, the **Pan-German** League had become the most vocal proponent of eastward expansion. The league and other Far-Right nationalists envisioned themselves as modern-day Teutonic knights who would "liberate" ethnic German communities from oppressive foreign rule and open up vast spaces for a growing German population. Hitler seems to have learned of living-space theorizing in the early 1920s and embraced it as the solution to a world in which the Bolshevik regime seemed here to stay.

From Hitler's perspective, Germany was not remotely as vast and rich in natural resources as the **United States**. Nor could it hope to possess a globe-spanning empire like Great Britain's. In Hitler's mind that left expansion within Europe as the only way to transform Germany into a self-sufficient world power. In typical fashion, he came to believe that obtaining living space was a matter of life or death for Germany.

The transformation in Hitler's thinking entailed characterizing Russia and **France** as Germany's mortal enemies and **Italy** and Britain as potential allies. Regarding Russia, his newfound animosity would deepen as **racism** and racialist anti-Semitism became central to his worldview. Indeed, the dream of eastward expansion dovetailed with the belief that the East was populated by "subhuman" Slavic peoples and **Jews**. The twinned obsession of race and space would drive his foreign policy and his leadership of the war effort. It also provided the strategic and ideological justification for the regime's murderous project of ethnic cleansing and reordering, a project that would come to include the **Holocaust**. *See also* GENERAL PLAN FOR THE EAST (GENERALPLAN OST); HIMMLER, HEINRICH (1900–1945); OPERATION BARBAROSSA (1941); SCHUTZSTAFFEL (PROTECTION SQUAD; SS); UKRAINE.

LUFTWAFFE (AIR FORCE). In the interwar years, everyone understood that the role of airpower would be decisive in any future great-power war. **World War I** had taught German military planners that the country could not hold out in a protracted war of attrition, so they focused on preparing to fight short, geographically limited campaigns in Europe. Essential to victory would be establishing air superiority as quickly as possible, mainly by destroying as much of the enemy's air force while it was still on the ground. With superiority achieved, airpower would then support ground forces in a series of fast-moving campaigns in which the operations of air and ground forces would be coordinated closely. The strategy, carried over into the Nazi period, precluded the development of airborne defense capabilities, with the military preferring to rely on ground-based anti-aircraft weapons.

Fortuitously for Hitler and the new Luftwaffe, the **Spanish Civil War** provided a uniquely valuable testing ground for new planes and pilots. The air superiority—close ground-air coordination—strategy worked remarkably well in the campaigns in **Poland** and Western Europe [*see* BLITZKRIEG (LIGHTNING WAR)]. The limitations were revealed in the failures in the **Battle of Britain** and the Blitz and in **Operation Barbarossa**. The ongoing war in the Soviet Union, combined with the British and American (*see* UNITED STATES OF AMERICA) ability to launch the **strategic bombing campaign** from bases in England, greatly reduced the Luftwaffe's size and capabilities. Making matters worse for the Germans was the underdeveloped state of the regime's ability to defend Germany in the air, though here the Luftwaffe proved capable of adapting to a fully defensive position quickly. Yet German wartime production—**Albert Speer**'s efforts notwithstanding—could not keep up with the capacity of the Americans and the Soviets to produce a seemingly endless supply of new (and superior) planes and pilots. Existing German models could not be upgraded quickly enough, and the development of jet fighters came far too late to affect the course of the war (*see* WONDER WEAPONS). Chronic fuel shortages were another major contributor to the Luftwaffe's declining effectiveness, a problem that plagued every dimension of Germany's increasingly desperate war effort.

The decisive blow against the Luftwaffe came in early 1944. The US Army Air Force had produced new, lighter-weight Mustang P51s equipped with supplemental fuel tanks. Superior to the now-outdated German Messerschmitts, the Mustangs could protect long-range bombers to a greater degree than ever before. One-third of the Luftwaffe's fighters were shot down in February alone. The following month, it lost half. Nearly all its fighter pilots were lost by May. Over a single week in February—the "big week" of air force lore—waves of US long-range bombers targeted German aircraft factories. Despite a doubling of aircraft production pulled off by Speer's armaments ministry, the Luftwaffe was no longer a significant factor in the war. *See also* GÖRING, HERMANN (1893–1946).

M

MADAGASCAR PLAN. From 1938 to the summer of 1940, the Foreign Ministry, Hitler, and the **Schutzstaffel** (Protection Squad; SS) eyed Madagascar as the most promising "solution" to the "**Jewish** problem." Since the beginning of his political career, Hitler had envisioned what he referred to in 1919 as the "uncompromising removal" of Jews from Germany. As he pushed the country toward war, he intensified the regime's efforts to push Germany's Jews out, mainly through a nationwide pogrom, the ensuing incarceration of thousands of Jewish men in **concentration camps**, and the acceleration of Aryanization [see ECONOMY; GÖRING, HERMANN (1893–1946)].

The idea of deporting European Jews to colonies was not new. It was probably German anti-Semitic writer Paul de Lagarde who first proposed Madagascar as a supposedly ideal destination in 1885, and it was debated extensively among European—especially **French**—colonial officials, anti-Semites, and Jews. French forces seized the island in 1895. While 13 were killed in combat in the 10-month campaign, nearly 6,000 succumbed to malaria and other tropical diseases. Following the conquest, colonial officials were incapable of controlling the spread of malaria among the European and non-European populations alike, so settling large numbers of French colonists on the island along the lines of Algeria was out of the question. A parallel development of signal importance was an influential though contested theory among European scientists and missionaries that the Malagasy were descendants of Jews. It was this idea that de Lagarde picked up on and popularized among anti-Semites, while some European Zionists embraced it, as well, albeit with somewhat different objectives in mind.

Combined with such ethnographic and religious quackery was the belief, one not limited to anti-Semites, that as "rootless" and "cosmopolitan," Jews could adapt to environments unsuitable to non-Jews. These currents, however, had some serious political pull, and in the late 1930s, the pro-**appeasement** French foreign minister and the anti-Semitic **Polish** government opened negotiations on resettling 7,000 Jewish families on the island. Deeply anti-Semitic French colonial officials succeeded in scuttling what was the first Madagascar plan.

It is unclear exactly how Hitler, the SS, and Foreign Ministry officials became fixated on Madagascar as opposed to some other non-European destination for "solving" the "Jewish question." Regardless of how, Hitler took up the idea enthusiastically. Increasingly anxious to remove Jews from Germany, **Joseph Goebbels** reported him insisting in April 1938 on negotiations with Poland and **Romania** about settling Jews in Madagascar. But the idea took on renewed urgency—and the possibility of actually being implemented—in the early summer of 1940 following the defeat of France and the expected capitulation of Great Britain. SS officials and the section of the Foreign Ministry responsible for Jewish affairs drew up plans to deport as many as 6.5 million Jews over a four-year period to the island, where it was presumed they would eventually perish. Assets stolen from the deportees would pay for the costs of resettlement.

The island's new settlement would be run by the SS and overseen by officials involved in the **Euthanasia Program**. Removing Jews from Germany and Europe was the most important objective of the scheme. Another other was to influence the actions of the **United States**, which Nazi officials assumed was controlled by Jews. With millions of Jews being in effect held hostage on Madagascar, the Americans could be deterred from entering the war.

The seriousness with which the regime took the plan is evinced not only by the flurry of planning activity but also by the fact that beginning after the armistice with France in June 1940, around 23,000 Jews from Alsace and Lorraine (reannexed to Germany) were deported to southern France, where they would presumably soon be transported to Madagascar. Also notable is that in July, Hitler ordered the deportation of Polish Jews to the General Government in Poland halted.

The plan had to be shelved in August, as it became clear that Britain was not going to leave the war, though regime officials continued to fantasize about realizing the plan until early 1942. That November, a British expeditionary force succeeded in taking control of the island, but by that point the possibility of a "territorial final solution" had already been superseded by mass executions and then gas chambers in the German-occupied East. Once again, the unforeseen course of the war determined the course of the **Holocaust**. *See also* BATTLE OF EL-ALAMEIN (1942).

MANSTEIN, ERICH VON (1887–1973). Contemporaries and historians alike have considered Manstein to be the **Wehrmacht**'s greatest general. He became an officer in 1906 and served on the western and eastern fronts in **World War I**. He remained in the Reichswehr, led the army general staff's operation section from 1935 to 1938, and served as **Gerd von Rundstedt**'s chief of staff during the invasion of **Poland**.

Manstein's first great success was to plan the daring attack on **France** through the heavily wooded Ardennes region of southern Belgium and then to lead the first German force to cross the Seine River. Hitler rewarded him with promotion to field marshal. In **Operation Barbarossa**, he led the German drive to the outskirts of **Leningrad** before being transferred to the Southeast, where his forces captured the Crimea. Hitler dispatched him to relieve the surrounded German Sixth Army at the **Battle of Stalingrad**, and while Manstein was too late, he did manage to temporarily stabilize this sector of the eastern front. But Hitler found his preference for staging tactical retreats to draw the enemy into traps unbearable, and the two clashed repeatedly over strategy. Hitler finally relieved him in March 1944, and Manstein retired to his East Prussian estate.

Like all other high-level commanders, Manstein was complicit in the Wehrmacht's war crimes and in the **Holocaust**. Though he argued constantly with Hitler, he remained loyal in the sense that he never joined the **opposition** and fought the war to the greatest extent of his considerable abilities. And like all other officers at his level, he accepted bribes from Hitler.

Having been forced to flee his estate, Manstein was arrested by British troops in August 1945 while convalescing in a hospital in Schleswig-Holstein. He then became one of the most influential architects of the myth of the "clean Wehrmacht," beginning with a long-written apologia prepared for the defense at the **International Military Tribunal** (IMT) and culminating with his 1955 war memoirs.

Manstein was tried by a British court in Hamburg in the second half of 1949, convicted on 9 of 17 charges related to the executions of prisoners of war and civilians and for coordinating with **Schutzstaffel** (Protection Squad; SS) mobile execution units. His 18-year sentence was reduced to 12 years in 1950, and he was released three years later, in part for health reasons but also because he had many influential allies inside and outside Germany, including West German chancellor Konrad Adenauer, **Winston Churchill**, and several well-known British military historians. The Cold War and the pressing question of West German rearmament also made keeping such a highly regarded former officer in prison impossible.

Immediately following his release, Manstein began consulting on the formation of a West German army. In 1955, he published his memoir, *Verlorene Siege* (*Lost Victories*), which became a best-seller and was translated into multiple languages. In 1958, he published a second volume—*Aus einem Soldatenleben* (*A Soldier's Life*)—covering the early years of his career. While contemporary historians still acknowledge Manstein's abilities as a field officer, they consider the memoir to be an unreliable, self-serving exercise in whitewashing his own record and that of the Wehrmacht. He died in Munich in 1973.

MAY, KARL (1842–1912). The German pulp fiction writer Karl May wrote more than 30 books set in the western **United States** telling stories of White settlers battling Native Americans. His two best-known characters are Winnetou, an Apache chief, and Old Shatterhand, a German immigrant. His first Winnetou–Old Shatterhand novel was published in 1893, late in May's life. They became wildly popular and continue to shape—for better and worse—popular perceptions of Native Americans in Germany.

Like thousands of other German-speaking boys, Hitler began reading May's books as a boy, and they seem to have made a lifelong impression on him. Unlike most, he never quite outgrew May's influence or at least a longing for the thrill devouring his books gave him. May's adventure stories informed Hitler's fantasies of an empire in the "wild East" of Europe, though it is difficult to discern precisely to what extent relative to other influences. According to **Albert Speer**, the stories may have taught him that it was not necessary to travel to a place to know what you need to know about it. A recollection from someone who knew Hitler in his **Vienna** days supports Speer's observation. When it was revealed that May, by then a celebrity, had never visited the places he wrote about, Hitler considered it unimportant because as a genius, May's depictions were "true to nature."

Much later, the stories may have influenced the way Hitler acted as a **military commander**. During the Second World War, he allegedly encouraged his generals to read May for inspiration and had 300,000 copies of the novel *Winnetou* printed (despite a shortage of paper) for distribution to German soldiers. Speer also recalled him rereading May's novels to lift his spirits as the war effort stalled.

May's longer-term influence on Hitler should not be overstated. Certainly, there were aspects of the Winnetou–Old Shatterhand adventures that he ignored. May's wildly inaccurate depictions of Native Americans romanticized them as "noble savages." Yet as poorly as he understood it, May admired Native American culture and expressly criticized White settler imperialism. And while Hitler supposedly praised Winnetou as a model company leader and even a "noble human being," his conception of Slavs as a "subhuman race" destined to be replaced by German farmer-warriors bore no relationship to May's distorted but sympathetic portrayal of Native American peoples.

Nor did Hitler seem to care or even remember that May was a pacifist. In Vienna in March 1912, he attended a lecture given by May in which the writer celebrated peace. Hitler is not known to have voiced any objections to a pacifist position he did not share. But he supposedly praised May's conjuring of a world divided clearly between "Ardistan," where the low and ignoble dwell, and "Djinnistan," the home of the pure and noble. May claimed that through his own efforts and despite the fact that many people stood in his way, he had reached "Djinnistan" and was at peace with himself. Ten days after the lecture, May died suddenly, the news of which allegedly saddened the young Hitler deeply.

MAYR, KARL (1883–1945). As an ambitious right-wing Reichswehr captain and counterintelligence officer in Munich after the collapse of the **Bavarian Soviet Republic** in May 1919, Mayr cultivated a then directionless Hitler as an anti-Bolshevist propagandist among returning soldiers. He was also responsible for Hitler's first contact with the **German Workers' Party** (Deutsche Arbeiterpartei; DAP).

The Far Right in postwar Bavaria was comprised of a fractious, loosely interconnected network of individuals and groups comprised of veterans; active-duty soldiers and officers; members of paramilitary groups; state officials; and a smattering of workers, journalists, and intellectuals. For a brief but crucial period, Mayr played a dual role in this network: He used his position to shape the political views of returning soldiers, and he farmed out reliable agents—Hitler being one of them—to monitor and influence right-wing groups like the DAP.

Between the fall of the Bavarian Soviet Republic and the restoration of civilian government in August 1919, the Reichswehr was in control of Munich and Bavaria. Mayr, then a captain, headed a counterintelligence unit tasked with monitoring the population for signs of the kind of popular uprising that produced the republic. He took note of Hitler's work on a commission investigating the behavior of soldiers and put his name on a list of potential agents who could be relied on to spread anti-Bolshevist messages and promote nationalism among the troops. This assignment required Hitler to take a training course, organized by Mayr, in July. Hitler attended lectures by conservative nationalist historian Karl Alexander von Müller and the **pan-German** engineer and amateur **economist Gottfried Feder**, whose attempt to link capitalism with supposed **Jewish** control of financial markets left a strong impression on him and informed the initial ideological orientation of the **National Socialist German Workers'** Party (Nazi Party; Nationalsozialistische Deutsche Arbeiterpartei; NSDAP).

It was apparently Müller who brought Hitler's potential as an effective agitator to Mayr's attention, and he subsequently assigned him as an instructor in anti-Bolshevik "classes" held in August at a makeshift Reichswehr camp in Lechfeld. It was here that Hitler recognized his own abilities as a public speaker. It was also in this capacity that he first conveyed in a quasi-public setting his emergent anti-Jewish worldview, the basic ideas of which he drew from Feder's lectures and the wider culture of conspiratorial anti-Semitism that was becoming pervasive in Munich in the wake of the Bavarian Soviet Republic.

On 12 September, Mayr ordered Hitler to attend a meeting of the DAP, most likely with an eye to exerting influence over it by having one of his best speakers join. At that meeting—one of the guest lecturers happened to be Feder—Hitler launched into a tirade against Bavarian separatism and in favor of a greater Germany and was approached by DAP leader Anton Drexler, who urged Hitler to consider working closely with the party. Hitler accepted the offer in less than a week.

The timing was felicitous. Hitler had just been rebuffed by the right-wing German Socialist Party as a contributor to its newspaper, the *Völkischer Beobachter*. He was seeking a political home in the aftermath of the ratification by the German government of the **Versailles Treaty**, and the DAP offered one in which Hitler could exert immediate influence.

Mayr's career as a behind-the-scenes promoter of the Far-Right's agenda was probably cut short by his determination to support a coup attempt led by Wolfgang Kapp [*see* KAPP PUTSCH (1920)] in Berlin in March 1920. He did so in defiance of General Arnold von Möhl, the de facto ruler of Bavaria, who was unwilling to support Kapp. In July, Mayr left the Reichswehr, possibly purged by Möhl. Indeed, Hitler's demobilization at the end of March may have been part of a move by Möhl to sideline Mayr and his allies after the Kapp fiasco.

Determined to remain an influential player on the Far Right, Mayr joined the NSDAP. Now he had become dependent on Hitler, his most important contact in the party. But by that point, Hitler had little use for his former superior officer. He had already distanced himself from Mayr and gravitated toward another prominent ideologue, **Dietrich Eckart**. Mayr left the party in March 1921 and then moved away from the radical Right entirely. He joined the **Social Democratic Party of Germany** (Sozialdemokratische Partei Deutschlands; SPD) in 1924 and its paramilitary wing, the Reichsbanner, and became an outspoken critic of Hitler and the NSDAP in articles for the SPD paper *Münchener Post*, where he also advocated Franco–German rapprochement. He fled to **France** in 1933 and lived quietly outside Paris until 1940, when he was arrested by the

Gestapo. Mayr was ultimately sent to Buchenwald and was forced to work in a munitions plant in Weimar. He was killed in a British air raid on 9 February 1945.

MEIN KAMPF (MY STRUGGLE). *Mein Kampf* is the single most important statement of Hitler's worldview and of his self-fashioning as the man destined to lead Germany back to greatness from the debacle of November 1918. He wrote the book during and after his brief imprisonment in **Landsberg Prison** [*see* BEER HALL PUTSCH 1923)]. He did not dictate the passages written in prison, as is often claimed, but typed them. The original title was *4½ Years of Struggle against Lies, Stupidity and Cowardice*. The intended audience was not every German but members of the **National Socialist German Workers' Party** (Nazi Party; Nationalsozialistische Deutsche Arbeiterpartei; NSDAP) who might be tempted to challenge his position or at least look to others for leadership. Only later would party propagandists attempt to give it canonical status for all Germans.

Mein Kampf was published in two volumes by the Franz Eher Verlag, the Nazi Party's publishing house, in 1925 and 1926. In the first, Hitler recounts his life to 1920. Shot through with distortions, half-truths, omissions, and outright falsehoods, it is not an accurate account of his early years. Rather, Hitler fashioned a story of an idealistic, highly intelligent boy and young man who learns how the world really works. His destiny to become a politician is finally revealed to him when he learns of Germany's capitulation in November 1918. Hitler also wrote this part of the book with more immediate and concrete political objectives in mind: to create something heroic from his rather unremarkable wartime service and to cover up his rank opportunism in the months after the armistice and not least his dalliance with the Munich Soviet in 1919.

The second volume is mainly an assemblage of political statements drawn extensively from his many speeches of the previous years. Yet it marks a significant change in his thinking about gaining power—a coup d'etat was now out of the question—and securing for Germany an unassailable position in Europe. He abandoned the idea of an alliance with an imagined post-Bolshevik Russia and embraced the idea of expanding Germany's Lebensraum (**living space**) into the vast expanses of the East. Also made clear is the centrality of race to his view of humanity (*see* RACISM).

The "Jewish question" is a prominent theme in both volumes. Since 1945, much attention has been paid to a sentence in which Hitler appears to predict the **Holocaust** by fantasizing about the gassing of **Jews**. In making this statement, Hitler was musing that killing a minority of Germany's Jews during **World War I** would have persuaded the rest to stop trying to sabotage the war effort, as he and many other anti-Semites falsely believed German Jews had done. But the prominence this statement has been given has overshadowed the numerous other references to the inevitability of a life-or-death conflict between Jews and the rest of the world and to the repeated use of terms like *eradication* and *extermination*.

Though the first print run of volume 1 sold out, sales of both were weak in the second half of the 1920s. Sales surged in 1930 with the party's electoral breakthrough and with the appearance of a cheap one-volume version. It became a national best-seller in 1933 and until 1945 was translated into 18 languages. It made Hitler a wealthy man. [*See* AMANN, MAX (1891–1957)].

Individual Germans were not required by law to buy the book, though libraries and schools were obliged to do so, and couples married in civil ceremonies were presented with copies by their officiators. After the war, the Allies authorized the Bavarian state government to hold the copyright. One of Germany's most prestigious institutes of historical research, the Institute for Contemporary History in Munich, prepared a heavily annotated version for publication when the copyright expired at the end of 2015.

MILITARY COMMANDER. One of the most durable postwar myths regarding Hitler was that he was an utterly incompetent military commander, a leader whose grandiose ambitions were undermined by his fanaticism, indecisiveness, and incessant meddling. That the source of this myth is the regime's surviving military leadership should not be surprising. Anxious to redeem themselves after a second lost war and, not least, avoid prosecution for war crimes and crimes against humanity, former officers directed all the blame to Hitler (and occasionally each other). Their main platforms were the Nuremberg trials, their memoirs, and their contributions to the US Army's massive series of studies on the German war effort. The fact that these same officers obeyed nearly every one of his orders to the very end and otherwise did everything they could to realize his imperial fantasies did not stop several generations of armchair generals and gullible historians from believing the myth.

Like all such myths, this one blends elements of truth, falsehood, and omission. Hitler had certain strengths as a military strategist. His instincts for bold offensive operations could pay off, no more so than in his enthusiastic support for **Erich von Manstein**'s plan to attack **France** through the Ardennes Forest in 1940. He was also highly attuned to the potential of mechanized warfare. And there was a period in which he was willing to give field officers considerable latitude, particularly in the opening months of **Operation Barbarossa**. Indeed, if Hitler was as completely inept as his generals claimed after 1945, then Germany's numerous victories through 1941 become difficult to explain. It certainly helped, of course, that Germany's opponents in these years were taken by surprise, overwhelmed, or led poorly.

That said, Hitler's liabilities far outweighed his strengths. He had no professional training and therefore little appreciation for the enormous complexities of modern military operations. Making himself supreme commander of the armed forces in 1938 precluded the creation of a professional command staff that could coordinate the operations of the three branches [*see* BLOMBERG–FRITSCH AFFAIR (1938); LUFTWAFFE (AIR FORCE); WEHRMACHT]. Because it was he alone who shaped German strategy, his unshakable belief in the infallibility of his own instincts and capabilities proved to be a fatal liability. His fixation on constantly taking the offensive and never retreating had truly disastrous consequences, as did his growing propensity to intervene even at the tactical level. The former characteristic was particularly dangerous after the **Battle of Stalingrad**, when Germany was on the defensive everywhere. The latter stands in sharp contrast to his style of domestic political leadership, which prioritized delegation and the expectation that loyal subordinates would "work toward the Führer," as one Agricultural Ministry official put it in 1934. Added to all this was his willingness to keep blindly loyal but subpar commanders in their posts when far more competent (but independent-minded) choices were available. *See also* HALDER, FRANZ VON (1884–1972); JODL, ALFRED (1890–1946); KEITEL WILHELM (1882–1946); RUNDSTEDT, GERD VON (1875–1953).

MUSSOLINI, BENITO (1883–1945). From the earliest years of his career as a politician, Hitler admired Mussolini for his successes in seizing power and creating a dictatorship. In the early 1920s, the **National Socialist German Workers' Party** (Nazi Party; Nationalsozialistische Deutsche Arbeiterpartei; NSDAP) mimicked multiple practices of the **Italian** Fascist Party, such as the straight-right-arm salute and its response (right arm raised but bent at the elbow) and the practice of using standards to bear flags and banners. Mussolini's 1922 March on Rome was the single most important inspiration for Hitler's **Beer Hall Putsch** [*see* ATATÜRK, MUSTAFA KEMAL (1881–1937). The leader cult being built up around the Italian dictator also prompted Hitler and his most fervent party supporters to transform the meaning of the term *leader* (*Führer*) from a matter-of-fact description of Hitler's position in the party to the quasi-mystical dimension of Hitler as *the* leader of Germany. After 1933, several prominent domestic programs of the Nazi regime were modeled on those of fascist Italy, notably the Strength through Joy recreational program for workers and the national highway system [Autobahn; *see* ECONOMY; GERMAN LABOR FRONT (DEUTSCHE ARBEITSFRONT; DAF); REARMAMENT].

In drawing up plans for the conquest and settlement of Eastern Europe, numerous Nazi officials studied fascist Italian colonial practices in Libya and Ethiopia. It was not, however, inevitable that Italy under Mussolini's fascist regime and Germany under Hitler's would become allies. In the 1920s, Mussolini and other Italian fascists did not think much of the Nazi Party, and there were strategic reasons to distrust German nationalists of any stripe. **Austria**'s majority German-speaking South Tyrol region had been transferred to Italy after **World War I**, and Mussolini pursued an aggressive policy of Italianization, to the intense displeasure of even moderate German nationalists. More worrisome for Mussolini was the prospect of a unified Germany and Austria.

But Hitler, alone among prominent Far-Right leaders, dismissed the need to "recover" the South Tyrol. As he saw it, Italy's biggest problem was **France**, not Germany, and conflict over the tiny region was not worth preventing the formation of an Italo-German alliance. The question of Austro-German unification was another matter. A "greater Germany" was, after all, the first demand in the **Nazi Party Program** (25-Point Program). In 1933, Hitler dispatched **Hermann Göring** to Rome to assure Mussolini that while unification was inevitable at some point, it would not take place anytime soon. In his first meeting with the Italian leader in June 1934, Hitler reassured him that he knew he could not pursue annexation at that moment but then approved of a plot by Austrian Nazis to attempt a coup in **Vienna** in July. It was a fiasco, in part because Mussolini backed the Austrian government from the start. He also deployed troops to the Austrian border in case Hitler missed the point. Though he denied any involvement in the coup attempt, Hitler had suffered a humiliating diplomatic setback. Progress toward an alliance was temporarily derailed.

Hitler recovered quickly from this setback and became steadily bolder, his public statements about desiring peace in Europe notwithstanding. He was not intimidated by the signing in May 1935 of a Franco–Soviet Mutual Assistance Treaty designed to deter German aggression in Eastern Europe. A month later, his foreign minister negotiated a bilateral **Anglo–German Naval Agreement** with Great Britain on terms surprisingly favorable to Germany. Italy's invasion of Ethiopia in October 1935 offered Hitler the chance to repair the damage done by the Austrian coup attempt. The brutal attack revealed both the weakness of the **League of Nations**, which did little more than denounce the invasion, and the hollowness of the Stresa Front, an informal agreement between Italy, France, and Britain to guarantee Germany's western borders and Austria's independence.

With Hitler emboldened and Mussolini now relatively isolated, the two leaders drew together in the second half of the 1930s. Mussolini began to retreat from his previously steadfast defense of Austrian independence. His denunciation of the Stresa Front further encouraged Hitler to plan and carry out the remilitarization of the **Rhineland** in March 1936. The two dictators then agreed to support General **Francisco Franco** and the nationalists in the **Spanish Civil War**. On 1 November, Mussolini proclaimed the creation of a "Rome-Berlin Axis."

A year later, after signing on to the **Anti-Comintern Pact** with Germany and **Japan**, Mussolini visited Germany and came away awestruck by the spectacle carefully staged for him by Hitler. The Italian fascist regime became increasingly imitative of Nazi Germany—notably in its implementation of brutal anti-**Jewish** measures—apparently in an effort not to be outdone ideologically. But the seeming dynamism of Hitler's Germany and the fact that he went ahead with the annexation of Austria in March 1938 without securing Mussolini's explicit approval in advance made it clear that his partnership with Hitler was not remotely one of equals.

Fascist Italy's ideologically subordinate status in the domestic sphere was replicated on a disastrous scale during the war: The regime's interests, like those of Germany's other allies and collaborators, would be subordinated to Hitler's. In the last years of the 1930s, Mussolini and Italian military officials had become reluctant to keep pace with Hitler's accelerating diplomatic revolution and march to war.

It was Mussolini who played peacemaker in the crisis over the Sudetenland and **Czechslovakia** in the fall of 1938. He had no success a year later, when he offered to play a similar role in the face of the imminent invasion of **Poland**.

As a military ally to Germany, fascist Italy was of little value. Italian forces did poorly against the Anglo–Indian and British–allied **African** forces in Africa. Indeed, a string of major Italian defeats in the Mediterranean Sea, Egypt, Abyssinia, Eritrea, and Somaliland in late 1940 through the spring of 1941 permanently damaged the two leaders' relationship. In southeastern Europe, where Mussolini expected to exert dominance, German interests prevailed. To right what he considered an intolerable imbalance in the region, Italian forces invaded Greece in October 1940, a fiasco that required a German bailout, followed by an unstable division of the **Balkans** into Italian and German spheres (*see* BULGARIA). By May 1943, Axis forces in North Africa had been routed. The Allied invasion of Sicily in July (Operation Husky) provoked Mussolini's overthrow by the normally supine Grand Council of Fascism and imprisonment. Despite all this, Hitler remained loyal to his former idol: He had Mussolini rescued by **Schutzstaffel** (Protection Squad; SS) commandos and installed as a puppet dictator of the short-lived **Italian Social Republic** (Republic of Salò) in northeastern Italy.

Mussolini's example would influence Hitler to the end of his life: His decision to commit **suicide** in the bunker and have his remains burned may have been bolstered by news of Mussolini's fate. On 28 April 1945, Mussolini and his mistress were executed by Italian partisans. Their bullet-ridden corpses were strung up outside a gas station in Milan. If Hitler indeed knew about this, then it could only have intensified his desire to avoid a similar fate.

Hitler and Benito Mussolini, Rome, 1938. *Courtesy of Bridgeman Images.*

N

NATIONAL SOCIALIST GERMAN WORKERS' PARTY (NAZI PARTY; NATIONALSOZIALISTISCHE DEUTSCHE ARBEITERPARTEI; NSDAP). On 24 February 1920, Hitler announced the renaming of the **German Workers' Party** (Deutsche Arbeiterpartei; DAP) to Nationalsozialistische Deutsche Arbeiterpartei and the **Nazi Party Program** (25-Point Program). Its members would not use the term *Nazi*, a derogatory contraction that probably emerged in the 1920s as a counter to *Sozi*, referring to Social Democrats [see SOCIAL DEMOCRATIC PARTY OF GERMANY (SOZIALDEMOKRATISCHE PARTEI DEUTSCHLANDS; SPD)]. In October, the party's paramilitary wing, the **Sturmabteilung** (Stormtroopers; SA), was formed. Two months later, it purchased what would be its official newspaper, *Völkischer Beobachter*. Hitler became the party's sole leader in July 1921, when its executive committee was disbanded.

The NSDAP's pre-1933 history can be divided into two distinct periods. The first ran from 1920 through 1924, and the second, from 1925 to 1933. In the first, the small, obscure party struggled to raise its profile amid the welter of Far-Right groups in Munich and Bavaria. The failed **Beer Hall Putsch** in 1923 and Hitler's subsequent **trial** was the turning point. The trial made Hitler a national figure, and he decided while in **Landsberg Prison** that the party would pursue a legal route to power. In the second half of the 1920s, the party built itself up at the national level and resisted being drawn into large Far-Right "fronts." Parallel to the legal path to power was intensifying violence, much of it initiated by the SA. Here, Hitler's authority was less absolute than it was over the party. But the SA was a necessary tool of recruitment and for maintaining ideological militancy within the "movement."

The party built on a nationwide local-level mobilization that had its roots in the experience of **World War I**, when millions of Germans entered either military service or a kind of home-front mobilization and widely shared sacrifice that cut across regional, confessional, and class lines. The NSDAP funded itself mainly through membership fees, small donations, the sales of newspapers and pamphlets (the party maintained its own publishing house), and fees to hear Hitler speak. With very few exceptions, Germany's business elite did not support Hitler or the party before 1933.

Though the Nazi Party remained on the political fringes until 1930, it drew members and voters from a surprisingly wide range of German society. Support was strongest among lower-middle-class Protestants living in smaller cities and towns or in rural areas: small business owners, shopkeepers, craftsmen, farmers, and other agricultural workers. But the party made significant inroads among workers. To be sure, most industrial workers remained committed to either the SPD or the **Communist Party of Germany** (Kommunistische Partei Deutschlands; KPD). By the early 1930s, however, about one out of four workers were voting Nazi. The party also made significant gains among middle- and upper-class professionals: engineers, architects, doctors, lawyers, and civil servants. It attempted, with marginal success, to appeal to **women** voters, who got the right to vote after World War I. Many university students (then overwhelmingly male) were increasingly drawn to the party and the SA. Attracting politically engaged Catholics was more difficult: They had their own party—the **Center Party** (Zentrum).

For a brief period in the mid-1920s, the **German National Peoples' Party** (Deutschnationale Volkspartei; DNVP) would become the largest conservative nationalist party, winning 20 percent of the vote in May 1924 **elections**. But it could not hold that position. It had no cross-class appeal and lacked the kind of local organizational presence that the NSDAP was building rapidly. For a growing number of Germans from various backgrounds, the Nazis could be counted on to oppose Marxist socialism and revolutionary communism and at the same time offer the prospect of national renewal. Renewal would take place across classes and along ethnoracialist lines, and it would restore Germany to greatness. No other party could offer this combination. The Left wanted class conflict, not national unification. All other parties were narrowly focused and associated with the prewar period. And no other party had a leader like Hitler.

The NSDAP had almost 850,000 members in January 1933. That number increased dramatically over the following months, leading long-term members to refer to newcomers as "March violets." New memberships in the party were blocked after 1 May, though Germans could still join the SA and auxiliary organizations, and millions did, though it should also be remembered that these auxiliaries absorbed the members of competing groups as the latter were banned. Germans joined the party and its organizations voluntarily or quasi-voluntarily for a variety of reasons. One was material: Membership could be helpful to an individual's career, and in some cases belonging to a party-sponsored association was required to work legally. Some, particularly the young and idealistic, supported the regime's ideologies and goals and wanted to contribute to the creation of a true Volksgemeinschaft (people's community). Another was social, in the sense that belonging offered at least some of the comradeship and association formerly provided by the country's many independent associations and clubs.

Beginning in 1933, Hitler built up party institutions that paralled and thus duplicated the funcations of many state ministries [*see* LEADERSHIP PRINCIPLE (FÜHRERPRINZIP)]. The duplication was extended across the country. During the 1920s, the party divided Germany into districts for the purposes of building up the party and election campaigns. The term for these districts was *Gaue*, a word going back to the days of the Holy Roman Empire. Beginning in 1933, Hitler maintained the Gaue system. He appointed Gauleiter (regional leaders) to each Gau to represent the party at the local level. These leaders in turn appointed subordinates throughout their districts—to towns, villages, or neighborhoods in larger cities.

This system had the effect of turning local governments—which continued to exist—into rubber stamps. It also meant that there were party officials all over the place. Some were reasonably competent, while many others were corrupt party hacks. Many ordinary Germans came to resent their presence and tried to avoid dealing with them as much as possible.

Reich ministers and supreme Reich authorities all answered to Hitler directly, so these subordinates competed with each other for resources, more power, and—especially—access to the leader. Hitler would often intervene to settle a dispute and, of course, to reassert his authority. As one of Hitler's biographers argued, Hitler was the crucial integrative figure whose authority (backed as it was by a fearsome security apparatus) held the system together until his **suicide**.

By May 1945, the party had 8 million members, or 1 out of every 10 Germans. The Allies abolished the party and its affiliated organizations and by chance captured its membership records intact. These became an essential source for denazification and postwar trials and, not least, historical research.

NATIONAL SOCIALIST WELFARE ORGANIZATION (NATIONALSOZIALISTISCHE VOLKSWOHLFAHRT; NSV). In Germany, the tradition of state-sponsored welfare provisions dates back to the imperial period (1871–1918). It was Chancellor **Otto von Bismarck** who pioneered the world's first comprehensive system of state welfare. Shared sacrifices and losses experienced during **World War I** had also revealed to millions of Germans the unifying possibilities of mutual support across class lines. The constitution of the Weimar Republic, moreover, included guarantees of generous welfare benefits. Indeed, it was the failure of the state to meet these obligations in the early 1930s that precipitated the political deadlock that resulted in Hitler's appointment as **chancellor**.

The official **Nazi Party Program** (25-Point Program) of the **National Socialist German Workers' Party** (Nazi Party; Nationalsozialistische Deutsche Arbeiterpartei; NSDAP) was thus hardly original in listing several demands for the provision of various forms of state-sponsored aid, though these were to be restricted to members of the Volksgemeinschaft (people's community). The matter became more pressing as the Great Depression hit the country and the NSDAP became the single largest party in the **Reichstag**. The NSV was created as a Berlin-based party-affiliated organization in April 1932. Two months later, Hitler ordered that every one of the party's regions sponsor an NSV branch.

When he became chancellor, the NSV took over nearly all independent welfare associations. The exceptions were those affiliated with the Christian churches or those sponsored by the Red Cross [see COORDINATION (GLEICHSCHALTUNG); RELIGION]. But another important exception was the popular Winterhilfswerk (Winter Help Works; WHW), which fell under the authority of the Propaganda Ministry. The WHW was more than an empty propaganda tool. It attracted thousands of volunteers. Even **Heinrich Himmler** ordered policemen and members of the **Schutzstaffel** (Protection Squad; SS) and Gestapo to do their part. The WHW collected more than 1 billion Reichsmarks and operated for the entire period of Nazi rule.

The NSV's leader proclaimed that his organization existed only to help "healthy" Germans make it through a period of crisis, after which they would be expected to return to work. Yet with more than 14 million members by 1939, the NSV became one of the largest party-sponsored organizations. And its aid and outreach activities were not miserly. Its workers and volunteers fed thousands of unemployed and destitute Germans. It hired tens of thousands of nurses, midwives, family counselors, and kindergarten teachers. The NSV sponsored rural outings and even trips abroad for hundreds of thousands of children. There is a considerable amount of evidence—from supporters and opponents of the regime alike—that the work of the NSV and WHW was highly effective in generating a sense of cross-class solidarity and mutual care, especially among young and idealistic Germans. But the seriousness and meaningfulness of these programs for the social consensus behind the regime were undercut by the fact that they became two of the largest cesspools of corruption.

NAZI PARTY PROGRAM (25-POINT PROGRAM). For a year after its founding in January 1919, the **German Workers' Party** (Deutsche Arbeiterpartei; DAP) had no formal, written program. To raise the tiny party's profile in Munich's crowded Far-Right scene and to expand its membership, its executive committee wrote a program and schemed to present it unannounced and dramatically to a large audience at the Hofbräuhaus beer hall on 24 February 1920. This was also the occasion in which the party's new name was revealed: the **National Socialist German Workers' Party** (Nazi Party; Nationalsozialistische Deutsche Arbeiterpartei; NSDAP). Hitler was the one who read out the program. In *Mein Kampf*, he proclaimed that it was greeted with rapturous and unanimous approval, which was not in fact the case. Also untrue was his boast that it was the moment when a new nationalist fire had been ignited, a fire that would someday "free" Germany and avenge the humiliation of November 1918 [see "STAB IN THE BACK" LEGEND (DOLCHSTOSSLEGENDE)].

Though the city's major newspapers paid little attention to the event, it does appear that Hitler's characteristically theatrical performance heightened public interest in him as a speaker. The identity of the program's principal author remains unclear, but it almost certainly was not Hitler [see ECKART, DIETRICH (1863–1923); FEDER, GOTTFRIED (1883–1941)]. It contains 25 points and is exclusively national in orientation on every one of them. This was a matter of some significance for a party based in a German state with a strong separatist tradition, and the program ends with the demand for a strong central government, in case anyone missed the point. The first five call for the creation of a "greater Germany"; the rejection of the **Versailles Treaty**; the expansion of Lebensraum (**living space**) for food and settlement; a citizenship **law** based on **race**, in which **Jews** were to be excluded; and "guest only" status for any non-Germans in Germany. The only other mention of Jews is in point 24, which implicitly rejects Judaism and "Jewish materialism," though some of the anticapitalist points are implicitly anti-Semitic. In advance of May 1928 **Reichstag elections**, when Hitler hoped to draw more votes in rural areas, he amended a vaguely worded point (number 17) on land reform to target Jewish businesses that had speculated on land and thus acquired it "illicitly."

Most of the remainder present demands for the creation of a kind of socialism. Point 7 proclaims that the state's first duty was to provide for the well-being of its citizens, with specific calls for a new national education system, provisions for the elderly, and state assistance for mothers. Others reject the individualism of liberalism and free-market capitalism. Though the program calls for government officials to be appointed on the basis of qualifications and for equality before the law, it also stresses the duties of individuals and, notably, prioritizes the "general good" over the needs and desires of the individual. Roman law is rejected as "materialist" and was to be replaced by "German law." There is a call for **religious** freedom and a pledge not to favor any denomination. Most of the others are aggressively anticapitalist: the confiscation of interest income and war profits, the nationalization of large-scale business trusts, profit sharing in major industries, an undefined reform of land ownership; and a ban on speculation on land. The state would also privilege small businesses and tradespersons over large department stores.

The program remained the party's official platform until May 1945. Hitler would state repeatedly that it was a "guiding" document, the expression of an idea rather than something to be taken literally. This position gave him a kind of cover to be selectively flexible while at the same time insisting that the program could never be changed. On certain matters, such as a race-based definition of citizenship that excluded Jews or the demand for a greater Germany or the rejection of the Versailles Treaty, there could be no compromise. Others, above all the most strident anticapitalist demands, could be ignored or discarded outright, as they eventually were. Even with an expanding state role in the **economy**, private property remained intact. But in the 1920s, if Hitler could be selective about some of the program's points, then so could others, and the anticapitalist points were the most controversial within the party. Those party and **Sturmabteilung** (Stormtroopers; SA) members who were intent on dismantling capitalism as part of a national socialist revolution were repeatedly beaten back by Hitler in the 1920s and repressed conclusively in the summer of 1934 [see RÖHM PURGE (1934); STRASSER, GREGOR (1892–1934)].

But this did not mean that there was never any "socialism" in "national socialism." Nazi socialism came to be defined against Marxist-Leninist-Stalinist socialism and against free-market capitalism for similar reasons. The Nazis viewed the latter two as internationalist, divisive along class lines, and "Jewish." What Nazi socialism stood *for* was a society in which the individual was subordinate to the interests of the Volksgemeinschaft (people's community) and the state was obliged to provide for all who belonged to this community. While it is true that Hitler never implemented the program's anticapitalist points, the regime did make a number of substantive attempts to realize the ideals of a distinctly "German national socialism," such as a national welfare agency [**National Socialist Welfare Organization**

(Nationalsozialistiche Volkswohlfahrt; NSV)], relief measures for unemployed workers, and recreational programs (including the popular Strength through Joy) sponsored by the **German Labor Front** (Deutsche Arbeitsfront; DAF). Much of the welfare work was undertaken not by regime bureaucrats but by ordinary German **women** and men, many of them young and idealistic. The effect of this form of socialism was to bond millions of Germans to the regime and its ideology.

NAZI–SOVIET NONAGGRESSION PACT (MOLOTOV–RIBBENTROP PACT; 1939). After German troops occupied Prague in March 1939 and **Czechoslovakia** ceased to exist, it was clear to any reasonably well-informed observer that another European war was all but inevitable. A nonaggression pact between Germany and the Soviet Union, concluded in Moscow on 23 August, was the trigger. On 3 April, Hitler ordered the military to be ready to invade **Poland** by 1 September. But he faced the same problem as his predecessors: the prospect of a two-front war. Without question in his mind, Poland had to be struck, either first or at the same time as an offensive against the West. Complicating matters was the fact that armaments production could not keep up with his most recent demand for an increase, making a short war in 1939 or 1940 an imperative (see REARMAMENT). If Germany invaded Poland, then would the British and **French** really attempt to defend it? And what were the prospects of quick German victory over the latter two? Another problem was alliances or rather the lack of them. The **Japanese** government was unwilling to commit to a war on Germany's side, and **Benito Mussolini** had made it clear—pronouncements of an "axis" and a "pact of steel" notwithstanding—that his country was not prepared to enter a major war anytime soon.

Poland, as always, was caught in the middle. But Warsaw would agree neither to allow Soviet troops transit rights in case of war nor to enter an anti-Soviet alliance with Germany. These positions left the country vulnerable to being carved up by its neighbors. And after Czechoslovakia, Polish officials could hardly be blamed for not putting much faith in an Anglo–French security guarantee.

Then there was the possibility of an Anglo-French-Soviet alliance, with talks between the respective governments beginning in April. The negotiations stretched out over the spring and summer. Perhaps the only thing on which all sides could agree was that nobody except Germany wanted a war. Otherwise, mistrust was pervasive on both sides. For London and Paris, forming an alliance with **Joseph Stalin**'s Soviet Union was tempting only because the prospect of a two-front war might deter Hitler. But it was also undesirable for ideological and practical reasons. And such an alliance would entail selling out the **Baltic** states, Finland, and Poland. The post–Czechoslovak crisis reality was clear and brutal: Defending Eastern Europe against either German or Soviet aggression with anything other than words was politically and logistically impossible.

For his part, Stalin suspected the British and French would be content to allow Germany to occupy the states on his western borders and then invade his country. Not unreasonably, he could not understand why both would object to friendly—admittedly meaning Soviet-dominated or even occupied—states on the Soviet Union's most vulnerable borders. And he was also becoming convinced that Britain and France would not put up serious resistance to Japan's ambitions in China and the eastern reaches of the Soviet Union.

The nightmare scenario for Poland, Britain, and France was the other possibility: a German–Soviet alliance. It would mean that Eastern Europe would be lost to one or both, and Japan would be free to turn to its aggression to Southeast Asia. Hitler would have a free hand to attack Western Europe without risking a two-front war. For Stalin, a pact with Hitler offered him what the untrustworthy and dilatory British and French could not: regaining territory lost in 1918 and time to prepare for war with Germany.

Berlin and Moscow seemed to be moving toward an alliance, even as Stalin allowed talks with the British and French to continue. In early May, he replaced the foreign minister, Maxim Litvinov, with Vyacheslav Molotov in what seems to have been a clear signal to Berlin. Litvinov was **Jewish**, relatively independent minded, and open to dealing with the West, whereas Molotov was slavishly devoted to Stalin and an Anglophobe. Another opening came at the end of the month, when Soviet-German trade talks resumed. In early August, **Joachim von Ribbentrop** made it clear to the Soviet charge d'affaires in Berlin that Hitler was open to a deal with Stalin that would give the latter control of Finland, Latvia, Estonia, Bessarabia, and eastern Poland in exchange for German control of the rest of Poland (see BALTICS).

At the same time, British and French officials were dragging their feet in discussions with their Soviet counterparts on a coordinated military response to a German invasion of Poland or **Romania**. It is easy to see how the lead Soviet negotiator, Kliment Voloshilov, could not take them seriously. They had not even thought through how the defense of those countries would actually be coordinated without the Germans first occupying one or both, a prospect that rendered a mutual defense treaty pointless. And even if they had shown more serious interest in a deal, the fact was that only Germany could give Stalin what he wanted and vice versa.

Hitler, moreover, was in hurry to get his war underway by the fall of 1939, which gave Stalin extra leverage. On 19 August, the same day a new trade agreement between the two states was concluded, Molotov presented a draft of a nonaggression pact to the German ambassador. Hitler responded directly to Stalin the next day, agreeing to the terms and asking for meeting between the two countries' foreign ministers to work out a secret protocol. An invitation to Ribbentrop to visit Moscow was extended three days later. Hitler was ecstatic. His biggest fear in those days was a repeat of the peaceful resolution to the Czechoslovak crisis. But time would now be on his side, as he was determined to invade Poland in about a week's time.

The pact was concluded on 23 August 1939 with Stalin raising a glass to Hitler. Germany and the Soviet Union agreed not to go to war with each other for 10 years. That part was public. Secret protocols divided up Poland and granted Finland, Latvia, Estonia, and Bessarabia to the Soviets, with Lithuania added in a subsequent agreement. German forces invaded Poland on schedule, and Soviet forces entered Polish territory on 17 September. The occupation of the Baltic states and Bessarabia began the following June. Only the invasion of Finland proved far more difficult than Stalin expected and concluded with a treaty rather than occupation.

The signing of the pact completed Hitler's diplomatic revolution in Europe, which began with the remilitarization of the **Rhineland** in March 1936, an alliance with **Italy**, the annexation of **Austria**, and the dismemberment of Czechoslovakia, all without a war that most Germans did not want. In four years' time, the terms of the post–**World War I** treaties were trampled, collective security dismantled, and the **League of Nations** proven useless.

NERO ORDER (19 MARCH 1945). On 19 March 1945 Hitler issued the Decree Concerning Demolitions in the Reich Territory, commonly known as the Nero Order for the Roman emperor who allegedly started a major fire in Rome in 64 CE. The decree ordered the destruction of any kind of infrastructure that might be used by the soon to be victorious enemy. Gauleiters, or regional leaders of the **National Socialist German Workers' Party** (Nazi Party; Nationalsozialistische Deutsche Arbeiterpartei; NSDAP), would oversee the destruction as newly designated "Reich defense commissioners."

Allied offensives on both fronts stalled briefly in the last months of 1944, before resuming with a vengeance at the beginning of 1945. On 15 March, **Albert Speer** urged Hitler to allow the **Wehrmacht** to disable rather than destroy what remained of Germany's industrial infrastructure in the West. Three days later, he recommended instead that the territory of Germany still held by the Wehrmacht be defended to the end, believing that the production of armaments could be maintained for two more months and that the Allies would be convinced by this display of resolve to end the war on terms more favorable to Germany than they would be otherwise.

According to Speer, Hitler proclaimed the German people, having been unable to vanquish a nation of Slavs, was no longer worthy of survival. By the end of the month, however, Speer had convinced him to make some exceptions and to put him in charge of carrying out the decree. Without informing Hitler, Speer then ordered that industries and essential services be preserved. It seems clear that Speer understood that even if he had relayed the modified decree to local officials, it would not have been carried out. In retrospect, the last desperate year of the war, when continuing to fight was resulting in millions more deaths and massive physical destruction, amounted to Hitler having given the real Nero Order.

NEURATH, KONSTANTIN VON (1873–1956). Born into a Swabian noble family, Neurath studied law and worked in the Foreign Ministry in Berlin and in the German embassies in London and Constantinople before serving with distinction in **World War I**. After the war, he served as minister to Denmark and then ambassador to **Italy** and Great Britain. In 1932, he was appointed foreign minister in the cabinet of **Franz von Papen**. He held the position during Kurt von Schleicher's short-lived tenure as **chancellor** and then, at President **Paul von Hindenburg**'s insistence, in Hitler's first cabinet.

Neurath embodied the aristocratic conservative nationalist establishment that Hitler detested yet needed to obtain and consolidate power. For his part, Neurath welcomed the end of the republic and the suppression of the **Communist Party of Germany** (Kommunistische Partei Deutschlands; KPD). Like other conservative nationalists, he wanted Germany rearmed and the entire **Treaty of Versailles** revoked. He had not been amenable to Germany's membership in the **League of Nations** or participation in a league-sponsored **Geneva Disarmament Conference**. Tellingly, he did not support the 1925 Pact of Locarno. These views made him amenable to serving in Hitler's cabinet, despite his dislike of the party's violent methods, which he believed would soon be restrained.

Like other influential conservative nationalists, Neurath enabled Hitler's consolidation of power. In his case, while he was not directly involved in the explosion of domestic terrorism directed at the KPD in the early months of 1933 and the decrees and legislation following the **Reichstag fire** or the murder of fellow conservative nationalists in the **Röhm purge**, he did not resign, an act that might in those months have had a more-than-symbolic effect. As for the regime's early anti-**Jewish** measures, notably the April 1933 boycott, Neurath stated during his postwar trial that such measures were necessary in order to reduce the allegedly excessive influence of Jews in Germany.

More directly, he was an essential figure in laying the foundations for Hitler's diplomatic revolution in the second half of the 1930s. He supported every one of Hitler's initiatives, including the extremely risky remilitarization of the **Rhineland**. The break with Hitler began in the fall of 1937, when Hitler laid out his longer-term strategy to senior officials [see HOSSBACH MEMORANDUM (1937)]. Neurath believed **Czechoslovakia** should be destroyed as a state, but he joined with War Minister Werner von Blomberg and army commander in chief Werner von Fritsch in believing that Great Britain and **France** would go to war with Germany to defend the country. In the wake of the **Blomberg–Fritsch affair**, Hitler replaced Neurath with the far less competent but pliable **Joachim von Ribbentrop**.

In response to the international outrage following the dismemberment of Czechoslovakia in March 1939, Hitler chose the seemingly respectable and moderate Neurath as the first protector of Bohemia and Moravia. But Neurath was moderate only by the standards set by the **Schutzstaffel** (Protection Squad; SS), and he consolidated Nazi rule in the protectorate, cracked down harshly on large-scale student protests in the fall of 1939, and made sure the **Nuremberg race laws** were implemented. Still, Hitler did not consider him radical enough and in September 1941 appointed **Reinhard Heydrich** as his deputy, knowing that Heydrich would really be in charge. Neurath held the title in name only until August 1943, when he retired to a huge estate after accepting a tax-free gift from Hitler of 250,000 Reichsmarks.

Among those prosecuted by the **International Military Tribunal** (IMT) in Nuremberg, Neurath seemed like something of an outlier. In sharp contrast to **Hermann Göring**, Julius Streicher, and Ernst Kaltenbrunner, he appeared to be an elderly aristocratic gentleman. While the tribunal convicted him on all four counts, he received only a 15-year sentence. As one historian of the trial's aftermath noted, Neurath was the only prisoner in Spandau whom a majority of West Germans could find sympathetic. He was released in 1954.

Somewhat surprisingly, the proposal to grant him early release came from the Soviets, who had been subjecting Neurath to middle-of-the-night cell searches that the American prison physician believed would kill the dying old man if they continued. While conventional wisdom had it that the seeming act of mercy was part of a larger "peace offensive" by Moscow aimed at softening anti-Soviet public opinion in West Germany, the more likely reason is that Soviet officials did not want him or any other Spandau inmate buried in a prison gravesite, which they feared could become a pilgrimage site for neo-Nazis. Neurath died at his family estate two years later.

NEW ORDER. For Hitler, as one historian put it, empire began at home with the realization by 1939 of the old **pan-German** dream of a "greater Germany." Further conquest in the East and the removal of its resident Slavic and **Jewish** populations would provide **living space** for an expanding German population and enough resources—especially food—to become truly self-sufficient. But trade deals favorable to Germany in Central and Eastern Europe, followed by the 1939 and 1940 military campaigns, demonstrated that more territory and resources in Europe would be required if Germany was to become powerful enough to take on both Great Britain and the **United States**. Hence the idea of a New Order: a bloc of **economically** integrated European states dominated by Germany and mobilized against the Anglo-Americans in the West and Judeo-Bolshevism in the East.

As German forces rolled into **France** in May 1940, all the major ministries concerned with economic affairs convened to plan how this vision of European integration was to be realized. When it came to Western Europe, the key was to ensure German hegemony without resorting to the kind of brute-force subjugation already being implemented in **Poland**.

Yet plunder prevailed over the intricate weaving together of national economies, especially after the failure of **Operation Barbarossa** in the winter of 1941–1942. In the end, the economies of Western Europe (and Greece) were treated largely as supply depots for Germany. And the bounty would come to include conscripted labor. The German war effort and home front benefitted, while the outcomes for the other members of the New Order were entirely predictable: shortages, rationing, malnutrition, inflation, and proliferating black markets. And German propaganda trumpeting its "European mission" to unite the continent against the Jewish-Bolshevik menace was revealed for the self-serving lie that it was. The conscription of more and more young men as forced laborers in Germany spurred the proliferation of underground resistance movements across the continent.

The New Order was also a cultural project. Unsurprisingly, Hitler intended to roll up the rich prewar tapestry of international cultural organizations and establish Berlin as the center of a new "international" (as one historian put it recently) network of state-sanctioned **artistic** output. The model was to be **Joseph Goebbels**'s Reich Chamber of Culture, with its subchambers for **cinema**, music, literature, and theater. Like the economic and political project, this attempt to exert a form of what later became known as "soft power" was a failure.

The New Order did leave behind one important legacy. The postwar project of unifying Western Europe's major economies was driven primarily by the need to reconcile former enemies and rebuild shattered economies, as a new, increasingly postcolonial world of superpower competition dawned. While the founders of what became the European Union were men with impeccable anti-Nazi credentials, there is no doubt that much of the lower-level work of early economic integration was undertaken by people who had attempted—willingly or otherwise—to realize Hitler's New Order.

NIGHT AND FOG DECREE (NACHT UND NEBEL; 1941). When **Operation Barbarossa** led to a reduced **Wehrmacht** presence in German-occupied Western Europe, resistance activity increased. The resulting crackdown burdened local military courts (*see* LAW). As a workaround, on 7 December 1941, Hitler ordered armed forces high command chief Field Marshal **Wilhelm Keitel** to implement a decree authorizing the transfer of anyone considered to be engaging in **oppositional** activities to Germany to be tried by special courts. Those deported would simply disappear and not be permitted to contact friends or family members. The operation was codenamed Night and Fog after a line from Johann Wolfgang von Goethe. In addition to its practical benefits, the decree would instill fear among populations in occupied states.

The decree was applied mostly in Western Europe (**France**, Belgium, Luxembourg, the Netherlands, Denmark, and **Norway**) and led to the arrests of around 7,000 people, the vast majority in France. Following the 20 July 1944 **assassination attempt**, Hitler issued a follow-up decree (Terror and Sabotage) that expanded the powers of the Wehrmacht, **Schutzstaffel** (Protection Squad; SS), and police to arrest and deport anyone suspected of engaging in acts of violence, now defined as "terror." Keitel broadened the authority of the army and SS to arrest anyone suspected of doing anything—violent or not—that could be considered in opposition to the German war effort.

In 1955, French filmmaker Alain Resnais borrowed the *Night and Fog* code name for the title of one of the earliest documentaries on the **concentration camps** and death camps, though the film was about life and death in the camps and not the decree itself. *See also* HOLOCAUST.

NIGHT OF BROKEN GLASS (REICHS-KRISTALLNACHT; 9–10 NOVEMBER 1938). The Nazi regime's anti-**Jewish** measures intensified beginning in 1935, with interruptions around the **Olympic Games** in 1936 and during the **Czechoslovakia crisis** in 1938 (*see* NUREMBERG RACE LAWS). New **laws** and restrictions were accompanied by eruptions of violence against Jews and attacks on Jewish institutions by party radicals at the local level.

Hitler's desire to see the complete departure of Germany's Jewish population became acute in the second half of the decade. Though 150,000—close to one-quarter of Germany's Jewish population in 1933—had emigrated by 1938, the annexation of **Austria** added 185,000 Jews, and they were finding it increasingly difficult to leave. The policies of purging Jews from the civil service and professions, along with the development by the **Schutzstaffel** (Protection Squad; SS) of an efficient machinery of expropriation, made it harder for Jews to emigrate. In the summer of 1938, an international conference was held in Evian, **France**, to discuss the fate of Jewish refugees from Germany, but its attendees offered no more than statements of sympathy. At the **Nuremberg party rally** in September, Hitler cynically excoriated Western states for criticizing Germany while refusing to take in more refugees.

An incident in Paris provided the opportunity for the regime to accelerate emigration and the expropriation of Jewish assets. On 26 October, **Joseph Goebbels** ordered the expulsion of **Polish**-born Jews from Germany. In just a few days, around 18,000 were arrested and deported to Poland. In response, on 7 November, Herschel Grynszpan, the 17-year-old child of two deportees, shot a German embassy official in Paris, Ernst von Rath, who died two days later. The timing was propitious for Goebbels. His relationship with Hitler, who was personally close to the Goebbels family, had been damaged by an affair Goebbels had been having with a well-known actress. Goebbels had also been among those who had wanted to avoid war during the Czechoslovakia crisis, as he understood that there was no public enthusiasm for it.

Given these setbacks for Goebbels and the fact that Hitler had been signaling his determination to accelerate the emigration of Jews for months, Grynszpan's act was a godsend. It allowed him to remedy a number of problems all at once: repair his relationship with Hitler, stir up enthusiasm for war by blaming "international Jewry" for attempting to incite war on Germany, and accelerate Jewish emigration. Even the date of Grynszpan's act was well timed for Hitler and Goebbels, as it coincided with the annual gathering of party officials to honor comrades killed in the **Beer Hall Putsch** in 1923. That party leaders were gathered in Munich and also celebrating the putsch's anniversary around the country undoubtedly facilitated the launching of the pogrom.

Immediately after Rath's shooting, anti-Jewish riots began locally, mainly in Kassel and Dessau. Hitler and Goebbels understood they would have to act quickly and decisively to leverage Rath's death to maximum advantage. This meant orchestrating from behind the scenes a national pogrom and making it appear to be a spontaneous outburst of righteous anger rather than the premeditated attack on a vulnerable, demonized minority that it was.

Goebbels had already ordered the press to present the shooting as part of a wider conspiracy of "international Jewry." During celebrations in Munich on the night of 9 November, Hitler, informed of Rath's death, told Goebbels that the demonstrations must be allowed to continue. Goebbels then conveyed the order to police and party officials. The latter in turn transmitted the order to the local level. Hitler immediately secluded himself in his Munich apartment.

Across Germany, party radicals, **Sturmabteilung** (Stormtroopers; SA) men (most wearing civilian clothes), and **Hitler Youth** (Hitlerjugend; HJ) robbed and set fire to synagogues and vandalized, burned, and looted Jewish-owned businesses. Home invasions took place in which inhabitants were robbed and abused. SS Reich Security Main Office chief **Reinhard Heydrich** had the chief of the Berlin Gestapo order police all over Germany not to interfere, only to prevent rampant looting and acts of extreme violence. Fire brigades were only permitted to save Aryan properties.

Germany had witnessed nothing like it since the Middle Ages. At least 91 Jews were killed, though this is almost certainly an undercount. Perhaps 300 more committed suicide. Nearly every synagogue in Germany (then including Austria and the Sudetenland) was gutted by arson attacks—around 1,000 synagogues and prayer spaces in total. Even orphanages were not spared. Cemeteries were desecrated. Between 7,000 and 7,500 businesses were looted, damaged, or destroyed. Late on the night of 9 November, Hitler ordered the Gestapo to begin arresting thousands of Jewish men. Around 30,000 were swept up the following day, nearly all of them imprisoned in the Dachau, Buchenwald, and Sachsenhausen **concentration camps**, where hundreds more were killed or died from causes related to their internment. In most cases, release was contingent on a formal agreement to leave the country and the forfeiture of most of what assets they had left.

Hitler did not want the destruction and plunder to spiral out of control and on 10 November had Goebbels issue an order halting the pogrom that day. At the same time, Hitler demanded that the pogrom bring about the total elimination of **economic** life for Jews in Germany. For starters, he prohibited the payment of insurance claims to Jewish claimants. **Hermann Göring**, in his capacity as head of the **Four-Year Plan** organization, was given responsibility for implementing Hitler's order. Germany's Jews were held collectively responsible for the damages, which the regime eventually calculated to be just over 1 billion Reichsmarks, or roughly 400 million US dollars in 1938.

The pogrom did indeed accelerate emigration: Around 115,000 left Germany between 10 November 1938 and 1 September 1939. A new wave of expropriations and restrictions on German Jews accompanied the surge in departures. As all this was still not enough to force Germany's remaining Jews out, forced labor and population concentration, or ghettoization, schemes were developed in what could be characterized as an "intermediate solution" to the Jewish "question."

Hitler was intent on using the pogrom as way of preparing the public for war, a point he made in an unusual in-person address to some 400 German journalists in Berlin. An extended press campaign was necessary for another reason: A majority of Germans did not participate in the pogrom and did not seem to approve of it. Authorized by Hitler at the top, it was carried out by a relatively small number of local-level party radicals and HJ. Yet the vast majority of Germans certainly did not know of Hitler's central role, and there is evidence that some believed he had not wanted it. It certainly did not have the effect of whipping up the public's enthusiasm for a war of territorial conquest.

Though the Propaganda Ministry had provided a clear explanation of the pogrom for Germany's newspapers, the press was instructed to downplay the attack. Hence newspapers reported that a few windows were broken and synagogues somehow managed to set themselves on fire. No photos of any damage were printed. The opposite was the case outside Germany, especially in the **United States**, where no other anti-Jewish measure during the entire period of Nazi rule received as much coverage. US President **Franklin D. Roosevelt** denounced the pogrom and recalled the American ambassador. Anti-Nazi protests broke out in some American cities. Yet the quota system for immigrants remained unchanged. A bipartisan bill proposing to admit 20,000 children to the country went nowhere. The best Roosevelt could do was make it easier for refugees already in the United States to remain.

In contrast, the British government eased some immigration restrictions and authorized the famous Kindertransport operation, which brought some 10,000 children, most of them Jewish, to Britain between the pogrom and the outbreak of the war. The parents of nearly all of those rescued would be murdered in the **Holocaust**.

NORWAY. With its long North Sea coastline and excellent natural harbors (fjords), Norway was a crucial strategic target for Hitler in the spring of 1940. After a harder-than-expected fight to secure control of the country, Hitler installed a Reichskommissar, Josef Terboven, to oversee the occupation [*see* NEW ORDER; WESER EXERCISE (WESERÜBUNG)].

It was a terrible choice. An "old fighter" from the days of the **Beer Hall Putsch**, the crude, ruthless Terboven abolished the monarchy (the king had already fled to London to form a government in exile) and put the deeply unpopular fascist Nasjonal Samling (NS) party chief Vidkun Quisling in charge of a commission to manage the country's day-to-day affairs. Terboven would have been better suited for service in the East, where Hitler and **Heinrich Himmler** planned to remove the local "subhuman" populations of Slavs and **Jews** and replace them with German settlers [*see* GENERAL PLAN FOR THE EAST (GENERALPLAN OST)]. But they had a very different future in mind for Norway. Hitler, Himmler, and other Nazi ideologues considered the "racial stock" of Norwegians to be superior to that of Germans. Along with Sweden, Denmark, the Netherlands, and Flanders in northern Belgium, Norway was to become part of the new Germany.

The project of Germanization would entail the settlement of Germans (though not the replacement of the local population) and a series of massive construction projects, the centerpiece of which was a new city on the fjord near the town of Trondheim. Hitler chose the name *Nordstern* (*North Star*), before changing it to Drondheim, and commissioned **Albert Speer** to design it. It was to serve as the northernmost regional outpost of German cultural imperialism, the others being Strasbourg, Königsberg, Munich, and Linz. A superhighway would connect the new city to Berlin and run all the way to Klagenfurt on the border with **Italy**.

The **racist** imperial project extended to the bodies of Norwegian **women**. Norway became the most important site of Himmler's Lebensborn (Fount of Life) project, in which local women were recruited to bear children fathered by SS officers. Ten Lebensborn nurseries were built in Norway, more than any other country, and some 8,000 children were registered. After the war, their mothers were treated by the government and Norwegians as collaborators and abused, arrested, and ostracized. An attempt by the postwar Norwegian government to deport all the children to

Germany was blocked by Allied officials. To this day, the Norwegian government has resisted acknowledging its actions and paying compensation to survivors.

Most Norwegians deeply resented the German occupation and engaged in acts of resistance, both quotidian and clandestine. As elsewhere in German-occupied Europe, an underground resistance movement formed (Milorg), though it kept a low profile to avoid harsh reprisals against civilians. Though Quisling's regime and Norwegian police assisted in the attempt to round up and deport the country's small Jewish population (around 1,700 in 1940, including some 200 refugees from Germany and **Austria**), local networks of resistance managed to save around 900, mainly by assisting their escape to neutral Sweden. Most of the rest were deported and murdered in Auschwitz.

Norway was spared extensive physical destruction, with the well-prepared Milorg preventing the extensive implementation of scorched-earth measures by the retreating **Wehrmacht** and quickly seizing control of Oslo. Following Hitler's **suicide**, the successor government led by Grand Admiral **Karl Dönitz** ordered the commander of German forces in Norway, General Franz Böhme, to surrender. Böhme complied, while Terboven and the local SS leader committed suicide. A new Norwegian government was installed by the first week of June 1945. A massive purge of collaborators followed, with Quisling tried and convicted of high treason and other crimes and executed on 24 October 1945.

NUREMBERG MILITARY TRIBUNAL (NMT).

Also known informally as the Subsequent Trials or Subsequent Proceedings, the NMT was a US court that presided over 12 trials between October 1946 and April 1949 in Nuremberg. The NMT was created after the Allied Control Council, the four-power body responsible for governing occupied Germany, agreed in December 1945 to authorize member states to conduct war crimes trials in their respective zones.

Unlike the **International Military Tribunal** (IMT), then, the NMT was not an international court. Nor was it strictly speaking a military tribunal, as the judges were all civilians. While the IMT tried the surviving individual regime officials and military officers, the NMT prosecuted members of institutions: physicians in the **Euthanasia Program** (Action T4), judges, officials in government ministries, directors of the IG Farben and Krupp industrial conglomerates, **Wehrmacht** officers, and various branches of the **Schutzstaffel** (Protection Squad; SS; *see* LAW). And while the IMT focused on the crime of aggressive war, the NMT emphasized what one historian characterized as "crimes of atrocity" committed against civilian populations.

The NMT indicted a total of 185 individuals and prosecuted 177 defendants, convicting 142 and sentencing 26 to death. It was hamstrung by budget cuts imposed by the US Congress, and its procedures, prosecutors, and legal bases became the target of a great deal of criticism inside and outside occupied Germany. As the trials touched Germany's professional, legal, industrial, and military elite, it became the target of an amnesty campaign spearheaded by ex-Nazi lawyers, veterans' groups, and prominent clergymen. This campaign and domestic criticism of the NMT and trials held by the US Army in Germany in the context of the emerging Cold War put American officials—particularly Military Governor General Lucius D. Clay and his successor, High Commissioner for West Germany John J. McCloy—under pressure to halt all executions and free the convicted men.

Largely in response to domestic (US) criticism and out of a desire to model American-style procedures to the post-Nazi West German population, McCloy and other American officials built a clemency and parole system as a substitute for a court of appeals. In the end, only 12 of the death sentences were carried out, and by 1958 every convicted defendant had been released from **Landsberg Prison**.

Yet by producing a massive record of individual and institutional criminality, the NMT made a contribution of incalculable value to the historical record. One prosecutor called it the "greatest history seminar ever held." While the **Holocaust** did not play a prominent role in the IMT's proceedings, it very much did in the NMT's. In the longer term, the NMT set important precedents. The court's records, proceedings, and emphasis on "crimes of atrocity" informed the 1948 UN Genocide Convention and influenced the conduct of war-crimes and crimes-against-humanity cases to a greater extent than the IMT. See also UNITED STATES OF AMERICA.

NUREMBERG PARTY RALLIES (1923–1938). To this day, few, if any, images of Hitler are more familiar than those of him at the 1934 party rally in Nuremberg: standing outdoors before thousands of uniformed supporters arrayed in perfectly ordered formations. The notoriety of this image is no accident. Though this rally was 1 of 10, it is the most famous of them, all thanks to **Leni Riefenstahl**'s film *Triumph of the Will*.

The first such event was held in Munich at the end of January 1923. The catalyst was the occupation of the Ruhr earlier that month by **French** and Belgian troops. Always at best ambivalent about alliances with other Far-Right groups, Hitler resisted the chance to join them in staging a protest action in response to the incursion and the national outcry it had generated. Doing so, he feared, would dilute the distinctive profile for the **National Socialist German Workers' Party** (Nazi Party; Nationalsozialistische Deutsche Arbeiterpartei; NSDAP) he had been working for three years to create. Besides, in his mind, the problem wasn't really foreign troops on German soil but the "November criminals" in Berlin, whose treachery had made such a humiliating violation of the country's sovereignty possible in the first place. So he ordered several days of marches, ceremonies, and meetings of regional party officials to take place in Munich. Beyond keeping the party at arm's length from other Far-Right groups, he used the occasion to have himself ostentatiously proclaimed its undisputed leader.

The next rally was held three years later in Weimar, as Hitler was still banned from speaking in Bavaria [see BEER HALL PUTSCH (1923)]. Attended by 7,000–8,000 people, Hitler orchestrated it in a way that displayed party unity and his unassailable position as leader. It also marked the first major public appearance of the recently created **Schutzstaffel** (Protection Squad; SS), the leader of which Hitler presented a party flag supposedly stained with the blood of a comrade killed in the Beer Hall Putsch. The rally concluded with a long speech by Hitler and a march that precipitated a riot in the center of Weimar. The pattern—including violence—was set for future rallies: They would be pure political theater, emphasizing Hitler's command over a unified party. He had in fact secured neither total authority nor party unity, as a split between its "left" and "right" wings and the question of the **Sturmabteilung**'s (Stormtroopers; SA) future role remained serious unresolved problems.

Hitler selected Nuremberg, which he considered an exemplary medieval German city, as the site for future rallies, and the remaining eight were held there. Hitler would drive himself to the point of physical collapse in presiding over what became weeklong spectacles of speeches, marches, parades, and ceremonies ultimately involving several hundred thousand people. Even observers unsympathetic to the regime were stunned by what they witnessed. Very much true to form, Hitler had been involved closely with every aspect of their design and execution. His enlistment of Riefenstahl and **Albert Speer** to film and carry out his designs, respectively, cemented their relationships with him. Hitler and Speer planned the transformation of an 11-square-kilometer space outside the old city, which was to include a huge parade ground and viewing stand (the Zeppelinfeld) modeled on the Pergamon Altar, a massive stadium and congress hall, a separate parade ground for a half-million soldiers (the March Field), and a 2-kilometer-long parade avenue. Only the Zeppelinfeld was completed, and part of it and a portion of the congress hall remain standing today.

The rallies served several purposes. Hitler would use them to announce new policies and laws, most notoriously the **Nuremberg race laws** in 1935. The popular success of *Triumph of the Will* notwithstanding, the rallies were first and foremost designed to impress upon party members, from the highest-level officials to thousands of **Hitler Youth** (Hitlerjugend; HJ) and SA recruits, that the party was unified behind the leader. Hitler also intended them to demonstrate the new German army's subservience to him. Beyond the party and the army, the rallies were to give expression to Germany's unity and its subordination to the leader. And just as Hitler was performing for Hitler when he subjected subordinates, visiting dignitaries, and members of his inner circle to his monologues, the rallies served the same purpose on a massive scale, one made indelible by Riefenstahl's film. *See also* ART; FÜHRER MYTH (FÜHRER MYTHOS).

NUREMBERG RACE LAWS. Jews had been targeted by Hitler, the **National Socialist German Workers' Party** (Nazi Party; Nationalsozialistische Deutsche Arbeiterpartei; NSDAP, the **Sturmabteilung** (Stormtroopers; SA), and the Far Right more generally long before Hitler was appointed **chancellor**. As early as 1919, Hitler had advocated replacing what he called "emotional anti-Semitism" with an "anti-Semitism of reason," or "scientific anti-Semitism," so that all "true" Germans would fully understand the supposedly widespread pernicious influence of Jews. Less than year later, he backtracked somewhat, allowing that the two strands would have to coexist. Intentionally or not, Hitler foreshadowed the mixture of sadistic violence and bureaucratic and legal measures that characterized his regime's anti-Jewish measures and, later, the **Holocaust**.

The first two major stages in the policy category were the attempted nationwide boycott of Jewish-owned businesses in April 1933, which was not particularly successful, and the first purge of the civil service, which was. At the same time, party radicals and SA men humiliated, assaulted, and sometimes killed Jews, and **Joseph Goebbels** was eager to whip up as much anti-Jewish resentment as possible. But the boycott and the violence were damaging Germany's reputation abroad and hindering diplomacy for the still-isolated country, notably that around negotiations for a **Anglo–German Naval Agreement** with Great Britain. In early May 1935, Economics Minister **Hjalmar Schacht** warned Hitler that anti-Jewish violence and the negative publicity it generated abroad was damaging the economy at a time when ordinary Germans were trying to cope with food shortages, stagnant wages, and rising prices. The unsettled relationship between the regime and the churches was another irritant for Hitler. It was at this juncture that he acted decisively to restrain "emotional anti-Semitism" and promote "anti-Semitism of reason." On 9 August 1935, he ordered an end to unsanctioned acts of violence and promulgated the Nuremberg race laws a month later.

The measures comprising the laws had been debated for several years within various ministries. Since the summer of 1933, swarms of Nazi officials had been grappling with the task of defining Jews in legal terms. Academic "race scientists" were of little help, as they could not seem to agree on what "race" was. The first formal attempt came on 7 April 1933 with the promulgation of the **Law** for the Reestablishment of a Professional Civil Service, which defined anyone with at least one grandparent as not of "Aryan ancestry" [*see* COORDINATION (GLEICHSCHALTUNG)].

The main problem for the regime was that Germany's Jewish population was deeply embedded in German society. Intermarriage and conversions to Christianity had become increasingly common since the turn of the 20th century. In 1933, almost 40 percent of all marriages contracted by Jews were mixed, and there were about 35,000 mixed couples in Germany at that time. Would the "uncompromising removal" of all Jews—as Hitler had put it in 1919—be possible without alienating a significant segment of non-Jewish German society? How would the churches that had blessed conversions react? Yet for party radicals, the problem had to be addressed. Otherwise, the Germanic "race" would be hopelessly diluted and ultimately replaced.

In the regime's early years, some of the most radical officials demanded an expansive legal definition of Jews. In making their case, they looked to an unexpected source for inspiration and legal models: the segregated **United States**. They were not the first

German imperialists to be influenced by the American model. At the turn of the 20th century, German colonial administrators in **Africa** had been inspired by the US example to ban miscegenation. Germany was the only European colonial power to take this step. By the early 1930s, the United States remained a world leader in race segregation, which was implemented through a web of laws, informal customs, and extreme violence. Mixed-race marriages were a crime in 30 states. In addition, America's immigration policy was race based, and non-white Americans were second-class citizens in the United States and its colonies.

For radical Nazis, there was a clear causal connection between legal segregation and the fact that the United States was a vast industrial and agricultural great power. That it had not built a discriminatory legal apparatus against American Jews was irrelevant. The important thing was that the Americans had shown the world how to keep the races separated, above all by limiting civil rights and restricting intermarriage.

The radicals' desire for an expansive definition ran up against strong resistance from more moderate officials, who were without question anti-Semites but who had more traditional legal instincts. More to the point, they understood that most Germans of mixed ancestry came from the educated and skilled middle class. Persecuting a significant number of professionals, including military officers, would be counterproductive, particularly because so many members of this class were inclined to support the regime. Another concern was Germany's reputation abroad, already damaged by the boycott and violence, as the 1936 **Olympic Games** neared.

Yet the moderates could not ignore surges in grassroots anti-Semitic agitation and violence. So the divide between party radicals and more cautious figures in the state ministries had to be bridged soon. The result was a compromise in the form of the Nuremberg race laws. At the annual **Nuremberg party rally** in September, Hitler announced a ban on sex and marriage between Jews and non-Jews and decreed a distinction between citizens and subjects of Nazi Germany. Officials then scrambled to finalize a legal definition of *full Jews*, so-called *mixed-race Jews (mischlinge)*, and *non-Jews*.

On 15 September, Hitler announced the new laws to a special session of the **Reichstag**, which convened for the first and only time in the city of Nuremberg. The laws, supplemented and clarified on 14 November, defined *full Jews* as those with three Jewish grandparents. They were to be subjects and not citizens. *Mischlinge* remained citizens and were divided into two categories: *Mischlinge* of the second degree had one Jewish grandparent and could marry Germans. *Mischlinge* of the first degree had two Jewish grandparents, did not belong to the Jewish faith, and were not married to a Jewish person. Mischlinge in this category could not marry Germans or *Mischlinge* of the second degree. If they were married Jews, then they would be considered full Jews (*Geltungsjude*). The regime had to produce simple charts clarifying the definitions and restrictions for the public.

The Interior Ministry estimated that according to the laws, in April 1935, there were around 775,000 full Jews and 750,000 *Mischlinge* in Germany, or 2.3 percent of the population. The figure of 750,000 *Mischlinge* was grossly inflated, with the actual number most likely around 200,000.

Hitler's announcement of the laws appeased both party radicals—even if many believed the decrees did not go far enough—and those who wanted the violence curtailed. There was no public protest, and the churches kept silent. Germany's Jewish communities turned even further inward, with many feeling relieved at the prospect of a more clearly defined legal existence and an end to seemingly random violence. It is telling in this regard that there was not a surge in emigration after the fall of 1935, though it is clear that more German Jews accepted that leaving the country—or at least getting their children out—at some point was inevitable. The minority of Orthodox Jews and Zionists were more enthusiastic, as the decrees required a greater degree of separation from Gentile Germans, which suited their **religious** and political interests.

For German Jews, then, the laws formed a juncture rather than a turning point or rupture. And that was the problem for Hitler. The tensions within the party and regime leading up to his pronouncement of the laws were only partly relieved. Indeed, radical grassroots anti-Semitism had to be further suppressed before and during the Olympic Games. The pent-up frustrations coincided with Hitler's determination to accelerate emigration and prepare the public for war, thereby creating a combustible situation that catalyzed into a nationwide pogrom in November 1938 (*see* NIGHT OF BROKEN GLASS (REICHS-KRISTALLNACHT; 9–10 NOVEMBER 1938).

OLYMPIC GAMES (1936). In 1931, the International Olympic Committee (IOC) selected Germany as the site of the 1936 winter and summer games. Held in Garmisch-Partinkirchen and Berlin in February and August, respectively, it was the last year in which both were held in the same country. Though Hitler had no interest in sports and no doubt found the IOC's pacifist internationalism odious, he was highly attuned to the political value of mass spectacles. His intense interest in design, moreover, prompted him to become closely involved in the construction of a massive sports complex for the summer games. As early as January 1934, **Joseph Goebbels** created a special committee within his ministry to prepare a domestic and international propaganda campaign.

As it turned out, circumstances in 1935 and 1936 offered a unique opportunity to use the games to project an image of Germany as a proud but peaceable and stable nation united behind its leader. The signing of the **Anglo–German Naval Pact** in June 1935, **rearmament**, the accelerating rapprochement with **Italy**, the remilitarization of the **Rhineland**, and the decision to back the right-wing rebels in the **Spanish Civil War** all incentivized Hitler to find a way to display German power and confidence in a nonmilitary setting. The games offered just such a setting.

To be sure, Italy's invasion of Ethiopia, a new prowar government in **Japan**, and the unfolding nightmare of **Joseph Stalin**'s purges in the Soviet Union would make Hitler's job relatively easier. But the fact that the games followed a wave of popular anti-Semitism and the promulgation of the **Nuremberg race laws** in September 1935 presented Hitler with a significant international public relations problem. The IOC had already demanded that he pledge not to discriminate against any athlete. Nonetheless, an international campaign to boycott the games was gathering momentum. In response, Hitler made sure anti-**Jewish** propaganda and popular expressions of anti-Semitism were tamped down for both games. Rather grudgingly, he allowed two Germans, now defined as "half-Jews" and not then even residing in the country, to compete for the national team in Garmisch and Berlin.

With nearly 4,000 athletes representing 49 nations (only the Soviet Union boycotted), the Berlin games were the most successful Olympics to date. There were a number of notable firsts. The tradition of runners relaying a lit torch from Olympia in Greece to the opening ceremonies was introduced. Others were high tech, such as live telex and radio transmissions and a limited television broadcast. In addition to the massive new sports complex, the regime festooned the city with **swastika** flags and banners. After some reporters in Garmisch spotted a military training exercise, soldiers were nowhere to be seen in Berlin.

The party again commissioned the indefatigable **Leni Riefenstahl** to make a film of the event, *Olympia*, which showcased the Nazi aesthetic in building, mass spectacle, and human bodies. Hitler appeared prominently in the film, which premiered on his 49th birthday in 1938. It was the IOC that commissioned

Richard Strauss to compose the games' official anthem, which was performed with a choir of 3,000 in the gigantic new Olympic stadium before 110,000 spectators. Though by that point Strauss had fallen out of favor with the regime, Goebbels was astute enough to allow Germany's best-known living composer to accept the honor.

Hitler performed effectively as a generous host, greeting IOC officials and foreign dignitaries in the **chancellery**, presiding ostentatiously over the opening ceremonies, and attending multiple events. Other high-level officials held enormous, lavish parties. German athletes performed very well, taking away the largest number of gold medals. Hitler and Goebbels were, however, unhappy about the stellar performances of Black American athletes, most notably Jesse Owens, the winner of four gold medals. Their victories must have been all the more galling given that German boxer Max Schmeling had knocked out the presumably unbeatable African American Joe Louis in New York City just two months earlier. Regardless, it is not true that Hitler snubbed Owens by refusing to shake his hand. IOC president Count Henri de Baillet-Latour informed Hitler that protocol dictated he not congratulate any victorious athletes in person.

The extent to which the games were a massive propaganda victory for the regime has probably been overstated. Those who wished to see a stable and "normal" Germany saw what they wanted to see. But many others inside and outside Germany were not fooled. The regime, as American reporter William Shirer noted, had only put up a very good front. Dresden scholar Victor Klemperer, now defined as Jewish by the race laws, predicted in his diary that the pent-up frustration of party radicals at the temporary official suppression of anti-Semitism would soon have to find release. He was right. And following the closing ceremonies, the drive to war would go into high gear.

OPERATION BAGRATION (1944). On 22 June 1944, the Red Army launched one of the largest and most successful surprise offensives in modern military history. In the Second World War, its success was rivaled only by the Allied invasion of German-occupied **France** two weeks earlier [*see* OPERATION OVERLORD (1944)].

That spring, Red Army planners calculated, correctly, that the Germans would not expect an attack on the army group occupying a well-defended position along the 1,300-kilometer-long center of the eastern front. But by skillfully applying a range of deceptions, they encouraged the German assumption that any Soviet counterattack would come in **Ukraine**. For good measure, they also planned a feint in the North. Meanwhile, **Joseph Stalin** and his top generals planned Bagration—named by Stalin in honor of a Georgian prince who fell while defending Moscow from Napoleon—at levels of secrecy that were extraordinary even for such a secretive dictatorship.

Hitler had speculated that Stalin would launch a counterattack on **Operation Barbarossa**'s anniversary, and the attack was launched on 22 June. The timing was in fact a coincidence. Germany's intelligence apparatus had been completely fooled, as was the region's **Wehrmacht** commander, though he had tried and failed to convince Hitler to allow him to bolster the front by shortening it. The Wehrmacht paid tribute to the effectiveness of Soviet deceptive measures by diverting armor to the South. When Bagration was launched, the Soviet-German imbalances in tanks and self-propelled guns was around 10 to 1; in aircraft, 7 to 1; and in manpower, 3 to 1.

It was over in a matter of days. Staying true to form, Hitler prohibited the evacuation of four "stronghold" cities behind the front. They were quickly surrounded and captured, along with tens of thousands of irreplaceable German troops and officers, 57,000 of whom were paraded through Moscow a month later. Red Army officers noted with considerable satisfaction that their forces had overcome a larger German force than the one that was still bottling up Allied armies in Normandy.

The Wehrmacht's once-mighty army group center was smashed—its losses over the following weeks were greater than those sustained by the Germans at the **Battle of Stalingrad**. By early August, Soviet forces were on the outskirts of Warsaw. **Joseph Goebbels** considered it Germany's greatest single military defeat to date. Hitler, who had been at the **Berghof** when Bagration began, became determined to return to the **Wolf's Lair** and departed his alpine compound on 14 July. Less than week later, a group of conspirators among his officers attempted to **assassinate** him. *See also* MILITARY COMMANDER.

OPERATION BARBAROSSA (1941). Hitler's strategic calculations in the summer and fall of 1940 set in motion planning for the invasion of the Soviet Union. He decided on an invasion in the summer, despite the fact that **Winston Churchill** refused to come to terms. Hitler suspected that Churchill was holding out for a major strategic realignment to take place. That realignment would involve bringing the **United States** and the Soviet Union together in an anti-German alliance with Britain. One way to prevent this would be the creation of a massive anti-Western bloc of states stretching from Spain to **Japan** and "including" the Soviet Union. If such a thing could be constructed, then Britain would be forced out of the war, and the United States would have to turn its full attention to the Pacific [*See* ANTI-COMINTERN PACT (1936); BALKANS; BULGARIA; FRANCO, FRANCISCO (1892–1975); HUNGARY; ITALIAN SOCIAL REPUBLIC (REPUBLIC OF SALÓ); ROMANIA; TRIPARITE PACT). But the attempt failed at every turn.

Hitler's pursuit of the key component of the envisioned megabloc—an alliance with the Soviet Union rather than just a **Nazi–Soviet Nonaggression Pact**—was serious and involved several face-to-face meetings in Berlin with Soviet foreign minister Vyacheslav Molotov in November 1940. But this should not be read as ambivalence on Hitler's part about an eventual war of territorial conquest against the Soviet Union, something he had been committed to since the mid-1920s [*see MEIN KAMPF (MY STRUGGLE)*]. Rather, he likely saw such an alliance as a stopgap measure intended to prevent **Joseph Stalin** from joining up with Britain.

Stalin's interest, of course, was also serious, or he would have never dispatched Molotov to Berlin with a detailed list of questions. Hitler was dangling the possibility of removing Britain's presence from the Mediterranean entirely and offering Stalin the possibility of expansion to the Persian Gulf and India, all without having to worry about a war with Germany or Japan. But the price demanded by Stalin was beyond what Hitler was willing or even able to pay.

Thus a German invasion of the Soviet Union had to begin as soon as possible. And quick victory was essential: the United States was officially neutral, though the administration of President **Franklin D. Roosevelt** was taking an increasingly strident anti-German position and would soon find ways of circumventing neutrality laws to increase material assistance to Britain. Hitler gambled that a rapid victory in the East would bring the British to heel. In this scenario, Germany would gain control of the entire Mediterranean and the Persian Gulf. The **Wehrmacht** having done its job, long-range bombers and a massive buildup of naval forces could commence. Bases in West **Africa** and on Atlantic islands would secure German control of the Atlantic Ocean. All of Europe, North and West Africa, and the Middle East would be invulnerable to American intervention.

On 16 December 1940, Hitler ordered Operation Barbarossa—in honor of the 12th-century Holy Roman Emperor Friedrich Barbarossa, or Friedrich I—to be launched in mid-May 1941. From the planning stages, Barbarossa was a criminal enterprise on a massive scale. Hitler was driven by more than strategic calculations. Barbarossa was planned and executed based on his twin core obsessions: obtaining Lebensraum (**living space**) in the East and his belief that the communist regime in Moscow was at the center of a conspiracy by **Jews** to destroy Germany and take over the world. In late February and early March came the first orders that the "Jewish Bolshevik intelligentsia" was to be exterminated (the Commissar Order). Further guidelines laid out plans for a war of unrestrained brutality in which distinctions between uniformed combatant and civilian were erased (the Barbarossa Decree). As Wehrmacht high command chief of staff General **Franz Halder** noted on 30 March, the war in the East would be completely different from the war in the west.

A month before the invasion, the Wehrmacht and the **Schutzstaffel** (Protection Squad; SS) worked out respective spheres of operation. On Hitler's orders, **Heinrich Himmler** organized the deployment of Einsatzgruppen (mobile SS execution squads) to follow the army into the Soviet Union. These units would operate behind the front lines independently of but in coordination with the army. Broadly, they were directed to eliminate any form of real or suspected civilian **opposition**. Specifically, they were ordered to kill "Jewish Bolsheviks," but by the late summer, in some areas, they were murdering every Jewish person they encountered.

On 30 April 1941, the date for the attack was moved to 22 June. Hitler expected the war to last four months. On the morning of 22 June, **Joseph Goebbels** broadcast a statement written by Hitler justifying the attack as a response to an alleged attempt by the Soviet Union to collude with Britain to erode Germany's preponderant position in Europe. A day later, he moved to his headquarters in East Prussia [see WOLF'S LAIR (WOLFSSCHANZE)], where he would reside for most of the war's duration.

Operation Barbarossa was the single largest military operation of its kind in history. Four million troops attacked along a massive front. The invasion force was divided into three groups aimed at **Leningrad** in the North, Moscow in the center, and **Ukraine** in the South. The objective was to take control of the entire territory from Archangel in the North to Astrakhan in the South. In the invasion's initial phase, Hitler prioritized the capture of Leningrad and Ukraine over Moscow.

It nearly succeeded. Stalin ignored multiple reliable intelligence reports that an invasion was imminent, and the Red Army's losses of men—5 million casualties—and matériel were staggering and seemingly catastrophic. Behind the lines, Himmler's SS task forces initiated what would become the first stage of the **Holocaust** (now often referred to by historians as the "Holocaust by bullets"). To manage and exploit the conquered territory, the Germans created two massive civilian-run occupation zones (Reichskommisariats): Ostland, encompassing the **Baltics** and western Belorussia, and Ukraine [see GENERAL PLAN FOR THE EAST (GENERALPLAN OST); ROSENBERG, ALFRED (1893–1946)].

By August, German forces approached Leningrad and Kiev, and Odessa fell in September and October, respectively. On 6 September, Hitler gave the order for the capture of Moscow (Operation Typhoon). By early December, German soldiers on the front line could see the city's skyline. But Stalin could draw on a practically unlimited supply of reinforcements from the East, and Moscow remained in Russian hands. German forces, their supply lines stretched thin and unprepared for the brutal Russian winter, dug in. Barbarossa had failed, and the eastern front had been created. More than two long, destructive years of war lay ahead.

In retrospect, the failure of Typhoon was the European war's most important turning point. Allied victory was achieved at colossal human cost on multiple land, air, and sea fronts stretching from Moscow to the shores of the US Eastern Seaboard and from Norway to North Africa. But it would be the extraordinary military-civilian mobilization in the Soviet Union after its initial losses that produced the Grand Alliance's single greatest victory. *See also* ASSASSINATION ATTEMPT (20 JULY 1944); BATTLE OF STALINGRAD (1942–1943); BATTLE OF KURSK (1943); KEITEL, WILHELM (1882–1946); OPERATION BAGRATION (1944).

OPERATION OVERLORD (1944). The battle for control of the Atlantic [see BATTLE OF THE ATLANTIC (1939–1945)], the victory in North **Africa**, the invasions of Sicily and then the **Italian** Peninsula, and the **strategic bombing campaign** notwithstanding, **Joseph Stalin** would not consider the Anglo-American (*see* UNITED STATES OF AMERICA) contribution to the war adequate until a second major land front was opened. The Americans and the British, however, faced several daunting problems. Considering it took British forces seven months to capture the weakly defended island of **Madagascar** in 1942, the paramount question was one of capability. Could an Anglo-American force pull off a massive amphibious and airborne invasion of German-occupied Europe at the most strategically significant—and increasingly heavily defended—point: northern **France** [see FORTRESS EUROPE (FESTUNG EUROPAS)]? A second involved disagreement between Washington and London over where to open a second front, with British officials skeptical about northern France and **Winston Churchill** pressing for an invasion of the **Balkans**.

The third became the greatest challenge: keeping the date and above all the location of the invasion a secret from the Germans. Not only did the Americans and British accomplish that, but they also pulled off the greatest military deception and misinformation campaign in history—Operation Bodyguard. In the Second World War, Bodyguard was matched only by the buildup to the Red Army's attack on the center of the front in Russia launched two weeks after Allied forces landed in Normandy on 6 June 1944 [see OPERATION BAGRATION (1944)].

Planning for a cross-channel invasion of France to take place in the spring of 1944 began in April 1943. Hitler and his generals (and the German public) certainly knew an attack was coming. Hitler ordered networks of defensive installations along the channel coastline built up in early 1944. So pleased was he with his own designs for some of the fortifications that he allegedly declared himself history's greatest fortification builder. He also installed one of the few generals he trusted, the highly competent **Erwin Rommel**, in charge of the region's defense. By March, he boasted to **Joseph Goebbels** that the Allies would be unable to establish a foothold anywhere along the northern coast, an opinion shared by the army's leadership, including Rommel. But by that point in the war, even the usually overconfident propaganda minister had his doubts.

Ultimately, German forces were split up along the coast (with some units sent to southern France, where Hitler suspected an invasion might take place). The dispersal was the result of disagreements between Rommel and other generals and because Hitler became unshakably convinced the Allies would land at Calais, at the narrowest stretch of the English Channel. He also retained personal command of 4 of the 10 armored divisions stationed in France. In the end, the preponderance of available German forces was concentrated around Calais, some 350 kilometers north of Normandy. Hitler persisted in believing this was to the focal point of the Allied attack until early August, shortly before German forces were driven out of France entirely [see MILITARY COMMANDER; RUNDSTEDT, GERD VON (1875–1953)].

Operation Overlord was one of the greatest Allied victories of the war. A convergence of factors made it possible: the success of Bodyguard, Allied logistical ingenuity and its practically limitless material resources, a fortuitously timed window of good weather, a German response hamstrung by dispersed forces and Hitler's insistence on maintaining the defense of Calais, and Allied control of the skies being the most important. The fighting capabilities of Allied soldiers, many who up to that point had little or no combat experience, must also be taken into account.

When the late-sleeping Hitler was informed of the landings, his confidence was undiminished, and he seemed to be beside himself with joy. He was unconcerned enough with the situation to devote several hours on 6 June to badgering the new **Hungarian** prime minister about the urgent necessity of rounding up his country's **Jews**. **Schutzstaffel** (Protection Squad; SS) internal security reports suggest that many Germans shared Hitler's sense of relief that the expected attack had finally taken place, though it's doubtful they had nearly as much faith in the ability of the **Wehrmacht** and what was left of the **Luftwaffe** to throw the invaders back into the channel.

Within days, it was clear that the invasion was a success and that Fortress Europe had been breached. Hitler's confidence remained high because he had already ordered the launching of the first supposed **wonder weapons**—V-1 rockets—at London. But as terrifying as these were for Londoners, they did nothing to alter the course of the war. Finally convinced of the seriousness of the situation by mid-June, Hitler traveled to Northeast France to consult with his commanders. Now he appeared distinctly cowed and, in typical fashion, blamed them for the unfolding calamity. The overall strategic situation worsened a few days later with the Red Army's surprise attack in central Russia. By early August, Anglo-American forces had broken out of Normandy (Operation Cobra), and the Red Army stood outside Warsaw.

OPERATION TORCH (1942). On 8 November 1942, Anglo-American forces invaded North **Africa** at multiple locations in Morocco and Algeria. It was the opening of the first Allied offensive of the war. The broad objective was to open a second front in the west, long demanded by **Joseph Stalin**, with the more immediate goal of putting pressure on German and **Italian** forces in Libya and Egypt [*see* BATTLE OF EL-ALAMEIN (1943)]. An added benefit would be securing bases in Northwest Africa as the **Battle of the Atlantic** was reaching a crucial stage.

The landings were successful, and resistance by **French** forces loyal to the Vichy regime was uneven and overcome quickly. The relatively untested Americans gained valuable experience in conducting amphibious assaults. With the **Afrika Korps** finally defeated in May 1943, the way was open to the invasion of Sicily and then the Italian Peninsula. Torch did not, however, succeed in drawing significant German forces away from the eastern front.

The operation caught Hitler by surprise. He was informed of the landings as he traveled to Munich for the annual ceremony honoring the **Beer Hall Putsch**. **Joachim von Ribbentrop** asked for permission to approach Stalin about a settlement via the Soviet embassy in Stockholm, but Hitler would not hear of it, and in his address to the party faithful in Munich, he ruled out any possibility of making peace with anyone. **Schutzstaffel** (Protection Squad; SS) internal security reports noted that morale in Germany—already shaken by the desperate fight for Stalingrad—took another hit. As the landings in North Africa continued and Hitler learned of **Erwin Rommel**'s desperate situation in El-Alamein, he ordered the **Wehrmacht** to occupy southern France (Operation Anton). *See also* MILITARY COMMANDER.

OPPOSITION. Assessing the extent of opposition to Hitler and the regime within Germany has always been difficult. Much of the difficulty has resulted from differing definitions of *opposition*. Restricting the definition to the activities of members of Germany's military, diplomatic, and church elite excludes those who took enormous risks attempting to subvert the regime's policies and ideology and to protect **Jews**. But defined too broadly, the concept becomes meaningless and, at worst, serves as a kind of alibi for those who outwardly conformed or otherwise supported the regime.

Whether undertaken by elites or ordinary Germans, opposition was in fact relatively rare. To some extent, this reflects Hitler's and the regime's genuine popularity through the 1930s and in the war's first year [*see* COORDINATION (GLEICHSCHALTUNG); REICHSTAG FIRE (27–28 FEBRUARY 1933)]. But the ruthless effectiveness of coercive measures must also be taken into consideration. The organized Left was decimated in the three months following Hitler's appointment as **chancellor** [*see* COMMUNIST PARTY OF GERMANY (KOMMUNISTISCHE PARTEI DEUTSCHLANDS; KPD); SOCIAL DEMOCRATIC PARTY OF GERMANY (SOZIALDEMOKRATISCHE PARTEI DEUTSCHLANDS; SPD)].

The **Röhm purge** of June 1934 eliminated the **Sturmabteilung** (Stormtroopers; SA) as an independent power center and sent an unmistakable message to conservative nationalists and politically active Catholics that Hitler could not be controlled and would not share power (*see* RELIGION). With all police forces placed under the control of the **Schutzstaffel** (Protection Squad; SS) in 1936, the regime greatly expanded its coercive and surveillance capabilities. And while the Gestapo was a relatively small organization, its officials could rely on the willingness of Germans to denounce each other and betray Jews in hiding. Small pockets of oppositional activities, such as those undertaken by the White Rose group in Munich during the war, were constantly broken up, often because of denunciations [see CANARIS, WILHELM (1887–1945)].

Opposition among young people became a significant concern of the Gestapo, and a **concentration camp** for youth was constructed in Neuwied in the Rhineland. Networks of self-proclaimed Edelweiss Pirates (Edelweiss Piraten) and Swing Youth (Swingjugend) attempted to break away from the **Hitler Youth** (Hitlerjugend; HJ), adopted certain forms of dress, took to camping and hiking excursions or staking out territories in cities, and embraced forms of music and dance banned by the regime.

No serious opposition formed within Germany's business elite or the legal and medical communities. The same was true of the country's scientific establishment and the professoriate at its once-great universities. The vast majority of Protestant and Catholic officials conformed and never engaged in oppositional activity. Outspoken opposition to the medical murder of the handicapped (**Euthanasia Program**) was exceptional and limited to a very small number of high-ranking and popular clergymen. Far more numerous were those clergy, physicians, civil servants, and caregivers who facilitated the mass murder of the handicapped.

And while the regime's attempt to get Germans to boycott Jewish-owned businesses in 1933 failed and there is evidence of widespread disapproval of the **Night of Broken Glass** pogrom in November 1938, substantial opposition to the persecution, deportation, and then mass murder of Jews was virtually nonexistent. Those Jews who did survive in Germany were saved by sheer luck and the willingness of individual Gentile Germans to protect them. One German historian estimated that it took at least seven people to save a single Jew in Berlin, though accounts by survivors suggest the number is most likely much larger.

A surge of surprise roundups of Jews that began in Berlin in late 1942 produced one of the rare instances of successful public protest against the regime. In February 1943, the Nazis arrested Jews, who were then used as forced labor in Berlin factories. About 1,500 Jewish men and a few **women** in mixed marriages and some *Mischlinge* (mixed race) were held in a building on Rosenstrasse, in the city's center (see NUREMBERG RACE LAWS). In response, several hundred—perhaps a few thousand—of their Aryan spouses, friends, relatives, and even a few strangers took to the streets and demanded the release of the prisoners. They were not deterred by threats from SS and Gestapo officers. The regime released the prisoners. It was the only public protest staged in Nazi Germany against the deportation of Jews.

With the crushing of political opposition, elite conformity, a strong popular consensus behind the regime, and organized opposition rendered practically impossible, the best chance at removing Hitler belonged to the upper echelons of the military [see ELSER, GEORG (1903–1945)]. Hitler's diplomatic successes in the prewar years—the remilitarization of the **Rhineland**, the annexation of **Austria**, and the dismemberment of **Czechoslovakia**—all precluded a coup attempt by the military, as did the early military victories in **Poland**, Western Europe, and Russia.

But a conspiracy to **assassinate** Hitler took shape after the loss at the **Battle of Stalingrad**. The plotters of multiple assassination attempts in 1943 and 1944 were motivated mainly by a desire to avert a catastrophic defeat. But it would not be correct to dismiss them as nothing more than deeply compromised men desperate to save their own skins. Some of them did act on the basis of principled opposition based their revulsion at Germany's barbaric war in the East.

In the end, what opposition did exist had no significant impact on the regime, the course of the war, and the **Holocaust**. It would take several decades after 1945 for a majority of West Germans to regard those who resisted—whether elite or ordinary—as martyrs rather than traitors.

P

PAN-GERMAN IDEOLOGY. The pan-German movement had its roots in the 19th-century liberal nationalist dream of uniting all German-speaking peoples in a "greater Germany." This objective was blocked by **Otto von Bismarck**'s creation of a German nation-state in 1870–1871 that excluded **Austria** and other ethnic German regions. Pan-Germanists remained undaunted, and by the end of the century, they had become thoroughly reactionary. Its adherents in the multiethnic Austro-Hungarian Empire responded to the perceived threats of Slavic nationalism, high birth rates among Slavic peoples, and the westward migration of **Jews** fleeing persecution in the Russian Empire. At the same time in imperial Germany, the Pan-German League was created as a small but well-funded and well-connected lobbying group advocating for the creation of a greater Germany, for expansion into Eastern Europe for the purposes of settling ethnic Germans, and for building an overseas empire of bases and colonies.

The movement's central figure in Austria was Georg von Schönerer, a member of the Austrian House of Deputies. Schönerer founded the League of German Nationalists in 1882 to promote the unification of Austria and imperial Germany. The league's platform was also militantly anti-Jewish, with Schönerer embracing a conspiratorial anti-Semitism that underpinned his demand for the elimination of Jews and "Jewish influence" from all areas of public life. The model for the legislation to achieve this was the American Chinese Exclusion Act of 1882 (*see* UNITED STATES OF AMERICA).

Hitler had grown up influenced by a milder form of German nationalism predominant in northern Austria, one that promoted a more prominent role for ethnic Germans in the empire but was otherwise loyal to the crown. He came to embrace Schönerer's more extreme pan-German ideology as a teenager in Linz. Though Schönerer's influence in Austrian politics had waned by the time Hitler moved to **Vienna**, his ideology and program left a permanent impression on him.

After **World War I**, the Pan-German League would become an important early source of funding for the **German Workers' Party** (Deutsche Arbeiterpartei; DAP) and the **National Socialist German Workers' Party** (Nazi Party; Nationalsozialistische Deutsche Arbeiterpartei; NSDAP). Its leader, Heinrich Class, would become one of Hitler's early mentors, introducing him to members of Munich's **economic** and political elite. Hitler and the NSDAP would resurrect key elements of Schönerer's and the league's platforms, and Hitler would later describe national socialism as the latter's "child."

PAPEN, FRANZ VON (1879–1969). Apart from **Paul von Hindenburg**, no other conservative nationalist politician played a more important role in facilitating Hitler's appointment as **chancellor** than Papen. Despite the fact that he was neither Prussian nor a Protestant, the urbane, elegant Papen personified Germany's aristocratic elite. The son of a Westphalian

167

nobleman and a devout Catholic, he became a professional officer and a diplomat and served with distinction in Turkey during the later years of the war.

Though he opposed the revolution, Papen joined the **Center Party** (Zentrum) in 1921 and served in the **Reichstag**. He was not a particularly knowledgeable or talented politician. A **French** diplomat observed acidly that neither Papen's friends nor his enemies took him seriously. He did not fit well within the Zentrum and aligned himself more closely with Hindenburg. In May 1932, Hindenburg and General Kurt von Schleicher engineered then chancellor Heinrich Brüning's resignation, and Hindenburg appointed Papen as his replacement. Papen was nothing more than the well-dressed and socially acceptable puppet of the nationalist establishment. His cabinet was prestacked with other aristocrats and earned the derisive nickname Cabinet of Barons. But it was Hindenburg and Schleicher who were the most important figures behind Papen's chancellorship.

By the late summer of 1932, the nationalist conservatives were boxed in. The July Reichstag **elections** netted the **National Socialist German Workers' Party** (Nazi Party; Nationalsozialistische Deutsche Arbeiterpartei; NSDAP) 37 percent of the vote, making it the single largest political party. The ideal solution for the conservatives, whose representation in the Reichstag had dwindled considerably, was to form a coalition with the Nazis. The problem was that this would necessitate giving in to Hitler's demand for the chancellor's office, something Hindenburg remained unwilling to do. At the same time, the **Sturmabteilung** (Stormtroopers; SA) had intensified its campaign of violence against its opponents, and to many, civil war seemed like a real possibility. Hitler was certainly keen to play up this possibility as leverage against Hindenburg's intransigence.

Papen's position weakened considerably following a massively lopsided vote of no confidence against him in the Reichstag on 12 September and Hindenburg's decision to call for new elections. Though the Nazis lost seats, the political impasse remained unbroken. A turning point came on 3 December, when Schleicher convinced Hindenburg that if he appointed him chancellor, then Schleicher could cleave away a large enough faction of Nazi Party delegates disaffected with Hitler's all-or-nothing position and form a majority that would include the **Social Democratic Party of Germany** (Sozialdemokratische Partei Deutschlands; SPD). Civil war could be avoided, and the **economic** recovery that had already begun could be accelerated. Hindenburg agreed.

But Schleicher's plan failed almost immediately. The Nazis would not be split, and the SPD refused to cooperate with Schleicher's government. Enraged and humiliated, Papen was determined to do what was necessary to dislodge his successor. The situation made an alliance, albeit an uneasy one, between Hitler and the vengeful Papen possible, and in January 1933, the two schemed against Schleicher. Because Hitler remained committed to the chancellorship or nothing, Papen had to accept a subordinate position for himself, that of vice chancellor. But the result of their negotiations was a cabinet stacked with non-Nazis. On 30 January, Hindenburg's closest advisers convinced him to go along with the plan and appoint Hitler chancellor.

It was Papen who wrote of Hitler, "We have hired him." The opposite was in fact the case. Though he was bypassed by Hitler as the Nazis crushed the Left and laid the legal basis for the dictatorship following the **Reichstag fire**, Papen was not completely powerless. Until the summer of 1934, he remained in a position to give voice to growing conservative nationalist discontent over Hitler's consolidation of power and especially the radicalism of the SA. His incendiary speech at the university in Marburg on 17 June denouncing Nazi extremism and the cult of personality around Hitler (whom he wisely did not name) accelerated Hitler's plans to purge the SA and send an unmistakable message to conservatives and politically active Catholics.

Papen's prominence most likely saved his life in **Röhm purge**—his three closest associates were murdered—and he was shunted off to **Vienna** as Germany's ambassador. There, he became useful to Hitler by helping pave the way to annexation in 1938 (see AUSTRIA). Beginning in 1939, Papen served as ambassador to Turkey, where he had some success in drawing the officially neutral government away from closer ties to the Allies. Papen returned to Germany in August 1944 after Ankara severed diplomatic ties with Berlin. He was arrested by American soldiers in April 1945 and was charged by the **International Military Tribunal** (IMT). Acquitted of charges related to crimes against peace, he was indicted by a German denazification court in 1947 and sentenced to eight years' hard labor. Released two years later following an appeal, he enjoyed a comfortable retirement. His memoirs and many other writings in the years before his death in 1969 attempted to justify his actions in the early 1930s and otherwise revived his conservative Catholic political positions.

PERSONALITY. There have always been significant obstacles to assessing Hitler's personality. We lack evidence like an introspective diary or an extensive personal correspondence. He was assertively secretive about his past and kept what few **family** members he had at a distance. As an adult, he had no close personal friends. The story of his formative years in *Mein Kampf*—maintained skillfully by his acolytes and propagandists—is greatly at odds with what is known to be true. Aspects of his personality and private life were also the subject of rumors, speculation, and outright falsifications by his opponents or opportunists seeking to cash in on what was often not much more than a fleeting acquaintance. Like the personal mythology of *Mein Kampf*, these have left their traces on popular perceptions and the pages of historical accounts alike.

No qualified psychologist analyzed Hitler in person, though there have been many attempts to do so at a distance. Among the earliest and most influential were undertaken by the wartime American intelligence agency, the Office of Strategic Services, in 1943. These were based on flimsy evidence and theories of childhood development that have long since been discredited. Hitler's biographers have either drawn from the more recent and reliable of these analyses, or they have avoided extended speculation about his personality, private life, or mental **health**. Most have emphasized the way he wielded power or the contingencies and contexts that made it possible for a destitute nobody to become the world's best-known dictator.

Yet there is no way to avoid considering the role that traits formed in his youth played in his career as politician and dictator. At a young age, he evinced the qualities of a narcissistic personality, namely a lack of empathy, an extremely high self-regard, and a propensity to dwell in a fantasy world. He had a high level of native intelligence and was extremely articulate, but as his Realschule (vocational school) teacher recalled, Hitler was lazy, "contrary, high-handed, self-opinionated, and irascible." Seemingly unable to form close personal relationships, he was a loner. His single friend, **August Kubizek**, recalled that Hitler spent much of his time fantasizing, reading, drawing, and becoming swept up in performances of **Richard Wagner**'s operas. The passive Kubizek—Hitler could not have tolerated any companion who was not passive or at least willing to be browbeaten into submission—was also a frequent victim of Hitler's propensity to deliver lengthy monologues, a practice he would carry into politics and his private sphere.

According to Kubizek, Hitler seemed uninterested in **women** and sex. But there is reliable evidence that as an adult, he had relationships with several women that involved conventional heterosexual sex. Conversely, there is no convincing evidence that he indulged in sexual fetishes. In general, he combined assumptions of male superiority and female weakness with his all-consuming determination to control and dominate. Both temperamentally and in terms of his self-conception as Germany's political savior, he could never conform to the standards of a middle-class heterosexual marriage.

Hitler's aversion to structures and authority vanished during **World War I**. He adapted to the discipline and ascetic existence of the soldier, not least because it provided him with the bare necessities of existence. He nonetheless remained a loner and resisted being drawn into powerful bonds of camaraderie commonly formed between soldiers. As a politician and dictator, he seemed to be constantly performing, whether giving speeches or delivering hours-long monologues. Cultivating his public image was one of the few areas in which he could devote sustained and disciplined effort. An autodidact, he read voraciously but not systematically nor very deeply and, like many people, sought confirmation of preexisting beliefs and prejudices (see RACISM). His self-certainty, combined with an extraordinary capacity to retain facts, fueled his lengthy monologues. These were performances designed to impress, intimidate, or simply wear out anyone who might be tempted to reveal his beliefs to be ill-informed nonsense. His monologues also kept him at the center of attention in his favorite cafés and later in official settings and the **Berghof**.

Of course, Hitler was also performing for Hitler, with his monologues an essential component of maintaining his mythology in his own mind. Also performative were his bursts of seemingly uncontrollable rage. For someone as repressed as Hitler, it may seem surprising that he was rather finely attuned to the emotional impact of an encounter with another person, though one might also conclude his simplistic conception of people as slaves to their emotions was a reflection of his own underdeveloped and immature personality. He was, after all, utterly devoid of empathy.

Though unable to form close relationships, his insatiable need for an audience meant that he often surrounded himself with people. Only among a very few—such as the families of **Joseph Goebbels**; Winifred Wagner; **Ernst Hanfstaengl** and his wife, Helene; and **Heinrich Hoffmann**—was he capable of seeming at ease. He could be charming and witty and capable of entertaining members of his entourage with his talent for mimicry. But his personal inapproachability became another performance, this one designed to heighten the mystique and allure of the savior and artist he believed himself to be. The image of this kind of leader—one devoted totally to Germany—was used to explain the lack of a conventional marriage and children.

A candid photo of Hitler, who was afraid of flying, in his personal plane, Bremen, 1932. *Courtesy of the United States Holocaust Memorial Museum.*

The related image of a man who lived simply was belied by his tastes for expensive cars and expensive, expansive residences. He was well known to be fastidious, if not very imaginative, about his clothing. After the war, he abandoned foppish accessories for traditional suits or Stormtrooper garb. Later he adopted a simple military-style jacket-and-tie combination, which became a party uniform. He never became the kind of dictator who bedecked himself in medals and wore only his Iron Cross. Unlike **Benito Mussolini**, who liked to appear shirtless for propaganda stunts, Hitler never allowed himself to be seen in any state other than fully dressed.

Obsessed with dying at a relatively young age, Hitler believed a vegetarian diet and avoidance of tobacco and alcohol would prolong his life. It is also clear that he was a germophobe, a fear that would carry over into his political ideology and belief that **Jews** were a form of human bacteria that threatened to infect the otherwise healthy "body" of Germany. *See also* DRUG USE; HOLOCAUST.

PERSONAL WILL AND POLITICAL TESTAMENT (1945). Hitler dictated a political testament and his final personal will to one of his secretaries, Traudl Junge, on the night of 28–29 April 1945, immediately before his marriage to **Eva Braun**. These are not to be confused with *The Political Testament*, a published collection of notes allegedly taken by **Martin Bormann** of Hitler's monologues delivered in the last months of his life and almost certainly a forgery.

In the personal will, Hitler declared that Braun's years of faithful companionship would be rewarded by his agreement to marry her, followed by her death at his side. Together, they would avoid the humiliation of surrender and captivity. Naming Bormann as executor, he left his personal possessions to either the **National Socialist German Workers' Party** (Nazi Party; Nationalsozialistische Deutsche Arbeiterpartei; NSDAP) or the state. The political testament was a self-pitying rehash of his conspiratorial anti-Semitism. He blamed "international **Jewry**" and those who served "Jewish interests" for starting a war he claimed he never wanted. By boasting that Jews were being "called to account" for starting a world war, he was confirming the realization of his **Prophecy Speech** from January 1939 (*see* HOLOCAUST). Despite the looming defeat, he declared that national socialism will never be forgotten and will live on. He confirmed his decision to remain in Berlin and that he would "choose death voluntarily," as he had no desire to allow Jews to make a spectacle of him.

Finally, he named the leading figures of the government that would come to power following his death—Grand Admiral **Karl Dönitz** would be Reich president, and **Joseph Goebbels** would be Reich chancellor—and did not miss the chance to repeat that **Hermann Göring** and **Heinrich Himmler** had been expelled from the party and removed from their positions. Most important was that this new leadership maintain Germany's **Nuremberg race laws** and continue the fight against "international Jewry," the "universal poisoner of all peoples."

Hitler seemed to be in a hurry and ordered Junge to type up her notes immediately. Meanwhile, Hitler and Braun were married. During what must be one of the most macabre wedding receptions ever held, Hitler discussed appointments to the new government with Bormann and Goebbels, who relayed the names to Junge as she typed three copies of each. Hitler signed the documents around 5:00 a.m.

With Soviet forces less than a quarter mile from the **chancellery**, three couriers were dispatched from the bunker, each carrying a copy of the will and testament. They were ordered to deliver them at all costs to Dönitz and Field Marshal Ferdinand Schörner, now the **Wehrmacht** commander in chief. It is unclear who was to receive the third set. Hitler told Junge that he would not commit **suicide** until it could be confirmed that the couriers had completed their missions. He did not wait, and in any case, confirmation never arrived. All three had given up after disguising themselves as foreign laborers and reaching areas controlled by Western Allied forces. They split up and hid the documents. British and American (*see* UNITED STATES OF AMERICA) intelligence agents—one of them was Hugh Trevor-Roper—soon recovered all three sets, one of which included Hitler's and Braun's marriage certificate [see DIARY HOAX (1983); *TABLE TALK* AND *THE TESTAMENT OF ADOLF HITLER* (1941–1944; 1945)].

British Foreign Office and US State Department officials made copies for other Allied governments, the US chief of counsel at the **International Military Tribunal** (IMT), and the press. They were reluctant to see the texts disseminated widely in occupied Germany. The two sets of originals held by the British were eventually deposited in Britain's national archives. In April 1946, after authentication by the Federal Bureau of Investigation, the set held by the US Military Intelligence Service was displayed to the public at the US National Archives in Washington, DC.

PHONY WAR. Also known as the Twilight War, Sitzkrieg (Sitting War), and *drôle de guerre* (Funny, or Bizarre, War). American (*see* UNITED STATES OF AMERICA) newspapers first used the term to describe the period from the German invasion of **Poland** in September 1939 to the attack on Western Europe that commenced in April 1940, an eight-month stretch during which British, **French**, and German armies did not engage each other in Western Europe or over the British Isles.

In a speech to the **Reichstag** on 6 October 1939, Hitler made a peace offer to France and Britain. Eager to attack in the West, however, he started discussing an offensive with top military officers the next day and ordered the **Wehrmacht**'s high command to prepare for an invasion in five weeks' time (Case Yellow). His senior officers were appalled. The Polish campaign had drained the military's human and material resources. And they expected that fighting the French and British—in the winter, no less—would be an entirely different matter than fighting the overmatched Poles, even if neither had yet fully rearmed.

The generals' reluctance enraged Hitler. In his mind, the window of opportunity to invade the Soviet Union was closing fast, and it had to be preceded by the conquest of the Low Countries and France (and hence control of the English Channel coast) and subduing Britain one way or another. In late November, he reminded them that his boldness had been justified by the string of diplomatic victories beginning with the remilitarization of the **Rhineland** in March 1936. Hitler's faith in his own destiny was further bolstered by the fact that he had narrowly missed being **assassinated** in Munich two weeks earlier [see ELSER, GEORG (1903–1945)].

The chief of the Army General Staff, General **Franz von Halder**, was so shocked by Hitler's demand that he briefly revived the poorly organized assassination plot abandoned when the **Czechoslovakia crisis** was resolved peacefully the previous fall. But Halder lost his nerve. It would be the worsening weather—rain and mud were the two biggest problems—that forced Hitler to postpone the invasion until the spring. And there was another serious problem—the German public's enthusiasm for war in the West was clearly lacking.

The delay ultimately worked to Hitler's advantage, as it made a surge in arms production possible (*see also* ECONOMY; REARMAMENT). It had the opposite effect on French forces dug in behind the Maginot Line. Unwilling to take offensive action, discipline eroded as they waited. Alone among high-ranking French officers urging preparations for war was then-unknown General Charles de Gaulle. Though France and Great Britain had declared war on Germany on 3 September, the twin pillars of **appeasement**, Prime Minister Neville Chamberlain and French prime minster Eduard Deladier remained in office until March and October 1940, respectively. The Phony War, then, was a continuation of appeasement.

Outside Western Europe and the British Isles, the period was hardly as quiet as monikers like *Sitzkrieg* suggested. Germany's war on Poland's elite and **Jewish** population was just beginning, as was the mobilization of the Polish underground army, which numbered around 100,000 fighters by mid-1940. On 17 September 1939, Soviet forces invaded Poland from the East, initiating **Joseph Stalin**'s war of revenge against the Poles. After the Finnish government refused to agree to Stalin's demands for territorial concessions, Soviet forces invaded Finland on 29 November, though here, the Finns fought them to a standstill in the Winter War. What would become a titanic battle for control of the Atlantic Ocean [see BATTLE OF THE ATLANTIC (1939–1945)] began almost immediately after Germany invaded Poland.

German aggression in the Atlantic had another important result in this period: the passage of "cash and carry" legislation by the US Congress in late October and early November. The law represented a major revision of the Neutrality Act of 1937, which had expired in May 1939, by allowing the sale of arms to a belligerent able to pay cash and pick up the purchase. Easing the bill's passage was the swing in public opinion against Germany and the neutrality laws when a month earlier the pocket battleship *Deutschland* captured an American cargo ship. See also DUNKIRK (26 MAY–4 JUNE 1940); NAZI–SOVIET NONAGGRESSION PACT (MOLOTOV–RIBBENTROP PACT; 1939); ROOSEVELT, FRANKLIN DELANO (1882–1945); WESER EXERCISE (WESERÜBUNG).

PIUS XII, POPE (EUGENIO PACELLI; 1876–1958). On 9 February 1939, Pope Pius XI died. His successor was Cardinal Eugenio Pacelli, the Vatican's secretary of state. An archconservative in church and secular political affairs, he was determined to defend and extend the Vatican's authority. He had extensive experience in Germany, serving as papal nuncio to Munich during the tumultuous period of the **Bavarian Soviet Republic** and then as nuncio to Berlin through most of the 1920s. As secretary of state, he played a central role in the negotiations for the concordat with the Nazi regime concluded in Rome in July 1933 and seems to have supported the decision by the leadership of the **Center Party** (Zentrum) to dissolve itself.

Pacelli became pope after years of tension between the Nazi regime and the German Catholic Church (*see* RELIGION). Though he found Hitler distasteful, his main objective as pope was to appease him, which he attempted to do from the very beginning of his papacy. A year before his death, Pius XI charged an American Jesuit priest and antiracist activist, John LaFarge, with drafting an encyclical denouncing Nazi **racism** and anti-Semitism. LaFarge delivered the draft, which was controversial among high-ranking Vatican officials. They delayed its presentation to Pius XI, and most copies were destroyed, possibly on Pacelli's orders, immediately after his death.

Pacelli issued several statements denouncing the regime's **Euthanasia Program**, pleading for humane treatment of Poles, and one on Christmas Eve in 1942 alluding tepidly to people being victimized "sometimes only because of their nationality or race." But he never denounced in public the ongoing persecution and mass murder of Europe's **Jews**. He ignored a private plea from Konrad Preysing, the bishop of Berlin, on 17 January 1941 to issue a statement on behalf of the persecuted Jews of Germany and Europe. When the leader of the collaborationist Vichy regime in **France**, Marshal Philippe Petain, inquired about the Vatican's position on his regime's proposed anti-Jewish laws, he received an encouraging response via his ambassador to the Holy See.

Though informed as early as 1941 from multiple reliable sources about deportations and mass murder, Pacelli never denounced the ongoing genocide nor took other potentially important steps, such as threatening Catholic perpetrators with excommunication. The moral nadir of Pacelli's papacy arrived in the fall of 1943, when he chose to remain silent as the Germans rounded up **Italian** Jews for deportation to Auschwitz. The first time Pacelli made a public attempt to help Jews was on 25 June 1944, when he objected to **Hungarian** leader Miklos Horthy, albeit in rather general terms, to the deportation of his country's Jews. It had little effect, and most of Hungary's half-million Jews were murdered in Auschwitz.

Pacelli's defenders have argued that he was obliged to protect Catholics everywhere and that he was concerned that public criticism of Hitler and the Nazis would provoke retaliation against Catholics, a concern that may have felt particularly pressing when it seemed likely that Germany would win the war. Then there was Pacelli's ardent anticommunism. As papal nuncio in Munich after **World War I**, he witnessed the Soviet Republic up close, and the experience seems to have left a lasting impression on him. His fears of a communist tide swamping Italy and Europe were heightened when the war turned against Germany decisively in 1943. There is little evidence that Pacelli was more than a garden-variety Catholic anti-Semite, but documents released in 2020 by the Vatican reveal that he was strongly influenced by ardent anti-Semitic officials who advised him, for instance, to keep silent as Italian Jews were being rounded up and deported in the fall of 1943.

Pacelli alone cannot be blamed for the Catholic Church's complacency and largely passive collaboration in the **Holocaust** nor for the role numerous church officials played in protecting German and other European war criminals or in the postwar kidnapping of Jewish children of Holocaust victims. But he does not deserve the credit he has often received for the actions of hundreds of individual priests, nuns, and lay Catholics who protected and rescued Jews, actions he never even encouraged. As pontiff, he was in a uniquely powerful position to use the church's authority to denounce the raw inhumanity of Nazi anti-Semitism and then do something to call attention to the Holocaust as it was taking place. Though Pope Francis authorized the early release of the Vatican's archives relating to Pius XII's papacy and undoubtedly more will be learned about what he and high-ranking officials thought and did during and after the war, Pius's silences and inaction may be the most damning evidence against him and much of the Vatican establishment.

POLAND. The modern Polish state was a creation of **World War I** and the postwar settlement. In 1915, German forces conquered Russian Poland. At first, they presented themselves as liberators from Russian oppression but then subjected the nascent country to a brutal occupation, foreshadowing what was to come beginning in September 1939. As in other parts of Europe, armed conflict continued here for years after 1918, with **Jewish** communities frequently targeted by whatever forces happened to be in control. In the wake of the German army's collapse in the West, its remnants in the East, joined by right-wing paramilitary units (Free Corps), fought Russian, **Baltic**, and Polish forces to hold on to as much territory as possible. At the same time, Polish forces pushed eastward but were driven back to Warsaw's outskirts by the new Red Army. The Polish army, led by Józef Piłsudski, defended the city, and in March 1921, the Bolsheviks were forced to cede portions of **Ukraine** and Belorussia to the new Polish state.

The situation across the country stabilized, and after more than a century of partitions, invasions, and foreign rule, Polish nationalists realized their dream of an independent Poland. But the wars that made it possible had taken a terrible human, physical, and economic toll. The new state, moreover, contained multiple mutually hostile ethnic minority groups and was surrounded by neighbors harboring irredentist designs and, not least, powerful desires for revenge. This was particularly true for Germany. To make Poland a viable state, the victorious allies carved a "corridor" of land through what had been German territory (Pomerania) to the Baltic coast. The port city of Danzig (now Gdańsk) was declared an "open city" under the supervision of the new **League of Nations**. The Polish corridor, as it became known, also separated East Prussia from the rest of Germany. Poland's independence was supposed to be guaranteed by **France**, but the weakness of this connection was becoming evident by the mid-1920s.

Like millions of other Germans, Hitler found this situation intolerable. But much more than lost territory animated his hatred of Poles and Poland. The country was populated by Slavs, whom he considered subhuman, and millions of Jews, whom he considered Germany's mortal enemy (*see* RACISM). And not only were its fertile lands targeted for ethnic cleansing and the settlement of millions of Germans, but it also was the gateway to even greater territorial bounty farther east. Hitler's hatreds and imperial fantasies did not, however, prevent him from pursuing temporary arrangements with Warsaw, notably a non-aggression pact signed in 1934, to secure Germany's eastern borders. But his efforts to recruit the cautious Polish government to the **Anti-Comintern Pact** failed, as did his attempts to get it to trade the corridor for a future gift of Ukrainian territory.

The quick negotiation of the **Nazi–Soviet Nonaggression Pact** late August 1939 gave Hitler the green light to invade. After pretending to seek a last-minute negotiated solution with Great Britain and then hastily faking a minor Polish attack on German territory, 1.5 million German troops began a rapid and extremely well-coordinated invasion [see BLITZKRIEG (LIGHTNING WAR)]. Polish forces were overwhelmed, and Warsaw capitulated on 27 September. Britain and France declared war but did nothing else. Soviet forces invaded on 17 September, and while the Red Army and People's Commisariat for Internal Affairs (Naródnyy komissariát vnútrennikh del; NKVD) were not as brutal and destructive as the **Wehrmacht**, **Luftwaffe**, **Schutzstaffel** (Protection Squad; SS), and local ethnic German militias, **Joseph Stalin** shared Hitler's pathological hatred of the Poles and his determination to eliminate the country's elite. In October, the leadership of the Polish government, its diplomatic corps, the surviving leadership of the military (including its commander in chief), and the country's Catholic primate fled first to **Romania**, then to Britain, where it formed a government in exile.

Shortly before the invasion, Hitler told his military commanders that he intended to destroy Poland and ordered them to behave with extreme brutality. They complied willingly and enthusiastically. The brutality of the Wehrmacht and the Luftwaffe was matched and exceeded by that of the SS. Hitler ordered Einsatzgruppen (SS mobile execution units) and the Waffen SS to follow the Wehrmacht, ostensibly to secure newly conquered territory but in reality to murder as much of Poland's elite and middle-class leaders, like priests and teachers, as possible. He also authorized the mobilization of local ethnic German militias, which would serve under the command of the SS. By the end of the year, the militias and SS units had killed around 50,000 Poles, among them 7,000 Jews.

Hitler had Polish and former German territory annexed to Germany, which became East and West Prussia, Wartheland, and Upper Silesia. Two more districts, Bialystok and Galicia, were added following the invasion of the Soviet Union, and what had been Poland's eastern reaches converted to Reichkommisariats Ostland and Ukraine [see OPERATION BARBAROSSA (1941)]. The remaining territory, which included Warsaw, Kielce, Lublin, and Krakow, was named the General Government and placed under the control of Hans Frank. Like other regional leaders appointed by Hitler, Frank was a **National Socialist German Workers' Party** (Nazi Party; Nationalsozialistische Deutsche Arbeiterpartei; NSDAP) "old fighter," a party member of long standing. Other regional leaders were also veterans of the post–World War I paramilitary campaigns in the East. Hitler chose them first and foremost because he knew they could be counted on to be brutal and to act in accordance with his wishes without his constant supervision and intervention.

The plan for Poland, to be overseen by **Heinrich Himmler**, was to deport Poles—who constituted the majority of the population of the annexed territories—and Jews to the General Government and resettle the territories with ethnic Germans from the Baltic states, eastern Poland, and the Tyrol. A severe labor shortage in Germany in 1940 complicated Himmler's plans for a clear reordering of populations, and hundreds of thousands of Poles were brought into Germany, where they lived and worked in conditions of what one historian called "penal apartheid." In the General Government, the draconian measures required to conscript and transport thousands of people generated widespread resistance, to which the Germans responded with extreme brutality.

The war and occupation resulted in the deaths of 5 million Poles, or about 17 percent of the prewar population, and physical destruction on a massive scale. Following an uprising in Warsaw by the Polish underground Home Army in August and September 1944, the Germans demolished nearly all of Warsaw. Poland also became the epicenter of the **Holocaust**. The country's 3.3 million Jews comprised about 10 percent of its prewar population. Only an estimated 380,000 survived.

Polish Jews were targeted by the Wehrmacht and SS from the beginning of the war. When the occupation began, they were imprisoned in ghettos, the largest of which was in Warsaw. Systematic mass murder began in December 1941 and continued until the summer of 1944. All the death camps—Chelmno, Auschwitz, Treblinka, Sobibor, Belzec, and Majdanek— were located in Poland (*see* CONCENTRATION CAMPS).

As in other parts of the East and in the **Balkans**, organized underground resistance by Polish Catholics and Jews alike was extensive though of minimal impact on the German occupation and riven by factions. Poles also constitute the largest number of those designated by Yad Vashem, Israel's Holocaust memorial authority, as belonging to the "righteous among the nations" for risking their lives to protect Jews. Yet collaboration, including in the dispossession, robbery, and murder of Jews, was more widespread than has long been acknowledged in Poland.

As Poland had been the gateway for three invasions of Russia since the early 19th century, Stalin was determined to install a subservient postwar government. But security meant more than a loyal communist regime. The country's borders were altered to an extent greater than in any other postwar state, save Germany: Nearly 180,000 square kilometers of eastern Poland were annexed by the Soviet Union, while 103,600 square kilometers were added from Germany to western Poland. With the knowledge and approval of the wartime Allied governments, 3.1 million ethnic Germans would be expelled by the postwar Polish government by 1950.

PROPHECY SPEECH (30 JANUARY 1939). Hitler gave an annual speech on 30 January, the date of his appointment as **chancellor** in 1933. Six years later, he was at the height of his power, visibility, and popularity in Germany. His 1939 speech came after a year of intensified German aggression in Europe and accelerated preparations for war. Not coincidentally in Hitler's and other party leaders' minds, these developments were accompanied a radicalization of anti-**Jewish** actions, culminating in the horrific **Night of Broken Glass** (Reichskristallnacht) pogrom in November.

Hitler used the occasion to give vent to a number of accumulating frustrations. A major target was the **United States**. Reacting to the strong American response to the pogrom and sharp public criticisms of the Nazi dictatorship by President **Franklin D. Roosevelt** and his outspoken antifascist secretary of the interior, Harold Ickes, Hitler mocked democracy and boasted of his achievements in returning Germany to greatness. He even proclaimed that no one in Germany was persecuted for his or her **religious** beliefs.

Hitler also had domestic targets. His lingering displeasure over the peaceful settlement of the **Czechoslovakia crisis** led him to lash out at unnamed German diplomats and military officials who he believed had restrained him in September. Then he made a well-publicized promise for which the two-and-a-half-hour speech became best known: "I have often been a prophet in my life, and I was mostly laughed at. . . . I want to be a prophet again today: If international finance Jewry in Europe and beyond should succeed once more in plunging the peoples into a world war, then the result will not be the Bolshevization of the earth and thus the victory of Jewry, but the annihilation of the Jewish race in Europe."

Here Hitler was encouraging more German Jews to emigrate. By extension, he was trying to pressure other countries to accept more Jewish émigrés. As for those Jews who remained, they would be hostages, their fate dependent on the United States remaining out of a European war Hitler had no doubt Germany would win. His logic only made sense, of course, if one accepted as factual the fantasy of Jewish control of the American government. Finally, the threat was part of an ongoing effort to prepare the German public for the outbreak of another war, something most Germans did not want. A war, Hitler was saying, would not be the result of German aggression but that of "international finance Jewry" with its bases of power "in Europe and beyond."

Hitler made repeated references to his prophecy to regime officials but also in future speeches broadcast by radio or reprinted in the German press. On 12 December 1941, the day after he declared war on the United States, he informed a large assembly of officials in the chancellery that now that the world war had arrived, his prophecy would be realized [*see* WANNSEE CONFERENCE (1942)].

Hitler's private boasts about its ongoing realization were duly recorded by **Joseph Goebbels** in his diary, tellingly in August 1941, with Hitler's full knowledge that **Schutzstaffel** (Protection Squad; SS) Einsatzgruppen (mobile execution units) had greatly expanded the murder of Jews in German-controlled areas of the Soviet Union. Three months later, Goebbels issued in print and on radio the first public confirmation by a high-ranking regime official that Hitler's prophecy was at that moment being realized.

There is abundant evidence that Hitler's words resonated not only among mid- and lower-level regime officials but also with German civilians and soldiers. Numerous letters from soldiers advancing deep into Russia in 1941 referred to the unfolding realization of Hitler's "prophecy." Historians have long searched for a single written or verbal order for the genocide of Europe's Jews. If such an order ever existed, then it was almost certainly given in secret with reference to the speech made in full public view on 30 January 1939. *See also* DIETRICH, OTTO (1897–1952); HOLOCAUST.

PROTOCOLS OF THE ELDERS OF ZION. *Protocols* is a collection of documents forged in imperial Russia in the late 19th and early 20th centuries. It purports to expose a conspiracy by a group of **Jews** to take over the world and became one of the most influential anti-Semitic tracts ever written. Russian émigrés fleeing the Bolshevik regime brought copies to Germany, where they were translated and published by one of their members, Fyodor Vinberg, and by a wealthy German right-wing fanatic. The postwar Far-Right scene in Germany was already laced with paranoid anti-Semitism, and the circulation of *Protocols* certainly fueled the fire. The German versions sold well: 120,000 copies in 5 editions by 1920, with 33 editions published by 1933.

Beginning in 1920, journalists in Germany, Great Britain, and the **United States** exposed *Protocols* as a fake. Even **Joseph Goebbels** admitted in 1924—in his diary—that it was a forgery. But he asserted that it possessed an "inner" truth about the supposed inherent nature of Jews everywhere. When more evidence of a forgery emerged from Switzerland in 1937, the Propaganda Ministry prevented German newspapers from defending *Protocols*' authenticity, presumably on the grounds that Goebbels and other officials knew it was faked and they would prefer to manufacture (and control) their own stream of lies and conspiracy theories.

Hitler's first known reference to *Protocols* is in notes he made for a speech on 12 August 1921, and he mentioned it to a **National Socialist German Workers' Party** (Nazi Party; Nationalsozialistische Deutsche Arbeiterpartei; NSDAP) chapter meeting near Munich a week later. But *Protocols* was not the singularly important influence on his conception of Jews and a supposed conspiracy of "international Jewry" as some historians have claimed. In the only reference Hitler makes to *Protocols* in ***Mein Kampf***, he defends it against revelations about its provenance but takes a position similar to Goebbels's. Its authenticity was for Hitler beside the point because it exposes the true "nature and activity" of the Jews, their "inner logic," and their "final aims."

He repeated a version of this view in a conversation with Goebbels in mid-May 1943, a point in the war in which the regime's narrative of a conspiracy of "international Jewry" to take over the world and exterminate the German people was reaching a fever pitch. Again, Hitler insisted *Protocols* was authentic but again claimed that the most important point was that because of the Jews' supposed "racial" nature, they would always behave as they did. The only two officials of any significance to embrace and propagate *Protocols* as both genuine and a document of fundamental importance were **Alfred Rosenberg** and the publicist Julius Streicher. *See also* HOLOCAUST.

RACISM. Racism was foundational to Hitler's worldview, the **National Socialist German Workers' Party** (Nazi Party; Nationalsozialistische Deutsche Arbeiterpartei; NSDAP) ideology and policies, and the regime's war of territorial conquest.

Racism pervaded Western nations, shaping political, **economic**, and social life at every level. It was a driving force in imperialism and colonialism. Two forms of modern racism predominated in the White Western world by the end of the 19th century. One was cultural and anthropological. The other was biological. The latter was based on the idea that each "race" bore hereditarily determined characteristics and displayed a range of distinct physical features and intellectual capacities. Individual and group behaviors could thus be ascribed to a given race. By the late 19th century, White Westerners had come to accept that the existence of "races" was both a feature of all human cultures and a scientific fact.

In Great Britain and the **United States**, "race science" was known as "eugenics." In Germany, the term was *Rassenhygiene* (*racial hygiene*). As a matter of public policy, eugenics and *Rassenhygiene* took two forms: positive and negative. The former denoted policies designed to encourage healthy behaviors, clean environments, and reproduction among healthy couples. The latter took two main forms: forced sterilization and "euthanasia," also known as "mercy killing."

It was to be in Nazi Germany that *Rassenhygiene* was taken to its deadliest extent. This was above all because of the centrality of race to Hitler's worldview. He was an avid but not systematic reader, and like many people, he read to reinforce preexisting beliefs and prejudices. On the issue of race, to which he devotes an entire chapter of ***Mein Kampf***, he drew from a variety of then-current pseudoscientific thinking and joined his belief that humanity was comprised of unequal "races" to the social Darwinist view of the inevitability and necessity of the struggle for survival. It was also crucial that in its formative years, the party attracted devoted biological racists. Other than Hitler, the most influential racist was **Heinrich Himmler**, who would ensure that the **Schutzstaffel** (Protection Squad; SS) would become the main institutional enforcer of racist policies.

There was also a party-sponsored agency, the Office for Enlightenment on Population Policy and Racial Welfare (Aufklärungsamt für Bevölkerungspolitik und Rassenpflege), which was renamed the Office of Racial Policy (Rassenpolitisches Amt) in 1934. Headed by young physician and early Nazi Party member Walter Gross, the agency's purpose was to educate the general public about *Rassenhygiene*, the necessity of forced sterilization, and other matters related to the "racial health" of Germans. Gross's office published a glossy magazine, *Neues Volk* (*A New People*), and his office also produced materials for soldiers, **Sturmabteilung** (Stormtroopers; SA) men, and medical school students. Gross directed the office until his death in the **Battle of Berlin**.

There were numerous radical *Rassenhygienists* in Germany's medical and university establishments. In the latter, *Rassenhygiene* institutes became common and received support from the regime or major German research institutions. Though a minority before 1933, radical *Rassenhygienists* would enjoy the new regime's favor, while more moderate or **oppositional** voices were silenced. They would provide the expertise, institutional infrastructure, and much of the personnel to carry out the forced sterilization and medical murder of hundreds of thousands of Germans and non-Germans.

From December 1946 to August 1947, the **Nuremberg Military Tribunal** (NMT) presided over the "Doctors' Trial." Twenty-three defendants, nearly all physicians and mostly SS officers, were charged with one of more of the following: conspiracy to commit war crimes and crimes against humanity, war crimes (which included medical experiments and medical murder), crimes against humanity (the court included German nationals of the **Euthansasia Program** as victims), and membership in a criminal organization (the SS). But the vast majority of Germans who had committed medical crimes went unpunished. Since the end of the war, forced sterilization has been banned in most countries but is still practiced, including in the United States.

RAUBAL, ANGELA (GELI; 1908–1931). Angela "Geli" Raubal was Hitler's half-niece. She was the daughter of his half-sister Angela and Leo Raubal. Hitler had a brief and intense relationship with Geli from 1928 to 1931, when she committed suicide in the apartment they shared in Munich.

Raubal was born in Linz in 1908. Her father died two years later, and in 1915, the family moved to **Vienna**, where she attended a prestigious Gymnasium (a preparatory school for university-level study). Multiple accounts describe her as intelligent, sociable, and attractive. She first met Hitler during his incarceration in **Landsberg Prison** in 1924 and met him again following her graduation in 1927, when he invited her class to Munich and greeted them at afternoon tea. That summer and fall, Geli, along with her mother and **Rudolf Hess**, accompanied Hitler as he toured the country.

In the fall of 1927, Geli moved to Munich, ostensibly to study medicine, though she spent much of her time socializing with Hitler and his entourage in Munich's Café Heck. She had a short-lived and secret engagement to Hitler's chauffeur, Emil Maurice, who around Christmas 1927 made the mistake of asking for Hitler's permission to marry her. The request elicited such a furious response that Maurice recalled fearing his boss might shoot him. Hitler sacked Maurice and drummed him out of his inner circle.

By the spring of 1928, Geli had become a fixture in this circle. She and Hitler seemed to be very close, and her Uncle Alf, as she called him, clearly enjoyed being seen with her in cafés, at private parties, at the theater, and even at events of the **National Socialist German Workers' Party** (Nazi Party; Nationalsozialistische Deutsche Arbeiterpartei; NSDAP). In October 1929, she moved into his Munich apartment; abandoned her studies; and—at Hitler's urging—began training to be a singer.

It is also clear that Hitler became increasingly possessive and that Geli chafed at the restrictions he placed on her. They quarreled frequently. In September 1931, he refused Geli's request to travel to Vienna. On 18 September, after another row, Hitler left Munich to campaign in northern Germany. The following morning, Geli was discovered dead in her room. She had apparently shot herself with a pistol belonging to Hitler.

Hitler, who had spent that night in Nuremberg, was informed of Geli's death as he was being driven north. He returned to Munich immediately and saw her body while it was still in his apartment. The police, including a police physician, had been summoned and had already conducted an investigation. No suicide note was found.

Hitler's opponents and the anti-Nazi press pounced on the story and generated rumors that Hitler killed Geli or perhaps had her killed. These rumors persist to the present. Particularly influential were Otto Strasser's claims to credulous American intelligence officers in 1943 that Hitler indulged in sexual fetishes, and that the demands he placed on

Geli to accommodate his desires induced her to kill herself. These claims became a principal source of enduring speculation about Hitler's allegedly warped sexuality (see PERSONALITY).

Rumors aside, the true nature and significance of Hitler's relationship with Geli, who was 19 years his junior, has long puzzled historians. While he had conducted several short-lived and platonic relationships with other young **women**, multiple independent sources confirm that Hitler treated Geli differently than he treated these and other women not employed by him. Some of those close to Hitler in this period believed that he had fallen hopelessly in love with her, while his housekeeper insisted that he only saw himself as the fatherless Geli's male guardian, an interpretation that comports with Hitler's tendency to treat most adult women with infantilizing condescension. Most likely, his personality and the way he defined his messianic role as the leader of a movement unconstrained by his era's social norms ruled out a conventional heterosexual relationship.

Regardless, there is no reason not to believe that Hitler's grief over Geli's death was genuine and that it lingered for months. Yet within a few days, he was back to giving crowd-rousing speeches. Moreover, he had not refrained from pursuing relationships with other women while Geli was alive. He had met **Eva Braun** in 1929 and pursued her over the following year, and their relationship only grew closer following Geli's death. In the summer of 1931, he and Magda Quandt conducted a flirtatious dalliance before **Joseph Goebbels** informed him right before Geli's death that he and Magda were engaged. And it seems that Hitler used the tragedy to his political advantage by portraying himself henceforth as devoted solely to Germany.

REARMAMENT. The terms of the **Versailles Treaty** put severe constraints on Germany's military. The army (Reichswehr) was to be limited to 100,000 officers and enlisted men. The general staff was abolished, as was a peacetime draft. The navy was restricted to 15,000 men and a small number of capital ships and no submarines. The air force was abolished completely. Armaments production was to be strictly limited.

With the German government's tacit acquiescence, the military's leadership began subverting the treaty's terms immediately after it was ratified in July 1919. Training and the development of new tactics and weapons (such as tanks) were conducted in the Soviet Union. The creation of a domestic commercial airline (Lufthansa) and an aircraft industry laid the foundation for a future air force [see LUFTWAFFE (AIR FORCE)]. Only a building program for a new navy was effectively blocked.

A week after his appointment as **chancellor**, Hitler informed government ministers that rearmament was to be the nation's highest **economic** priority. Given widespread resentment among Germans at the Versailles Treaty and the Nazi Party's stated intention to reject it, a rearmament program—hidden or open—should have surprised no one [see NATIONAL SOCIALIST GERMAN WORKERS' PARTY (NAZI PARTY; NATIONALSOZIALISTISCHE DEUTSCHE ARBEITERPARTEI; NSDAP); NAZI PARTY PROGRAM (25-POINT PROGRAM)]. In October, he took Germany out of the **League of Nations** and the **Geneva Disarmament Conference**, albeit on the spurious grounds that Hitler simply wanted his country to be accorded equal status with all others when it came to national defense. Nonetheless, in the regime's first two years, he attempted to conceal the extent of the rearmament drive and, for good measure, gave several speeches proclaiming an interest in peace. So while work-creation programs like the construction of a national highway system (Autobahn) were ostensibly civilian projects, their real purposes were military.

In March 1935, he announced rearmament (and compulsory military service three months later), a move that resulted in the formation of the short-lived Stresa Front between Great Britain, **France**, and **Italy**, in which the three states reaffirmed their intention to uphold the terms of the 1925 Pact of Locarno guaranteeing Germany's western borders and the **Rhineland**'s demilitarization. Yet by June, Germany and Britain had concluded a treaty on limits to their respective navies' sizes. The agreement amounted to an indirect admission by the British government that it had no intention of enforcing the Versailles Treaty's disarmament clauses [see ANGLO–GERMAN NAVAL AGREEMENT (1935)].

At the same time, the German military was given control of its own budget and flooded related industries with new orders. To pay for the spending spree, economics minister and Reichsbank chief **Hjalmar Schacht** devised a number of ingenious schemes, but massive deficit spending, the unavoidable heavy reliance on imports, low levels of exports, and a shortage of foreign currency put unsustainable pressures on the economy. And consumers certainly felt the pinch in the form of shortages of basic goods and foodstuffs, poor-quality substitutes, and rationing. Hitler's response to Schacht's increasingly urgent warnings was to sack him and hand over the authority for rearmament to **Hermann Göring** and a new **Four-Year Plan** organization. A true military-industrial complex came into existence.

What Göring lacked in an understanding of how modern industrialized economies worked was more than compensated for by his utter ruthlessness and loyalty to Hitler. The pressures on the economy only intensified. By 1939, the share of Germany's economic output devoted to military spending had reached 20 percent, up from less than 1 percent just six years earlier. For a country of Germany's size, it was completely unsustainable if domestic living standards were to be maintained at a level the population would tolerate.

Unwilling to adjust the "guns and butter" imbalance in favor of the latter, Hitler's solution was to accelerate his timetable for war. In a crucial meeting with his military chiefs on 5 November 1937 that produced the **Hossbach Memorandum**, he demanded the military be prepared for war between 1943 and 1945 and ideally before then, should the opportunity present itself. The international arms race set off in the second half of the 1930s by German rearmament provided more incentive to accelerate the march to war. A short, victorious war initiated as soon as possible would, Hitler remained convinced, resolve all the economic problems caused by rearmament.

Though the production of armaments never came close to the levels demanded by Hitler, in relatively short order, the regime had ended the unemployment crisis and created a formidable new fighting force. In the process, as a recent history of the Nazi economy pointed out, it redistributed production at a speed and scale unprecedented in the history of capitalist economies.

REICHSTAG. To a greater extent than any other single building in Germany, the Reichstag in Berlin symbolizes the country's political triumphs and traumas. Completed in 1894, it was designed by architect Paul Wallot, who took inspiration from Philadelphia's Memorial Hall. Its iconic dedication—"*Dem Deutschen Volke*" ("To the German people")—was added in 1916. It was from one of its balconies that **Social Democratic Party of Germany** (Sozialdemokratische Partei Deutschlands; SPD) politician Philipp Scheidemann proclaimed the creation of a republic on 9 November 1918.

A fire that gutted much of the interior provided the pretext for Hitler to lay the legal foundations for his dictatorship. Though a young Dutch communist was arrested at the scene and confessed to setting the fire, it was most likely a **Sturmabteilung** (Stormtroopers; SA) and Gestapo operation [see REICHSTAG FIRE 27–28 FEBRUARY 1933)]. While the Reichstag as a political institution continued to exist even after all non-Nazi political parties were banned in the summer of 1934, it was nothing more than a glorified rubber stamp and adulatory audience for Hitler. It convened only occasionally in Berlin's Kroll Opera House. The Reichstag building remained largely unrepaired and suffered even more damage in air raids and during the **Battle of Berlin** (*see* STRATEGIC BOMBING CAMPAIGN).

Following Germany's formal division into two states in 1949, the Bundestag of the Federal Republic of Germany (West Germany) was established in Bonn, while the Volkskammmer, the parliament of the German Democratic Republic (East Germany), convened in the new Palace of the Republic in East Berlin.

Restoration work on the Reichstag was undertaken in the early 1960s, but the building was largely unused until 1990, when on 3 October it was the site of the formal reunification ceremony. After considerable debate, the Bundestag voted to return to Berlin. British architect Normal Foster won an international contest to redesign the Reichstag, and in 1999 its reconstruction was completed. Foster's enormous glass dome acknowledged both the original building's design and the necessity of transparency to a healthy democracy.

REICHSTAG FIRE (27–28 FEBRUARY 1933). On the night of 27–28 February 1933 a fire gutted much of the **Reichstag** building in Berlin. What is indisputable is that 24-year-old Dutch communist Marinus Van der Lubbe was arrested in the building and confessed to acting alone. As the fire raged, Hitler and **Joseph Goebbels** raced to the scene, where they found **Hermann Göring** and **Franz von Papen**. Hitler, Goebbels, and Göring immediately proclaimed the fire to be the opening act of a communist attempt to seize power, though they did not believe this was the case. They then accelerated an ongoing nationwide crackdown on German communists, and thousands were arrested over the following days, including **Communist Party of Germany** (Kommunistische Partei Deutschlands; KPD) leader Ernst Thälmann. The crackdown extended to members of the **Social Democratic Party of Germany** (Sozialdemokratische Partei Deutschlands; SPD) and its press and a handful of other notable regime opponents.

The fire also provided the pretext to establish the legal basis for Hitler's dictatorship. Two cabinet meetings on 28 February produced the Decree of the Reich President for the Protection of People and State (also known as the Reichstag Fire Decree), which suspended civil liberties. President **Paul von Hindenburg** signed it that day. The passage of the **Enabling Act** by the intimidated members of a truncated Reichstag followed on 24 March.

The question of who set the fire has been the subject of intermittent and intense debate ever since. Given the timing and what followed, it was easy for many people inside and outside Germany to assume that the Nazis were responsible. The problem has always been the lack of conclusive evidence one way or the other. A conspiracy by the KPD, however, can be ruled out definitively. Not even the regime's own prosecutors could prove this at the September–December 1933 trial in Leipzig of Van der Lubbe and four other communists and no supporting evidence has emerged since. Already under attack at the time of the fire, the KPD was in fact preparing to go underground, not planning a Bolshevik-style revolution, something **Joseph Stalin** would not have authorized.

But then matters become murkier, starting with the alleged sole arsonist. Van der Lubbe, a mentally disturbed man, maintained that he was acting alone from the time of his arrest until his execution in January 1934. However, he was nearly blind, and was not familiar with the layout of the darkened building's interior. Further, the oak wood construction of the huge main chamber could not have been set ablaze the way it was in a matter of minutes by the simple fire starters he claimed to have used. The police discovered traces of other substances that Van der Lubbe stated he did not use in parts of the building he could not have accessed. The official investigation was also seriously flawed. The chief of Berlin's fire department was prevented from conducting a full investigation at the scene. He was sacked for questioning the official version of fire and later murdered under mysterious circumstances.

There is credible evidence that the fire was a **Sturmabteilung** (Stormtroopers; SA) operation. At the **International Military Tribunal** (IMT), two former Gestapo officers claimed the culprit was Hans-Georg Gewehr, the SA's specialist in arson at the time of the fire. A recent extensive investigation by an American historian into Gewehr's wartime and postwar career supports but does not prove the case for his involvement. In July 2019 a copy of an affidavit was discovered in a German archive that also points to an SA operation. In the affadavit written in 1955, former SA member Hans-Martin Lennings swore that he and a few comrades drove Van der Lubbe to the Reichstag, where fires had already been set. He and the other SA men were then sworn to secrecy, and in his affidavit, Lennings claimed they had later been executed, a fate he avoided by escaping to the former **Czechoslovakia**.

Debate about whether there was a Nazi conspiracy to frame the hapless KPD for a terrorist attack in order to justify establishing a dictatorship will likely continue. There is a consensus that Hitler was not involved with any such conspiracy, if one in fact existed. Multiple independent accounts suggest he was genuinely surprised by news of the fire. Whether the opportunity the fire presented was manufactured or not, Hitler, Goebbels, Göring, Minister of the Interior **Wilhelm Frick**, and the SA were ready to seize the opportunity to destroy what was left of the KPD and lay the legal basis for the dictatorship.

RELIGION. Born and raised in a predominantly Catholic region of **Austria**, Hitler was baptized as a Catholic. He was never observant as an adult, but he was not an atheist. Nor did he ever renounce his Catholicism. And while he made numerous references to scripture in *Mein Kampf*; peppered his speeches with references to God, providence, or divine intervention (as did some of his acolytes, notably **Rudolf Hess**); and deployed elements of the Christian liturgy in party rallies, he never wanted national socialism to become a religion, and he did not want to be worshipped as some kind of messiah or deity.

He was exposed to currents of occultism, astrology, and various esoteric belief systems in prewar **Vienna**—they were very popular in the years Hitler lived in the city—but they did not play a significant role in shaping his political beliefs or practices. His obsession with **Richard Wagner**'s operas notwithstanding, he never embraced the mania for Nordic mythologies that gripped some on the nationalist Right before and after the war. After 1933, he had little patience for indulging those in the party—notably **Heinrich Himmler** and **Alfred Rosenberg**—who tried to construct a cult of worship around ancient Germanic mythologies. What he does seem to have appreciated was that many people believed in supernatural phenomena and that such beliefs could be instrumentalized for political purposes. As for his anti-Semitism, Hitler categorically rejected the idea of **Jews** as adherents of a religious faith. They were, he believed, a "race" and one way or another had to be removed from Germany and ultimately the world.

Hitler occasionally made references to non-Christian religions. As he believed the Christian Church had become weak and pacifist, he seemed enamored of religions he considered to possess martial values, such as Shinto in **Japan**. And while there are relatively few reliable sources regarding Hitler's views of Islam, several firsthand accounts suggest that he embraced the cliché of Islam as a fighting faith. **Albert Speer** recalled Hitler musing about what might have been had Islam overtaken Europe in the 8th century: Convinced that Arabs could not have survived northern Europe's climate, he imagined that Germany would have been Islamized, and all to the good, as a supposed religion of the sword was far better suited to the Aryan race than Christianity.

During the war, the regime's attitude toward Muslim-majority lands it controlled or expected to control was purely instrumental. The regime hosted a contingent of native Arabic speakers who broadcast pro-Nazi propaganda to North **Africa**. German forces in the Caucasus reopened mosques closed by the communist regime and authorized the previously banned observance of religious holidays. The regime formed an alliance with Haj Amin al-Husseini, an influential Sunni political and religious leader who hated the British and Jews with equal fervor. Husseini contributed to the propaganda campaign and helped the **Schutzstaffel** (Protection Squad; SS) recruit Bosnian and Albanian Muslims to Waffen SS units.

In Hitler's mind, national socialism was first and foremost a secular political ideology based on his unshakable belief that humanity was divided hierarchically into biological "races" engaged in a life-and-death struggle for supremacy. As a party leader, politician, and dictator, he opposed mixing politics and religion, a position he made clear on multiple occasions in the 1920s and 1930s. But keeping the two completely separate proved impossible.

Hitler and the **National Socialist German Workers' Party** (Nazi Party; Nationalsozialistische Deutsche Arbeiterpartei; NSDAP) shared a bundle of animosities with the Protestant and Catholic Churches, namely anticommunism, antisocialism, antiliberalism, and anti-Semitism. The Prussian monarchy, aristocracy, and military establishment identified closely with Protestantism, and it was among Germany's roughly 45 million Protestants that the party enjoyed its strongest electoral support. But the situation with regard to the disunited Protestant Churches—there were 28 sects in 1933—was complicated. Once he became **chancellor**, Hitler pursued a unified Reich church with a single state-appointed leader supported by the German Christian movement, a branch of Protestantism that claimed Jesus was an Aryan and attempted to excise the Old Testament from the Scriptures. The entire enterprise foundered and generated considerable friction with mainstream Protestant clergy. In response, the Confessing Church formed in 1934. Its members rejected the German Christians and sought to block the regime from interfering in religious matters. The Confessing Church did not, however, become a bastion of political **opposition**.

In contrast to Protestants, the party never had substantial success with Catholic voters, and before 1933, numerous church officials issued statements condemning national socialism. Conversely, as much as Hitler might have admired the reach and power of the Catholic Church, he did not trust it for the old reason that he was convinced its allegiance to the German nation was not total.

Somewhat paradoxically, the party's first move to separate politics and religion involved an appeal to unity. The **Nazi Party Program** (25-Point Program) advocated what it called "positive Christianity—that is, religious freedom for all denominations as long as none posed a threat to the state or the "moral senses of the German race"—and refused to bind itself to any one denomination. All this was simply an expression of the party's general desire to unify Germany and all "true" Germans.

The next major step was the signing of a concordat with the Vatican in July 1933. In exchange for the church's agreement to stay out of politics, Hitler promised not to interfere with the church's religious affairs, including religious instruction in schools, and to respect its legal status and properties. But he did not hold up his end of the bargain. There were strongly anti-Christian currents within the party, and some local radicals had been persecuting priests and otherwise deliberately offending the sensibilities of devout Catholics. Hitler reneged on the concordat's terms and allowed harassment of church officials to continue. In March 1937, Pope Pius XI issued an encyclical, written by German cardinal and archbishop of Munich Michael Faulhaber, denouncing the violations of the concordat and the regime's **racism**. Hitler banned its circulation in Germany and retaliated by ordering the prosecution of hundreds of priests for the alleged sexual predation of children. At one point, he contemplated renouncing the concordat.

A kind of equilibrium between the two sides obtained during the war. The church as an institution—including Pope **Pius XII**—was unwilling to condemn the regime for its crimes, while a few individual Catholics, priests, and higher-level officials occasionally aided persecuted persons or, in the case of the popular bishop of Münster, used the pulpit to denounce the regime's **Euthanasia Program**.

As for Hitler and the party, there was no master plan to eliminate Christianity or Christian Churches from Germany, despite outbursts in which Hitler cursed the perfidy of the Catholic Church and made ominous statements about a postwar settling of accounts. Those relatively few priests and pastors who engaged in overt opposition were indeed persecuted, usually with imprisonment in **concentration camps**, and sometimes killed, but the regime did not engage in the wholesale repression of devout Christians or the churches to the extent claimed by Catholic and Protestant leaders after the war. An exception was the tiny community of Jehovah's Witnesses, the members of which were persecuted because of their pacifism and unwillingness to recognize the absolute authority of the state. In the end, most church officials and ordinary Catholics and Protestants conformed, and the regime's perpetual violations of Christian doctrine, teachings, and morality never inspired collective resistance.

RHINELAND, REMILITARIZATION OF THE
(1936). The remilitarization of the Rhineland in March 1936 was a turning point for Hitler, the regime, and Europe, both in terms of accelerating the diplomatic revolution of the second half of the 1930s and solidifying his position domestically. The **Versailles Treaty** stipulated that the region would be occupied by Allied forces until 1935 and that a zone along the Rhine River's right bank remain demilitarized in perpetuity. Governments of the Weimar Republic worked to revise these widely despised provisions, and in June 1930, Allied occupation forces withdrew, though demilitarization remained in place.

Full-scale rearmament and war were unthinkable without complete German control of the region. In addition to its position along the Franco–German border, it contained most of Germany's industrial infrastructure, an abundance of raw materials, and the crucial transportation artery of the Rhine River. It's reasonable to speculate that Hitler could have reached an agreement over the issue of demilitarization with more patient diplomacy, but in the spring of 1936, he sensed the moment was right to make a bold though risky move that if successful stood to greatly bolster his standing at home and abroad. He was right on both counts.

The operation began on 6 March. Acting against the advice of the High Command of the **Wehrmacht** and his foreign minister, Hitler had ordered the mobilization of 30,000 troops, though only 3,000 were authorized to march well into the territory. These had orders to retreat if confronted with armed resistance from Allied forces. Hitler later admitted knowing at the time that this force would have been no match for even small-scale armed opposition. Yet, as he predicted, neither the British nor the **French** governments were willing to enforce the treaty's terms, a prediction based in part on intelligence estimates and in part on his low regard for the stiffness of French and British spines. The leaders of both states simply had no desire to fight, a sentiment shared by most of their countries' citizens. Logistical problems also impeded a quick, decisive response. But British and French officials had assumed that Hitler would make a move on the Rhineland, so there was plenty of time to have warned him off and prepared an armed response. The most they could muster were statements condemning the action after the fact.

As the troops crossed the river from Cologne, Hitler gave a speech to the **Reichstag** that whipped the audience into a wild frenzy of screaming and saluting. The adulation was not limited to the Reichstag's chambers. A squad of reporters selected by **Joseph Goebbels** recorded the equally genuine joyful responses of German civilians and clergymen on the west bank of the Rhine. But the rejoicing spread to every corner of Germany. Demoralized opponents of the regime conceded that Hitler had won a major victory without firing a shot.

British and French acquiescence confirmed something Hitler already knew: Liberal democracies were weak and cowardly. The reticence of the high command and Foreign Ministry were neither forgiven nor forgotten. Hitler's sense of his own infallibility assumed even greater proportions. In retrospect, it was the last opportunity for either determined opponents within the German military or the remnants of the wartime alliance to halt the march to war at minimal cost. *See also* REARMAMENT.

RIBBENTROP, JOACHIM VON (1893–1946).
Born in Wesel in the Rhineland, Ribbentrop served on the eastern and western fronts during **World War I** and ended the war as a staff officer in Istanbul, where he got to know **Franz von Papen**. After the war, he married the daughter of a wealthy vintner and worked as a traveling wine merchant. Arrogant, pretentious, and ambitious, he procured the nobiliary particle *von* as a means of ingratiating himself with Germany's aristocracy and economic elite.

A former comrade introduced him to Hitler in 1928. More opportunist than ideologue, Ribbentrop and his wife joined the **National Socialist German Workers' Party** (Nazi Party; Nationalsozialistische Deutsche Arbeiterpartei;

NSDAP) in 1932. His first important service to Hitler was to offer his home in an exclusive Berlin suburb as the place where the final negotiations involving Hitler's appointment as **chancellor** and a new cabinet took place in late January 1933.

The provincial Hitler took the multilingual and seemingly aristocratic Ribbentrop to be a well-connected businessman, the kind of person whose support Hitler needed. Ribbentrop became his chief foreign policy adviser. His slavish loyalty mattered far more to Hitler than the fact that he had no experience as a diplomat. That Ribbentrop created a kind of shadow Foreign Ministry staffed with ambitious toadies only increased his appeal to Hitler. In return, Hitler consistently defended the almost comically inept Ribbentrop—he allegedly nearly struck King George VI in the face while giving the Hitler salute—against his many enemies.

His incompetence notwithstanding, Ribbentrop was involved in every one of the regime's major diplomatic negotiations, culminating in the **Nazi–Soviet Nonaggression Pact** with the Soviet Union that is commonly known as the Molotov–Ribbentrop pact [*see* ANGLO–GERMAN NAVAL AGREEMENT (1935); ANTI-COMINTERN PACT (1936); TRIPARTITE PACT (1940)]. After serving for two years as ambassador to Great Britain, an experience that turned Ribbentrop into an Anglophobe, Hitler appointed him foreign minister in the shake-up following the **Blomberg-Fritsch affair**. His Anglophobia led him to attempt to dissuade Hitler from pursuing an Anglo–German alliance, but his influence on this and all other matters of diplomacy should not be overstated. Ribbentrop was nothing more than Hitler's tool, much the same way Vyasheslav Molotov was **Joseph Stalin**'s, the main difference being that Molotov was a more competent negotiator.

Ribbentrop brought a large number of similarly incompetent party hacks into the Foreign Ministry. Their presence made it easier for career officials to claim after the war that it had, on the whole, been a bastion of relative moderation and restraint, even resistance. But recent research has illuminated the ministry's deep complicity with the regime and its crimes, including the **Holocaust** and widespread looting in German-controlled Europe. Ribbentrop's leadership alone was not entirely to blame.

During the war, Ribbentrop compensated for his waning influence with increasingly aggressive displays of anti-**Jewish** zeal. He was not an initiator of deportation and extermination policies but did what he could in his increasingly limited spheres of authority to pressure foreign governments—especially those of **Hungary**, Slovakia, and Croatia—to round up and deport Jews as quickly as possible (*see* BALKANS).

Following Hitler's **suicide**, Ribbentrop sought a position in Grand Admiral **Karl Dönitz**'s short-lived successor government, but Dönitz wanted nothing to do with him. He was arrested in Hamburg on 14 June 1945. He was charged and convicted on all four counts by the **International Military Tribunal** (IMT) and was the first defendant sentenced to death by hanging.

RIEFENSTAHL, HELENE BERTHA AMALIE (LENI; 1902–2003). After an injury ended her first career as a dancer, Helene "Leni" Riefenstahl turned to acting and filmmaking. She became the single most influential visual propagandist for Hitler and the regime. Riefenstahl made five films. The first, *Das Blaue Licht* (*The Blue Light*, 1932), was a feature film in the hugely popular genre of films involving courageous exploits in the mountains (she had already acted in several of these). It was a hit and won a gold medal at the Venice Film Festival.

Claiming to have no knowledge of or interest in politics, she nonetheless attended a **National Socialist German Workers' Party** (Nazi Party; Nationalsozialistische Deutsche Arbeiterpartei; NSDAP) rally in Berlin in February 1932 after returning from a publicity tour. What impressed her, she recalled in her memoirs, was not Hitler so much as the response to him. But what most likely drove her to Hitler was opportunism. Supremely self-confident and highly effective at self-promotion—particularly important qualities for any woman wanting to break into an industry completely dominated by men—Riefenstahl contacted Hitler. He was an admirer of *Das Blaue Licht*, and the two met in person in May and again in November. Whether sex was involved in these encounters remains a matter of dispute. Hitler had her commissioned to make a documentary of the 1933 **Nuremberg party rally**, which was released as *Victory of Faith*.

Suitably impressed, he had her commissioned to make another film of the following year's rally, only this time she was given practically unlimited resources. The result was *Triumph of the Will*, the single most influential film ever made about Hitler (*see* CINEMA AND TELEVISION, REPRESENTATIONS IN). She made one more propaganda film, *Olympia*, a four-hour party-financed account of the 1936 Berlin **Olympics**. Released in two parts, it premiered on Hitler's 49th birthday in 1938. *Triumph of the Will* and *Olympia* both received awards in Venice.

The making of her second feature film, *Tiefland* (*The Lowlands*) further illuminates the nature of her close ties to the regime and Hitler. The film was based on an opera (a favorite of Hitler's) by Eugen d'Alambert, which was derived from an 1896 play by a Catalan writer. It centers around the fate of a Spanish **woman**, played by Riefenstahl, who appears to be—though is not identified as such in the script—a "Gypsy." Riefenstahl wanted to shoot the film in Spain and **Italy**, but financing and then the war interfered with scheduling the shoots. She made repeated requests to Hitler via **Martin Bormann** for foreign currency to finance the filming in Spain and Italy, and Hitler approved them. She was still scrambling for resources and actors in early April 1945, though now working on the film in the Tyrolean Alps.

Before finally being allowed to film in Spain, Riefenstahl shot extended scenes in the Bavarian Alps in the fall of 1940 and summer of 1941. As stand-ins for Spaniards, she requested permission to use **Romani** and Sinti ("Gypsy") children and adults then imprisoned in one of two internment camps for Romani in Germany, Maxglan.

It is likely that the fastidious Riefenstahl visited Maxglan personally to select her extras, though this has not been confirmed. Fifty-one are known have been used in the filming. The costs were borne by Riefenstahl's company, including the costs of the armed guards who segregated them from the local population and the crew. As local farmers (with one exception) refused to house them, they were locked in a single barn at night. They were never paid the wages they had been promised.

When an injured Riefenstahl offered to reward one of the extras for standing in for her, the young woman (known publicly only as Anna) asked that she arrange for the release of her siblings from **concentration camps**. Riefenstahl heartlessly countered with an offer to get one released. The others were eventually murdered in Auschwitz. An additional 66 were taken from the second detention facility (Marzahn) for shoots in Berlin studios in 1942. At least 48 of the 117 were murdered in Auschwitz.

Tiefland became the third-most-expensive film made in the Nazi period. It was not a propaganda film but a passion project undertaken by a megalomaniacal director and funded by a grateful and indulgent Hitler. The end of the war and the occupation delayed the film's completion and release. An Allied denazification tribunal categorized Riefenstahl—who never joined the party—as a "fellow traveler." But her notoriety and connections to the regime prevented her from resuming work in Germany. She sank into obscurity until interest in her work was revived in the 1950s by the French artist Jean Cocteau, though he was unable to persuade the West German government to allow *Tiefland* to be screened at the Cannes Film Festival. It was finally released in 1954 and was a commercial and critical flop.

Meanwhile, her reputation as a pioneering filmmaker was reestablished and bolstered in the 1960s and continued well into the 1990s, mainly outside Germany. It was accompanied by the construction and aggressive maintenance of a self-exculpating narrative of her Nazi-era career and not least her relationship with Hitler. Her basic position was that her three documentaries had been nothing more than matter-of-fact visual accounts of two party rallies and an Olympic Games. She had no interest in politics and knew nothing of the regime's crimes. Her assertion that her most famous film, *Triumph of the Will*, was nothing more than a visual recording of an event was demolished in the mid-1970s by one of her sharpest critics, American writer Susan Sontag. Riefenstahl, Sontag argued, did not simply record reality on film but shaped reality to suit her medium, producing a distinctive "fascist aesthetic," a comment that enraged Riefenstahl. Yet Sontag's characterization was spot on.

While Riefenstahl is best known for her undoubtedly innovative camera work and direction, her genius lay in her abilities as an editor. The technical virtues of her work confounded the comforting claim that propaganda produced by totalitarian regimes never amounts to anything more than mind-numbing kitsch.

With the important exception of **Albert Speer**, no other individual associated closely with the regime at its highest levels was able to manage their postwar image as effectively as Riefenstahl. She spun a tale similar to Speer's. He had cast himself as an apolitical technocrat who had come under Hitler's spell. She, by her own admission, was struck by Hitler's ability to connect with and sway large audiences, but she was first and foremost an apolitical filmmaker.

It would be *Tiefland* that would cause her the most problems after the war. She pursued multiple libel suits against journalists who as early as 1949 attempted to reveal her complicity in exploiting the extras. In 2000, she stated that the accusations amounted to the worst falsehood ever spread about her. Two years later, she let slip that every one of them survived the war. With that lie, the legal tables were turned on her: She was sued by one of the last living extras and issued a retraction. The state prosecutor in Frankfurt considered taking further action but suspended the inquiry due to Riefenstahl's advanced age. She died a year later at age 101.

Hitler congratulates Leni Riefenstahl at the premiere of Olympia, Berlin, 1938. *Courtesy of Bridgeman Images.*

RÖHM, ERNST (1887–1934). The son of a railway official, Röhm was a lieutenant in the Royal Bavarian Army when **World War I** began. He served on the western front, where he received multiple serious wounds. Decorated and promoted to captain, he was transferred to the Bavarian War Ministry. The assignment, along with a posting late in the war as an ordinance officer for the 12th Bavarian Infantry Division, were important to his postwar career as a highly effective middleman between the Reichswehr, Far-Right paramilitaries, and then the **German Workers' Park** (Deutsche Arbeiterpartei; DAP) and **National Socialist German Workers' Party** (Nazi Party; Nationalsozialistische Deutsche Arbeiterpartei; NSDAP). That he was highly regarded by his superior officers was yet another crucial factor.

Röhm remained in the Reichswehr following the armistice. He also served in one of the most important right-wing paramilitary groups, Freikorps (Free Corps) Epp, which participated in the suppression of the **Bavarian Soviet Republic** and the suppression of a leftist rebellion in the Ruhr industrial region. Following the dissolution of Freikorps Epp and other paramilitary units, Röhm put his experience as an ordinance officer to effective use by hiding and supplying weapons to subversive groups. In October 1919, he joined the DAP, and he and Hitler formed a close bond quickly.

Röhm's experience and connections were essential to Hitler and the party in these formative years, most notably in establishing the **Sturmabteilung** (Stormtroopers; SA) in September 1921 as a force for protecting party officials and assaulting political opponents and **Jews**. He played a major role in the failed **Beer Hall Putsch** in 1923 and was one of the 10 defendants in the subsequent **trial** of the main conspirators in 1924. Following his release, he formed a new paramilitary group, the Frontbann, to replace the banned SA. But his ambition to transform it into a huge force outside the party's control conflicted with Hitler's insistence on the exact opposite. Their disagreement led Röhm to resign from the party in 1925. After relocating to Bolivia and working as a military adviser, Hitler recalled him in 1930. It was a risky move, but Hitler needed Röhm's experience and authority over the rank and file of the SA. That Röhm's **homosexuality** was well known and a cause of some resistance to his return in the party and SA did not concern Hitler, and he would repeatedly attempt to deflect homophobic attacks on Röhm.

The fundamental problem was that neither man's position on the relative roles of the party and the SA had changed. Röhm was one of the few powerful Nazi Party figures whose loyalty to the ideal of a national socialist Germany and to the paramilitary culture he saw as essential to establishing and dominating it exceeded that of his loyalty to Hitler personally. The conflict came to a head in the summer of 1934, when Hitler created an excuse to have Röhm and other past and present political opponents arrested and murdered. A truncated SA ceased to play any significant role in the regime, and Röhm's memory was effectively purged from the party's official histories and celebrations. *See also* RÖHM PURGE (1934); RIEFENSTAHL, HELENE BERTHA AMALIE (LENI; 1902–2003).

RÖHM PURGE (1934). A purge of the **Sturmabteilung** (Stormtroopers; SA); the murder of its leader, **Ernst Röhm**; and the killing of at least 90 others in June and July 1934. Also known as the Röhm affair and the Night of the Long Knives, it was one of two murderous purges conducted almost entirely within the regime, the other taking place in the aftermath of the failed July 1944 **assassination attempt** on Hitler.

The Röhm purge was a single response to a three-pronged challenge to Hitler's position. One was the intertwined problem of the SA and the Reichswehr. This was not simply a matter of competition for influence and resources between sectors of the party and state. For Röhm and many SA "old fighters," the very meaning of national socialism was at stake. In their eyes, the revolution was unfinished. Having played a crucial role in the party's victory in January 1933, Röhm was determined that the SA would drive the true national socialist revolution forward. Accordingly, he expanded its membership—by the summer of 1934, it had around 4.5 million men—with the intention of replacing the Reichswehr with an SA militia. He also planned for SA functionaries to take up prominent positions within Germany's civil service. This agenda found strong support within the SA's increasingly embittered rank and file, who had expected their victory in January 1933 to produce a bounty of rewards in the form of jobs and real political power.

For the leadership of the much smaller Reichswehr—including its commander in chief, President **Paul von Hindenburg**—the bloated SA and its powerful leader posed an existential threat. It was this threat that connected the first problem to the second: A handful of conservative nationalists around Vice Chancellor **Franz von Papen** had become determined to curtail Hitler's power or even replace him with a military dictatorship. The SA's growing challenge to the Reichswehr and public order seemed to offer conservative nationalists a window of opportunity to act against Hitler with the support of the army and the ailing Hindenburg.

But it was not only Reichswehr officers and a tiny stratum of conservatives who saw the SA as a threat. By the summer of 1934, the wave of enthusiasm that followed Hitler's appointment as **chancellor** had passed. While Hitler remained popular, there was growing discontent among Germans with the corruption of local party bosses. And though the number of unemployed had fallen, there were other **economic** problems plaguing business owners, workers, farmers, and consumers. Currents of discontent also coursed through the Protestant and Catholic Church establishments at a time when the relationship between both churches and the regime was unsettled (*see* RELIGION). The unruly and violent behavior of SA thugs, who felt free to accost anyone at will, including foreign diplomats, provided another reason for Germans to become more disillusioned with a regime that had promised to restore **law** and order.

Hitler had been courting the loyalty of the Reichswehr and, more generally, trying to assuage conservative nationalists that the "revolution" was definitely over, a message he began asserting to the **National Socialist German Workers' Party** (Nazi Party; Nationalsozialistische Deutsche Arbeiterpartei; NSDAP) as early as the summer of 1933. But Röhm and the SA also had to be handled carefully. He and Hitler remained loyal to each other into the first months of 1934, if largely on a superficial level. Nonetheless it was becoming clear to Hitler that the SA had outlived its usefulness and posed a serious threat to his plans for **rearmament**. At the same time, frustration within the SA with Hitler, the party, and the Reichswehr was intensifying rapidly and would reach a boiling point in the summer of 1934.

Matters came to a head in mid-June. On 17 June, Papen gave an incendiary speech at the university in Marburg, in which, without naming Hitler, he denounced leadership cults, the regime's violent methods, and social revolution. Around the same time, the SA had been stockpiling weapons, but it was the **Schutzstaffel** (Protection Squad; SS) that circulated rumors that the SA was preparing a coup attempt. On the 21 June, Reich war minister General Field Marshal Werner von Blomberg warned Hitler in person that if he did not act to stabilize the situation, then Hindenburg would declare martial law and transfer his authority to the Reichswehr.

Over the following week, Hitler decided to strike at both Papen's clique and the SA. The SS, with logistical support from the army, mobilized a sweep-up of SA leaders and conservative nationalists. On the morning of 30 June, Hitler personally arrested a shocked Röhm. An SS officer shot him in his jail cell the following day. Other SA officers were arrested and summarily executed. The circle around Papen was arrested, and a few prominent personalities of the nationalist Right, notably Edgar Jung, were murdered. Only Papen's prominence as a former diplomat ensured his survival that night.

Hitler authorized most of the executions personally, though a few local SS officers took the opportunity to settle old scores. Hitler did the same when he ordered the murders of **Gregor Strasser**; former chancellor Kurt von Schleicher; and his old nemesis from the **Beer Hall Putsch**, Ritter von Kahr. Three prominent politically active Catholics who had been critical of the regime were also killed.

On 2 July, an exhausted Hitler proclaimed the end of the operation. To the party and the public, he and **Joseph Goebbels** justified the shocking spasm of violence against the party's own paramilitary wing and one of Hitler's oldest comrades as necessary to prevent an insurrection and to expunge **homosexuality** from the ranks of the SA. Privately, Hitler told party officials in 1937 that he had acted mainly to demonstrate his strong support of the Reichswehr and because he believed an SA militia would have been worse than useless as a military force.

The purge was a seminal moment in the consolidation of Hitler's dictatorship. The SA continued to exist, but its membership was nearly halved, and its influence was reduced to almost nil. A particularly momentous outcome was that the door was now open for the ascendance of the SS to a position similar in some ways to what Röhm imagined for the SA. A small but influential cell of conservative nationalist opponents was decimated, and Catholics were warned to steer clear of political activism. It assuaged the leadership of the Reichswehr and even earned Hitler the personal gratitude of Paul von Hindenburg. And while the purge didn't resolve the problem of discontent about corrupt party officials and did nothing to address Germany's systemic economic problems, many Germans were relieved that the SA had been brought to heel.

ROMANI ("GYPSIES"). The Romani (or Roma) ethnic group originated in what is today India and Pakistan and migrated to Europe beginning in the 8th century CE. The term *Gypsy* probably originated when Europeans mistakenly identified Roma as Egyptians. German speakers used the term *Zigeuner*, derived from the Greek *atzinganoi*. Romani people self-identified as Kaldarashi, Lalleri, and (in German-speaking Europe) Sinti. Across Europe over the following centuries and up to the present day, Roma have been subjected to formal and informal discrimination and persecution.

By the outbreak of the Second World War, there were about 1 million to 1.5 million Roma in Europe, with the vast majority living in central, southern, and eastern nations. Around 30,000 resided in Germany, where most were citizens. Hitler did not take a particular interest in them. But Nazi "race scientists" and **Schutzstaffel** (Protection Squad; SS) officials obsessed with the biological health of the "people's community" did, as did some fascists and Nazi collaborators outside Germany (*see* RACISM). Though the Racial Hygiene Division of the Ministry of Health created a special unit to determine on "scientific" grounds whether Romani were in any way Aryan or "subhumans," regime policies were based on the assumption that the latter was the case.

Before the war in Germany, Roma were denaturalized, and sex or marriage with Aryans was banned. Regime officials repeatedly characterized **Jews** and Romani together as members of "alien races" and wrote of a "total" and "final solution" to the "Gypsy problem." In December 1938, **Heinrich Himmler** decreed the "combating of the Gypsy plague" on the grounds that most Gypsies were members of an inferior "race." The treatment of Roma in prewar and wartime Germany paralleled that of Jews closely and also that of Germans with hereditary disabilities, as some Roma were subjected to forced sterilizations. During the war, Roma were segregated within Jewish ghettos or in areas designated for them, deported to **concentration camps** and death camps, and deployed as slave labor [*see* RIEFENSTAHL, HELENE BERTHA AMALIE (LENI; 1902–2003)]. Thousands were murdered in local killing operations and in the camps. Perhaps one-quarter to one-half of Europe's Roma population perished in the war, though precise figures can be difficult to confirm.

Historians have debated the extent to which the Nazi and wider European wartime persecution of the Roma is similar to that of the Jews. The evidence is clear that Nazi intentions, policies, and practices were genocidal. In the 1990s, a Romani scholar and activist popularized the Romani-based term *Porajmos* (suggesting "devouring") to characterize the attempted genocide of the Roma, though other scholars prefer the neologism *Samurdaripen* (mass murder). In terms of recognition and restitution in Germany, the West

German government did not acknowledge Roma as targets of Nazi racial discrimination (see RACISM) until 1979. Formal recognition of genocide came three years later. A public memorial to Roma victims of the Nazis was dedicated in central Berlin in 2011.

ROMANIA. For Hitler, drawing Romania into an anti-Soviet alliance in the late 1930s and ensuring it remained a reliable ally was complicated by the Romanian government's determination to hold territory it had been awarded after **World War I**, particularly Transylvania,

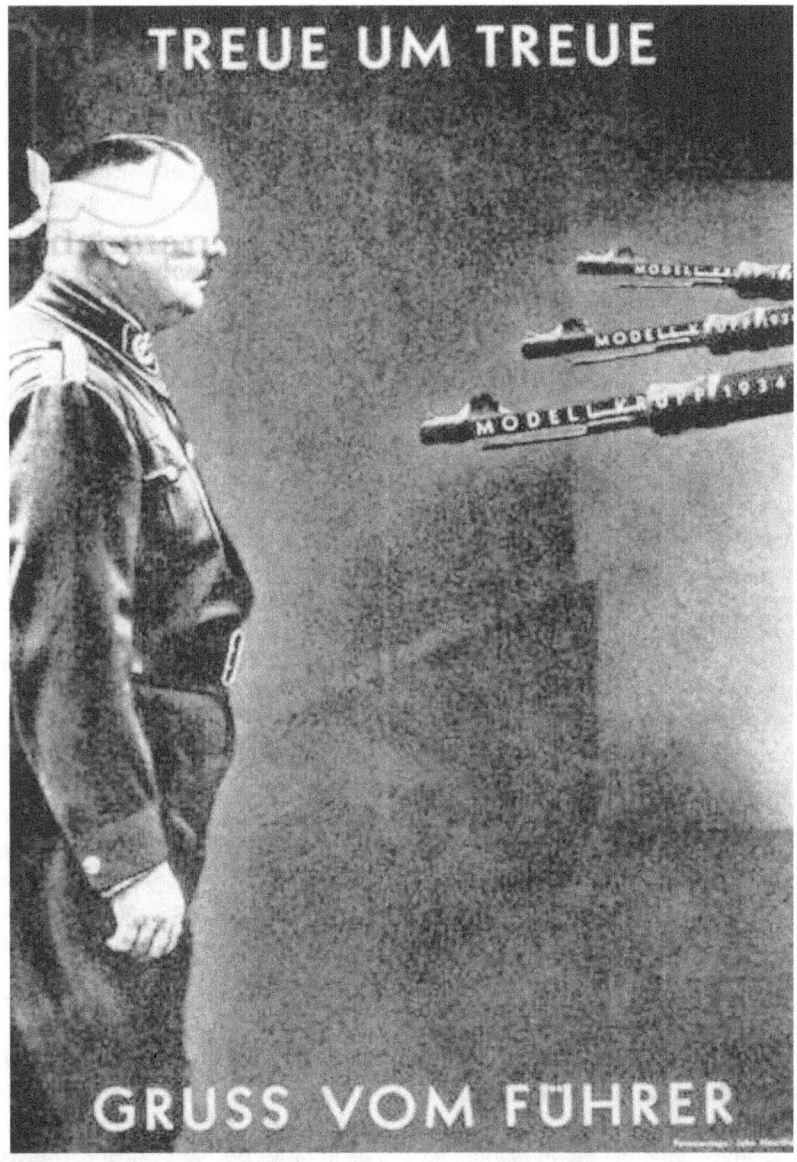

The Prague-based *Arbeiter-Illustrierten Zeitung* published the anti-Nazi German artist John Heartfield's poster following the violent purge of the Sturmabteilung (SA) and the execution of its leader, Ernst Rohm, in June 1934. The text reads "Loyalty for Loyalty—Greetings from the Leader." The rifle barrels are labeled "Model Krupp 1934." *Courtesy of Bridgeman Images.*

which was coveted by **Hungary**. Yet the presence of significant quantities of oil and an extensive refinery complex at Ploieşti, roughly 50 kilometers north of Bucharest, meant that of all southeastern European states, Romania was of the greatest significance to Hitler. The extension of direct German influence in the country came on 23 March 1939—just over week after German troops occupied Prague—when he signed a trade agreement ensuring a steady supply of Romanian oil [see CZECHOSLAVAKIA CRISIS (1938–1939)]. That move, along with **Italy**'s invasion of Albania in early April, led the British and then the **French** governments to extend a security guarantee to Romania, Greece, and Turkey.

A turning point came in the summer of 1940, when as a result of a secret protocol of the **Nazi–Soviet Nonaggression Pact**, the Soviet Union annexed Bessarabia and northern Bukovina. Sensing Romania's weakness, Hungary and **Bulgaria** demanded territorial concessions to their states. To prevent a regional conflict that might tempt **Joseph Stalin** to seize the all-important Ploieşti oil fields, Hitler intervened and strong-armed the Romanian king, Carol II, to turn over northern Transylvania to Hungary and southern Dobruja (also known as South Ossuja) to Bulgaria. The king assented but then abdicated in protest, and a regime led by General Ion Antonescu and the fascist Iron Guard came to power in September. At Antonescu's request, Hitler dispatched a German military mission to Bucharest, and Romania joined the Axis on 20 November. Along with the attention Hitler was paying to Finland, Germany's moves in Romania helped to sink any possibility that Stalin might be tempted by Hitler's offer to join the **Tripartite Pact**.

The partial dismemberment of Romania had other serious implications. As Hitler had not consulted with **Benito Mussolini** about the Bucharest mission, the enraged Italian dictator launched an ill-fated invasion of Greece in late October. The consequences of Mussolini's folly soon required Hitler to invade Greece via Romania and Bulgaria, an operation that was accompanied by a daring but costly airborne operation in Crete. When the Yugoslav government was impertinent enough to refuse Hitler's demand for transit rights for German forces, Hitler unleashed the **Luftwaffe** on Belgrade and dismembered the entire state. The ensuing occupation of Greece was a catastrophe for that country, leaving behind a legacy that has poisoned the relationship between Athens and Berlin to the present day. Bailing out Mussolini in the **Balkans** delayed the launch of **Operation Barbarossa** by six weeks.

No other country contributed more forces to Barbarossa than Romania. The government's hope that a hefty contribution to the invasion would be repaid in territory was partly realized when Hitler returned control of Bessarabia and northern Bukovina to Bucharest. Romania's **economic** and strategic importance to Germany made the country a target of Allied air raids, notably a major but not terribly effective American attack on Ploieşti on 1 August 1943 (Operation Tidal Wave) and major raids on Bucharest in April 1944. With the Red Army closing in on the ground, King Michael engineered a successful coup against Antonescu's regime on 23 August 1944, declared war on Germany, and offered to join the Allies. Stalin recognized the new government, and a month later, Michael agreed to an unconditional surrender. Meanwhile, Romanian forces fought alongside the Red Army for the duration of the war.

Though the country was technically under joint Allied occupation, it was the Soviet Union that was clearly in near-total control. After the war, Romania regained northern Transylvania though lost territory to the Soviet Union and Bulgaria. In 1947, Michael was forced from the throne, and a one-party communist-led state was created. Unlike other Eastern European states, ethnic Germans were not forcibly expelled by the Soviets or postwar Romanian government.

Powerful currents of anti-Semitism were present in Romania long before the alliance with Nazi Germany came into existence, and as in other parts of Europe, there was extensive local collaboration in the **Holocaust**. The savagely anti-Semitic Iron Guard was the driving force in the persecution, robbery, and murder of **Jews** after it took power with Antonescu in September 1940. The city of Iaşi was the site of a particularly brutal pogrom in June 1941. The territories returned to Romania in the aftermath of Barbarossa—Bessarabia and northern Bukovina—along with the land between the Dniester and Bug Rivers in **Ukraine** (renamed Transnistria) became the center of the Holocaust in Romania. Here, German and Romanian forces cooperated closely in carrying out mass executions and deportations to regional ghettos and **concentration camps**. Hungarians were largely responsible for the deportation of around 90,000 Jews from northern Transylvania to Auschwitz. Historians estimate that 220,000 Jews—about one-third of Romania's prewar Jewish population—were murdered or perished in the Holocaust. The vast majority of local perpetrators were never brought to justice.

ROMMEL, ERWIN (1891–1944). Born in Heidenheim in what is today Baden-Württemberg, Rommel was the son of a schoolmaster and former artillery officer. He entered an officer training cadet school in Danzig (now Gdańsk in **Poland**) in 1910 and would serve with great distinction on multiple fronts in **World War I**. He became a professional officer after the war and gravitated to Far-Right politics. Though he never joined the **National Socialist German Workers' Party** (Nazi Party; Nationalsozialistische Deutsche Arbeiterpartei; NSDAP), he became an admirer of Hitler and a **Hitler Youth** (Hitlerjugend; HJ) military instructor.

Rommel came to Hitler's attention in 1937 following the publication of what would become a best-selling book on infantry tactics (*Infanterie greift an*, published in English as *Infantry Attacks*). He was given command of Hitler's headquarters during the Sudetenland crisis and the invasion of Poland and developed a strong rapport with Hitler, who came to admire and respect Rommel to a greater degree than any other general [*see* CZECHOSLOVAKIA CRISIS (1938–1939)].

But Rommel's reputation as a brilliant tank commander and as a German general who operated within the confines of international **law** was made in the campaign in **France** and then as commander of the **Afrika Korps** (Africa Corps) from 1940 to 1943. He was lionized by the Propaganda Ministry not only as a uniquely talented general but, much more problematically from Rommel's perspective, also a military leader who supposedly demonstrated that sheer willpower could overcome any obstacle. As Rommel well understood during his campaign in **Africa**, all the willpower in the world could not overcome a deficiency in resources, overextended supply lines, dysfunctional leadership, poor strategic thinking, and—not least—the Allies' growing material superiority.

Following the evacuation of the Afrika Korps, Rommel was assigned to northern **Italy**, where his reputation as commander who respected the laws of war was compromised by his treatment of Italian soldiers who joined partisan units. As he never served on the eastern front, the extent to which he would have followed other professional officers in committing war crimes is unknowable. His final assignment was to prepare the Atlantic coastline for the expected Allied invasion [*see* FORTRESS EUROPE (FESTUNG EUROPAS)]. Rommel's preference was to prevent the Allies from establishing a beachhead anywhere on the coast rather than hold armored forces away from the beaches in reserve.

With the success of **Operation Overlord**, Rommel pleaded with Hitler to come to terms with the Allies. He then made contact with some members of the military **opposition**, though there is no evidence he was involved directly with the 20 July 1944 **assassination attempt**. In the ensuing crackdown, the Gestapo connected him to the plot. But his status in Germany (thanks in part to Propaganda Ministry) made persecuting him, as other plotters were, extremely difficult. So Hitler gave him the option of taking his own life or facing dismissal from the military and trial by the People's Court. Rommel, who had been badly wounded in an Allied air raid three days before the assassination attempt, chose suicide and received a military burial with honors, with complications from his recent injuries given as the official cause of death.

No other Nazi-era German general has been regarded as highly inside and outside Germany than Rommel, though some scholars have challenged what became known as the

Rommel myth. For many Germans after the war, he could be recalled as both a highly competent and decent soldier whose reputation was never stained by service in the East. And because he was not involved directly in the assassination attempt, he could avoid the accusations of treason that many Germans long after the war leveled at men like Colonel Claus von Stauffenberg. For many non-Germans, Rommel's well-documented reputation for observing the laws of war facilitated postwar Anglo–**French**–German reconciliation. The Rommel myth, however, did contribute—if indirectly—to the wider myth of the "clean Wehrmacht."

ROOSEVELT, FRANKLIN DELANO (1882–1945). Roosevelt was inaugurated as the 32nd US president on 4 March 1933, just as Hitler, the **National Socialist German Workers' Party** (Nazi Party; Nationalsozialistische Deutsche Arbeiterpartei; NSDAP), and the **Sturmabteilung** (SA) were destroying the Weimar Republic. Though Roosevelt did not much care for Germans and Germany, he hoped to maintain good relations with Hitler's regime. And while Roosevelt was a true internationalist, his priority was the economic Depression, and the isolationism that emerged in the **United States** after **World War I** was only growing stronger as a political force. On 31 August 1935—between Hitler's announcement of **rearmament** in March and **Italy**'s invasion of Ethiopia in October—Roosevelt signed the first of several increasingly expansive neutrality acts prohibiting the United States from exporting arms to any nation at war.

But he was becoming keenly aware of another rising political force: dictatorship. When the neutrality acts were enacted, liberal democracy was on the defensive everywhere, including in the United States, while dictatorships of the Far Right and Left seemed dynamic, increasingly popular, and highly aggressive. Roosevelt's first major public response was to give what became known as the Quarantine Speech on 5 October 1937 in Chicago, not coincidentally a bastion of isolationist sentiment. He likened the spread of dictatorships and what he called "world lawlessness" to a contagious disease that, if gone unchecked, would infect the United States. What this speech would produce in terms of new policies was unclear even to Roosevelt. Whatever he did at that point, however, would have to be done quietly, as the public's and Congress's resistance to greater involvement in the world outside the Western Hemisphere was stronger than ever.

By 1939, he was signaling—quietly—to opponents of **appeasement** in London and Paris that he was on their side. The crucial year was 1940. In June, he and British prime minister **Winston Churchill** began corresponding in secret. Roosevelt perceived Hitler as the single greatest long-term threat to American security and was convinced that it was essential to keep Great Britain in the war. The fact that it was an election year in the United States only increased the necessity of acting discreetly. In early September, he announced a deal with the British to exchange access to British bases in the Caribbean and Atlantic for 50 obsolete American destroyers, a deal that proved popular with the American public. He also introduced peacetime conscription, stationed American soldiers in Greenland and Iceland, and extended the projection of US naval power into the mid-Atlantic, guaranteeing an undeclared shooting war with the Germans [*see* BATTLE OF THE ATLANTIC (1939–1945)]. After he won reelection, he announced Lend-Lease, which lasted until August 1945 and provided a total of $50 billion in war-related aid and materials, including weapons, to Britain, the Free **French**, China, and the Soviet Union. These policies greatly facilitated cooperation with Britain after Pearl Harbor and Hitler's declaration of war [*see* ATLANTIC CHARTER (1941)].

Roosevelt's ability to respond to international crises was particularly constrained when it came to immigration. In this case, isolationism fused with **racism** and nativism to make it extremely difficult to admit more **Jewish** refugees from Germany. Roosevelt's legacy when it comes to this question is still debated by historians. But he faced resistance to revising immigration laws not only from Congress and right-wing nativists but also from labor unions and from within the State Department. And nearly every other country in the world resisted taking in more refugees. Nonetheless, Roosevelt, with Eleanor Roosevelt's strong support, attempted to bypass restrictions with executive orders and initiated an international conference on refugees held in Evian, France, in July 1938. But none of this made much difference. Following the **Night of Broken Glass** in November 1938, he recalled the American ambassador from Berlin and made it easier for refugees already in the United States to remain. Increasingly, Germany's Jews were trapped. During the war, there was nothing the Western Allies could have done militarily to stop or even significantly impede the **Holocaust**. As Roosevelt understood, only defeating Germany would end the genocide.

Roosevelt was without question the dominant partner in the Anglo–American alliance. But despite the imbalance and frequent disagreements, the partnership between Roosevelt and Churchill and their respective governments functioned remarkably well, mainly because both leaders remained fixated on defeating Germany as quickly as possible. Just as Roosevelt was finding ingenious ways to aid Britain without provoking a powerful isolationist backlash, Hitler was trying to keep America out of the war. But he was well aware of the emerging transatlantic alliance, and his hatred of Roosevelt became intense. Predictably, the Propaganda Ministry portrayed him as a tool of the Jews. **Albert Speer**'s account of Hitler's elated response to Roosevelt's death on 12 April 1945 is probably exaggerated.

An American soldier replaces Adolf Hitler Street, Krefeld, 9 March 1945. *Courtesy of the United States Holocaust Memorial Museum.*

ROSENBERG, ALFRED (1893–1946). Rosenberg's career presents a paradox. A committed national socialist, he influenced the **National Socialist German Workers' Party** (Nazi Party; Nationalsozialistische Deutsche Arbeiterpartei; NSDAP), and Hitler's early ideological orientation and became the party's purported chief ideologue. He held multiple putatively high-ranking positions, most notably Reich minister for the occupied eastern territories, and was in close regular contact with Hitler for 25 years, remaining loyal to the very end. All of this earned him a place among the 21 defendants standing before the **International Military Tribunal** (IMT), a conviction on all four counts, and a death sentence. Yet with few exceptions, Rosenberg's real influence was rather limited after 1933 and particularly during the war.

Like a number of other fanatical national socialists, Rosenberg was born on the far periphery of German-speaking Europe, in Estonia, then a part of the Russian Empire. He studied architecture, engineering, and painting and taught at a gymnasium (high school) in Tallinn. In 1918, in the wake of the Bolsheviks' seizure of power, he moved to Munich. Virulently **racist**, anticommunist, and anti-Semitic, he became involved with the Far-Right Thule Society and was an early member of the **German Workers' Party** (Deutscharbeiter Partei; DAP). Along with Max Erwin von Scheubner-Richter and **Dietrich Eckart**, Rosenberg became one of the most important figures linking the community of **Baltic** Germans and White Russian exiles to Bavarian national socialists. Rosenberg and other representatives of the former encouraged Hitler to embrace the idea of a future German–Russian alliance once Russia had rid itself of the Bolsheviks. Hitler's emerging belief that Slavic peoples were "subhuman" would eventually render that strategy untenable.

Of more lasting significance was Rosenberg's influence on Hitler's still-evolving ideological and strategic orientation. Rosenberg's anti-Semitism was based on the belief in a global conspiracy of "**Jewish** finance capitalism" that had managed to seize power in Russia under the guise of Bolshevism. This belief would come to occupy a central position in Hitler's anti-Semitism.

By the time of the **Beer Hall Putsch**, Rosenberg had become a member of Hitler's inner circle of confidants. In 1923, Hitler appointed him editor of the party's newspaper, the *Völkischer Beobachter*. Following his conviction for treason in 1924, Hitler selected Rosenberg to lead the Grossdeutsche Volksgemeinschaft (Greater German National Community), the stand-in for the banned NSDAP. He either chose him knowing he would be incapable of being an effective leader and hence no threat, or he simply made a quick, poorly thought-out decision. In either case, Rosenberg was soon pushed aside by more assertive party figures.

During and after his release from **Landsberg Prison**, Hitler kept Rosenberg close, eventually bestowing on him a slew of important-sounding titles. He became head of the party's Foreign Affairs Office, and in January 1924, Hitler made him responsible for the ideological instruction of party officials. One of Rosenberg's particular concerns was culture, defined broadly, and Hitler made him one of several high-level party officials responsible for "**coordinating**" German culture with the leader's preferences. This entailed denouncing and eventually banning works of Jewish and Marxist literature and any form of modernism. Only in his hostility to Christianity and interest in paganism did his views deviate from Hitler's.

In July 1941, Hitler appointed Rosenberg as Reich minister for the occupied eastern territories but kept the **Schutzstaffel** (Protection Squad; SS), **Hermann Göring**'s **Four-Year Plan** organization, and the **Wehrmacht** outside the new ministry's control. Moreover, while Rosenberg supported the objectives of conquering the East and vanquishing Bolshevism, he differed with Hitler and other officials on the means to these ends, favoring alliances with anticommunist Slavs and the creation of buffer states. Like Hitler, however, he advocated the removal and extermination of the Jews.

Along with his early ideological influence on Hitler and editorship of the *Völkischer Beobachter*, his only other significant success was heading a special task force responsible for plundering books and art from German-controlled Europe. Rosenberg was highly intelligent, industrious, and loyal to Hitler. But he lacked charisma. Unlike Göring, **Martin Bormann**, **Joseph Goebbels**, **Heinrich Himmler**, and such wartime imperial overlords as Erich Koch, he did not have the drive or talent for amassing real power and influence.

Rosenberg kept a diary, which was stolen by Robert Kempner, a German-born lawyer who had emigrated to the **United States** and served as a prosecutor at the IMT and in the **Nuremberg Military Tribunal** (NMT). The diary, only portions of which had been published, was recovered in 2013 by an American archivist and an agent of the US Federal Bureau of Investigation. Its contents, however, did not offer any significant revelations about Hitler or the regime. *See also* PROTOCOLS OF THE ELDERS OF ZION.

RUNDSTEDT, GERD VON (1875–1953). One of Hitler's most competent and successful field commanders, Rundstedt personified the deep complicity of the Prussian officer elite's subservience to Hitler and its complicity in the Nazis' genocidal war of conquest. Born into a family of Prussian nobility and professional officers, Rundstedt was a general staff officer in Turkey and **France** in **World War I**. He remained in the Reichswehr and was promoted to lieutenant general in 1929 and full general in 1932.

Though he fully supported rearmament, Rundstedt found Hitler and the **National Socialist German Workers' Party** (Nazi Party; Nationalsozialistische Deutsche Arbeiterpartei; NSDAP) distasteful. Like many other professional officers, he feared the **Sturmabteilung** (Stormtroopers; SA) and was relieved when Hitler purged its leadership [*see* RÖHM, ERNST (1887–1934); RÖHM PURGE (1934)]. He was, however, incensed that two officers had been murdered (Kurt von Schleicher and Ferdinand von Bredow). He attempted, with little success, to defend then **Wehrmacht** commander in chief Colonel General Werner von Fritsch in the **Blomberg–Fritsch affair** and subsequently declined the opportunity to be appointed as his replacement. Though concerned about the planned dismemberment of **Czechoslovakia**, Rundstedt resisted being drawn into a plot hatched by a handful of officers to depose Hitler should France and Great Britain take military action.

After commanding an army group in the occupation of the Sudetenland, Rundstedt retired. Hitler recalled him to lead one of the army groups in the invasion of **Poland** and then in the attack on France through the Ardennes region [*see* DUNKIRK (26 MAY–4 JUNE 1940)]. In July 1940, Hitler promoted him to general field marshal. He was given command of one of the three army groups (South) in **Operation Barbarossa** but was relieved by Hitler in November 1941 when he disobeyed an order not to stage a tactical retreat from Rostov. His later claims to the contrary, he knew about **Schutzstaffel** (Protection Squad; SS) Einsatzgruppen (mobile execution units) operations and endorsed in writing an October 1941 order by Sixth Army commander Field Marshal Walter von Reichenau ordering Wehrmacht troops to take revenge on "subhuman" **Jews**.

Hitler recalled him once again in 1942 to prepare the West for the expected Allied invasion. Though he failed to prevent the successful landings in Normandy, he did succeed in halting the Allied advance in the fall of 1944 [*see* OPERATION OVERLORD (1944)]. His final contribution to Germany's by then doomed war effort was to command the surprise **Ardennes Offensive** in December 1944. Hitler replaced him as commander in chief in the West with Field Marshal **Albert Kesselring** in March 1945.

As with the earlier plot against Hitler, of which he was aware, Rundstedt knew about the 1944 **assassination** conspiracy. And as in 1938, he neither joined nor betrayed the conspirators. In the aftermath of the 20 July 1944 assassination attempt, he presided over the military honor court that dismissed officers accused of participating in the plot so they could be tried by the Volksgerichthof (People's Court) and executed (*see* LAW).

Rundstedt's obedience and complicity in war crimes and the **Holocaust** made a mockery of his references to honor, duty, and a supposedly unbreakable oath of loyalty. He was also corrupt. Like other high-ranking officers, Rundstedt accepted gifts from Hitler, in his case, a 250,000-Reichsmark check on his 65th birthday in December 1941. He delayed cashing it in hopes of dodging a small tax liability.

Having taken refuge in a sanatorium in Bad Tölz, Rundstedt was taken into custody by American soldiers on 1 May 1945. Field commanders were not charged by the **International Military Tribunal** (IMT), and Rundstedt testified in defense of the army's high command. His insistence that the army acted honorably in all theaters contributed to the myth of the "clean Wehrmacht." After the conclusion of the IMT's trials, American officials wanted him prosecuted for war crimes, and the Soviets wanted him extradited, but their British counterparts resisted releasing Rundstedt from their custody. In 1949, however, British foreign minister Ernest Bevin succeeded in getting Rundstedt and two other high-ranking officers charged as war criminals by the British government. But prosecuting Rundstedt was unpopular in Britain, including among several prominent officers, and in any case, he was declared medically unfit to stand trial. Rundstedt died in Hannover in 1953.

S

SCHACHT, HORACE GREELEY HJALMAR (1877–1970). A talented, well-connected banker, Schacht became one of the single most important conservative nationalists in the crucial first five years of Hitler's dictatorship. Indeed, outside of the military, his influence outlasted all other major conservative figures responsible for putting Hitler in the **chancellor**'s office and then making his consolidation of power possible.

Schacht was born in Tingleff, Schleswig-Holstein (now Tinglev in Denmark), and earned a doctorate in **economics** at the University of Kiel. Multilingual and cosmopolitan, he worked for several major banks and was appointed the Weimar Republic's currency commissioner in November 1923. His success in confronting the hyperinflation crisis earned him a promotion to the leadership of the Reichsbank.

In 1918, Schacht had cofounded the German National Party. Like other conservative nationalists, he rejected the **Versailles Treaty**, especially reparations, and supported the restoration of Germany's great power status. He resigned from the Reichsbank in 1930 when he disputed the government's renegotiations of reparations payments. A year later, he met Hitler and seemed to be impressed—though Schacht was one of many members of the elite establishment who assumed he could be tamed and controlled. He never joined the **National Socialist German Workers' Party** (Nazi Party; Nationalsozialistische Deutsche Arbeiterpartei; NSDAP), though he was awarded honorary membership. Schacht was, however, intent on seeing Germany **rearmed**. He was also an anti-Semite, albeit one who wanted the expropriation of German **Jews** and their removal from German life to be carried out in a legal and orderly manner.

Hitler recognized Schacht's value as a financial wizard. He returned him to leadership of the Reichsbank in March 1933 and appointed him economics minister and general plenipotentiary for the war economy in 1934 and 1935, respectively. Schacht excelled at devising ingenious ways to fund the initial phase of rearmament off book, his single most important contribution to Hitler's consolidation of power. Schacht's New Plan envisioned rearmament taking place in two four-year phases, the first devoted to defense capabilities, the next to offensive. But neither Hitler nor **Wehrmacht** leaders were willing to wait.

Never radical enough for Hitler, Schacht had outlived his usefulness by 1936. The pace of rearmament accelerated to the point where he was issuing repeated warnings to Hitler that the economy, dependent as it was on imports of raw materials but increasingly short on foreign currency reserves, could not withstand the strain. Hitler's dream of autarky was unachievable, and for Schacht, that meant returning to the world economy and restoring exports. Hitler would hear none of it, believing that a victorious war would resolve all of Germany's economic problems. From 1936 to 1939, he removed Schacht from his various posts and made **Hermann Göring** the rearmament supremo (*see* FOUR-YEAR PLAN).

Schacht retreated from political life. He was stripped of his minister without portfolio title in

1943 and arrested in the aftermath of the 20 July 1944 **assassination attempt**. Though he had connected with members of the elite resistance around Admiral **Wilhelm Canaris**, General Hans Oster, and former mayor of Leipzig Carl Goerdeler in the late 1930s, Schacht had played no role in the 1944 conspiracy. He spent the remainder of the war in a succession of **concentration camps** before being arrested and charged on two of four counts (common plan or conspiracy and crimes against peace) by the **International Military Tribunal** (IMT). The prosecution's case was weak, and he was acquitted. He was soon arrested by German police and jailed pending his trial before a denazification court. He successfully appealed his sentence of eight years' hard labor. Charged by another denazification court in a different occupation zone, he was acquitted again in 1950. Now destitute and 73 years old, he published two memoirs, founded a bank, and served as an adviser to various Third World governments. He died in Munich in 1970.

SCHUTZSTAFFEL (PROTECTION SQUAD; SS). The SS was created in March 1925, immediately after Hitler's release from **Landsberg Prison**. Concerned about his personal security, Hitler charged Julius Schreck, a paramilitary veteran and **Sturmabteilung** (Stormtroopers; SA) tough who belonged to Hitler's entourage of drivers and bodyguards, with creating a small protective force that would answer to Hitler. Though it would operate under the command of the SA, from the start he imagined the SS as something distinct, smaller, and more disciplined (and hence easier to control) than the SA. The SS remained very small through the remainder of the decade, in part because of lackluster leadership.

The first turning point came in January 1929, when Hitler appointed **Heinrich Himmler**, an SS member since 1925, to lead the organization. Though still subordinated to the much larger SA (the SS had just under 300 members at that point), Himmler quickly built it up into a nascent police force. In the process, tensions between the expanding SS—Himmler recruited around 700 new members in 1929 alone—and the SA occasionally boiled over into violence. Hitler's worsening problems with the SA led Himmler to make the SS responsible for monitoring and policing the party, namely the SA.

Thus its profile was nothing like the SA. For one thing, from its beginnings, SS members wore distinctive black uniforms. When Himmler, a talented administrator and recruiter, took over, he gave the SS a quasi-military organizational structure. But he never intended it to be just another paramilitary formation, let alone a gang of street brawlers. He imagined it forming the basis of a new, "racially pure" German elite. Himmler was inspired by another fanatical racialist, **Richard Walther Darré**, to implement strict hereditary requirements for SS recruits.

Perhaps most important, Himmler was loyal to Hitler. In 1931, following a minor revolt against Hitler's leadership by elements of the SA in Berlin during which the SS supported Hitler, the SS adopted its motto: *Meine Ehre heisst Treue* (My honor is called loyalty; see BOXHEIM DOCUMENTS). The SS again proved its loyalty in June 1934, when it played a crucial role in the **Röhm purge**. The purge not only freed the SS from SA control, but it also opened the door for Himmler to expand its size and powers.

The growing network of **concentration camps** was already under SS control. In 1936, it took over all police functions. Himmler also transformed the small detachment of "disposition troops" created by Hitler in 1933 into the Waffen SS, the organization's armed forces division that would eventually number 1 million men and serve under the operational command of the **Wehrmacht**. Some Waffen SS units would be comprised substantially of non-German volunteers and conscripts. A special unit, the Totenkopf (Death's Head), supplied guard detachments to concentration camps and would form its own combat division.

The SS became the principal tool of domestic repression and, through its management of the camp system, social-biological engineering. During the war, it bore the greatest responsibility for all phases of the

Holocaust—roundups, "ghettoization," deportations, slave labor, mass shootings, the death camps, and the death marches. And wherever Waffen SS field units were deployed, they demonstrated a greater willingness relative to their counterparts in the Wehrmacht to fight fanatically, even suicidally, and murder prisoners of war and civilians.

Outlawed by the occupying powers, the SS was labeled a criminal organization by the **International Military Tribunal** (IMT). Though only one high-ranking SS officer (Ernst Kaltenbrunner) was a defendant in the main trial at Nuremberg, numerous SS officials were prosecuted in the 12 successor trials of the **Nuremberg Military Tribunal** (NMT), which included a trial for Einsatzgruppen (mobile execution units) personnel. A high-profile trial of 40 SS personnel who served at Auschwitz was held in **Poland** in 1947, and around 37,000 former SS members were prosecuted by Soviet courts. From December 1963 to August 1965, a West German court tried 22 former SS members who had served at Auschwitz.

In the end, most SS members who survived the war lived out their lives in the postwar Germanys, undisturbed by any court, intelligence service, or independent Nazi hunter. A few managed to flee to Spain, the Middle East, and the Americas, often with the assistance of the Red Cross and sympathetic Catholic clergy and Vatican officials [see PIUS XII, POPE (EUGENIO PACELLI; 1876–1958)], while a small number served the postwar American and Soviet intelligence services. And while former SS members ably aided and protected their own, there never was an international clandestine organization of ex-SS called ODESSA.

SECOND BOOK. Following **Reichstag elections** in May 1928, in which the **National Socialist German Workers' Party** (Nazi Party; Nationalsozialistische Deutsche Arbeiterpartei; NSDAP) did poorly, Hitler decamped to Berchtesgaden in the Bavarian Alps to recuperate. There he rented the then modest house that he would later purchase and transform into the **Berghof**. He had toyed with the idea of writing a memoir specifically about his wartime experiences but instead set to work on a new book dealing with foreign policy questions. Unlike *Mein Kampf*, which Hitler wrote himself, he dictated what would become a 234-page manuscript to **Max Amann**, the head of Franz Eher Verlag, the party's publishing house.

The impetus to write the book seems to have been provoked by nationalist criticism of his willingness to give up all claims on the majority ethnic German South Tyrol region, then part of **Italy**, if doing so created the possibility of an alliance with that country [see MUSSOLINI, BENITO (1883–1945)]. The manuscript, however, is not specifically about the Tyrol or Italy, though Hitler devotes a significant part of it to justifying his controversial position on the contested region. Most of it covers some of the same ground as the second volume of *Mein Kampf* by identifying **Jews** as Germany's eternal and deadliest enemy and justifying the need for Lebensraum (**living space**) in the East. He calls for **rearmament**, the rejection of the **Versailles Treaty**, alliances with Great Britain and Italy, and the rapid conquest of Eastern Europe in advance of a war with the Soviet Union.

Most striking is the attention he pays to the **United States** as a potential long-term threat. His views on the United States had clearly evolved from the time he wrote *Mein Kampf*. In general, Hitler knew very little about the rest of the world, particularly the United States [see MAY, KARL (1842–1912)]. The presence of millions of ethnic Germans and their descendants, of course, appealed to his belief in the existence of a hierarchy of human "races." He was also aware of America's natural resources and industrial potential. It may also be the case that he had learned something about racial segregation, the eugenics movement, and the race-based Immigration Act of 1924 [Johnson-Reed Act; see GERMAN AMERICAN BUND (AMERIKADEUTSCHER VOLKSBUND)].

Though much of what the manuscript contained drew from speeches Hitler had been giving in public, it was never published in his lifetime. *Mein Kampf* was not selling well, and Amann—whose business acumen Hitler respected—may have convinced him that a second book would further dampen sales of the first. Another factor may have been his growing interest in allying with the conservative nationalists he had attacked in the manuscript.

The manuscript was hidden away in an Eher Verlag safe in Munich and confiscated by the US Army in May 1945. In 1958, Gerhard Weinberg, a young German-born American historian microfilming German documents captured by the Allies, discovered it, and it was published in German as *Hitlers zweites Buch: Ein Dokument aus dem Jahr 1928* (1961) and in English as *Hitler's Second Book: The Unpublished Sequel to* Mein Kampf (2003).

SOCIAL DEMOCRATIC PARTY OF GERMANY (SOZIAL DEMOKRATISCHE PARTEI DEUTSCHLANDS; SPD).

Established in 1890, the SPD of Germany became the country's single largest political party in terms of representation in the **Reichstag** until it was surpassed by the **National Socialist German Workers' Party** (Nazi Party; Nationalsozialistische Deutsche Arbeiterpartei; NSDAP) in the summer of 1932.

A year after its founding, the SPD rejected violent revolution and committed itself to achieving socialism through legal participation in the political process. The strict adherence to legality was inspired not only by the belief that capitalism would inevitably produce a revolution but also by the need to deliver tangible benefits to Germany's growing industrial working class in the here and now. If the party stuck to legality, then the state and other parties would be unable to repeat the attempt by Chancellor **Otto von Bismarck** in the 1880s to suppress organized socialism.

More than Reichstag seats and influence over organized labor was at stake. Like other parties, the SPD's influence extended to a wide range of publications, clubs, associations, youth groups, and venues like pubs, where the like-minded could debate, socialize, and in general maintain a sense of community and shared purpose. Legality would block the state from attempting to suppress this essential component of organized working-class culture.

Currents of **opposition** to the Social Democrats ran deep and wide in Germany. Liberal parties had supported Bismarck's antisocialist campaign, something SPD leaders never forgot. Conservative nationalists, of course, were uniformly hostile. The Left fractured during **World War I** and in the aftermath of the 1918 revolution, when the SPD-dominated government supported multiple violent crackdowns on the radical Left by the army and right-wing paramilitaries. The resulting legacy of mutual animosity prevented unified opposition to the Far Right.

The basis of Nazi hostility to the SPD was primarily ideological: The socialists were internationalists and sought to divide Germany by class. The **German Workers' Party** (Deutsche Arbeiterpartei; DAP) had been created to break the SPD's seemingly viselike grip on German workers [the **Communist Party of Germany** (Kommunistische Partei Deutschlands; KPD) was not yet a mass party]. But the NSDAP would make notable gains among working-class voters as the Great Depression devastated the **economy**. The SPD and the KPD remained the dominant parties for workers and organized labor. The end came in the spring of 1933, as it did for all other non-Nazi parties: through violence, intimidation, confiscations, and a legal ban.

Throughout, the SPD held to the principle of legality, and to its enduring credit, its delegates were the only ones to vote against the **Enabling Act** in March. The vote, courageous as it was given the circumstances, was at that point purely symbolic. As party chairman Otto Wels proclaimed on the day of the fateful vote, the new regime could strip away freedoms and kill at will, but the SPD's honor would remain intact.

Wels fled the country for Prague, where he and a handful of other party leaders formed a party in exile, known as Sopade, which soon had to relocate to Paris and then London. It attempted to monitor conditions inside Germany, and its reports have provided historians with valuable insights into daily life under Nazi rule.

Only around 6,000 SPD officials left the country. Most former SPD members and the millions who had formed its wider culture remained in Germany and went into what is often termed "internal exile." They stayed out of politics or at most maintained clandestine contacts with each other through informal clubs and groups. Organized oppositional activities, not all of which were directed by Sopade, were extremely risky, and the Gestapo proved extraordinarily effective at shutting them down.

Hitler was fully aware of the appeal of socialism to many Germans. While the regime could dismantle the SPD, the KPD, and their affiliated organizations and trade unions, the resulting economic and social vacuum would have to be filled. Not least, there was the pressing matter of the ongoing unemployment crisis. Hence the regime not only embarked on make-work programs but also created the **German Labor Front** (Deutsche Arbeitsfront; DAF) to represent workers and introduced a raft of social welfare measures. To the dismay of Sopade officials, these were effective in creating a strong consensus behind the regime [see NATIONAL SOCIALIST WELFARE ORGANIZATION (NATIONALSOZIALISTISCHE VOLKSWOHLFAHRT; NSV)].

Following the regime's collapse in May 1945, Allied governments authorized the reformation of political parties. The SPD was the only democratic party that could claim that it had supported the republic and resisted the Nazis to the very end.

SPANISH CIVIL WAR (1936–1939). In July 1936, right-wing military officers in Spain rebelled against the democratically elected left-wing government with the intention of replacing it with a military dictatorship. In the ensuing civil war, the rebels, or nationalists, received Hitler's and **Benito Mussolini**'s support almost immediately. Great Britain and **France** declared neutrality, as did the **United States**. Only Mexico and the Soviet Union supported the republican side.

The timing of the rebellion could hardly have been better for Hitler. **Italy**'s invasion of Ethiopia in October 1935 had driven a wedge between Mussolini and the Western powers, which worked to Hitler's advantage. He then capitalized on Italy's estrangement from Britain with his bold move to remilitarize the **Rhineland** in March 1936. The civil war in Spain offered another chance to improve relations with Rome. And there were other potential benefits to backing the nationalists. If the nationalist side won, then it would further weaken France's position vis-à-vis Germany. This calculation was driven in part by Hitler's intensifying obsession with the spread of communism. A republican victory in Spain, he believed, would result in a communist takeover there and then in France. With Paris and Moscow having recently concluded a mutual assistance pact, Germany would be almost completely surrounded by communist states.

But the civil war offered a more immediate and highly practical benefit: a unique opportunity to test new German weapons. At the request of General **Francisco Franco**, the leader of nationalist forces, Mussolini and Hitler sent planes to transport him and rebel troops from North **Africa** to the Spanish mainland. They then dispatched thousands of troops to advise and fight with nationalist forces. As the summer **Olympic Games** were scheduled to open in Berlin in August, Hitler prohibited German troops from engaging directly in the war until the games ended. Germany's most notorious contribution was the deployment of an air force unit soon to be known as the Condor Legion [see LUFTWAFFE (AIR FORCE)]. Its personnel carried out bombing raids that included civilian targets; the best known was an attack on the Basque town of Guernica on 26 April 1937. The operation killed 1,600 people and inspired Pablo Picasso to paint his antiwar masterpiece *Guernica*. In the dock in Nuremberg in 1946, **Hermann Göring** admitted what everyone had long known about the horrific attack in which German planes bombed and strafed the strategically meaningless town for three hours on market day: It was an experiment in destroying a city from the air and terrorizing its civilian population.

As the conflict dragged on, however, Hitler resisted sending even more forces. He sensed that a prolonged war would be to his advantage. It would generate instability on France's border, and it would distract attention from accelerating **rearmament** in Germany. German business interests in Spain would also benefit, as would the military, should it gain access to essential raw materials. The wedge between

Italy and Great Britain and France would remain and deepen, while German–Italian relations would improve, the latter a prerequisite for any German attempt to annex **Austria**. Hitler's strengthening position allowed him to rebuff British efforts to revive the Pact of Locarno.

SPEER, ALBERT (1905–1981). The son of an architect from Mannheim, Albert Speer was training to take up his father's profession when he attended one of Hitler's speeches in December 1930. He recalled being transfixed, and he applied for membership in the **National Socialist German Workers' Party** (Nazi Party; Nationalsozialistische Deutsche Arbeiterpartei; NSDAP) a month later, though he had in fact already been active with the party. Speer would also join the **Sturmabteilung**'s (Stormtroopers; SA) automobile corps and the party's Action Group of German Architects and Engineers.

His attraction to Hitler and the NSDAP was not unusual for a member of his generational cohort. Political conviction and ambition drew many talented and well-educated middle-class professionals to the party and the **Schutzstaffel** (Protection Squad; SS). But two things made Speer unique. One was the nature of his personal relationship with Hitler, rivaled only by that of Hitler with **Joseph Goebbels** and **Martin Bormann** in its closeness and duration. The other was his success after the war in creating and maintaining the myth of a contrite technocrat who had been hypnotized by the devil rather than having eagerly sold him his soul.

Speer sought commissions from the party as he struggled to establish himself as a professional architect during the **economic** crisis. The first were relatively small in scale, but they brought him to Goebbels's and then Hitler's attention. For the first Day of German Labor on 1 May 1933, Speer overhauled the design of the spectacle by adding displays of enormous banners and making innovative use of searchlights. He repeated this success on an even greater scale the following year, when Goebbels commissioned him to design the setting for the 1934 **Nuremberg party rally**.

But it was the death of Hitler's favored architect, Paul Troost, in 1934 that opened the door to his inner circle. Unlike the older and well-established Troost, Speer was 16 years younger than Hitler. He was also handsome, ambitious, and competent and possessed a seemingly boundless capacity for work. Most important, Speer was devoted to Hitler personally. For nearly 12 years, they were in regular contact with each other, and Speer enjoyed a place among the small circle of habitués at the **Berghof**. He may have been the closest thing to a personal friend that the adult Hitler ever had.

To this day, Speer is usually referred to as Hitler's favorite architect. This characterization is misleading. Hitler's favorite architect was Hitler. It was Hitler who determined the aesthetic of Nazi-era construction projects: neoclassical in inspiration, spare in ornamentation, and elephantine in scale. His ideas, often sketched by him, were carried through to the formal design phase or partial or total completion under his close supervision. He retained about a dozen professional architects and did not hesitate to play them off one another. It took Speer several years to be entrusted with the highest-profile commissions.

Speer was particularly skillful at indulging Hitler's fantasy of rebuilding Germany's cities, above all Berlin and Linz. In January 1937, Hitler created a new position just for him: inspector general of building for the Reich Capital Berlin. This was not an honorary title but a position of real power, mainly thanks to the fact that Speer reported to Hitler directly. The office was given an enormous budget, the authority to bypass municipal authorities, and a staff that grew to 1,400 by 1942. Speer enriched himself and his private firm in the process. But very little of their grand design for the capital city was ever realized. Speer's most significant architectural accomplishment was a massive new Reich **chancellery**, completed in 1939 on a grueling schedule and constructed in part by laborers imprisoned in the Mauthausen, Flossenbürg, and Sachsenhausen **concentration camps**. Hitler engaged with the project closely, spending hours poring over blueprints and a tabletop scale model of the new capital—to be renamed Germania—that Speer built for him.

It would be another unexpected death that propelled Speer into the most important role he would play in the regime. When **Fritz Todt** was killed in a plane crash in early February 1942, Hitler appointed Speer minister of armaments and production. This position, accompanied as it was by Hitler's seemingly unshakable trust, made him one of the regime's most powerful officials. Though Speer manipulated statistics and proved masterful at deploying propaganda boasting of an "armaments miracle," production did in fact increase under his direction. But it was never going to be enough to prevent total defeat. As the country's war effort disintegrated in the spring of 1945, Speer managed to convince Hitler to modify his demand that what was left of Germany's industrial infrastructure be completely destroyed [see NERO ORDER (19 MARCH 1945)]. This was not the brave act of resistance that Speer later claimed, as **opposition** to the order was widespread, and there was little chance it would have been obeyed.

Speer was one of the last people to see Hitler alive. He had attended a desultory birthday celebration in the bunker below the chancellery on 20 April 1945 and then fled Berlin. He returned three days later, possibly in hopes of convincing Hitler to appoint him as his successor rather than Grand Admiral **Karl Dönitz**, whom Hitler had given control of a successor government based near the German border with Denmark. Speer swallowed his pride and served the short-lived regime as its minister of industry and production.

Speer's extremely dangerous last-minute foray into Berlin notwithstanding, the scale of his ambition was ultimately greater than his personal devotion to Hitler. He did not, after all, end his own life in the bunker or while awaiting arrest by Allied soldiers. Nor did he attempt to escape to South America. Rather, he expected to play a major role in postwar Germany.

He was arrested by British officers on 23 May 1945 but not before being interrogated for seven days by American officials of the US Strategic Bombing Survey (see UNITED STATES OF AMERICA). The war with **Japan** was still grinding on, and plans for a **strategic bombing campaign** were on the table. But American officials needed to know about its impact—or lack of it—on Germany's ability to keep fighting, and Speer was the man with whom they needed to speak. He proved to be a selectively candid subject, the first in a series of successful mythmaking performances that Speer would spend the rest of his life giving. He remained cooperative over the following weeks, ever more convinced of his importance to Germany's future, and was stunned to learn that he would be one among the 21 living defendants to face the **International Military Tribunal (IMT)**.

Charged on all four counts, he pled not guilty. Unlike his co-defendants, he expressed some remorse and asserted the "leaders must accept a common responsibility." While he admitted he knew about and approved of the use of forced labor from concentration and prisoner-of-war camps, he insisted real responsibility for the brutality of the work overseen by his ministry fell to his fellow defendant, former general plenipotentiary for labor deployment Fritz Sauckal. As to the fate of Europe's **Jews**, Speer claimed total ignorance. The tribunal convicted him on two counts (war crimes and crimes against humanity), but the judges spared his life and sentenced him to 20 years' imprisonment in Spandau Prison. Sauckal was hanged (see HOLOCAUST).

Speer's limited admission of responsibility did not stop him from working tirelessly, if unsuccessfully, with a network of supporters to get his sentence reduced. With the knowing assistance of prison officers, he succeeded in smuggling a large quantity of written material out of Spandau, material that would become the basis for his two best-known books, *Inside the Third Reich* (1969) and *Spandau: The Secret Diaries* (1975). In these books, he built on the myth of the apolitical technocrat ignorant of the regime's worst crimes that he had laid out in Nuremberg. *Inside the Third Reich* became a worldwide best-seller and one of the most influential books ever published about Hitler—the person and the dictator—and the inner workings of the Nazi regime. No other party figure at that level was willing or able to write a memoir like it. Many Germans could identify with Speer's claim that he had fallen under Hitler's spell, along with his expression of a general but not personal sense of responsibility and a degree of remorse, albeit for the destruction inflicted on Germany rather than for the suffering of the regime's millions of victims. It mattered, too, that he seemed to bear no resemblance—not in his appearance, his temperament, or his purported role in the regime—to figures like **Hermann Göring**, Goebbels, or **Heinrich Himmler**.

It was not until the early 1980s that historians began to disentangle the truth from the densely woven web of lies, omissions, and carefully worded rationalizations that underpinned his reputation as the repentant Nazi functionary who had served his time (most West Germans considered his sentence unjust) and become a respectable member of the bourgeoisie. Speer played an active role in the eviction by his inspectorate of thousands of Berlin Jews from their homes, at one point in September 1938 advocating their incarceration in camps. He also knew far more than he admitted about the use of slave labor and the persecution and systematic murder of Europe's Jews. Beginning in the fall of 1941, the inspectorate worked closely with the Gestapo in the deportation of 50,000 Jews from Berlin to the East. In 2007, a cache of letters he wrote to the widow of a Belgian resistance leader came to light, and one of them included his admission to her in 1971 that he was in fact present at Himmler's 1943 speech at Posen, in which Himmler discussed the ongoing genocide of the Jews.

As armaments minister, he was not the miracle worker most historians had long assumed. His most significant contribution to the doomed war effort was to have been the driving force behind the accelerating conscription of slave laborers. Perhaps the most important achievement of Speer's mythmaking was to have convinced many people that a technocrat could not at the same time be an ideologue. In reality, Speer was both, and nothing better demonstrated his fanatical devotion to Hitler than his determination to prolong a war he knew to be lost.

"STAB IN THE BACK" MYTH (DOLCH-STOSSLEGENDE). In November 1918, Germany lost **World War I**. The defeat had been months in the making. Russia's departure from the war allowed the Germans to transfer a significant number of forces to the western front, where they launched a series of major offensives in the spring of 1918. Yet it was not enough to defeat the entente, now joined by the **United States**. The infusion of American troops and the effective deployment of tanks halted and reversed the German advance into northern **France**. In the fall, **Bulgaria** and the Austro-Hungarian Empire collapsed. Morale among German troops crumbled. On the home front, years of war and a British naval blockade had taken a severe material and psychological toll, seeding the ground for the revolution that began with a mutiny at a German naval base on 3 November.

On 2 September, First Quartermaster General Erich Ludendorff had admitted the truth to civilian officials: The war was lost. By the end of the month, he conceded the same to the army's leadership and recommended that a new, democratically elected government sue for peace. It was as cynical a political maneuver as one could imagine. Ludendorff had by no means become a convert to liberal democracy. He was well aware that his demand would saddle a new government with the blame for whatever happened next. And what happened next was a revolution in Germany, an attempted communist seizure of power, and the imposition of what most Germans would consider unacceptably harsh settlement [see also VERSAILLES TREATY (1919)].

No one person is responsible for formulating what became known as the "stab in the back" legend, though Ludendorff and former chief of the great general staff **Paul von Hindenburg** were two of its most important instigators. The accusation was simple: The German army was undefeated until socialists, leftists, and "pacifists" at home deliberately sabotaged the war effort. Anti-Semites would soon add **Jews** to the roster of alleged traitors. None of this was remotely true, but several versions of the conspiracy theory spread like a virus among conservatives and military and civilian circles and across the Far-Right scene. Over the following decade, it remained a cornerstone of the nationalist conservative–Far Right opposition to the republic, and no evidence to the contrary could change the minds of those who had embraced it.

The willingness of the Right to perpetuate the lie, along with the willingness of millions of Germans to believe it, undermined the republic's legitimacy from its very beginnings. Refusing to accept the fact of military defeat, Germans looked to other explanations for the unexpected news of the armistice. The lie also fueled preexisting hatreds of democrats, leftists, and Jews.

Hitler and the **National Socialist German Workers' Party** (Nazi Party; Nationalsozialistische Deutsche Arbeiterpartei; NSDAP) did not deploy one or more of the most common versions of the legend to attract supporters or votes. In Hitler's version of events, profit-seeking Jews had undermined Germany's **economy** and thus the war effort. For his part, according to Hitler, the Kaiser had proven too weak to do what was necessary to win. Then what Hitler would call the November criminals betrayed Germany by submitting to a humiliating treaty. Taking these positions was a shrewd political move. Blaming a vulnerable minority allowed him to avoid alienating Germans who might resent hearing their wartime sacrifices described as part of a treasonous conspiracy. His take on events also emphasized the forward-looking nature of national socialism. The point was not to dwell on the reasons for the 1918 armistice but to take revenge on the November criminals; purge Germany of Jews; and forge the German people into a cohesive, "racially pure" entity capable of fighting and winning a new war.

STALIN, JOSEPH (1878–1953). As many observers pointed out at the time and since, Stalin bears a degree of responsibility for putting the Nazis in power. After taking control of foreign communist parties, he prevented the **Communist Party of Germany** (Kommunistische Partei Deutschlands; KPD) from allying with the **Social Democratic Party of Germany** (Sozialdemokratische Partei Deutschlands; SPD) in the late 1920s and early 1930s. When he finally did approve of "popular front" coalitions of left and liberal parties in the mid-1930s, it was far too late for Germany.

Stalin believed the Soviet Union was surrounded by enemies, and he was not wrong. Better to prepare the motherland for the inevitable showdown with the capitalist-imperialist world than try to export revolution. Hence his turn inward and the policy of building "socialism in one country." At the same time, he sought good relations with Berlin. He was not blind to the threat a rearmed and virulently anticommunist fascist regime posed to his nation. Yet as the Nazi threat became clearer, Stalin turned to a form of **appeasement** by spurning an Anglo–French–Soviet alliance in favor of a **Nazi–Soviet Nonaggression Pact** with Germany negotiated with remarkable speed in August 1939.

Certainly, the latter option was from strategic and economic standpoints the preferable choice, if only in the short term. He was in a good position to bargain with Hitler, as only he could give him a free hand in the East to attack Western Europe. It also allowed Stalin to retake, or attempt to retake, much of the territory lost to the Russian Empire in 1918 and avenge the defeat of the Red Army by **Polish** forces in 1921. And it bought time and economic benefits; a flood of high-quality machine tools was particularly important in the latter category. A war between capitalist states would be another plus. There is no convincing evidence that he was planning an offensive against Germany in 1941.

Hitler is known to have expressed a kind of admiration for Stalin, as did **National Socialist German Workers' Party** (Nazi Party; Nationalsozialistische Deutsche Arbeiterpartei; NSDAP) officials who encountered their Soviet counterparts. Hitler's sense that at some level he understood the famously inscrutable Soviet dictator may have contributed to his utter mystification at Stalin's behavior during the purges of the mid- to late 1930s. Insanity was the only explanation that made sense to him. More generally and catastrophically, Hitler's belief that Slavs were "subhumans," along with the bizarre spectacle of the purges and the failure of the Red Army in the Winter War with Finland in 1939, led him to expect the Soviet Union to collapse like a house of cards following the German invasion.

Stalin's most disastrous error was to assume that Hitler was a rational leader and a practitioner of realpolitik. In June 1941, Stalin persisted in believing multiple independent and reliable public and secret reports of a German invasion were German and British disinformation. He knew a war between Nazi Germany and the Soviet Union was coming, but he seems to have been engaging in wishful thinking. Perhaps Hitler would not risk the string of victories he had just achieved. Given that Britain remained undefeated, would it make sense to risk a two-front war? Nor would it be sensible for Hitler to jeopardize the **economic** benefits of the nonaggression pact, given the resource-starved state of the German economy. And Stalin perhaps also expected Hitler to issue a series of demands before sending more than 4 million soldiers across the border.

A shocked Stalin quickly recovered his capacity for ruthless leadership and led the extraordinarily effective mobilization of the Soviet Union that allowed it to survive the German onslaught. As a military leader, the most important difference from Hitler was that Stalin was willing to listen to his generals—especially the exceptionally talented Georgi Zhukov—and support their decisions. Despite the precariousness of his country's position in 1941 and 1942, Stalin drove a hard bargain with Britain over the terms of an alliance in demanding that he retain control of the territories gained in the nonaggression pact. Britain and the **United States** provided a substantial amount of material aid, but the main thing the ever-mistrustful Stalin wanted was the opening of a second front as soon as possible. The hard reality was that the Western Allies were simply not in a position to launch an invasion of German-occupied **France** until the summer of 1944. In the end, what kept the alliance together was a shared determination to defeat Nazi Germany as quickly as possible, a commitment that included the steadfast unwillingness of all three leaders to consider a separate peace at any point in the war.

Historians continue to debate Stalin's intentions as the Red Army occupied half of Europe in 1944 and 1945. Russia had withstood two German invasions in the space of a single generation's life span, the second one resulting in the loss of some 26 million people, most of them civilians. The bulk of the war in Europe was fought and won for the Allies on the eastern front. Stalin—not unreasonably—expected that the governments along his country's western borders would be friendly. That meant controlled by Moscow. Moreover, Stalin had watched the Western Allies set up an occupation regime in **Italy** without consulting him. In October 1944, he met one on one with British prime minister **Winston Churchill**, and the two agreed to divide up much of Eastern Europe into spheres of influence, with Britain dominant in Greece; the Soviet Union dominant in **Hungary**, **Romania**, and **Bulgaria**; and influence split in Yugoslavia (the only Eastern European state not completely occupied by the Red Army; *see* BALKANS).

As for the rest of Eastern Europe, with the notable exceptions of Germany and Poland, there were no major border changes. The region's demography, however, was altered radically by years of war, the **Holocaust**, and the expulsion of perhaps 12 million ethnic Germans from across Eastern Europe. The **Baltics** would remain Soviet republics, and Poland's eastern and western borders would be altered substantially. In 1948, Stalin engineered a local communist party overthrow of **Czechoslovakia**'s democratically elected government.

Yet Stalin found the Soviet Union again surrounded by potential enemies. The extent of his control over Eastern Europe, while achieved quickly, came at a considerable short- and long-term cost for Stalin and his successors. Both anticommunism and anti-Russian sentiment were powerful in Eastern Europe, and Stalin's determination to control the region's postwar governments would quickly alienate him from the United States and its new president, Harry Truman, who was far less ambivalent about Eastern Europe's fate than his predecessor. But Stalin also perceived the United States as a global threat, considering the extent of its military power and especially economic power, and not least the fact that with **Japan**'s defeat in August, American military bases did in fact surround the Soviet Union.

STEEL HELMETS (STAHLHELM). Most German veterans of **World War I** returned to their prewar lives. A sizeable minority joined paramilitary groups of the Right and Left. In the former category, one of the most significant was the Stahlhelm, Bund der Front Soldaten (Steel Helmets, League of Frontline Soldiers). Established on 13 November 1918 by Franz Seldte, a decorated and badly wounded veteran of the western front, it became a hybrid of paramilitary, social welfare organization for veterans, and political party. Seldte and the Stahlhelm's other principal leader, Theodor Duesterberg, looked back to the patriotic spirit that supposedly pervaded Germany in August 1914. Reviving that spirit, they believed, was the key to unifying the nation. The organization's program was largely reactionary: the rejection of the **Versailles Treaty** and restoration of the monarchy, though its manifesto also demanded the expansion of Lebensraum (**living space**). It also became increasingly anti-Semitic, banning **Jewish** veterans from its ranks in the mid-1920s.

By then, the Stahlhelm had around 300,000 members who regularly made their presence known in parades and fights with other paramilitaries. There was also overlap and cooperation with various right-wing groups. Hitler's attitude was ambivalent. By the late 1920s, he had to balance the demands of the more radical elements of the **National Socialist German Workers' Party** (Nazi Party; Nationalsozialistische Deutsche Arbeiterpartei; NSDAP) and its hostility to "reactionaries" with the practical need to form strategic partnerships with conservative nationalists, including the Stahlhelm. Such partnerships were shaky and short lived [*see* HARZBURG FRONT; YOUNG PLAN REFERENDUM (1929)]. The one that mattered most, however, resulted from the negotiations that led to Hitler's appointment as **chancellor**: In the conservative-nationalist-dominated cabinet, Seldte was given the Labor Ministry, a position he held through Hitler's regime and then the short-lived successor regime of Grand Admiral **Karl Dönitz**.

Hitler, however, had no confidence in Seldte, who was quickly marginalized by the far more talented and ruthless **Hermann Göring**. Like the alliance with conservative politicians, the Stahlhelm was doomed from the moment Hitler became chancellor. In April, Seldte agreed to give control of the organization to Hitler and sacked Duesterberg. At the same time, its membership was absorbed by the **Sturmabteilung** (Stormtroopers; SA). In 1935, it was unceremoniously disbanded. In retrospect, the Stahlhelm had played a double role for Hitler, first by contributing to the destabilization of the Weimar Republic and then as a soon-to-be-dispensed-with adjunct to Hitler's seizure of power.

STRASSER, GREGOR (1892–1934). Strasser was born in Geisenfeld, Bavaria, in 1892. He was training to be a pharmacist when **World War I** broke out, and he served in an artillery regiment and was promoted to lieutenant. After the war, he joined a right-wing paramilitary unit (Freikorps; Free Corps) and then the **National Socialist German Workers' Party** (Nazi Party; Nationalsozialistische Deutsche Arbeiterpartei; NSDAP) in 1922. After participating in the **Beer Hall Putsch**, he abandoned street-level militancy and became a prominent Far-Right politician during the period of Hitler's imprisonment.

Strasser was an unusual figure among prominent party officials. He looked every bit the **Sturmabteilung** (Stormtroopers; SA) tough that he in fact was. But he was also highly intelligent and an effective public speaker and political organizer. Even some on the Left considered him relatively reasonable, and industrialists who donated money to the party after the NSDAP's electoral breakthrough in 1930 singled out Strasser because they considered him among the few who might be able to restrain Hitler's radicalism.

Most important was his unwillingness to devote himself mindlessly to Hitler. While Strasser considered Hitler to be a political genius and understood his importance to the movement, he refused to become a sycophant.

His independence of mind extended to his vision of national socialism. Strasser was serious about implementing the socialization measures as stated in the **Nazi Party Program** (25-Point Program), an agenda pursued even more aggressively by Gregor's younger brother, Otto. But it was Gregor's abilities as an organizer and not an ideologue that would make him the second-most powerful figure in the party until 1932. His first major success was achieved in 1925, when he built up the reconstituted NSDAP in western and northern Germany.

In September of that year, he founded the Working Association North West. His secretary and the group's chief publicist was a recent recruit to the party, **Joseph Goebbels**. Based in Elberfeld in the heart of Germany's industrial Northwest, the group was an informal association of regional party leaders. Strasser intended to use it to add substance to the party program, particularly on **economic** matters. He also proposed the creation of a "greater German Empire" as the core of a regional customs union and a "United States of Europe" and advocated an alliance with the Bolsheviks based on their mutual anticapitalism and opposition to the post–**Versailles Treaty** system. It was not Strasser's intent to use the Working Association to challenge Hitler's position as leader, though it did portend the deepening of an emerging division between the party in northern Germany and its base in Munich.

At first, Hitler seemed uninterested in these developments, devoting the second half of the year to enjoying his first visit to the **Wagner** Festival in Bayreuth and then retreating to Berchtesgaden to work on the second volume of *Mein Kampf*. But he sensed a challenge to his leadership after reading a draft of Working Association proposals in January 1926. He hastily ordered party leaders to assemble in Bamberg on 14 February, where he subjected them to a lengthy tirade in which he rejected every one of the Working Associations's recommendations. A shocked and cowed Strasser did not manage to mount an effective defense of his agenda, and the group ceased to have any influence on the party's direction.

The incident did not, however, spell the end of Strasser's career as an influential party leader and **Reichstag** deputy. Indeed, Hitler was magnanimous after Bamberg. He brought Strasser to Munich to direct the party's propaganda work and then put him in charge of the party's organizational structure. Strasser abandoned his pursuit of a more socialist national socialism and broke with Otto, who remained a stubborn advocate of nationalizing German industries and forming an alliance with the Soviet Union until he was forced to resign from the party in the summer of 1930.

For the next two years, Gregor's organizational abilities again served him and the party well, especially because Hitler never gave up his dilettantish approach to work. His break with Hitler occurred in late 1932 over the question of how to finally achieve power. Hitler would accept nothing less than the **chancellorship**, while Strasser advocated a more flexible approach. This flexibility included a willingness to form a coalition government without Hitler as chancellor. Conservative nationalists sensed an opening and approached Strasser. In a secret meeting in Berlin on 3 December, General Kurt von Schleicher, who had just been appointed chancellor, proposed making Strasser vice chancellor and minister president in Prussia. But Strasser realized that despite his stature within the party, he did not have sufficient support to stage what would in effect be a palace coup against Hitler. On 8 December, he resigned from his party offices and warned a handful of regional party leaders that Hitler's intransigence on the matter of the chancellorship threatened to wreck the party.

By that time, Hitler had already pushed Strasser out of his inner circle. Their relationship was also poisoned by a jealous Goebbels, who had come to detest his powerful former mentor, suspecting him of using his talents to slowly marginalize Hitler. Yet word of Strasser's resignation stunned Hitler, who immediately assembled the same regional party officials who had just met with Strasser to justify his all-or-nothing strategy and demand their personal allegiance. Still badly shaken—at Goebbels's residence that night, he threatened suicide—he met with Goebbels, **Ernst Röhm**, and

Heinrich Himmler; ordered a reorganization of the party's structure; appointed himself head of its political organization; and soon after set out on a nine-day speaking tour to make personal appeals to any wavering party officials. A purge of Strasser supporters followed, along with a campaign vilifying the man who had done so much to rebuild the party after the Beer Hall Putsch and demands for declarations of personal loyalty to Hitler.

Strasser remained a party member, though he was now completely marginalized and began working for a Berlin subsidiary of IG Farben. He was murdered in the Gestapo's Berlin headquarters during the **Röhm Purge**, possibly on Hitler's orders. *See also* HARZBURG FRONT.

STRATEGIC BOMBING CAMPAIGN. Hitler was the first leader of the belligerent states in the Second World War to order a strategic bombing campaign. The **Luftwaffe** had developed significant capabilities during the **Spanish Civil War**. The German Condor Legion and the **Italian** air force attacked Madrid and other civilian centers (most notoriously the small Basque town of Guernica) and key industrial facilities [*see* FRANCO, FRANCISCO (1892–1975)]. The strategy previewed the twinned objectives of future strategic bombing campaigns: the destruction of war-supporting infrastructure and the erosion of morale. Luftwaffe officials noted that while the bombing of infrastructure clearly helped the nationalist war effort, it did not undermine civilian morale. Rather, it boosted it. They also noted the importance of effective civilian defense measures in maintaining morale in the face of this terrifying new form of warfare.

Despite this and the minimal impact on morale in **Poland** during the Luftwaffe's short-lived bombing campaign against Warsaw, both senior officers and Hitler persisted in believing that hitting population centers by air would fatally undermine civilian morale. Hence the decision to switch from extremely costly—for the Luftwaffe—attacks on British Royal Air Force (RAF) installations in 1940 to the bombing of London and other population centers beginning in August. Though morale in Great Britain did take a hit in the winter of 1940–1941, it never crumbled [*see* BATTLE OF BRITAIN (1940)].

The RAF had first bombed Berlin in August 1940. A systematic campaign followed with attacks on war-related industries and infrastructure. Civilian centers became the focus of the campaign in the summer of 1941. Like their counterparts in the Luftwaffe, RAF Bomber Command was convinced morale would not hold up. But there was another reason: Forced to fly sorties at night, RAF bombers were mostly incapable of hitting their intended targets. They could more easily bomb towns and cities.

In 1943, the US Army Air Force (USAAF) joined the RAF's campaign. Initially, USAAF forces suffered enormous casualties, mainly because bombers were sent on missions in daylight without fighter escorts. By the beginning of 1944, however, the USAAF was able to deploy fighter planes with the range to escort the bombers. They shot down Luftwaffe fighters at a ratio of three to one. The bombers, now protected and being produced in huge quantities, inflicted enormous damage in Germany, and the campaign killed and injured an estimated 355,000 to 420,000 civilians, uniformed personnel, foreign workers, and prisoners of war.

Yet civilian morale did not, as expected, collapse. Nor did the German **economy**. Analysts for the postwar US Strategic Bombing Survey were shocked to learn that German industrial production actually increased as the bombing campaign intensified. Both morale and the German economy proved far more resilient than Allied officials believed. The attacks did, however, restrict German industrial production and caused major disruptions to transportation and supply networks. In the end, the campaign was just one of the fronts on which the Allies won the war.

The question of why civilian morale was not affected far more than it was has generated a good deal of debate among historians. Simple blind devotion to Hitler does not account for the resilience of German civilians. The regime managed to provide a significant amount of material goods, compensation for lost property, and other forms of welfare. Party and state officials relied on millions of civilian volunteers to distribute aid (including plunder): By 1944, a quarter of the population had volunteered to serve the Reich Air Defense League. More important factors as the attacks intensified were shared sacrifice, a sense of patriotic duty, and commitment to the ideal of a Volksgemeinschaft (people's community). And while food was rationed, deprivation never reached the levels experienced by millions of Germans in **World War I**. A steady stream of propaganda promising that **wonder weapons** would turn the tide provided a short-lived boost to morale. In the last months of the war, desperation and a campaign of terror by the regime against defeatism and desertion, in which thousands of Germans were summarily executed, kept the home front from disintegrating.

What is striking is how detached Hitler was from the destruction his war had unleashed on Germany and the Germans. He certainly knew of the bombing campaign's increasingly destructive impact but was far more concerned with the potential threat a precipitous decline in morale could pose to his regime. As for the human cost to his own people, he was callous and indifferent. Beginning in June 1941, he lived mainly at his East Prussian headquarters (the **Wolf's Lair**) with periodic stays at the secluded **Berghof**. His public appearances dwindled during the war's later years, and he never visited a city following a major bombing raid. In the end, having decided on suicide as the Red Army closed in on his well-protected bunker complex in Berlin, he would blame for the lost war the very people he claimed to have been chosen by destiny to lead.

STURMABTEILUNG (STORM SECTION; STORMTROOPERS; BROWN SHIRTS; SA). The Nazi Party's paramilitary division performed an essential role in Hitler's ascent to and consolidation of power. The unit was created in 1921 as the party's Gymnastics and Sports Section before being renamed. It reflected the fact that the party's leadership was becoming dominated by men with military backgrounds: **World War I** and Freikorps (Free Corps) paramilitary veterans. The brown uniforms were an accident: They were German East **Africa** troop surplus.

The SA was to serve several purposes. One was to protect party leaders at speeches, marches, and rallies. Another was to project power, purpose, and unity. As its early membership was comprised of many (often unemployed) war and Freikorps veterans, it was designed to appeal to more of them but also those who had been too young to serve in either. Its first leader was **Ernst Röhm**, a battle-scarred First World War and Freikorps veteran and capable organizer with good connections to the Reichswehr.

Röhm and the SA participated in the **Beer Hall Putsch**, and following its banning by the Bavarian state, Röhm attached the organization to the Frontbann, a paramilitary group comprised of war veterans. He broke with Hitler in 1925 and resigned his post, with the re-formed SA now led by Franz Pfeffer von Salomon. It expanded enormously in size over the next five years, counting around 60,000 members in 1930. The problem was that Salomon resisted Hitler's attempts to bring the organization under his and the party's direct control. Complicating matters was growing conflict between SA and **Schutzstaffel** (Protection Squad; SS) men, conflict that was sometimes violent. When Salomon insisted on adding SA men to electoral lists in **Reichstag elections**, Hitler balked, and Salomon quit. Hitler took the opportunity to make himself the SA's supreme commander and recalled Röhm, who had moved to Bolivia, as a chief of staff responsible for running its day-to-day operations.

Through the 1920s, the SA developed a distinctive culture, with songs and—increasingly—martyrs. The best known of these was Horst Wessel, a young SA leader in Berlin killed by communists in February 1930. **Joseph Goebbels**, who had personally sent Wessel to learn about grassroots organizing in **Vienna**, immediately created a national myth of a "martyr for the Third Reich." Conveniently for Goebbels, Wessel had written a marching song a few months before his death. Renamed "The Horst Wessel Song," it became the party's official anthem, and beginning in 1933, it was second only to "Deutschland, Deutschland über Alles" ("Germany, Germany Above All"). The attack on Wessel was but one instance of an epidemic of street-level violence between paramilitary groups, especially the SA and the Red Front Fighters League, the paramilitary arm of the **Communist Party of Germany** (Kommunistische Partei Deutschlands; KPD). The violence undermined the Weimar Republic's stability by heightening the mood of political crisis brought about mainly by the **economic** depression and the ensuing political gridlock.

For Hitler, recalling the capable Röhm was a blessing and a curse. Even more than Salomon, Röhm was intent on establishing a more independent profile for the SA. He also wanted to transform it into Germany's new army. As a kind of armed revolution vanguard, it would force through a more radical economic agenda than Hitler knew most Germans (and Germany's economic elites) would tolerate.

As tensions with Hitler, the SS, and the party, the SA—which counted a half-million members in January 1933 but quickly exploded in size to more than 4 million after it absorbed other paramilitary groups—provided one more crucial service to Hitler. It was mainly the SA that crushed the German Left in the spring of 1933. But it quickly became an intolerable liability as Hitler sought to bring the "national socialist revolution" to an end and turn his attention to **rearmament**.

In June 1934, Hitler had Röhm murdered, along with a number of prominent conservative nationalists and Catholic political activists [see RÖHM PURGE (1934)]. Röhm was replaced by Viktor Lutze, and the SA was disarmed and almost halved in size. It continued to exist and to perform ceremonial functions. It was periodically deployed to attack **Jews** (SA men played a major role in the November 1938 **Night of Broken Glass**). But it was henceforth politically powerless. Perhaps the most important result of the purge was that it cleared the way for the rapid ascendancy of the SS.

SUICIDE (30 APRIL 1945). On 30 April 1945, Hitler and **Eva Braun** committed suicide in his private study in the Berlin bunker complex. Hitler had moved into the lower, or main, bunker in March, where he was joined by party officials, military personnel, and members of his personal staff. He made his final public appearance on 20 March, when he emerged briefly to greet a handful of **Wehrmacht** and **Schutzstaffel** (Protection Squad; SS) soldiers and **Hitler Youth** (Hitlerjugend; HJ) members.

Hitler had considered evacuating to Berchtesgaden on 20 April, his 56th birthday. On 19 April, however, **Wehrmacht** chief of staff General Hans Krebs informed him that Soviet forces were only 30 kilometers from Berlin. They were in fact closer. On Hitler's birthday, they had reached its southernmost outskirts and had nearly surrounded the city. Only the west remained open, with Anglo-American forces still some 500 kilometers away. Upon hearing this, Hitler flew into a rage and decided to remain in Berlin and take command of the city's defense. A day after a desultory celebration of his birthday, he ordered a largely imaginary army to break the near-total Soviet encirclement. On 21 April, Wehrmacht officers and the highest-ranking regime officials—including **Hermann Göring**, **Heinrich Himmler**, **Joseph Goebbels**, **Albert Speer**, and **Martin Bormann**—begged Hitler to get out of the city while he still could. He refused, and nearly all of them fled the bunker immediately.

At the afternoon briefing on 22 April, Hitler was informed that the counteroffensive he had ordered had never been launched. One account describes him flying into another rage and proclaiming the war to be lost and that he would rather shoot himself than leave Berlin. Another recalled that he was relatively calm. Still others recount him threatening suicide to the dwindling number of personnel residing in the bunker.

There is no question that Hitler received two other major shocks over the following days. On 23 April, Göring informed him he would act to succeed him as per an agreement from June 1941. Hitler ordered him arrested and threatened to charge him with high treason unless he resigned from his positions, which Göring did immediately. Another came on 28 April, when Hitler learned that Himmler had attempted to open negotiations with the Americans (see UNITED STATES OF AMERICA) and the British via a Swedish intermediary.

Over the previous week, Soviet forces had cut off most reliable lines of communication with the outside world. By 28 April, the **chancellery** was under constant artillery bombardment, and Soviet troops were closing in. The scene in the bunker became a bizarre, macabre spectacle. A physically debilitated Hitler shuffled about, while the remains of his personal staff consumed copious quantities of alcohol and made plans to escape or take their own lives. The most ghastly moment resulted from Joseph and Magda Goebbels's decision to move into the bunker with their six children with the intention of killing them before taking their own lives, which they did on 1 May.

Shortly after midnight on 29 April, Hitler and Eva Braun were married, a decision Hitler apparently made quite suddenly. He then dictated a **personal will and political testament**. In the will, he stated that he and Eva had chosen death over capture or surrender and ordered that their remains be burned. He repeated his intention to commit suicide in the testament.

That afternoon, Hitler had a vial of prussic acid (hydrocyanic acid, a cyanide compound) tested on his dog. The animal suffered an agonizing death, which may have prompted him to choose suicide by gunshot rather than poison or perhaps to resort to both measures simultaneously. That evening, he learned of **Benito Mussolini**'s fate, though it is unclear whether he was informed that his bullet-ridden body had been strung up in public. If so, the news would have bolstered his decision to take his own life rather than risk being captured alive by the Soviets.

In the afternoon of 30 April, he said formal farewells to the remaining officials and staff and entered his private quarters with Eva. Hitler shot himself, while Eva took a prussic acid capsule. Some documentary and forensic evidence suggests that he may have also taken prussic acid. Per his orders, their bodies were burned in the chancellery courtyard. The ongoing artillery bombardment prevented a secure underground burial, so the remains were covered hastily with a thin layer of soil.

Krebs managed to reach a Soviet command post to speak with General Vasily Chuikov about a negotiated surrender—which Chuikov and General Georgy Zhukov refused to consider—and to inform him of Hitler's death. **Joseph Stalin** was awoken with the news and asked whether a body had been located. The next afternoon, Goebbels and Bormann informed Grand Admiral **Karl Dönitz** of Hitler's death. Dönitz announced the news by radio the same day.

On 2 May, Berlin's military commander ordered German troops to cease fighting. Soviet troops entered the bunker, followed by Red Army intelligence (SMERSH) officers charged with finding Hitler's remains. Two days later, officers discovered corpses so badly burned they could not be positively identified by sight. On the night of 5–6 May, the remains were transported to SMERSH headquarters in a Berlin suburb. There, an autopsy on what were presumed to be parts of Hitler's and Braun's corpses was conducted with an assistant to Hitler's dentist who had worked on his teeth. She confirmed the remains to be Hitler's.

What happened next comprises one of the stranger chapters of the war's end in Europe. Two competing Soviet intelligence arms, SMERSH and the NKVD, produced conflicting assessments of the cause of Hitler's death: either poison or gunshot. It seems clear that Stalin and NKVD chief Lavrenty Beria very much wanted a confirmation of the presumably more cowardly suicide by poison. Complicating matters was the fact that British intelligence conducted a separate investigation in which a young historian, Hugh Trevor-Roper, was charged with gathering as much information as he could, though he was denied access to any eyewitnesses in Soviet captivity. His conclusion, which he made public in his best-selling 1947 book *The Last Days of Hitler*, was that Hitler had shot himself in the mouth.

Stalin was kept informed of the Soviet investigation as it took place and knew that Hitler's remains had been identified. Yet he chose to proclaim repeatedly that Hitler was alive and hiding in an area controlled by Western Allied forces or had escaped to Argentina. Whatever his motives, it was Stalin who was responsible for propagating the first of what would be many equally baseless conspiracy theories that Hitler had survived the war.

The remains were buried and reburied in multiple locations in the Soviet occupation zone (after 1949, the German Democratic Republic, or East Germany) until 1970, when KGB chief Yuri Andropov ordered them destroyed. A fragment of Hitler's jawbone containing a few natural teeth and a segment of his dentures were spared destruction and are now held in a Russian security services (FSB) archive. In 2016 and 2017, researchers were able to compare images of the teeth and dentures to X-rays of Hitler's head. They also conducted tests on the remains to detect any evidence of either a gunshot wound to the mouth or prussic acid. There was no evidence of gunshot residue but some suggesting Hitler bit down on a glass prussic acid vial. It is unlikely that a bone fragment with what appears to be a bullet hole and held in the same archive is part of Hitler's skull, as claimed by Russian authorities.

Hitler was hardly alone among Germans—civilian, party, and military—in choosing suicide. The wave of suicides that accompanied Germany's defeat was unprecedented in modern history. Only a very few can be confirmed as having been inspired by Hitler's act. Nearly all the other highest-level regime officials took their own lives: Goebbels, Bormann, Himmler, **Robert Ley**, and Göring. At the local level, 20 percent of Gauleiters killed themselves, as did a strikingly large number of military officers: 10 percent of Wehrmacht generals and 14 percent of **Luftwaffe** generals. Fear of capture may have played some role, though many officers had surrendered or been captured alive by both Western Allied forces and the Red Army and then did not kill themselves in captivity. The more likely explanation is that they believed they were confronting a calamitous defeat in the only truly honorable manner.

Thousands of civilians also committed suicide. Their motives varied. For many, the fear

Hitler at an SA rally, Dortmund, 1933. *Courtesy of the United States Holocaust Memorial Museum.*

of what was to come in the occupation was certainly a factor. This fear was intensified by years of propaganda that told Germans that they were engaged in a life-or-death struggle with their enemies, above all the Slavs and their "**Jewish** Bolshevik" masters. Another factor was the widespread knowledge of the regime's and Wehrmacht's crimes. There was also a gendered dimension to the suicides, particularly in parts of Germany conquered and occupied by the Red Army. While the rape of German **women** by soldiers of the Western Allied armies was more common than once thought, Red Army soldiers and personnel assaulted women on a massive scale. The number of women who killed themselves as the Red Army approached is in the thousands. Ten thousand are known to have committed suicide in Berlin after being raped. But the same impulse that led Joseph and Magda Goebbels to murder their six children before taking their own lives was present among ordinary Germans: A life without Hitler was not worth living.

SWASTIKA (HAKENKREUZ). Nothing sinister should be read into the fact that the symbol Hitler selected to represent the **National Socialist German Workers' Party** (Nazi Party; Nationalsozialistische Deutsche Arbeiterpartei; NSDAP) had for centuries appeared in various forms in the iconographies of different cultures. The word is derived from Sanskrit (*svasika*), meaning "good fortune and wellness." German archeologist Heinrich Schliemann may have been the first to connect the symbol, which he noticed during his excavation of Troy in the early 1870s, to what appeared to be swastika symbols on pottery discovered in Germany. The belief that a great Aryan culture spanned the Eurasian continent became a common one in Germany and elsewhere in Europe.

By the beginning of the 20th century, it could be seen in various European countries. The nationalist Right in Germany transformed it into a symbol of alleged Germanic cultural and "racial" superiority. It was adopted by a strange secret society in **Vienna** founded in 1907 by Guido von List, a writer obsessed with legends of pre-Christian Germanic tribes and convinced of the existence of a "race" of Aryans chosen by God to dominate the world. Other such groups deployed the symbol, believing it to have been a rune of signal importance to ancient Aryans. It is most likely from reading List that Hitler embraced it in the earliest period of his public speaking in postwar Munich.

Highly attuned to the power of imagery, Hitler ensured the swastika became the party's official symbol in 1921. It would then appear on all kinds of party regalia, most notably on a flag of Hitler's design: a bold black swastika placed against a simple white-and-red background. The format blended elements of the new and the familiar red-black-white color scheme of the old imperial flag. During the years of Nazi rule, the symbol could be found on all kinds of consumer goods.

During the September 1935 **Nuremberg party rally**, Hitler demanded that the **Reichstag** enact a law making the swastika flag the legal flag of the Reich. The demand came in response to an act of protest against the regime's policies in New York City, during which anti-Nazi protestors boarded the German passenger ship *SS Bremen*, pulled down the swastika flag, and threw it in the river. Hitler used the incident to push through the full legal adoption of the symbol. Because the move finally eliminated the imperial flag, it was a symbolic step against the lingering influence of the traditional nationalist Right. **Jews** would be forbidden to display the new national flag (*see* NUREMBERG RACE LAWS; RACISM).

In 1945, the Allies outlawed the dissemination and display of Nazi symbols, a ban that remains in place in Germany, **Austria**, and a few other European states.

***TABLE TALK* AND *THE TESTAMENT OF ADOLF HITLER* (1941–1944; 1945).** Subjecting subordinates and members of his inner circle to long monologues was a habit Hitler, a narcissist and an autodidact, developed as a teenager and young man. Beginning in 1941, **Martin Bormann** ordered notes to be taken of Hitler's monologues in his wartime headquarters with the intent of preserving his words—more accurately, an approximation of them—for posterity. Three lawyers, Henry Picker, Heinrich Heim, and Hans Müller, are known to have taken the notes, with Bormann adding some of his own. Multiple versions have been published in Germany, Great Britain, **France**, and the **United States** since the early 1950s. *The Testament*—not to be confused with Hitler's final **personal will and political testament**, which he dictated the night before his **suicide**—is supposedly a continuation of the *Table Talk* notes and purports to cover Hitler's monologues of February and April 1945. Hitler's biographers and other historians of Nazi Germany have made extensive use of *Table Talk*, drawing on it for clues to Hitler's views on the ongoing war, his recollections of the **National Socialist German Workers' Party**'s (Nazi Party; Nationalsozialistische Deutsche Arbeiterpartei; NSDAP) early years, and insight into his **personality**. But the *Table Talk* is an extremely problematic source, and *The Testament* is almost certainly a forgery.

Regarding the former, the three lawyers—they were not stenographers—and Bormann did not take down what Hitler said verbatim, a fact that complicates the document's credibility and usefulness as a primary source. Then there is the matter of the original document's provenance, translations, and retranslations. The first version, covering the years 1941 and 1942, was published in Germany in 1951 with the assistance of historian Gerhard Ritter and the prestigious Institute for Contemporary History in Munich. It was based mainly on Picker's notes and a few of Heim's. A second edition appeared in 1963, this time edited by Percy Ernst Schramm, a history professor at the University of Göttingen and former Nazi Party member, **Wehrmacht** officer, and staff historian of the Wehrmachtführungsstab (German High Command Operational Staff). In 1952 and 1954, François Genoud, a Swiss lawyer and unrepentant Nazi and former Abwehr (German military intelligence) agent, published two volumes based on what he claimed was a more complete set of notes he had acquired under mysterious circumstances. Genoud, working with British historian Hugh Trevor-Roper, also oversaw the translation of the French version into English. Trevor-Roper was not given access to the alleged German original in Genoud's possession.

An edition based on these German documents appeared in Germany in 1980, though due to a legal dispute, it does not include notes taken by Picker. Complicating an already-murky situation is the fact that no one has been able to locate original copies of Picker's and Heim's notes. Only one set of notes that may be authentic, taken by Heim in January 1942, is known to exist and is held in a branch of Germany's federal archive system. It would not be until 2003 that an American historian would demonstrate that the English version, which was based on Genoud's French translation, contained statements attributed to Hitler that were in fact written by Genoud. In 2016, a Swedish historian confirmed that for more than 30 years, Trevor-Roper repeatedly withheld information that would have called the authenticity of both sources and the accuracy of their translations into serious question. Unlike his last-minute decision in 1983 to reverse his appraisal of the faked Hitler **diaries**, he kept what he knew about *Table Talk* and *The Testament* to himself. By cultivating Genoud, whom he knew to be an ex-Nazi and not entirely reliable, he hoped to gain access to other materials he suspected Genoud had collected. Trevor-Roper had already established himself as the English-speaking world's leading authority on Hitler, and his name on multiple editions of *Table Talk* further cemented this status.

Genoud was the first to publish an edition of *The Testament*, in French, in 1959. He claimed that **Walther Funk**, former Reich economics minister, gave him a photocopy of the original notes. English and German versions appeared in 1961 and 1981, respectively. Trevor-Roper never made public his strong doubts about the authenticity of these notes, supposedly taken by Bormann in the final months of Hitler's life. He preferred instead to profit from the credibility—and increased sales—his declaration of authenticity would impart to the English-language edition. But more scrupulous historians have suspected *The Testament* to be a forgery since the 1960s. It is full of erroneous statements or statements so out of line with what is otherwise reliably known about Hitler's views as to amount to clear evidence of forgery. *The Testament* was most likely written by Genoud, a lifelong Hitler admirer.

In the end, the *Table Talk* must be approached not as a singularly important and reliable primary source that allows the reader unmediated access to Hitler's true views, let alone his actual words. It is rather one of many contributions to Hitler mythology that continue to shape popular and even scholarly perceptions of him. That is, a version of Hitler the person and his views and accomplishments as he and one of his most devoted and powerful acolytes wanted them to be presented to the world. *Table Talk*, in short, is nothing more than Nazi propaganda.

TELEVISION. See CINEMA AND TELEVISION, REPRESENTATIONS IN.

***THE TESTAMENT OF ADOLF HITLER* (1945).** See TABLE TALK AND *THE TESTAMENT OF ADOLF HITLER* (1941–1944; 1945).

THIRD REICH. Depending on the historical context, the German word *Reich* can be translated into English as *kingdom*, *realm*, or *empire*. Drawing on the New Testament's Book of Revelation, a 12th-century Italian theologian, Joachim of Fiore, proposed the idea that a kingdom of God's reign on earth would emerge from a great conflict between good and evil. This third kingdom would follow what he considered to be the first and second (of the **Jews** and Christians, respectively). By the 19th century, the concept had been secularized to denote the replacement of an old, failing order with a new, ideal one. This interpretation became particularly appealing to frustrated nationalists in the German Empire, the state created by **Otto von Bismarck** in 1871. They looked back to the decline and eventual abolition of the first empire (the Holy Roman Empire) and were themselves living through what they perceived to be decline of the second.

The term *Third Reich* as the manifestation of national renewal became popular on the Far Right after **World War I**. Its best-known proponent was Arthur Moeller van den Bruck, a conservative writer whose 1923 book *Das Dritte Reich* (*The Third Reich*) drew on Joachim of Fiore's scheme and imagined the triumph of a new national order after a violent struggle with Marxism and liberalism. Even before the publication of *Das Dritte Reich*, **Dietrich Eckart** promoted the ideal, adding Jews to the list of enemies to be vanquished in the great coming struggle for Germany's national renewal.

The idea of a Third Reich found its way into the **National Socialist German Workers' Party**

(Nazi Party; Nationalsozialistische Deutsche Arbeiterpartei; NSDAP). In addition to Eckart, Otto Strasser, **Joseph Goebbels**, and **Alfred Rosenberg** took to using the term, and it appeared with increasing frequency in the party press as the NSDAP became a major force in German politics. While determined to overthrow the republic and return Germany to greatness, Hitler avoided references to a Third Reich until he was appointed **chancellor**. For the next five years, he used it repeatedly, first to describe the new regime being constructed and then, by 1937, to claim that it had been built. Two years later, however, he prohibited its formal use by the party. War and conquest were what Hitler desired, not a peaceable utopia contained within the borders of a German nation-state.

Since 1945, *Third Reich* has often been used by historians and journalists to denote Hitler's 12-year regime, though some avoid the term so as not to legitimize Nazi terminology. Not surprisingly, the idea of a Fourth Reich appeared in the 1930s among a wide range of anti-Nazis (or at least opponents of the direction Hitler had taken the party, such as Otto Strasser) as a vision of a post-Nazi order. At the end of the Second World War, the idea emerged in Allied states and among German anti-Nazis of a Fourth Reich to signify the possibility that a resurgent Nazism would undermine the democratic half of Germany.

TODT, FRITZ (1891–1942). A talented and ambitious engineer, Todt played a pivotal role in the construction of a new national highway system (Autobahn) before becoming a wartime armaments minister. Like numerous other engineers and educated professionals, Todt combined technical capabilities with a fervent attachment to Nazi ideology. He was a **National Socialist German Workers' Party** (Nazi Party; Nationalsozialistische Deutsche Arbeiterpartei; NSDAP) "old fighter," having joined the party in 1922, and **Sturmabteilung** (Stormtroopers; SA) officer. He shared Hitler's enthusiasm for motorization, roadway construction, and **rearmament**.

In December 1932, Todt presented Hitler with an ambitious plan to build a national highway network consisting of more than 6,000 kilometers of roadways. The plan earned Hitler's enthusiastic backing, and Todt was appointed inspector general for German roadways in July 1933. In May 1938, he replaced the inspector general's office with the new Organisation Todt (Todt Organization; OT), a hybrid state–private sector conglomerate responsible for construction projects in territories controlled by Germany, though its best-known projects were the Westwall (West Wall; also known as the Siefried Line), a 600-kilometer-long network of defensive installations running from Germany's border with the Netherlands to Switzerland, and the Atlantic Wall along the Atlantic coastline [see FORTRESS EUROPE (FESTUNG EUROPAS)]. In these and other projects—mostly roadway constructions in German-occupied Europe—hundreds of thousands of prisoners of war and civilians were deployed as slave labor.

In March 1940, with the enthusiastic support of the industrialists who stood to benefit, Hitler appointed Todt Reich minister for armaments and ammunition. Like **Albert Speer**, Todt was not the armaments miracle worker many held him to be. He was, however, effective at managing the state-military-industrial hybrid that dominated the wartime **economy**. On 8 February 1942, Todt was killed in an airplane crash. There is no evidence that he was assassinated. Hitler replaced Todt as armaments minister with Speer, another talented (if somewhat overrated) technocrat and devoted ideologue.

TRIAL (1924). In the spring of 1924, Hitler and nine other defendants were charged with high treason for their roles in the coup attempt, or **Beer Hall Putsch** of the previous November. Hitler used the trial to justify the coup, to place himself in the role of its architect and leader, and to expound his political agenda. He was convicted but received an astonishingly lenient sentence.

Following his arrest on 11 November 1923, Hitler was transferred to **Landsberg Prison**, about 40 miles west of Munich. After a brief period of despondency, during which he threatened suicide and went on a short hunger strike, he recovered his composure and delivered a long tirade to the deputy state prosecutor, Hans Erhard. Hitler made it clear that his actions were justified and that he would not recognize the court's authority. He also threatened to divulge what he knew about the involvement of Bavarian state leaders, notably Gustav Kahr, and the Reichswehr in supporting Far-Right elements and plotting, if not carrying out, their own coup attempt.

By **law**, the trial should have been held in the state court in Leipzig, and Hitler certainly hoped it would be, as he feared the conservative nationalist judiciary would protect Kahr and his associates. They in fact had no desire to have their activities made public. At the Bavarian government's insistence, the trial was held in the first district court in Munich and opened on 26 February 1924. The prosecution limited the charge to high treason and ignored the fact that the plotters had been involved in robbery and kidnapping and could be held responsible for the deaths of four Munich policemen. The other defendants were Erich Ludendorff; **Ernst Röhm**; three other **Sturmabteilung** (Stormtroopers; SA) leaders, Wilhelm Brückner, Robert Wagner, and Heinz Pernet; former Munich police president and longtime Hitler supporter Ernst Pöhner; Munich criminal police chief **Wilhelm Frick**; and two leaders of paramilitary groups, Hermann Kriebel and Friedrich Weber. The heavily guarded courtroom was packed, and the German and international press covered the proceedings closely.

As a well-known war hero and the symbolic leader of Germany's fractured Far-Right scene, Ludendorff was the highest-visibility defendant at the beginning of the trial. But Hitler put himself at the center of the proceedings. His supreme self-confidence was not simply an expression of his megalomania (*see* PERSONALITY). He knew enough to implicate the state's conservative nationalist establishment and senior Reichswehr officers. Just as important, the head judge was Georg Neidhardt, a right-wing nationalist who clearly sympathized with the Far Right and Hitler.

Defendants in the Hitler trial, Munich, 1924. The photograph of 9 of the 10 defendants was produced in Heinrich Hoffmann's studio. *Courtesy of the United States Holocaust Memorial Museum.*

The indictment named Hitler as the driving force of the conspiracy, and he did everything he could to confirm the accusation. Hitler took full advantage of the latitude offered by Neidhardt to turn much of the trial into a platform for justifying the coup attempt and promoting his political ideas. Hitler accepted responsibility, denied it was possible to commit treason against the republic, and blamed its failure entirely on forces out of his control (namely, that he was betrayed). He also insisted that Kahr and his associates were just as culpable and should be in the dock with him. Hitler's performance overshadowed all the other defendants and the culpable Bavarian state officials called as witnesses, who were happy to let him have the spotlight, as it diverted attention from their respective roles in the debacle.

The court announced the verdicts on 1 April. Ludendorff was, not surprisingly, acquitted, while Hitler, Krieger, Pöhner, and Weber each received five years, with the allowance that six months of good behavior would lead to the suspension of their sentences, and fined 200 gold Marks apiece. The judges also prevented Hitler from being deported to **Austria**, despite the provisions of a 1922 law that required foreigners convicted of high treason to be deported without exception. The other defendants received suspended sentences. The mainstream press in Germany and abroad denounced the trial as a travesty of justice, with the *New York Times* reporting that the widespread feeling in Munich was that the verdict made for an excellent All Fools' Day joke.

More than any other single event up to that point, the trial gave Hitler a prominent national and international profile. The downside for him, of course, was that the **National Socialist German Workers' Party** (Nazi Party; Nationalsozialistische Deutsche Arbeiterpartei; NSDAP) had been banned, and his impending imprisonment would take him out of circulation as an active political player. And though the Far Right in Bavaria was hardly vanquished, the end of the trial coincided with the beginnings of a period of general stability, during which Far-Right parties saw their worst **election** results before the Great Depression.

TRIPARTITE PACT (1940). Hitler intensified his efforts to secure a three-power alliance between Germany, **Italy**, and **Japan** in the aftermath of the German occupation of Prague and his decision to attack **Poland**. To entice **Benito Mussolini**, who was angered by not being informed about the move on Prague, Hitler took steps to accelerate full Italian control over the South Tyrol by informing the ethnic German population that it would have to either move to Germany or accept full Italian political and cultural dominance.

Hitler hoped that a mutual defense pact with Italy would deter Great Britain and **France** from moving against Germany following the invasion of Poland, as defending the Mediterranean would be a higher priority for both nations. The "Pact of Steel" was signed in Berlin on 22 May 1939, though Hitler continued to keep his plans for Poland a secret from his new ally. For his part, Mussolini informed Hitler that his country would be unprepared to enter a war before 1942. The "Pact of Steel" was in reality a pact on paper. Getting Japan onboard at that moment, however, was proving difficult, as the Japanese government was not interested in antagonizing the British, French, or Americans.

By the summer of 1940, Hitler's priority was knocking Britain out of the war and keeping the **United States** and the Soviet Union from entering the conflict. Concluding the Tripartite Pact with Italy and Japan was aimed primarily at deterring the United States from entering the war in Europe. For Japan, the German occupation of the Netherlands and victory over France opened new possibilities for closer ties with Germany, the easing of tensions with Moscow, and a drive into Southeast Asia. The agreement signed in Berlin on 27 September 1940 was not a traditional military alliance, then, but an agreement clarifying that Japan recognized German and Italian leadership in the creation of a new order in Europe while Germany and Italy acknowledged Japan's predominant position in Asia. More substantively, the signatories agreed to assist each other should one or more be attacked by a state not then involved in the war in Europe or in the Sino-Japanese War. As it was Japan that attacked the United States in December 1941, Hitler's and Mussolini's declarations on the United States were not technically related to the terms of the pact.

In the fall, Hitler also dangled the prospect of extending the pact to **Joseph Stalin**, though only to dissuade him from joining Britain in a new anti-German alliance that might also include the Americans. **Hungary**, **Romania**, and Slovakia joined the pact in late November 1940, and **Bulgaria** joined the following March. When the Yugoslav government joined on 25 March, pro-British officers staged a coup d'etat, and the new government backed out of the pact. An enraged Hitler had the **Luftwaffe** bomb Belgrade and occupy the country. The new Independent State of Croatia joined in June. *See also* BALKANS.

TRIUMPH OF THE WILL **(1935). Leni Riefenstahl**'s 1935 film became the most important propagandistic presentation of Hitler and his relationship to the German people as he wished both to be seen. Deeply impressed with Riefenstahl's film of the 1933 **Nuremberg party rally**, *Victory of Faith*, he commissioned her to make another of the rally scheduled for September 1934. Crucially, Riefenstahl had Hitler's personal support to make the film an "artistic creation." Equally important, she was given practically unlimited resources. The party funded the film (albeit surreptitiously), and Hitler chose the title.

That year's rally had two purposes: to demonstrate Hitler's position as Germany's unquestioned leader and, as **Rudolf Hess** put it at several points in the film, that "Hitler is Germany, just as Germany is Hitler." Two momentous events of the previous summer only intensified the stakes for the Propaganda Ministry and Riefenstahl: the violent **Röhm purge** in June of the **Sturmabteilung** (Stormtroopers; SA) and the killing of its leader, **Ernst Röhm**, and the death of President **Paul von Hindenburg** in August, which gave Hitler the opportunity to merge the offices of the **chancellor** and president. With the elimination of the last significant internal threat to his rule and the consolidation of his position as Führer and Reich chancellor, the annual party rally offered the perfect opportunity for a theatrical demonstration of his total political power.

The Propaganda Ministry planned a massive weeklong spectacle to take place again in Nuremberg, a city of 350,000. A half-million **National Socialist German Workers' Party** (Nazi Party; Nationalsozialistische Deutsche Arbeiterpartei; NSDAP) members would be joined by 200,000 guests. And for the first time, **Wehrmacht** personnel would participate. **Albert Speer** had been commissioned to design expanded rally grounds.

Riefenstahl understood what Hitler wanted done. Her crew of more than 170 people formed a parallel infrastructure to the highly choreographed rally, with her cameramen shooting 400,000 feet of footage. Highly innovative camera placements made it possible for her to create a film that would not be anything like a conventional, newsreel-style documentary. Rather, it was a work of pure political propaganda that would bring the spectacle and its twin messages to millions of Germans and non-Germans alike.

Though after the war she would insist repeatedly that she had made nothing more than a "historical document" without a "single reconstructed scene," *Triumph of the Will* was as highly choreographed as the rally itself. The film opens with Hitler's arrival by plane in Nuremberg and his motorcade's progression past thousands of cheering residents. His speeches are interspersed with those of party officials, but most scenes not focused solely on Hitler show thousands of SA and **Schutzstaffel** (Protection Squad; SS) men standing in formation, marching, or wildly saluting Hitler. There is no voiceover narration, only speeches and an ongoing musical score synchronized to the movements of the participants in a manner reminiscent of Busby Berkeley's musicals.

Hitler and **Joseph Goebbels** were overjoyed with the results. *Triumph of the Will* premiered in Berlin on 28 March 1935. The party press, not surprisingly, published fawning reviews. Hundreds of thousands of Germans saw it, making it the most popular film of the year. It also received multiple international awards, including for best foreign documentary film at the 1935 International Film Festival in

Venice and the Grand Prix at the Paris World's Fair in 1937.

Neither Riefenstahl nor any other filmmaker during the dictatorship made another film of this kind, suggesting that Hitler held it to be the ultimate visual expression of the "strength and beauty of our movement," as he put it in 1935. Yet *Triumph of the Will* would soon be put to other purposes. In 1939, Spanish surrealist Luis Buñuel assembled a condensed version in hopes of convincing American government officials (*see* UNITED STATES OF AMERICA) that film could be a powerful tool of propaganda. Perhaps more important, Buñuel's montage may have incited Charlie Chaplin to make *The Great Dictator* (1940), the greatest of all **cinematic** Hitler satires. During the war, British and American officials also used portions of *Triumph* as anti-Nazi propaganda, mostly notably in Frank Capra's *Prelude to War* (1942). *See also* FÜHRER MYTH (FÜHRER MYTHOS).

U

UKRAINE. It would be difficult to overstate the ideological and strategic significance of Ukraine to Hitler's vision for the East. The territory had been the object of German imperial fantasizing long before Hitler came to power. By the early 20th century, a powerful current of thought among German nationalists had fixated on expansion into Eastern Europe and the settlement there of millions of Germans. Those swept up in this current—Hitler, **Heinrich Himmler**, and other Nazi ideologues would soon be among them—believed that the process of settlement would be both a demonstration and an incubator of racial superiority.

Ukraine had already once come under Germany's control for six months in 1918, after being ceded by the new Bolshevik regime in the Treaty of Brest-Litovsk. The German army set up a puppet regime, intending to transfer forces to the western front and grain harvests to Germany, which was being subjected to a British naval blockade. Then, as would be the case during the Second World War, the German occupation provoked widespread resistance by Ukrainians. But after Hitler came to power, fantasies of creating an imagined Garden of Eden for millions of Aryan farmer-warriors crowded out what practical lessons this short-lived imperial venture might have imparted about the treatment of the local civilian population or the potential benefits of collaborating with Ukrainian nationalists eager to break free of the Soviet Union.

Hitler found it intolerable that a territory as vast and fertile as Ukraine was ruled by Bolsheviks and populated by Slavs and **Jews**. Space for German settlements and grain were the principal treasures to be taken at the expense of millions of lives. But there was even more. East of Kiev was the industrial city of Stalino (now Donetsk) and huge deposits of coal. Further east was Stalingrad (now Volgograd), the gateway to the Caucasus and its oil reserves.

In **Operation Barbarossa**, Ukraine was the main target of the **Wehrmacht's** Army Group South, commanded by General Field Marshal **Gerd von Rundstedt**. The drive into this region produced one of the Wehrmacht's greatest successes. Kiev was captured on 19 September 1941. More than 600,000 Soviet soldiers were captured in the area around the city alone. The administration of Ukraine was then turned over to the Reichskommissariat Ukraine under the command of the brutal Erich Koch. A German-created region in the Northeast, Zhytomir, became the occupation's administrative center and also a kind of laboratory for implementing the **General Plan for the East**. Hitler established a headquarters here, nicknamed Werewolf, as did Himmler and **Hermann Göring** [see WOLF'S LAIR (WOLFSSCHANZE)]. It was in Zhytomir that Himmler had a prototype constructed—Hegewald—of the kind of settlement community he envisioned for all of Ukraine.

The Germans had Ukrainian collaborators at the ready when Barbarossa was launched. As elsewhere in German-controlled Europe, collaborators formed an essential component of the local infrastructure of the Nazi Empire. Yet the extent of collaboration should not obscure the horrific suffering endured by the vast majority of Ukrainians. The territory had not recovered from the catastrophe of Stalin's forced collectivization of agriculture and the resulting famine when the Germans invaded a decade later. Around 4 million Ukrainians perished under German rule. Nearly all the 2.8 million inhabitants of Soviet territories deported to Germany as slave laborers were Ukrainians. By rejecting any possibility of co-opting anti-Soviet nationalism and turning Ukraine into a quasi-independent or puppet state, Hitler, Himmler, Göring, and legions of lower-level officials on the ground revealed the great depth of the regime's ideological commitment to **racism** and genocidal imperialism.

As Ukraine was home to Europe's largest Jewish population in the summer of 1941, it would become the demographic epicenter of the **Holocaust**. At least 1.5 million Ukrainian Jews were murdered, most in the occupation's first year, by **Schutzstaffel** (Protection Squad; SS) mobile execution squads (Einsatzgruppen) assisted by local collaborators. The murder of 33,771 Jews on 29–30 September 1941 near Kiev at Babi Yar was one of the single largest massacres of Jews by firing squads. Only 29 people are known to have survived. Thousands more, along with Soviet prisoners of war, local civilians and officials, and **Roma** people were murdered by the Germans and their collaborators here over the following months.

The German invasion provoked armed resistance from the start. Disorganization and divisions among partisan groups, along with the effectiveness of German antipartisan measures, limited their effectiveness in 1941 and 1942. But partisan activity increased dramatically in 1943 as the German occupation unraveled. By June, partisans had killed more than 2,500 German officials, German settlers, and collaborators and controlled much of the territory of Zhytomir alone. In the end, of course, it was the Red Army that drove the Germans out of Ukraine. Hitler canceled the General Plan for the East in July. By November, Soviet forces had overrun Zhytomir and captured Kiev.

As elsewhere in Europe, there was never a unified **opposition** in Ukraine to German rule. Existing divisions were only exacerbated by Hitler's and Himmler's attempt at empire building, and resistance was paralleled by civil conflict between different political and ethnic groups seeking to fill the growing vacuums of local authority as the German occupation weakened and then ended. The arrival of the Red Army, which meant liberation but also reconquest, ensured that armed conflict between partisans, former collaborators, and Soviet forces would continue for years after 1945.

UNITED STATES OF AMERICA. To some extent, the warped way Hitler thought about America was shaped by the pulp fiction novels of **Karl May**. Like millions of other German boys before, during, and after Nazi rule, Hitler devoured May's stories of White settlers battling Native American peoples in the Wild West. As a politician and dictator, Hitler was hardly alone in the Anglo-European world in admiring and resenting the seemingly unstoppable growth of American power. For Hitler, the United States was a state to be envied and in some respects copied, a threat to be contained, and ultimately a mortal enemy to be vanquished.

As he and Nazi ideologues saw it, all this power had several sources beyond the obvious realities of America's size, boundless natural resources, and separation from Europe and Asia by two great oceans. One was the fact that millions of Americans were German born or descendants of German immigrants. Another was the US government's impressive record of exclusionary immigration **laws**, notably the Johnson-Reed Act of 1924. Yet another was that the United States had created a ruthlessly effective system of racial segregation, one that combined law, **economic** disenfranchisement, informal codes of behavior, and mass terror. Nazi ideologues saw a direct causal connection between these factors and America's status as great power. The dark underside, however, was "international **Jewry**," which Hitler believed controlled the US government, Wall Street, the American press, and Hollywood. And while Hitler is alleged to have remarked in 1940 that America was nothing more than "beauty queens, millionaires, stupid records and Hollywood," he had long been aware of the appeal in Germany of American consumer and popular culture.

Thus it was American power in all its past, present, and future manifestations that fueled much of the urgency he felt as early as the 1920s when it came to breaking the shackles of the postwar settlement, rearming, and creating a great European empire [see VERSAILLES TREATY (1919)]. This empire, he believed, would make Germany a world power on a par with the United States but without entangling it in global trade networks and international finance.

But all that lay in the future. The United States indirectly assisted Hitler's diplomatic revolution in Europe in the 1930s through its unwillingness to participate in a post–**World War I** collective security arrangement and through an increasingly stringent series of neutrality laws. The regime was less successful in influencing American public opinion in an overtly pro-Nazi direction. Throughout most of the decade it found some pockets of support, but the **German American Bund** and the fascist Silver Shirts remained at the fringes of American politics. **Racists** (membership in the Ku Klux Klan surged in the 1920s and 1930s), anti-Semitic populists, and anti-immigrant nativists were far more influential. But their high profiles, even that of the wildly popular aviator and pro-Nazi **Charles Lindbergh**, did not translate into substantial elite and grassroots support for homegrown fascists or Hitler's regime.

Nor did a concerted Nazi campaign in which German agents tried to get American congressmen to spread disinformation to influence public opinion. Antifascism and opposition to Nazi anti-Semitism proved stronger. This was particularly true of President **Franklin D. Roosevelt**. An internationalist and antifascist, he was consumed with the economic crisis and constrained from taking a more assertive role in Asia and Europe by powerful domestic currents of isolationism, nativism, and antirefugee sentiments. It would be the **Czechoslovakia crisis** in the fall of 1938 and the **Night of Broken Glass** that moved him to take a stronger anti-German posture. US-German relations deteriorated quickly as Roosevelt talked openly about mobilizing the world's remaining democracies against the fascist menace. He warned Americans that if Hitler conquered Europe, then the United States would become a militarized, totalitarian state akin to the Soviet Union and Nazi Germany.

In practical terms, this mean developing new naval and airpower capacities and focusing on the defense of the wider Atlantic Ocean region. It also meant finding ways to aid Great Britain without overtly violating US neutrality laws. Roosevelt managed to do both with extraordinary skill. In September 1940, he traded 50 obsolete US destroyers for access to British bases in the Atlantic and Caribbean. Having been warned by **Winston Churchill** that Britain would not be able to pay for its purchases in the United States with cash, as the law required, Churchill suggested a scheme by which the United States would supply other democracies with war matériel, food, and essential goods in exchange for whatever the president deemed to be equitable compensation. Passed by Congress in March 1941, the Lend-Lease Act gave the president the legal authority to "lend"—in reality, give—supplies first to Britain, then to China and the Soviet Union. Eventually, the United States provided nearly $50 billion worth of supplies to 40 nations. Protecting US and British ships was the other priority, and by the fall of 1941, the US Navy was engaged in an undeclared shooting war with Germany in the Atlantic [see BATTLE OF THE ATLANTIC (1939–1945)].

It was the acceleration of American rearmament along with the German invasion of the Soviet Union that incited **Japan** to strike at American naval forces in the Pacific. Four days after the attack on Pearl Harbor and other US bases in early December 1941, Hitler declared war on the United States. The declaration struck many observers then and since as impulsive, even irrational. But not acting would hardly have comported with his image of himself as a leader destined to return Germany to greatness. In more concrete terms, the declaration would serve as a welcome distraction from the situation on the eastern front, where the **Wehrmacht**'s advance had been stalled outside Moscow [see OPERATION

BARBAROSSA (1941)]. He also likely thought it would boost morale in Germany. Japan's stunning series of victories in Southeast Asia in late 1941 and early 1942 only confirmed the wisdom of his decision in his mind, as he believed—not incorrectly—that fighting Japan would prevent an exclusive Anglo-American focus on defeating Germany first.

In the **Reichstag** speech in which he declared war on the United States, Hitler repeated his claim that Roosevelt was backed by Jews who were intent on destroying Germany. This message was entirely in line with Hitler's conspiratorial anti-Semitism and would be amplified and repeated to the public by the Propaganda Ministry as a way of explaining the war, as it widened and dragged on, to the German public [see DIETRICH, OTTO (1897–1952); GOEBBELS, JOSEPH PAUL (1897–1945)]. Allied victory was the result of hard-won campaigns fought on multiple fronts. But the mobilization of American power, combined with the survival of the Soviet Union and the titanic struggle on the eastern front, must count among the most important factors that explain the total defeat of Nazi Germany. *See also* PROPHESY SPEECH; REARMAMENT.

V

VERSAILLES TREATY (1919). In January 1919 representatives of the victorious Allied states—the Bolshevik regime in Russia was excluded—met in Paris to draw up final peace treaties. The treaty with Germany was the most important of them.

It was to be a dictated settlement: Representatives of the new German government were not included in the deliberations. The terms were harsh. Germany lost 13 percent of its territory and 10 percent of its prewar population of 65 million, mostly through the return of Alsace-Lorraine to **France** and the transfer of territory in the East to the new **Polish** state, with two smaller territories given to Belgium and Denmark. The industrial Saarland was placed under the supervision of the new **League of Nations**, with a pledge to hold a plebiscite in 15 years on whether it would be returned to Germany or become part of France. In the meantime, France controlled its rich mines. The **Rhineland** was subjected to an occupation and was to be permanently demilitarized. Unification with the new state of **Austria** was prohibited. All of Germany's overseas colonies became League of Nations mandates. The Reichswehr (German army) was limited to 100,000 men, and conscription was prohibited. The navy could recruit no more than 15,000, no air force of any kind was permitted, and the production of armaments was strictly limited.

If these losses and restrictions were not offensive enough to German public opinion, there was the provision that forced the government to accept the country's full responsibility for starting the war. This article was the basis for a reparations bill totaling 132 billion gold Marks (equivalent to roughly US$ 400 billion in 2010). It was not the case that the German government could not pay that amount. The problem was the political impact of the announcement of the treaty's terms in May and its ratification by the German government on 9 July 1919. Not only did the vast majority of Germans not believe their country bore primary or even any responsibility for starting the war, but most did not accept the reality of military defeat [*see* "STAB IN THE BACK" MYTH (DOLCHSTOSSLEGENDE)]. Many had also held out great hope that President Woodrow Wilson of the **United States** would deliver on his call for a just and conciliatory peace.

With eerie accuracy, French marshal Ferdinand Foch, the wartime commander of Allied forces, termed the treaty nothing more than a 20-year armistice. But there is no direct causal connection between its imposition on Germany and Hitler's ascent to power, let alone the outbreak of another general European war in 1939. While it is true that most Germans across the political spectrum rejected the treaty, its terms were modified by diplomacy at several points in the 1920s. And while it became a particularly effective tool of mobilization for conservative nationalists and the Far Right, there were many other factors that account for the republic's loss of legitimacy and eventual demolition.

The treaty's ratification had a profound effect on Hitler. As for many other Germans, it drove home a hard reality: Germany had lost the war. And it took place at a moment in which he was still searching for a stable political identity and a vehicle for his frustrations and resentments. By chance, it was that month that **Karl Mayr**, who had already sensed Hitler's potential as a political agitator for the Right, had him begin taking a training course and in September would dispatch him to attend a meeting of the **German Workers' Party** (Deutsche Arbeiterpartei; DAP). It was only after this juncture that Hitler became obsessed with not only overturning the treaty and avenging Germany's humiliation but also in ensuring that the conditions that led to the armistice and revolution would never be repeated. The treaty's rejection became a principal point in the **National Socialist German Workers' Party** (Nazi Party; Nationalsozialistische Deutsche Arbeiterpartei; NSDAP) program, and Hitler began defying its provisions almost immediately after being appointed **chancellor**. He had, of course, considerable help from the wartime Allies, who increasingly refused to enforce its provisions. *See also* LUFTWAFFE; NAZI PARTY PROGRAM (25-POINT PROGRAM); REARMAMENT; WEHRMACHT.

VIENNA. Hitler first visited Vienna in the spring of 1906. For several weeks, he took in the city's architecture, theater, and opera performances. In September 1907, he rented a room in a central district and was soon joined by his only friend from Linz, **August Kubizek**. Hitler was determined to study at the Academy of Fine **Arts**, but he failed the entrance examination. After returning briefly to Linz to care for his dying mother, he failed the examination a second time.

Having received an inheritance that could support him for a year, he spent his time reading, drawing, attending the theater (especially performances of **Richard Wagner**'s operas), and subjecting Kubizek to long monologues. But the death of **Klara Hitler** and Hitler's second rejection by the academy in September 1908 affected him deeply. He changed addresses abruptly—he did not inform his family or Kubizek. A year later, without a job or money, he began staying in a series of hostels for homeless men. An acquaintance, Reinhold Hanisch, convinced him to start painting postcards, which Hanisch would sell on the streets and in cafés. The two made enough money to be able to stay in a reasonably comfortable men's hostel on the city's outskirts, and Hitler would reside here until he moved to Munich in the spring of 1913. He continued to paint, though not as much as Hanisch wanted, and otherwise spent his time reading and debating with other residents. After breaking with Hanisch, Hitler began selling his own paintings, mainly to two **Jewish** owners of a picture-framing shop.

There has been much debate about the significance to Hitler's life of the years he spent living on Vienna's economic and social margins. Disentangling the truth from the largely invented autobiographical account in *Mein Kampf* is an essential task, though one greatly complicated by the paucity of reliable sources independent of those solicited or influenced by **National Socialist German Workers' Party** (Nazi Party; Nationalsozialistische Deutsche Arbeiterpartei; NSDAP) officials. Hitler was no doubt exposed to the city's virulent anti-Semitic currents, but contrary to his claims in *Mein Kampf*, there is no convincing evidence that he experienced a kind of life-changing anti-Semitic epiphany in Vienna (*see* RACISM).

And there were many targets at which a narcissistic, introverted loner with no professional prospects could direct his seemingly bottomless reserve of indignation and contempt: Marxists, Social Democrats, artistic modernists, bickering parliamentarians, streets and neighborhoods swelling with non-German-speaking newcomers. In the atmosphere of this multiethnic capital of a multiethnic empire, Hitler's attraction to **pan-Germanism** that began in provincial Linz only deepened, even if the political influence of pan-German politicians had waned by the time Hitler arrived. His Vienna years, in short, provided a reservoir of impressions, ideas, inspirations, prejudices, and resentments that he would later draw on as he fashioned a new identity for himself in the 1920s.

VOLKSWAGEN (PEOPLE'S CAR). Along with expansive residences in Munich and eventually a huge retreat in the Bavarian Alps (the **Berghof**), Hitler admired and coveted expensive automobiles. As dictator, however, he placed a high priority on developing Germany's automotive industry, building a highway system (Autobahn), and making what had been a luxury available to ordinary Germans.

While an Autobahn was constructed and automobile production increased, the vast majority of Germans could not afford a car for personal use. Hitler intended from an early point in his rule to change this situation. At the International Motor Show in Berlin in March 1934, he announced that a modestly sized and relatively inexpensive car would be produced. Not surprisingly, the press made much of this. But Hitler, who did not really understand how advanced industrial **economies** worked, had not considered whether it would be possible to mass produce and sell the car to as many people as he envisioned. Nonetheless, two of Germany's leading automakers, Daimler-Benz and Auto Union, hired Ferdinand Porsche to develop a prototype. Porsche had produced a working model in 1936, officially the Strength-through-Joy car (KdF-Wagen, though known popularly as the Volkswagen, or People's Car).

The cost was far higher than Hitler had demanded, and as was so often the case, he blamed industry leaders and considered the problem one of willpower rather than limited resources. He then ordered the construction of an entirely new factory to produce the People's Car. Industry leaders were relieved when the entire project was transferred to the **German Labor Front** (Deutsche Arbeiterfront; DAF) in 1937. The transfer, however, did not resolve the basic problem: The car simply could not be mass-produced at the target price of 1,000 Reichsmarks, a price that was in any case still out of reach for a majority of Germans. Regardless, the DAF, under the leadership of the Hitler sycophant **Robert Ley**, scrambled to raise enough money to start the project, with one fundraising scheme involving Germans contributing a small amount in advance monthly and the DAF paying depositors no interest. The program was popular, with 340,000 accounts created by the end of the war. But no one ever received a People's Car. Production was derailed by the demands of accelerated **rearmament** and then the longer-than-expected war. Far more successful were the state-subsidized mass production of cheap and reliable radios and refrigerators.

Though a high-priority target for destruction by the Royal Air Force, the Volkswagen factory managed to survive the war largely intact. Under energetic and determined new management, the company achieved what Hitler and the DAF could not: It refined and mass-produced one of the most popular cars ever made, the Volkswagen Beetle.

W

WAGNER, RICHARD (1813–1883). Hitler became a devotee of Wagner's operas at a young age and attended performances in Linz, **Vienna**, and Munich regularly. No other composer or performing **artist** seems to have affected him so deeply and enduringly. In particular, Wagner's evocations of a mystical German past and his accounts of heroic, doomed protagonists left an indelible impression on Hitler. The fact that a genius like Wagner had been rejected by the Parisian opera establishment but then went on to become one of Germany's most revered artists must also have been a crucial factor in Hitler's attachment to his memory. Hitler also considered himself an unrecognized artistic genius, destined nonetheless for greatness (see ART; PERSONALITY).

Even before he became a prominent politician, Hitler was embraced by the most influential members of the Wagner family, whose affinity for him reflected more than opportunism. The relationship deepened through the 1920s, and the family was an important source of financial support and connections to Bavaria's political and cultural establishment [see HANFSTAENGL, ERNST (PUTZI; 1887–1976)]. As dictator, Hitler regularly attended the annual Wagner music festival in Bayreuth, Bavaria, the location of the composer's home. Because the festival was not profitable, Hitler ensured it received sufficient funds to continue.

The connection between Wagner's operas, his nationalism, anti-Semitism, Francophobia, the cult his work inspired, the Wagner family, and Hitler has been the subject of intense speculation since at least the late 1930s. At the most absurd extreme is the proposition that Wagner was Hitler's primary political inspiration and that his genocidal war of conquest and ultimately Germany's total defeat represented Hitler's attempt—consciously or not—to "stage" the operas that had made such a deep impression on his psyche.

The writings of Wagner's most influential interpreter for the German nationalist Right, Houston Stewart Chamberlin, seems to have bolstered Hitler's belief that Germany's return to greatness was more than a matter of replacing the hated republic and shredding the **Versailles Treaty**. Chamberlin was Wagner's son-in-law and one of Germany's most popular *völkisch* (nationalist populist) authors. He distilled and simplified Wagner's many writings and argued that the composer's greatest legacy to Germany was his conception of cultural renewal or regeneration. More than a new political regime was needed: The thorough cultural renewal Chamberlin believed Wagner had envisioned was essential to rescuing the nation.

This message resonated with Germany's conservative nationalist and Far-Right scenes, the members of which saw the country being consumed by defeatism, internal betrayal, division, and cultural decline. Like many others, Hitler read Chamberlin's work and at least some of Wagner's voluminous writings. The two met during Hitler's first visit to Wagner's home in Bayreuth in September 1923. A week after their meeting, Chamberlin wrote Hitler and told him he believed him to be Germany's savior.

To some extent, Hitler's highly emotional responses to Wagner's fantasias did shape how he saw himself and his role as Germany's leader. But too much should not be read into Wagner's influence on Hitler the dictator. For Hitler, Wagner was more than just a greatly admired composer. But he was not some kind of political-spiritual forerunner or posthumous mentor. Not least, Wagner—or, for that matter, any other single artist or writer—bears no responsibility for the catastrophe Hitler and his supporters visited on the world.

WANNSEE CONFERENCE (1942). In the late summer of 1941, Hitler had decided on a comprehensive "solution" to the "**Jewish** question" in Europe. On 31 July, **Hermann Göring** conveyed the decision to **Schutzstaffel** (Protection Squad; SS) Reich Security Main Office chief **Reinhard Heydrich** and charged him with implementing it. To this end, Heydrich invited regime ministers, **National Socialist German Workers' Party** (Nazi Party; Nationalsozialistische Deutsche Arbeiterpartei; NSDAP) officials, and SS officers to a conference scheduled for 9 December to discuss the geographic scope of the "solution" and how it would be carried out.

What is unclear is whether Hitler at that point meant total extermination. His intentions became clearer in early December, when the Red Army launched a counteroffensive on 5 December, and **Japan** attacked US bases in the Pacific Ocean on 7 December. In a speech to party officials on 12 December, Hitler invoked his **Prophecy Speech** of 30 January 1939: Now that the world war was at hand, the Jews would be exterminated. Five days later, he repeated the order to **Joseph Goebbels**, and a day after that, to **Heinrich Himmler**.

Having been forced to delay the conference, Heydrich rescheduled it for 20 January 1942. It was held in a villa then being used by the SS in the Berlin suburb of Wannsee. In attendance were 15 officials representing the Interior, Justice, and Foreign Ministries; the **Four-Year Plan** organization; the Reich **chancellery**; the civilian administrations of the occupied East; and the SS. After asserting that the Reich Main Security Office had principal responsibility for carrying out Hitler's order, Heydrich presented calculations of the size of Jewish populations by nation, which estimated that 11 million would be deported to the occupied East. The estimates included countries not yet conquered (Great Britain) or neutral (Sweden, Switzerland, Turkey).

Able-bodied Jews would be worked to death, while all others would be murdered. It was also assumed that a certain number would not survive deportation. Though the first fixed-installation extermination camp had been constructed in **Poland** the previous fall for the purpose of murdering Jews in the region, the details of how a much larger program of accelerated mass murder was to take place had yet to be determined. For practical and propaganda purposes, elderly Jews and **World War I** veterans would be imprisoned in the Theresienstadt **concentration camp**. Left unresolved was the fate of Jews designated as mixed race (*Mischlinge*) by the **Nuremberg race laws**.

Other than some debate about the perennially complicated *Mischlinge* question, no one is recorded as having raised any objections to what had been confirmed in just 90 minutes. Adolf Eichmann, the lead specialist on Jewish affairs for the Reich Main Security Office, wrote up the minutes. After the meeting, Heydrich and a few of the attendees shared glasses of cognac and relaxed in front of the villa's fireplace. Four months later, British-trained Czech commandos assassinated Heydrich in Prague, though not because of his role as a principal architect of the **Holocaust**.

In March 1947, investigators for the prosecution at the **International Military Tribunal** (IMT) discovered the record in Foreign Ministry files. West Berlin's mayor declared the villa a memorial site in 1982, and 10 years later it became a museum and educational center.

WEHRMACHT. The terms of the **Versailles Treaty** required the dismantling of Germany's armed forces. The Imperial German Army ceased to exist, but the country was permitted to maintain a kind of national guard, which became the Reichswehr in 1921, limited to 100,000 men. A general staff organization was forbidden, but leading officers maintained one anyway under the innocuous-sounding Truppenamt (Troops' Office). They also worked on new doctrines and carried out a clandestine training and weapons-development program with the Red Army in the Soviet Union.

On 10 November 1918, President Friedrich Ebert concluded an arrangement with Lieutenant General Wilhelm Groener, the wartime army's quartermaster general. In exchange for the army's support of the new republic, Ebert agreed to suppress the radical Left and allow the military to retain its status as a "state within a state": that is, independent of civilian control and with professional officers remaining in charge. It was a steep price to pay for the fledgling liberal democracy, and it earned Ebert the enduring enmity of the Left. But in the tumultuous circumstances of Germany's revolution, he had little ability to secure civilian oversight in a country in which the army had answered directly to the Kaiser.

The Reichswehr, then, remained a separate preserve of conservative nationalists who were not only anti-Left but also generally hostile to the republic. In the early 1920s, a clandestine wing—the Black Reichswehr—working with right-wing paramilitaries engaged in acts of sabotage against French occupation forces in the Ruhr and were behind a wave of assassinations of political opponents, known as the *Feme* murders. It was dissolved in October 1923, after attempting to instigate a coup d'etat. While Reichswehr officers subverted the Versailles Treaty's disarmament provisions, they largely stayed out of domestic politics until the early 1930s. They were correct in assuming that should Hitler become **chancellor**, he could be counted on to suppress the Left, dismantle the republic, extract Germany from the treaty, and **rearm**. But just like civilian conservative nationalist politicians, then including former officers like Kurt von Schleicher and **Paul von Hindenburg**, they were mistaken in believing that Hitler could be controlled.

The Reichswehr may have been the single biggest institutional beneficiary of the new regime in its first years. Hitler, as expected, persecuted the Left, destroyed the republic, and made rearmament his highest **economic** priority. The Reichswehr immediately began expanding in secret, though it remained far smaller than the massive **Sturmabteilung** (Stormtroopers; SA). But in the summer of 1934, Hitler eliminated the SA as a threat to a resurgent and rearmed Reichswehr [*see* RÖHM, ERNST (1887–1934); RÖHM PURGE (1934)].

The next major step was the announcement of conscription on 16 March 1935. The Reichswehr was dissolved and replaced by the Wehrmacht. Its personnel swore an oath of allegiance to Hitler personally. From 1934 to 1938, Hitler was the head of the armed forces, with General Field Marshal Werner von Blomberg serving the commander in chief and minister of war. In the wake of the **Blomberg–Fritsch affair** in 1938, Hitler assumed direct control of the armed forces and appointed General **Wilhelm Keitel** as chief of the Oberkommando der Wehrmacht (Wehrmacht High Command; OKW). He further consolidated his control in 1941, making himself supreme commander, minister, and commander in chief.

Some 17 million men and **women** would eventually serve in Germany's armed forces, most of them in the Wehrmacht. Some military historians consider it to have been soldier for soldier the single most effective fighting force of all belligerent states. The record of its highest-ranking officers is mixed, ranging from among the war's most brilliant, such as **Erich von Manstein**, Hermann Balck, and **Erwin Rommel**, to its most incompetent. The most dangerous and incompetent of them all was, of course, Hitler. He never really trusted the officer corps. And despite his involvement in the kind of decision making normally left to staffs and individual commanders, he blamed them for Germany's defeats (*see* MILITARY COMMANDER).

Quick elimination of political **opposition** in 1933, strong popular support for the regime, and the effectiveness of the Gestapo left the Wehrmacht as the only potential source of effective opposition to Hitler. Other than **Georg Elser**'s lone-wolf attempt to **assassinate** him in 1939, it was a small segment of the Wehrmacht's officer corps that planned multiple attempts, one of which nearly succeeded. But it should not be forgotten that the conspirators had all contributed to Germany's early victories and had turned to assassination only when it was clear that a catastrophic defeat was inevitable.

The **International Military Tribunal** (IMT) at Nuremberg did not declare the Wehrmacht to be a criminal organization, but it included the general staff and the OKW in this category, along with the **Schutzstaffel** (Protection Squad; SS) and the Gestapo. Keitel and chief of the OKW's Operations Division Colonel General **Alfred Jodl** were both found guilty on all four counts and hanged. The last of the 12 subsequent trials of the **Nuremberg Military Tribunal** (NMT), held from 30 December 1947 to 28 October 1948, was the High Command Trial. Fourteen former generals and field marshals were tried, with 11 convicted on one or more charges of crimes against peace, war crimes, and crimes against humanity and receiving sentences of time served to life.

Numerous Wehrmacht veterans of all ranks wrote memoirs or found other ways to whitewash its history, and veterans' organizations became a powerful force in postwar West Germany. Their lobbying on behalf of imprisoned comrades inside and outside Germany received strong support from the government of Chancellor Konrad Adenauer and the Bundestag (federal parliament). The Cold War and the question of West Germany's rearmament gave the amnesty lobby powerful leverage,

Der Führer im Hauptquartier des Oberbefehlshabers des Heeres, Generalfeldmarschall von Brauchitsch. Links Generalfeldmarschall Keitel, der Chef des Oberkommandos der Wehrmacht, rechts Generaloberst Halder, der Chef des Generalstabes des Heeres.

Hitler with army commander in chief Field Marshal Walther von Brauchitsch (at Hitler's right), chief of the high command Field Marshal Wilhelm Keitel (far left), and chief of the general armed forces staff Colonel General Franz Halder (far right). Early August 1941. *Courtesy of the United States Holocaust Memorial Museum.*

and by 1953, all of those convicted in the High Command Trial had been released.

Historians continue to debate the extent to which Nazi ideology permeated the Wehrmacht from the highest to the lowest ranks, but the evidence is clear that support for Hitler was extensive, as was support for national socialist ideology more generally. Nor is there any doubt that knowledge of the **Holocaust** was widespread. What is also not in doubt is that contrary to the claims of its veterans, several generations of gullible historians, and neo-Nazis, the Wehrmacht was deeply complicit in war crimes, crimes against humanity, and the Holocaust. The vast majority of these crimes were perpetrated in the East, where the Wehrmacht was responsible for killing many thousands of civilians—exact figures will never be known—and millions of Soviet prisoners of war.

By contrast, the Wehrmacht and Allied armies in the West generally adhered to the laws of war codified in the late 19th and early 20th centuries. But this fact also supports the seriousness with which Wehrmacht personnel took Hitler's ideas about supposedly "subhuman" Slavs and **Jews** as mortal enemies of the German "race." More evidence of the deeply ideological nature of the war in the East is suggested by the Wehrmacht's staggering losses in the war's final 17 months: more than 1.5 million killed, or 11,846 every day, most on the eastern front. The belief in Slavic "subhumanity" carried by millions of German soldiers into the East and expressed in countless war crimes had provoked what by that point had become a war of retaliation by the Red Army. It is a perverse irony of Hitler's ideology that the Wehrmacht, the SS, and legions of collaborators had turned his vision of a them-or-us war of annihilation into a self-fulfilling prophecy.

WESER EXERCISE (WESERÜBUNG). There were sound strategic reasons for Germany to occupy Denmark and **Norway** and exert some form of controlling influence over Sweden. Denmark was, despite its size, an important supplier of foodstuffs and concrete. In April 1940, the Swedish government—dependent on shipments of coal from Germany—assured Hitler of its willingness to supply iron ore even during wartime. But control of Norway's long North Sea coastline would allow Germany to protect shipments of the crucial resource in case of a British naval blockade, mainly through seizing the year-round port of Narvik. Norway's fjords also provided excellent natural harbors for submarines.

There was, in addition, an ideological dimension to Hitler's thinking. He and **Schutzstaffel** (Protection Squad; SS) ideologues considered Scandinavian peoples to be "racially" Germanic and envisioned their eventual absorption into what Hitler told **Joseph Goebbels** on 10 April would be a "Germanic Reich," the boundaries of which would far exceed those of the German Reich established by **Otto von Bismarck** in 1871 [see LIVING SPACE (LEBENSRAUM); RACISM].

Increasingly anxious to secure Norway's coastline, Germany's naval chief Admiral Erich Raeder made contact with the head of the country's fascist party, Vidkun Quisling. In a visit with Hitler in mid-December 1939, Quisling tried to convince him to back a coup d'etat. Given that Quisling's party had very little popular support, Hitler was doubtful about his chances. But he was persuaded that the Allies would soon invade the country. The Soviet Union's attack on Finland in late November also accelerated his decision to move on Scandinavia as soon as possible, given the possibility that an Anglo–**French** expeditionary force mobilized to aid the Finns would establish itself in Norway and disrupt transports of iron ore to Germany.

On 1 March, Hitler ordered preparations for the invasion and occupation of Denmark and Norway, code-named Weserübung. The operation began on 9 April, with the Danish government capitulating in just two hours. Taking control of Norway proved more difficult, even with Germany's military superiority and intelligence provided by Quisling. German naval forces suffered some significant losses, and for a few months, Norwegian and British troops put up tenacious resistance on the ground. Hitler's mood swung violently from euphoria on the operation's opening day to a loss of nerve when Narvik's capture was delayed and then back again to euphoria. Despite stumbling in Norway, Germany had secured control of the country—and continued shipments of iron ore—for the war's duration. *See also* HOLOCAUST; MILITARY COMMANDER.

WOLF'S LAIR (WOLFSSCHANZE). Hitler established 7 Führer Hauptquartier (leader's headquarters) in Germany, **France**, and **Ukraine**, giving them names like Wolf's Gorge and Eagle's Aerie. The most important of them was his East Prussian headquarters, where he began residing on 23 June 1941 to direct the war on the eastern front. Unexpectedly, it became his home for three and a half years. He rarely left, an exception being a three-and-a-half-month stay in 1942 near Vinnitsa in Ukraine, at a new compound known as Werewolf.

Hitler gave the East Prussian headquarters the informal name Wolf's Lair after his preferred nickname from the 1920s. Located in the Masurian Woods area near the town of Rastenburg, now Kętrzyn in **Poland**, the compound had been built on 600 acres over the previous winter and consisted of 200 structures, including 50 concrete bunkers and 70 wooden barrack huts. One of the huts would be the site of the 20 July 1944 **assassination attempt**. The site was well protected by its remote location deep in the woods, camouflage, and anti-aircraft batteries. After the war, Polish sappers cleared 50,000 mines from the surrounding landscape.

Two airstrips and a railway spur provided the only physical connections to the outside world. For its inhabitants, ultimately numbering up to 2,000, the compound became an eerily self-contained world, its daily life structured around Hitler's preferred routine. The day began at noon with a briefing, followed by a long late lunch; meetings to deal with matters unrelated to the war; another military briefing; a long dinner; films; and finally a late-night gathering dominated by Hitler's monologues, which sometimes lasted until dawn. Notes were taken on **Martin Bormann**'s orders and were later published as Hitler's *Table Talk*.

The monotonous routine notwithstanding, the mood in the compound in the first months of **Operation Barbarossa** was optimistic. Colonel General **Alfred Jodl**, chief of the **Wehrmacht**'s high command operations staff, characterized the atmosphere later in the war as a mixture of monastery and **concentration camp**. By October 1944, Soviet forces had reached German territory and were less than 100 kilometers from the compound, yet Hitler resisted efforts to convince him to evacuate. Increasingly resigned to the fact that the war would soon be lost and in need of a minor operation on his vocal cords, he finally departed by train for **Berlin** on 20 November. Chief of the armed forces high command Field Marshal **Wilhelm Keitel** ordered the compound destroyed, and its structures were dynamited on 24 and 25 January 1945, just two days before the arrival of Red Army troops.

As the bunkers were designed to withstand aerial bombardment (the roof of Hitler's personal bunker was more than seven meters thick), their destruction was incomplete, and to this day, the former compound remains littered with the hulking remains of the structures. The Polish Forestry Inspectorate took control of the site in 2012 and in 2017 began adding markers and exhibitions, including a replica of the wooden hut where Colonel Claus Shenk Graf von Stauffenberg and Major Ernst John von Freyend attempted to assassinate Hitler. The site received 330,000 visitors in 2019.

WOMEN. No other aspect of Hitler's life has attracted as much speculation as his relationship with women. As a young person in Linz and **Vienna**, he demonstrated little interest in pursuing women his age. In Vienna, he seems to have become briefly infatuated with the 17-year-old sister of a friend, but no relationship of any kind came of it. His living circumstances in Vienna precluded standard courtship rituals, and there's no evidence that Hitler visited brothels. His outward disinterest in women was one of the things about him that amused some of the men in his wartime regiment (*see* WORLD WAR I).

Once he entered politics, he became determined to avoid following a path to marriage. For one thing, the image he would project as a man devoted solely to his cause and to

Germany seems to have reflected what he really believed, and this self- and public image left no space for a conventional marriage. For another, it is clear that he considered women in general to be physically, emotionally, and intellectually inferior to men. Like many men at the time and since, he believed the professions and politics were exclusively male domains.

None of this meant that he avoided all contact and relationships with women. Many admired and were attracted to Hitler, who seems to have enjoyed being seen with attractive women in public, particularly after giving speeches. Multiple accounts describe him as unfailingly polite, even charming. But there is also evidence that his attempts at physical intimacy were extremely awkward and fumbled, which was probably the result of inexperience and the highly emotionally repressed nature of his **personality**. There is no evidence that Hitler had **homosexual** encounters or was same-sex oriented.

Hitler was thoroughly paternalistic, and it is notable that his closest relationships were with women who were much younger than he. In 1926, when he 37 years old, he courted Maria (Mimi) Reiter, a 16-year-old salesgirl. But Hitler ended the relationship, such as it was, a year later. Over the next several years, he became close with his much younger half-niece **Angela (Geli) Raubal**, but the relationship was most likely platonic. Hitler's opponents used her suicide in his Munich apartment in September 1931 as political ammunition against him, and the minor scandal seems only to have reinforced his general inclination toward extreme secretiveness when it came to his personal life.

Hitler did, however, demonstrate interest in women closer to his own age, such as Winifred Wagner, Helene Hanfstaengl, and Magda Quandt (the future wife of **Joseph Goebbels**), and it seems that the attraction was often mutual [see HANFSTAENGL, ERNST (PUTZI; 1887–1976); WAGNER, RICHARD (1813–1883)]. Perhaps Hitler's most interesting relationship with a woman was with filmmaker **Leni Riefenstahl**, which may have involved one or more sexual encounters. Whatever mutual physical attraction may have existed, ego and opportunism were the most important factors drawing the two together. Riefenstahl produced what Hitler considered to be the perfect **cinematic** representation of the **Führer myth**, and he remained an indulgent patron [see TRIUMPH OF THE WILL (1935)].

Given all of this, then, it may seem surprising that he became involved steadily with **Eva Braun**, whom he met in **Heinrich Hoffmann**'s studio in 1929 when he was 40 and she was 18. Hitler kept their relationship out of the public eye, and she would eventually accept and embrace the role of the leader's mistress (see BERGHOF). They seem to have had a conventional sexual relationship, and while the extent of their emotional bond is unclear, they were close, and Hitler clearly valued her companionship. His agreement to marry her right before their joint **suicide** was intended as a reward for her years of devotion.

WONDER WEAPONS. Since the beginning of the Second World War, Hitler had favored bold, decisive offensive operations of the kind that had achieved the first victories, above all over **France**, in the summer of 1940 and during the first months of **Operation Barbarossa**. This inclination meshed with his propensity to view overcoming all obstacles—political, **economic**, and military—as questions of will and loyalty to his supposedly infallible instincts. As Germany's momentum stalled in late 1941 and turned to holding conquered territory and then steady retreat on all fronts, Hitler invested increasing hopes in the production of an array of wonder, or miracle, weapons.

The first to be deployed was a pilotless flying bomb that had gone into production in the summer of 1942. Called the V-1 (for *Vergeltung*, or *retribution*), the bomb was supplied with just enough fuel to reach its target. It would then simply fall from the sky and explode upon impact with the ground. The first 10 were launched from Calais in northern France on the night of 12–13 June 1944 and aimed at London [see OPERATION OVERLORD (1944)]. Their engines were extremely loud, and Londoners could hear them coming. The V-1s were inaccurate, slow, and easily shot down by Royal Air Force fighters. Still, they were terrifying—nearly 6,000 were killed and almost 16,000 injured that summer—though the thousands eventually launched at Great Britain did not put a very serious dent in civilian morale.

Far more effective as a terror weapon was what came next: the V-2, a liquid-fueled rocket developed by German physicist Wernher von Braun. In addition to his abilities as a scientist, Braun was an extremely effective advocate for his program and convinced Hitler and **Albert Speer** of the weapon's potential to change the course of the war, a message to which Hitler had long been receptive.

The Allies were well aware of this and other high-tech weapons under development and in August 1943 nearly destroyed the main V-2 construction site at Peenemünde on the **Baltic** coast. This drove production underground. Abandoned mines in the Harz Mountains were converted into a makeshift rocket factory. Run by the **Schutzstaffel** (Protection Squad; SS) as Work Camp Dora, a subcamp of the Buchenwald **concentration camp** near the town of Nordhausen, prisoners labored in hellish conditions. One-third of the 60,000 men forced to work here did not survive. More slave laborers perished in producing both types of rockets than were killed as targets of them.

After considerable trial and error, Dora was producing up to 700 rockets every month. But this capacity was only achieved in the fall of 1944, when there was no chance of altering the war's outcome. Some 3,200 V-2s were eventually launched, most of them at targets in Belgium. They did relatively little physical damage, but the V-2 was a true terror weapon. The rocket could only carry a relatively small warhead but flew so fast it could not be stopped or even heard before it hit its target, and the V-2 was considerably more accurate than its precursor. The development of other new weapons was pursued, notably an **atomic bomb**, a new class of poison gases (including sarin), and high-capacity batteries for powering submarines, but in most cases, there was not enough time or resources to produce any or enough of them.

Competition between various party satraps or Hitler's amateurish preference for V weapons over potentially far more effective battlefield rockets of the kind deployed by the Red Army (the Katyushas) also blocked their development. In some cases, the technical problems were insurmountable, as with atomic weapons. Or, as in the case of poison gas, the weapon was simply too dangerous and unpredictable and might also be used against German soldiers and civilians.

The jet-propelled engine was a technology pioneered by German engineers and unmatched by any other belligerent. But Hitler's constant meddling and unwillingness to approve the production of a new generation of then unstoppable fighter planes in favor of long-range bombers greatly magnified the damage inflicted by the Allied **strategic bombing campaign**. Typically, he was unwilling to tolerate anyone displaying greater knowledge or better instincts for tactics and strategy. And bombers were primarily weapons of attack, whereas the fighters Speer and other officers were pleading with him to put into large-scale production were intended to defend Germany from Allied bombers.

In addition to being an armed conflict in the conventional sense, the Second World War was a war between engineers, technicians, and scientists. Though usually not at the cutting edge of new weapons technologies—with the notable exception of the atomic bomb—the governments of Allied states ultimately prevailed on this front, thanks mainly to huge resources, the ability to innovate quickly, and the willingness to develop new capacities when and where they mattered most.

Despite the fact that the Nazi regime never produced the wonder weapons necessary to ensure victory, German scientists and engineers had revealed the future of warfare. Hence, hundreds of them—along with tons of blueprints, documents, and machinery—became among the highest-value targets of Allied governments as Germany was occupied in 1945. The biggest catch was undoubtedly Braun, who surrendered to American forces in **Austria** on 2 May 1945. By the early 1950s, he was safely ensconced in the Redstone Arsenal army base in Alabama, where he led the development of a new generation of rockets and guidance systems, including the Jupiter-C rocket, which carried the first US satellite into space in 1958. Braun then became an indispensible driving force in the new National Aeronautics and Space Administration (NASA) and the program that built the system that put the crew of the Apollo 11 on the moon in July 1969.

Though his past was never a secret, Braun—along with many other German engineers who worked with him in Peenemünde and then for NASA—was never prosecuted as a war criminal or for his complicity in crimes against humanity. He died from cancer in 1977, at age 65.

WORLD WAR I. Perhaps no period in Hitler's life has been as widely and persistently misunderstood as his service in the German army in the First World War. Hitler was required by **law** to register for military service in **Austria** in 1909. He may or may not have done so, but in January 1914, Munich police acting at the behest of Austrian authorities delivered him to the Austrian consulate to answer for his alleged failure to register. The destitute and apologetic young man was not penalized and reported for a physical examination in Salzburg on 5 February, which he failed.

Deemed unfit for service, Hitler returned to Munich. The day after Germany declared war on Russia on 1 August, he may have attended a mass demonstration in Munich's Odeonsplatz celebrating the outbreak of the war. A famous photograph—allegedly discovered by his official photographer **Heinrich Hoffmann**—of what appears to be Hitler's face among the huge crowd is almost certainly a fake. Regardless, Hitler embraced Germany's cause and enlisted on 3 August, with the authorities apparently overlooking the fact that he was not a German national and that he had been found physically unfit six months earlier.

He served for four years on the western front in the 16th Bavarian Infantry Reserve Regiment, known informally as the List Regiment, in honor of its first commander. Hitler spent a month as an infantryman at the front before being assigned as a dispatch runner based at regimental headquarters. The assignment exposed him to some danger, though not of the kind endured by front-line infantry. Certainly, when not running messages between regimental and battalion headquarters, he was quartered in relative safety and comfort.

Hitler's wartime rank was that of Gefreiter, which was not, as is usually translated, the equivalent of a corporal but that of a private first class. He never sought promotions and reportedly pleaded with **Max Amann**, the staff sergeant at regimental headquarters, not to recommend him for one. He was awarded the Iron Cross, second class, for protecting a commanding officer, and first class, for serving honorably rather than in recognition of any particularly deserving act of bravery. He also received the wound badge (equivalent of an American Purple Heart) after being injured in an artillery attack in October 1916.

His former comrades recalled him as a dutiful soldier and something of an oddball, whose eccentricities were a source of friendly bemusement to them. While Hitler seems to have relished the comradeship of these years, he did not develop close personal friendships and refrained from participating in the typical leisure activities available to soldiers. It also seems likely that nostalgic recollections of front-line comradeship were at least embellished as his ideology was formed in the first postwar years. Comradeship came to represent more than bonds between soldiers; it represented the foundations for a new political order that would avenge Germany's humiliation and return the nation to greatness.

When the war ended, he was being treated in a military hospital in Pasewalk for injuries received during a British gas attack at Ypres, though there is evidence that he was admitted for "war hysteria." It was here that he learned of the armistice, and there is no reason to doubt he was as shocked and angered by the news as anyone else. But there is no evidence to support his claim in *Mein Kampf* that his destiny as a politician was revealed to him at that moment.

Like most other veterans, the war did not radicalize Hitler. What evidence exists of his wartime political views show him to have been a fervent nationalist, convinced that German victory was inevitable and gripped by the hope that the war would purge the homeland of unspecified international enemies. The three months total he spent away from the front in Germany recovering from his wounds or on leave left him embittered at what he perceived to be the replacement of the patriotic fervor of 1914 with rampant defeatism. There is no evidence that he expressed anti-Semitic views or treated his numerous **Jewish** comrades with hostility.

Hitler's radicalization took place in the first postwar years and were contingent on a number of developments, notably that he managed to remain in the army and that he caught the attention of a right-wing army counterintelligence officer, **Karl Mayr**, who believed the excitable and articulate Hitler could be of use in indoctrinating troops against communism. Hitler would invent a version of his wartime experiences that served his political purposes. In *Mein Kampf*, speeches, and monologues, he portrayed himself as an ordinary frontline soldier who, like millions of others, had been betrayed by socialists and Jews. They watched their country convulsed by revolution and were betrayed yet again by the "November criminals" who accepted the terms of a humiliating peace treaty [*see* VERSAILLES TREATY (1919)]. Many of the details of his service—he never mentioned in *Mein Kampf* that he was a dispatch runner—were omitted from this characterization. It was fitting, then, that he would keep most former comrades from his regiment at arm's length.

Hitler (on the far right) with two fellow dispatch runners and his dog, Foxl, Fournes, France, 1915. *Courtesy of Bridgeman Images.*

Y

YOUNG PLAN REFERENDUM (1929). Having received only 2.6 percent of the vote in the May 1928 **Reichstag elections**, the **National Socialist German Workers' Party** (Nazi Party; Nationalsozialistische Deutsche Arbeiterpartei; NSDAP) remained at the fringes of political power. But in state elections in the following spring and summer, it did well enough to enter into governing coalitions with conservative nationalist parties. For Hitler, this represented what he referred to in the party's newspaper as the lesser of two evils. The worse evil in his mind was to remain neutral, which would only benefit the Left. Willingness to participate in coalition governments at the state level formed part of a broader strategy of marginalizing the still-powerful "Left" elements within the party and attracting more middle-class voters, a strategy that would entail closer cooperation with the conservative nationalists.

Yet Hitler remained an ambivalent and reluctant ally. He rebuffed an approach by the leadership of the Stahlhelm (**Steel Helmets**) about joining a campaign for a plebiscite to change the constitution in a way that would empower the Reich president at the expense of the Reichstag. In public, he asserted the matter wasn't important enough to justify a plebiscite because even if successful, it would still leave the president at the mercy of the constitution, the legitimacy of which Hitler rejected. Behind the scenes, party radicals—**Joseph Goebbels** among them—were hostile to making common cause with the conservative "reactionaries."

Continuing reparations payments as dictated by the **Versailles Treaty**, however, was for Hitler one of those issues that could justify supporting a plebiscite. In June 1929, the government approved a new plan for rescheduling Germany's debts brokered by American businessman Owen Young. In response, a coalition of nationalist parties and groups calling itself the Reich Young Plan Committee and dominated by **German National Peoples' Party** (Deutschnationale Volkspartei; DNVP) chairman **Alfred Hugenberg** launched a campaign for another plebiscite, with the aim of rejecting it, along with the admission of Germany's responsibility for starting **World War I** and any more payments.

Hitler agreed to participate, though he was careful to justify it in the party's newspaper as a mere tactical move. He continued to maneuver between the wings of his party throughout the **Nuremberg party rally** in August [see STRASSER, GREGOR (1892–1934)]. He denounced conservatives for failing to support national unity based on "racial" criteria to satisfy one faction and refused to reject cooperation across the Right to push back against the other. Here, Hitler was practicing the kind of divide-and-rule tactics at which he excelled and which would be a key feature of his dictatorship. He exploited the deep animosity between the arch-radical Goebbels and the Strasser brothers while at the same time preventing the latter from splintering the party.

When the Young Plan plebiscite was finally held in December, it resulted in a strong defeat for the Right. But Hitler did not seem overly concerned. Allying more closely with the conservative establishment was more than about courting middle-class voters. Hitler also wanted access to more of Germany's business elites, who up to (and, as it turned out, beyond) that point had been wary of the NSDAP, particularly its "left" wing. While joining a coalition dominated by the conservative nationalists did not produce more business support for the party, it did help its leading officials make connections to the wider conservative establishment and more generally raised its national profile. The results could be seen in local elections in 1929, where support for the NSDAP jumped in several states, while the establishment parties continued to lose votes.

So Hitler's balancing act seemed to be paying off at the local level. To more and more German voters, the Nazi Party appeared assertively nationalist but also new and inclusive in a way the establishment parties were not. And none of them had a leader like Hitler. The party was already moving off the political fringes, just as the Great Depression hit Germany.

The partnership with the conservatives would not last long. Hitler withdrew from the Reich Young Plan Committee in the spring of 1930, after the DNVP refused to join it in backing a vote of no confidence in a new government. Hitler believed the new elections that would have resulted would build on the momentum achieved locally the previous year. His disappointment would not prevent him from entering into a revived and similarly short-lived version of the anti–Young Plan coalition in 1931 known as the **Harzburg Front** and then one final time in early 1933 as a condition for his appointment as **chancellor**. *See also* GERMAN PEOPLE'S PARTY (DEUTSCHE VOLKSPARTEI; DVP).

Appendix

Reichstag Elections, 1919–1933
Percentages rounded to the nearest tenth.

19 JANUARY 1919 CONSTITUENT ASSEMBLY ELECTIONS

Party	Seats	%
Social Democratic Party of Germany	165 seats	39.0%
Center Party	91 seats	21.5%
German Democratic Party	75 seats	17.7%
German National People's Party	44 seats	10.4%
Independent Social Democratic Party of Germany	22 seats	5.2%
German People's Party	19 seats	4.5%
Others	7 seats	1.7%

6 JUNE 1920 (FIRST REICHSTAG ELECTION OF THE WEIMAR REPUBLIC)

Party	Seats	%
Social Democratic Party of Germany	103 seats	22.4%
Independent Social Democratic Party of Germany	83 seats	18.0%
German National People's Party	71 seats	15.4%
German People's Party	65 seats	14.1%
Center Party	64 seats	13.9%
German Democratic Party	39 seats	8.5%
Bavarian People's Party	21 seats	4.7%
Communist Party of Germany	4 seats	0.9%
Others	10 seats	2.2%

4 MAY 1924 (KNOWN INFORMALLY AS THE INFLATION ELECTION)

Party	Seats	%
Social Democratic Party of Germany	100 seats	21.2%
German National People's Party	95 seats	20.1%
Center Party	65 seats	13.8%
Communist Party of Germany	62 seats	13.1%
German People's Party	45 seats	9.5%
People's Freedom Party/National Socialist German Workers' Party	32 seats	6.8%
German Democratic Party	28 seats	5.9%
Bavarian People's Party	16 seats	3.4%
Others	29 seats	6.1%

7 DECEMBER 1924

Social Democratic Party of Germany	131 seats	27.6%
German National People's Party	103 seats	21.7%
Center Party	69 seats	14.6%
German People's Party	51 seats	10.8%
Communist Party of Germany	45 seats	9.5%
German Democratic Party	32 seats	6.8%
National Socialist German Workers' Party	14 seats	3.0%
Others	29 seats	6.1%

20 MAY 1928

Social Democratic Party of Germany	153 seats	31.0%
German National People's Party	73 seats	14.8%
Center Party	62 seats	12.6%
Communist Party of Germany	54 seats	10.9%
German People's Party	45 seats	9.1%
German Democratic Party	25 seats	5.1%
Bavarian People's Party	16 seats	3.2%
National Socialist German Workers' Party	12 seats	2.4%
Others	54 seats	10.9%

14 SEPTEMBER 1930

Social Democratic Party of Germany	143 seats	24.8%
National Socialist German Workers' Party	107 seats	18.5%
Communist Party of Germany	77 seats	13.3%
Center Party	68 seats	11.8%
German National People's Party	41 seats	7.1%
German People's Party	30 seats	5.2%
German State Party (formerly the German Democratic Party)	20 seats	3.5%
Bavarian People's Party	19 seats	3.3%
Others	72 seats	12.5%

31 JULY 1932

National Socialist German Workers' Party	230 seats	37.8%
Social Democratic Party of Germany	133 seats	21.9%
Communist Party of Germany	89 seats	14.6%
Center Party	75 seats	12.3%
German National People's Party	37 seats	6.1%
Bavarian People's Party	22 seats	3.6%
German People's Party	7 seats	1.2%
German State Party	4 seats	0.7%
Others	11 seats	1.8%

APPENDIX

6 NOVEMBER 1932 (LAST ENTIRELY FREE ELECTION OF THE WEIMAR REPUBLIC)

National Socialist German Workers' Party	196 seats	33.6%
Social Democratic Party of Germany	121 seats	20.7%
Communist Party of Germany	100 seats	17.1%
Center Party	70 seats	12.0%
German National People's Party	52 seats	8.9%
Bavarian People's Party	20 seats	3.4%
German People's Party	11 seats	1.9%
German State Party	2 seats	0.3%
Others	12 seats	2.1%

6 MARCH 1933 (FIRST ELECTION HELD UNDER HITLER'S CHANCELLORSHIP)

National Socialist German Workers' Party	288 seats	44.5%
Social Democratic Party of Germany	120 seats	18.5%
Communist Party of Germany	81 seats	12.5%
Center Party	74 seats	11.4%
Battlefront Black-White-Red	52 seats	8.0%
Bavarian People's Party	18 seats	2.8%
German State Party	5 seats	0.8%
German People's Party	2 seats	0.3%
Others	7 seats	1.1%

Endnotes

1. Sebastian Haffner, *The Meaning of Hitler* (New York: Macmillan, 1979).
2. Gavriel D. Rosenfeld, "Who Was 'Hitler' before Hitler? Historical Analogies and the Struggle to Understand Nazism, 1930–1945," *Central European History* 51 (2018): 249–81.

Bibliography

CONTENTS

Speeches, Writings, and Monologues	253
Biographies	253
General Histories of Nazi Germany	254
Firsthand Recollections of Hitler	254
Principal Nazi Regime and Military Figures	255
Diplomacy and War	256
Hitler and the Holocaust	257
Hitler's Death	257
Resistance and Opposition	258
Memory and Popular Culture	258
Feature Films, Documentaries, and Television Productions	258
Websites	259
German-Language Sources	259
Speeches, Writings, and Monologues	259
Biographies	259
Firsthand Recollections of Hitler	260
Principal Nazi Regime and Military Figures, War, and Diplomacy	261

SPEECHES, WRITINGS, AND MONOLOGUES

Nilsson, Mikael. *Hitler Redux: The Incredible History of Hitler's So-Called Table Talks*. New York: Routledge, 2020.

Trevor-Roper, H. R., and Gerhard Weinberg, eds. *Hitler's Table Talk 1941–1944: His Private Conversations*. New York: Enigma Books, 2008.

BIOGRAPHIES

Bullock, Alan. *Hitler: A Study in Tyranny*. New York: Harper and Row, 1962.

———. *Hitler and Stalin: Parallel Lives*. London: HarperCollins, 1991.

Fest, Joachim. *Hitler*. New York: Harcourt Brace Jovanovich, 1974.

Fritz, Stephen. *The First Soldier: Hitler as Military Leader*. New Haven, CT: Yale University Press, 2018.

Haffner, Sebastian. *The Meaning of Hitler*. New York: Macmillan, 1979.

Heiden, Konrad. *Hitler: A Biography*. New York: Alfred A. Knopf, 1936.

Jäckel, Eberhard. *Hitler's Worldview: A Blueprint for Power*. Cambridge, MA: Harvard University Press, 1981.

Kershaw, Ian. *Hitler: A Biography*. New York: W. W. Norton, 2010.

———. *Hitler, 1889–1936: Hubris*. New York: W. W. Norton, 1998.

———. *Hitler, 1936–1945: Nemesis*. New York: W. W. Norton, 2000.

Longerich, Peter. *Hitler: A Biography*. New York: Oxford University Press, 2019.

Ryback, Timothy W. *Hitler's Private Library: The Books That Shaped His Life*. New York: Vintage, 2010.

Simms, Brendan. *Hitler: A Global Biography*. New York: Basic Books, 2019.

Spotts, Frederic. *Hitler and the Power of Aesthetics*. London: Hutchinson, 2002.

Stratigakos, Despina. *Hitler at Home*. New Haven, CT: Yale University Press, 2017.

Toland, John. *Adolf Hitler*. Garden City, NY: Doubleday, 1976.

Ullrich, Volker. *Hitler: Ascent 1889–1939*. London: Vintage, 2016.

———. *Hitler: Downfall 1939–45*. London: Vintage, 2020.

Weber, Thomas. *Becoming Hitler: The Making of a Nazi*. New York: Oxford University Press, 2017.

GENERAL HISTORIES OF NAZI GERMANY

Baranowski, Shelley, Armin Nolzen, and Claus–Christian W. Szejnmann, eds. *A Companion to Nazi Germany*. Hoboken, NJ: Wiley Blackwell, 2018.

Bendersky, Joseph W. *A Concise History of Nazi Germany*. Lanham, MD: Rowman & Littlefield, 2013.

Bessel, Richard. *Life in the Third Reich*. New York: Oxford University Press, 1985.

Burleigh, Michael. *The Third Reich: A New History*. New York: Hill and Wang, 2000.

Caplan, Jane, ed. *Nazi Germany*. Oxford, UK: Oxford University Press, 2008.

Childers, Thomas. *The Third Reich: A History of Nazi Germany*. New York: Simon and Schuster, 2017.

Epstein, Catherine. *Nazi Germany: Confronting the Myths*. Chichester, UK: John Wiley and Sons, 2015.

Evans, Richard J. *The Coming of the Third Reich*. New York: Penguin, 2004.

———. *The Third Reich at War*. New York: Penguin, 2008.

———. *The Third Reich in Power, 1933–1939*. New York: Penguin, 2005.

Fischer, Klaus. *Nazi Germany: A New History*. New York: Continuum, 1995.

Gellately, Robert. *Hitler's True Believers: How Ordinary People Became Nazis*. New York: Oxford University Press, 2020.

———. *Lenin, Stalin, and Hitler: The Age of Social Catastrophe*. New York: Alfred A. Knopf, 2007.

Hildebrand, Klaus. *The Third Reich*. London: Allen Unwin, 1984.

Kershaw, Ian. *The "Hitler Myth": Image and Realty in the Third Reich*. New York: Oxford University Press, 1987.

———. *The Nazi Dictatorship: Problems and Perspectives of Interpretation*. New York: Oxford University Press, 2000.

Kershaw, Ian, and Moshe Lewin, eds. *Stalinism and Nazism: Dictatorships in Comparison*. Cambridge, UK: Cambridge University Press, 1997.

Overy, Richard. *The Third Reich: A Chronicle*. London: Quercus, 2011.

FIRSTHAND RECOLLECTIONS OF HITLER

Below, Nicolaus von. *At Hitler's Side: The Memoirs of Hitler's Luftwaffe Adjutant*. Havertown, PA: Frontline Books, 2010.

Burdick, Charles, and Hans-Adolf Jacobsen, eds. *The Halder War Diary, 1939–1942*. Novato, CA: Presidio, 1988.

Carruthers, Bob, ed. *Ten Years at Hitler's Side: The Testimony of Wilhelm Keitel*. Barnsley, UK: Pen and Sword Military, 2018.

Ciano, Galeazzo, conte. *Diary 1937–1943: The Complete Unabridged Diaries of Count Galeazzo Ciano, Italian Minister for Foreign Affairs, 1936–1943*. London: Phoenix, 2002.

Dollmann, Eugen, *With Hitler and Mussolini: Memoirs of a Nazi Interpreter*. New York: Skyhorse, 2017.

Dönitz, Karl. *Memoirs: Ten Years and Twenty Days*. Annapolis, MD: Naval Institute Press, 1990.

Eberle, Henrik, and Matthias Uhl, eds. *The Hitler Book: The Secret Dossier Prepared for Stalin from the Interrogations of Hitler's Personal Aides*. New York: Public Affairs, 2006.

Eden, Anthony. *Facing the Dictators: The Memoirs of Anthony Eden, Earl of Avon*. New York: Houghton Mifflin, 1962.

François-Poncet, André. *The Fateful Years: Memoirs of a French Ambassador in Berlin, 1931–1938*. New York: H. Fertig, 1972.

———, ed. *The Memoirs of Field-Marshal Wilhelm Keitel: Chief of the German High Command, 1938–1945*. New York: Cooper Square, 2000.

Haffner, Sebastian. *Defying Hitler: A Memoir.* London: Hachette UK, 2012.

Hanisch, Reinhold. "I Was Hitler's Buddy." *New Republic*, April 5, 12, 19, 1939, 239–42, 270–72, 297–300, respectively.

Hitler, Adolf. *The Testament of Adolf Hitler: The Hitler-Bormann Documents, February–April 1945.* London: Cassell, 1961.

Hoffmann, Heinrich. *Hitler Was My Friend.* Barnsley, UK: Frontline Books, 2011.

Junge, Traudl. *Until the Final Hour: Hitler's Last Secretary.* London: Weidenfeld & Nicolson, 2003.

Kersten, Felix. *The Kersten Memoirs 1940–1945.* New York: Macmillan, 1957.

Krause, Karl Wilhelm. *Living with Hitler: Accounts of Hitler's Household Staff.* Barnsley, UK: Greenhill Books, 2018.

Kubizek, August. *The Young Hitler I Knew: The Memoirs of Hitler's Childhood Friend.* South Yorkshire, UK: Frontline Books, 2011.

Loringhoven, Bernd Freytag von. *In the Bunker with Hitler: 23 July 1944–29 April 1945.* London: Weidenfeld and Nicolson, 2006.

Lüdecke, Kurt. *I Knew Hitler.* New York: Scribner, 1938.

Manstein, Erich von. *Lost Victories: The War Memoirs of Hitler's Most Brilliant General.* Auckland, New Zealand: Pickle Partners, 2014.

Misch, Rochus. *Hitler's Last Witness: The Memoir of Hitler's Bodyguard.* South Yorkshire, UK: Frontline Books, 2014.

Morell, Theodor Gilbert. *The Secret Diaries of Hitler's Doctor.* London: Grafton, 1990.

Papen, Franz von. *Memoirs.* New York: Dutton, 1953.

Reuth, Ralf Georg, ed. *Joseph Goebbels Tagebücher 1924–1945.* Munich: Piper Taschenbuch, 2008.

Röhm, Ernst. *The Memoirs of Ernst Röhm.* Barnsley, UK: Frontline Books, 2012.

Schacht, Hjalmar. *Account Settled.* London: G. Weidenfeld & Nicolson, 1949.

Schroeder, Christa. *He Was My Chief: The Memoirs of Adolf Hitler's Secretary.* Barnsley, UK: Frontline Books, 2009.

Speer, Albert. *Inside the Third Reich.* New York: Simon and Schuster, 1970.

Strasser, Otto. *Hitler and I.* Boston: Houghton-Mifflin, 1940.

Trevor-Roper, Hugh, ed. *The Bormann Letters: The Private Correspondence between Martin Bormann and His Wife from January 1943 to April 1945.* London: Weidenfeld & Nicolson, 1954.

———, ed. *Hitler's War Directives, 1939–45.* London: Pan, 1966.

Weinberg, Gerhard L., ed. *Hitler's Second Book: The Unpublished Sequel to Mein Kampf.* New York: Enigma Books, 2006.

PRINCIPAL NAZI REGIME AND MILITARY FIGURES

Bramwell, Anna. *Blood and Soil: Richard Walther Darré and Hitler's "Green Party."* London: Kensal, 1985.

Fest, Joachim C. *The Face of the Third Reich: Portraits of the Nazi Leadership.* New York: Pantheon Books, 1970.

Gerwarth, Robert. *Hitler's Hangman: The Life of Heydrich.* New Haven, CT: Yale University Press, 2011.

Goda, Norman J. W. *Tales from Spandau: Nazi Criminals and the Cold War.* Cambridge, UK: Cambridge University Press, 2007.

Guderian, Heinz. *Panzer Leader.* Cambridge, MA: Da Capo, 2002.

Hancock, Eleanor. *Ernst Röhm: Hitler's SA Chief of Staff.* New York: Palgrave Macmillan, 2008.

Heineman, John. *Hitler's First Foreign Minister: Constantine Freiherr von Neurath, Diplomat and Statesman.* Berkeley: University of California Press, 1979.

Kitchen, Martin. *Speer: Hitler's Architect.* New Haven, CT: Yale University Press, 2015.

Lambert, Angela. *The Lost Life of Eva Braun.* New York: Macmillan, 2007.

Lang, Jochen von. *The Secretary: Martin Bormann—The Man Who Manipulated Hitler.* New York: Random House, 1979.

Longerich, Peter. *Goebbels.* New York: Random House, 2016.

———. *Heinrich Himmler.* Oxford, UK: Oxford University Press, 2011.

Melvin, Mungo. *Manstein: Hitler's Greatest General*. London: Hachette UK, 2010.

Overy, Richard. *Interrogations: The Nazi Elite in Allied Hands, 1945*. New York: Viking, 2001.

Reuth, Ralf Georg. *Rommel: The End of a Legend*. London: Haus Books, 2005.

Smelser, Ronald. *Robert Ley: Hitler's Labor Front Leader*. Oxford, UK: Berg, 1988.

Smelser, Ronald, and Rainer Zitelmann, eds. *The Nazi Elite*. New York: Palgrave, 2001.

Van der Vat, Dan. *The Good Nazi: The Life and Lies of Albert Speer*. London: Weidenfeld & Nicolson, 1997.

DIPLOMACY AND WAR

Baranowski, Shelley. *Nazi Empire: German Colonialism and Imperialism from Bismarck to Hitler*. New York: Cambridge University Press, 2011.

Bartov, Omer. *The Eastern Front, 1941–45: German Troops and the Barbarisation of Warfare*. New York: Palgrave Macmillan, 2001.

———. *Hitler's Army: Soldiers, Nazis, and War in the Third Reich*. New York: Oxford University Press, 1992.

Bessel, Richard. *Germany 1945: From War to Peace*. New York: HarperCollins, 2009.

Caddick-Adams, Peter. *Sand and Steel: The D-Day Invasion and the Liberation of France*. New York: Oxford University Press, 2019.

Claasen, Adam R. A. *Hitler's Northern War: The Luftwaffe's Ill-Fated Campaign, 1940–1945*. Lawrence: University Press of Kansas, 2001.

Fritz, Stephen G. *Ostkrieg: Hitler's War of Extermination in the East*. Lexington: University Press of Kentucky, 2011.

Goda, Norman. *Tomorrow the World: Hitler, Northwest Africa, and the Path toward America*. College Station: Texas A&M University Press. 1998.

Hart, Bradley W. *Hitler's American Friends: The Third Reich's Supporters in the United States*. New York: Thomas Dunne Books, 2018.

Herf, Jeffrey. *Nazi Propaganda for the Arab World*. New Haven, CT: Yale University Press, 2010.

Hett, Benjamin C. *The Nazi Menace: Hitler, Churchill, Roosevelt, Stalin and the Road to War*. New York: Henry Holt, 2020.

Jackson, Julian. *The Fall of France: The Nazi Invasion of 1940*. New York: Oxford University Press, 2004.

———. *France: The Dark Years, 1940–1944*. New York: Oxford University Press, 2001.

Kershaw, Ian. *The End: The Defiance and Destruction of Hitler's Germany, 1944–1945*. New York: Penguin Books, 2011.

Martin, Benjamin G. *The Nazi-Fascist New Order for European Culture*. Cambridge, MA: Harvard University Press, 2016.

Mazower, Mark. *Inside Hitler's Greece: The Experience of Occupation, 1941–44*. New Haven, CT: Yale University Press, 2001.

Megargee, Geoffrey. *Inside Hitler's High Command*. Lawrence: University of Kansas Press, 2000.

———. *War of Annihilation: Combat and Genocide on the Eastern Front, 1941*. Lanham, MD: Rowman & Littlefield, 2007.

Moorhouse, Roger. *Poland 1939: The Outbreak of World War II*. New York: Basic Books, 2020.

Motadel, David. *Islam and Nazi Germany's War*. Cambridge, MA: Harvard University Press, 2014.

Nagorski, Andrew. *1941: The Year Germany Lost the War*. New York: Simon and Schuster, 2019.

Overy, Richard. *The Battle of Britain: The Myth and the Reality*. New York: W. W. Norton, 2002.

———. *The Bombers and the Bombed: Allied Air War over Europe 1940–1945*. New York: Viking, 2014.

———. *Why the Allies Won*. New York: W. W. Norton, 1997.

Shepherd, Ben. *Hitler's Soldiers: The German Army in the Third Reich*. New Haven, CT: Yale University Press, 2016.

Stahel, David. *Operation Barbarossa and Germany's Defeat in the East*. Cambridge, UK: Cambridge University Press, 2009.

Stargardt, Nicholas. *The German War: A Nation under Arms, 1939–1945*. New York: Farrar, Straus and Giroux, 2015.

Stratigakos, Despina. *Hitler's Northern Utopia: Building the New Order in Occupied Norway*. Princeton, NJ: Princeton University Press, 2020.

Weinberg, Gerhard. *Germany, Hitler, and World War II: Essays in Modern German and World History*. New York: Cambridge University Press, 1995.

———. *Hitler's Foreign Policy 1933–1939: The Road to World War II*. New York: Enigma Books, 2006.

Wette, Wolfram. *The Wehrmacht: History, Myth, Reality*. Cambridge, MA: Harvard University Press, 2006.

HITLER AND THE HOLOCAUST

Aronson, Shlomo. *Hitler, the Allies, and the Jews*. Cambridge, UK: Cambridge University Press, 2004.

Bartov, Omer. *Germany's War and the Holocaust: Disputed Histories*. Ithaca, NY: Cornell University Press, 2003.

Bergen, Doris. *War and Genocide: A Concise History of the Holocaust*. London: Rowman & Littlefield, 2009.

Bloxham, Donald. *The Final Solution: A Genocide*. Oxford, UK: Oxford University Press, 2009.

Browning, Christopher R., and Jürgen Matthäus. *The Origins of the Final Solution: The Evolution of Nazi Jewish Policy, December 1939–March 1942*. Jerusalem: Yad Vashem, 2004.

Burrin, Philippe. *Hitler and the Jews: The Genesis of the Holocaust*. London: Hodder Education, 1994.

Confino, Alon. *Foundational Pasts: The Holocaust as Historical Understanding*. Cambridge, UK: Cambridge University Press, 2011.

Dawidowicz, Lucy. *The War against the Jews, 1933–1945*. New York: Bantam, 1986.

Friedlander, Henry. *The Origins of Nazi Genocide: From Euthanasia to the Final Solution*. Chapel Hill: University of North Carolina Press, 2000.

Herf, Jeffrey. *The Jewish Enemy: Nazi Propaganda during World War II and the Holocaust*. Cambridge, MA: Harvard University Press, 2008.

Himmelfarb, Milton. "No Hitler, No Holocaust." *Commentary* 77, no. 3 (March 1984): 37–43.

Ihrig, Stefan. *Justifying Genocide: Germany and the Armenians from Bismarck to Hitler*. Cambridge, MA: Harvard University Press, 2016.

Kershaw, Ian. *Hitler, the Germans, and the Final Solution*. New Haven, CT: Yale University Press, 2008.

Longerich, Peter. *Holocaust: The Nazi Persecution and Murder of the Jews*. Oxford, UK: Oxford University Press, 2010.

———. *The Unwritten Order: Hitler's Role in the Final Solution*. Stroud, UK: History Press, 2001.

Snyder, Timothy. *Black Earth: The Holocaust as History and Warning*. New York: Tim Duggan Books, 2016.

———. *Bloodlands: Europe between Hitler and Stalin*. New York: Basic Books, 2012.

HITLER'S DEATH

Brisard, Jean-Christophe, and Lana Parshina. *The Death of Hitler: The Final Word*. New York: Da Capo Press, 2018.

Daly-Groves, Luke. *Hitler's Death: The Case against Conspiracy*. Oxford, UK: Osprey, 2019.

Fest, Joachim. *Inside Hitler's Bunker: The Last Days of the Third Reich*. New York: Farrar, Straus and Giroux, 2004.

Joachimsthaler, Anton. *The Last Days of Hitler: The Legends, the Evidence, the Truth*. London: Brockhampton, 1995.

McKale, Donald. *Hitler: The Survival Myth*. New York: Stein and Day, 1981.

Petrova, Ada, and Peter Watson. *The Death of Hitler: The Full Story with New Evidence from Secret Russian Archives*. New York: W. W. Norton, 1995.

Trevor-Roper, Hugh. *The Last Days of Hitler*. New York: Macmillan, 1947.

Vinogradov, V. K. *Hitler's Death: Russia's Last Great Secret from the Files of the KGB.* London: Chaucer, 2005.

RESISTANCE AND OPPOSITION

Fest, Joachim. *Plotting Hitler's Death: The Story of German Resistance.* New York: Macmillan, 1997.

Hoffmann, Peter. *History of the German Resistance, 1933–1945.* Montreal, Canada: McGill-Queen's Press-MQUP, 1996.

———. *Stauffenberg: A Family History, 1905–1944.* Montreal: McGill-Queen's Press-MQUP, 2008.

Nicosia, Francis R., and Lawrence D. Stokes, eds. *Germans against Nazism: Nonconformity, Opposition and Resistance in the Third Reich: Essays in Honour of Peter Hoffmann.* New York: Berghahn Books, 2015.

Thomas, Gordon, and Greg Lewis. *Defying Hitler: The Germans Who Resisted Nazi Rule.* Toronto: Dutton Caliber, 2019.

MEMORY AND POPULAR CULTURE

Bendix, John. "Facing Hitler: German Responses to *Downfall.*" *German Politics and Society* 25, no. 1 (Spring 2007): 70–89.

Berghahn, Klaus L., and Jost Hermand, eds. *Unmasking Hitler: Cultural Representations of Hitler from the Weimar Republic to the Present.* Pieterlen, Switzerland: Peter Lang, 2005.

Evans, Richard J. *The Hitler Conspiracies.* New York: Oxford University Press, 2020.

———. *The Third Reich in History and Memory.* New York: Oxford University Press, 2015.

Frei, Norbert. *Adenauer's Germany and the Nazi Past: The Politics of Amnesty and Integration.* New York: Columbia University Press, 2002.

Fulbrook, Mary. *Reckonings: Legacies of Nazi Persecution and the Quest for Justice.* New York: Oxford University Press, 2020.

Haffner, Sabastian. *The Meaning of Hitler.* New York: Macmillan, 1979.

Herf, Jeffrey. *Divided Memory: The Nazi Past in the Two Germanys.* Cambridge, MA: Harvard University Press, 1997.

Herwig, Malte. *Post-War Lies: Germany and Hitler's Long Shadow.* London: Scribe, 2014.

Jäckel, Eberhard. *Hitler in History.* Hanover, NH: Brandeis University Press, University Press of New England, 1984.

Kansteiner, Wulf. *In Pursuit of German Memory: History, Television, and Politics after Auschwitz.* Athens: Ohio University Press, 2006.

Machtans, Karolin, and Martin A. Ruehl, eds. *Hitler Films from Germany: History, Cinema, and Politics since 1945.* New York: Palgrave Macmillan, 2012.

Maser, Werner. *Hitler: Legend, Myth and Reality.* New York: HarperCollins, 1973.

Mitchell, Charles P. *The Hitler Filmography: Worldwide Feature Film and Television Miniseries Portrayals, 1940 through 2000.* Jefferson, NC: McFarland, 2002.

Neiman, Susan. *Learning from the Germans: Race and the Memory of Evil.* New York: Farrar, Straus and Giroux, 2019.

Rosenbaum, Ron. *Explaining Hitler: The Search for the Origins of His Evil.* London: Hachette UK, 2014.

Rosenfeld, Gavriel D. *Hi Hitler! How the Nazi Past Is Being Normalized in Contemporary Culture.* New York: Cambridge University Press, 2014.

Smelser, Ronald, and Edward J. Davies II. *The Myth of the Eastern Front: The Nazi–Soviet War in American Popular Culture.* New York: Cambridge University Press, 2008.

Stelzel, Philipp. *History after Hitler: A Transatlantic Enterprise.* Philadelphia: University of Pennsylvania Press, 2018.

FEATURE FILMS, DOCUMENTARIES, AND TELEVISION PRODUCTIONS

Chaplin, Charlie, dir. *The Great Dictator.* 1940.

Chomsky, Marvin J., dir. *Inside the Third Reich.* 1982.

Concini, Ennio de, dir. *Hitler: The Last Ten Days.* 1973.

Dietl, Helmut, dir. *Schtonk!* 1992.
Duguay, Christian, dir. *Hitler—The Rise of Evil*. 2003.
Epperlein, Petra, and Michael Tucker, dirs. *The Meaning of Hitler*. 2020.
Farrow, John, dir. *The Hitler Gang*. 1944.
Fest, Joachim, and Christian Herrendoerfer, dirs. *Hitler: A Career*. 1977.
Hershey, Barry J., dir. *The Empty Mirror*. 1996.
Hirschbiegel, Oliver, dir. *Downfall*. 2005.
Holland, Luke, dir. *Final Account*. 2021.
Johnson, Alan, dir. *To Be or Not to Be*. 1983.
Leiser, Erwin, dir. *Mein Kampf*. 1960.
Levi, Dani, dir. *My Führer*. 2007.
Lubitsch, Ernst, dir. *To Be or Not to Be*. 1942.
Mueller-Stahl, Armin, dir. *Conversation with the Beast*. 1996.
Pabst, G. W., dir. *Der Letze Akt*. 1955.
Powell, Michael, Alexander Korda, Adrian Brunel, and Brian Desmond Hurst, dirs. *The Lion Has Wings*. 1939.
Riefenstahl, Leni, dir. *Olympia*. 1938.
———, dir. *Triumph of the Will*. 1935.
———, dir. *Victory of the Faith*. 1933.
Schaefer, George, dir. *The Bunker*. 1981.
Schaffner, Franklin J., dir. *The Boys from Brazil*. 1978.
Singer, Bryan, dir. *Valkyrie*. 2008.
Syberberg, Hans-Jürgen, dir. *Hitler, ein Film aus Deutschland*. 1977.
Tarantino, Quentin, dir. *Inglourious Basterds*. 2009.
Voorhis, Westbrook Van, dir. *The Secret Life of Adolf Hitler*. 1958.
Waititi, Taika, dir. *Jojo Rabbit*. 2019.
Wnendt, David, dir. *Look Who's Back*. 2015.
Yakin, Boaz, dir. *Max*. 2015.

WEBSITES

Dokumentationszentrum Reichsparteitagsgelände, Museen der Stadt Nürnberg. https://museen.nuernberg.de/dokuzentrum/.
German History in Documents and Images. http://germanhistorydocs.ghi-dc.org.
German Propaganda Archive. https://research.calvin.edu/german-propaganda-archive/.
The German Resistance Memorial Center. https://www.gdw-berlin.de/en/home/.
Institut für Zeitgeschichte. https://www.ifz-muenchen.de.
Stiftung Denkmal für die ermordeten Juden Europas. https://www.stiftung-denkmal.de/.
Topographie des Terrors. https://www.topographie.de/ihr-besuch/.
The United States Holocaust Memorial Museum. www.ushmm.org.
The Wolf's Lair. https://wilczyszaniec.olsztyn.lasy.gov.pl/.
Yad Vashem. www.yadvashem.org.

GERMAN-LANGUAGE SOURCES

Speeches, Writings, and Monologues

Erk, Daniel. *So viel Hitler war selten. Die Banalisierung des Boesen, oder warum der Mann mit dem kleinen Bart nicht totzukriegen ist*. Munich: Heyne, 2012.
Hartmann, Christian, Othmar Plöckinger, Roman Töppel, Thomas Vordermayer, eds. *Hitler, Mein Kampf. Eine kritische Edition*. Munich: Institut für Zeitgeschichte, 2018.
Hitler, Adolf. *Reden, Schriften, Anordnung—Februar 1925 bis Januar 1933*. Vols. 1–6. Munich: Insitut für Zeitgeschichte, 1992–2003.
Jäckel, Eberhard, ed. *Sämtliche Aufzeichnungen 1905–1924*. Stuttgart: Deutsche Verlags-Anstalt, 1980.
Jochmann, Werner, ed. *Monologe im Führerhauptquartier 1941–1944. Die Aufzeichnungen* Hamburg: A. Knaus, 1980.
Karlauf, Thomas. *Stauffenberg. Porträt eines Attentäters*. Munich: Blessing Verlag, 2019.

Biographies

Pyta, Wolfram. *Hitler: Der Künstler als Politiker und Feldherr. Eine Herrschaftsanalyse*. Munich: Siedler Verlag, 2015.
Reuth, Ralf Georg. *Hitler. Eine politische Biographie*. Munich: Piper, 2003.
Zitelmann, Rainer. *Adolf Hitler: Eine politische Biographie*. Göttingen: Muster-Schmidt, 1989.
———. *Hitler: Selbstverständnis eines Revolutionärs*. Munich: Olzog ein Imprint der Lau Verlag und Handel KG, 2017.

Firsthand Recollections of Hitler

Breker, Arno. *Im Strahlungsfeld der Ereignisse: Leben und Wirken eines Künstlers. Porträts, Begegnungen, Schicksale.* Preußich-Oldendorf: K. W. Schütz, 1972.

Brüning, Heinrich. *Memoiren 1918–1934.* Stuttgart: Deutsche Verlags-Anstalt, 1970.

Burckhardt, Carl J. *Meine Danziger Mission 1937–1939.* Munich: Callwey, 1980.

Dahlerus, Birger. *Der letzte Versuch, London–Berlin Sommer 1939.* Munich: Nymphenburger Verlagshandlung, 1948.

Dietrich, Otto. *12 Jahre mit Hitler.* Munich: Isar Verlag, 1955.

———. *Mit Hitler in die Macht: Persönliche Erlebnisse mit meinem Führer.* Munich: Franz Eher Verlag, 1934.

Dodd, Martha. *Meine Jahre in Deutschland 1933 bis 1938: Nice to Meet You, Mr. Hitler!* Berlin: Eichborn, 2005.

Duesterberg, Theodor. *Der Stahlhelm und Hitler.* Wolfenbüttel: Wolfenbütteler Verlagsanstalt, 1949.

Frank, Hans. *Im Angesicht des Galgens: Deutung Hitlers und seiner Zeit auf Grund eigener Erlebnisse und Erkenntnisse: Geschrieben im Nürnberger Justizgefängnis.* Munich: F. A. Beck, 1953.

Giesler, Hermann. *Ein anderer Hitler: Bericht seines Architekten: Erlebnisse, Gespräche, Reflexionen.* Leoni am Starnberger See: Druffel, 1978.

Goebbels, Joseph. *Vom Kaiserhof zur Reichskanzlei. Eine historische Darstellung in Tagebuchblättern (vom 1. Januar 1932 bis zum 1. Mai 1933).* Munich: Zentralverlag der N.S.D.A.P., Frz. Eher Nachf., G.m.b.H., 1934.

Görlitz, Walter, ed. *Generalfeldmarschall Keitel. Verbrecher oder Offizier? Erinnerungen, Briefe, Dokumente des Chefs OKW.* Göttingen: Musterschmidt-Verlag, 1961.

Hanfstaengl, Ernst. *15 Jahre mit Hitler. Zwischen Weißem und Braunem Haus.* Munich: R. Piper, 1980.

Hassell, Ulrich von. *Römische Tagebücher und Briefe 1932–1938.* Munich: Herbig, 2004.

———. *Vom anderen Deutschland: Aus den nachgelassenen Tagebüchern 1938–1944.* Zürich: Atlantis Verlag, 1946.

Hess, Rudolf. *Rudolf Hess Briefe, 1908–1933.* Munich: Langen Müller, 1987.

Hitler, Adolf, Lothar Gruchmann, Clemens Vollnhals, Klaus A. Lankheit, Christian Hartmann, Katja Klee, and Bärbel Dusik. *Der Hitler-Prozeß 1924: Wortlaut der Hauptverhandlung vor dem Volksgericht München I / 3 12.–18. Verhandlungstag.* Munich: Saur, 1998.

Hoffmann, Heinrich. *Hitler wie ich ihn sah: Aufzeichnungen seines Leibfotografen.* Munich: Herbig, 1974.

Hoßbach, Friedrich. *Zwischen Wehrmacht und Hitler, 1934–1938.* Göttingen: Vandenhoeck und Ruprecht, 1965.

Jochmann, Werner, ed. *Monologe im Führer-Hauptquartier 1941–1944.* Gütersloh: Orbis, 2000.

Kallenbach, Hans. *Mit Adolf Hitler auf Festung Landsberg.* Munich: Kress und Hornung, 1939.

Kempka, Erich. *Die letzten Tage mit Adolf Hitler.* Preußisch-Oldendorf: K. W. Schütz, 1975.

Kotze, Hildegard von. *Heeresadjutant bei Hitler 1938–1945.* Stuttgart: Deutsche Verlags-Anstalt, 1976.

Linge, Heinz. *Bis zum Untergang. Als Chef des persönlichen Dienstes bei Hitler.* Munich: Goldmann, 1983.

Meissner, Otto. *Staatssekretär unter Ebert, Hindenburg, Hitler: Der Schicksalsweg des deutschen Volkes von 1918–1945, wie ich ihn erlebte.* Hamburg: Hoffman und Campe, 1950.

Schirach, Baldur von. *Ich glaubte an Hitler.* Hamburg: Mosaik Verlag, 1967.

Schmidt, Paul. *Statist auf diplomatischer Bühne 1923–1945. Erlebnisse des Chefdolmetschers im Auswärtigen Amt mit den Staatsmänner Europas.* Bonn: Athenäum, 1950.

Strasser, Otto. *Ministersessel oder Revolution? Eine wahrheitsgemässe Darstellung meiner Trennung von der NSDAP.* Berlin: Verlag der Nationale Sozialist, 1933.

Wagener, Otto. *Hitler aus nächster Nähe. Aufzeichnungen eines Vertrauten: 1929–1932*. Frankfurt am Main: Ullstein, 1978.

Zoller, Albert, *Hitler privat. Erlebnisbericht seiner Geheimsekretärin*. Düsseldorf: Droste Verlag, 1949.

Principal Nazi Regime and Military Figures, War, and Diplomacy

Gräfe, Heinz. *Vom Donnerkreuz Zum Hakenkreuz: Die Baltischen Staaten Zwischen Diktatur und Okkupation*. Berlin: Organon, 2010.

Hartmann, Christian. *Halder. Generalstabschef Hitlers 1938–1942*. Paderborn: Ferdinand Schöningh Gmbh, 1991.

Lang, Jochen von. *Der Hitler-Junge: Baldur von Schirach, der Mann, der Deutschlands Jugend erzog*. Hamburg: Rasch und Röhring, 1988.

Neliba, Günter. *Wilhelm Frick. Der Legalist des Unrechtsstaates: Eine politische Biographie*. Paderborn: Schöningh, 1992.

Pätzold, Kurt, and Manfred Weissbecker. *Rudolf Hess: Der Mann an Hitlers Seite*. Leipzig: Melitzke Verlag, 1999.

Index

Abwehr, 45, 219
Adenauer, Konrad, 238
Adolf Hitler, Sein Leben, Seine Reden, 11, 34
Africa, 8, 12–13, 20, 23, 30, 32, 49, 69, 76–78, 142, 157, 161, 164, 184, 195, 205. *See also specific countries*
Afrika Korps, 12–13, 30, 32, 124, 164, 195
Albania, 12, 27, 184
Algeria, 12–13, 30, 135, 164
Allies, 7, 19, 20, 32, 37, 44–45, 60, 74, 97, 108, 113–15, 124, 130–31, 139, 144, 148, 163, 169, 173, 194–95, 197, 204, 210, 213, 218, 232, 239, 242
Amann, Max, 13–14, 89, 139, 203, 243
Anglo–German Naval Agreement, 14, 75–76, 125, 130, 141, 156, 159, 182, 187
Annexation of Austria (Anschluss), 7, 15, 24–25, 43, 56, 92, 111, 117, 141, 148, 151, 165, 169
Anti-Comintern Pact, 14–15, 111, 117, 141, 173, 187
Anti-Semitism, 2, 6–8, 11, 43, 59, 63–64, 70, 72–73, 86–87, 89–90, 98, 105, 111–12, 117–19, 120, 126, 131–33, 135, 138, 146, 156–60, 167, 171, 175–77, 184–85, 194, 198, 211, 229–30, 232, 235, 244
Antonescu, Ion, 194
Appeasement, 15–16, 25, 49, 55, 132, 135, 172, 196, 209
Ardeatine Massacre, 124–25
Ardennes Offensive, 16–17, 31, 199
Armenia, 17–18, 22
Armenian Genocide, 17–18, 22, 118
Arrow Cross, 112
art, 18–19, 90, 104–5, 117, 125, 156, 199, 235

assassination attempt, 19–21, 38, 45, 61, 67, 89, 92–93, 95, 97, 124, 151, 162, 165, 172, 190, 195–96, 199, 202, 237–38, 240
Atatürk, Mustafa Kemal, 17, 21–23, 34–35, 140
Atlantic Charter, 23, 196
Aufbau (reconstruction), 13
Auschwitz, 99, 107, 112–13, 154, 174–75, 188, 195, 203
Australia, 13, 120
Austria, 1, 3, 7, 11, 13–15, 18, 24–26, 35, 37, 46, 55–56, 70–72, 75, 80, 92, 94, 103, 105–6, 109–11, 117, 119, 124–25, 141, 148, 151–52, 154, 165–67, 169, 184, 206, 218, 223, 231, 242–43
Axis, 13–14, 27, 61, 117, 141–42, 147, 194
Axmann, Artur, 103

Backe, Herbert, 58
Bagdolio, Pietro, 115
Baillet-Latour, Henri de, 160
Balck, Hermann, 237
Balkans, 8, 27, 44, 49–50, 111, 142, 161, 174, 194, 210, 224. *See also specific countries*
Baltics, 23, 27–28, 58, 63, 87, 92, 99, 106, 120, 131–32, 147, 162, 173–74, 198, 210, 242. *See also specific countries*
Barnes, Djuna, 94
Battle of Berlin, 28–29, 47, 61, 103, 179, 182
Battle of Britain, 29–30, 77, 90, 124, 133, 213
Battle of El-Alamein, 12–13, 30, 32, 136, 164
Battle of Kursk, 30–32, 61, 162

INDEX

Battle of Stalingrad, 7, 20, 23, 30, 31–32, 44, 59, 71, 73, 89, 92, 112, 120, 131, 136, 140, 160, 162, 164–65
Battle of the Atlantic, 23, 30, 32, 50, 60, 89, 162, 164, 173, 196, 229
Battle of the Bulge, 17, 113
Bavarian People's Party, 32, 45
Bavarian Soviet Republic, 32–33, 52, 72, 137–38, 175, 190
Beck, Ludwig, 109
Beer Hall Putsch, 65, 67, 73, 78–79, 90, 94,
Belarus, 28, 81, 106, 120, 162, 173
Belgium, 12, 16–17, 31, 76, 136, 151, 153, 231, 242
Belzec, 107, 174
Beneš, Edvard, 56, 97
Berger, Gottlob, 99
Berghof, 15, 25, 35–37, 40, 42–43, 59, 72, 74, 89, 95, 161, 170, 203, 206, 214, 233, 241
Beria, Lavrenty, 216
Best, Werner, 41
Bevin, Ernst, 200
Bismarck, Otto Von, 37, 79, 105, 145, 167, 204, 220, 239
Blitzkrieg, 37–38, 77, 80, 92, 110, 133, 173
Bloch, Eduard, 102, 117
Blomberg–Fritsch affair, 38–39, 42, 45, 90, 108, 111, 123, 140, 149, 187, 199, 237
Blomberg, Werner Von, 38–39, 45, 74, 90, 108–11, 123, 140, 149, 187, 191, 199, 237
Böhme, Franz, 154
Bolivia, 41, 190, 214
Boris III, 43
Bormann, Martin, 2, 7, 32, 36, 39–40, 70, 72, 89–91, 95–96, 107, 114, 125, 127, 171, 188, 199, 206, 215–17, 219–20, 240
Bouhler, Philipp, 69
Boxheim Documents, 40–41, 66, 202
Brandt, Karl, 69
Brauchitsch, Walther Von, 39, 42, 62, 120
Braun, Eva, 36, 42–43, 79, 104, 171–72, 181, 215–16, 241–43
Braun, Wernher Von, 242
Briand, Aristide, 130
Brooks, Mel. *See* cinema and television, representations in
Brüning, Heinrich, 41, 94–95, 101, 168
Bulgaria, 15, 27, 43–44, 111–12, 115, 142, 161, 194, 208, 210, 224

Bunker, 8, 20, 40, 43, 46–47, 51, 89, 99, 102, 142, 171, 207, 214–16, 240
Buñuel, Luis, 225

Canada, 120
Canaris, Wilhelm, 20, 45, 78, 165, 202
Capra, Frank, 225
Center Party, 32, 37, 41, 45–46, 49, 65, 68, 94, 101, 144, 168, 175
Chamberlain, Neville, 15–16, 55–56, 172
Chamberlin, Houston Stewart, 235
Chancellery, 36–37, 39–40, 43, 48–49, 51, 69, 89, 109–10, 127, 160, 171, 117, 206–27, 216, 236
Chancellor, 4, 46, 130, 149, 171, 185, 201, 211–12, 224
Chancellor, appointment, as, 3–4, 24, 41, 46–49, 111, 119, 129–30, 145, 156, 164, 167–68, 176, 181, 187, 191, 211, 221, 232, 237, 246
Chaplin, Charlie. *See* cinema and television, representation in
Chelmno, 174
China, 15, 110, 117, 131, 147, 196, 229
Chuikov, Vasily, 216
Churchill, Winston, 7, 15–16, 23, 32, 49–50, 62, 113, 125, 136, 161, 163, 196–97, 210, 229
cinema and television, representations in, 50–51, 79, 84, 88, 94, 188, 220, 225, 241
Class, Heinrich, 167
Clay, Lucius D., 154
Cocteau, Jean, 188
Collaboration, 8, 27–28, 56, 76, 107, 115, 175–76, 194, 227
Communist International (Comintern), 14–15, 41, 52
Communist Party of Germany, 4, 33–34, 41, 46, 49, 51–52, 64–65, 67, 84, 88, 143, 149, 164, 183, 204, 209, 215
concentration camp, 4, 6, 21, 25, 45–46, 53–54, 67, 70, 84, 93, 98–99, 107, 109, 121, 135, 151–52, 165, 174, 185, 188, 192, 195, 202, 206, 236, 240, 242
Congo, 12
coordination (*Gleichschaltung*), 4–5, 7, 25, 49, 54–55, 68, 84, 119, 129, 145, 156, 164
Croatia, 15, 27, 187, 224
Cuba, 53
Cuno, Wilhelm, 34

264

Czechoslovakia, 7, 15–16, 25–27, 37, 45, 55–56, 75–76, 109–11, 117, 147–49, 165, 184, 199, 210
Czechoslovakia crisis, 14, 37, 42, 45, 55–56, 90, 93, 151, 172, 176, 195, 229

D'Alambert, Eugen, 188
Dachau, 53–54, 67, 84, 93, 98, 152
Darré, Richard Walther, 57–58, 65, 85, 99, 202
Dawin, Charles. *See* social Darwinism
De Lagarde, Paul, 135
death camp, 54, 99, 151, 174, 192, 203, 236
Deladier, Eduard, 172
Denmark, 15, 29, 60, 76, 149, 151, 153, 201, 207, 231, 239
diary hoax, 58–59, 172
Dietrich, Eckart, 33, 63, 73, 87, 103, 123, 138, 146, 198, 220
Dietrich, Otto, 14, 59–60, 89, 177, 230
Dollfuss, Engelbert, 24, 46
Dönitz, Karl, 32, 40, 60–61, 91, 100, 121, 124–5, 154, 171, 187, 207, 211, 216
Drexler, Anton, 73, 87, 138
drug use, 61, 96. *See also* health
Duesterberg, Theodor, 95, 211
Dunkirk, 61–62, 124, 173, 199

Ebert, Friedrich, 100, 237
economics, 3–4, 6–7, 12, 24, 27, 34, 39, 41, 43, 46, 49, 55, 58, 63–68, 72–75, 77, 80, 86, 90, 94, 101, 106, 109–11, 114, 119, 130, 135, 138, 140, 146, 150, 152, 156, 167–68, 172–73, 179, 181–82, 191–92, 194, 201, 204, 206, 209–10, 212–13, 215, 221, 228–29, 232–33, 237, 241
Eden, Anthony, 14
Egypt, 12–13, 30, 96, 142, 164, 192
Eichinger, Bernd. *See* cinema and television, representations in
Eichmann, Adolf, 26, 112, 236
Einsatzgruppen, 28, 30, 99, 107, 162, 174, 177, 199, 203, 228
Eisenhower, Dwight, 29, 61
elections, 3–4, 24, 32, 41–42, 47, 52, 65–68, 78, 84–86, 95, 98, 101, 105, 128, 130, 144, 146, 168, 203, 214, 223, 245–46
Enabling Act, 4, 41, 46, 67–68, 86, 95, 183, 204
Estonia, 27–28, 148, 198
Ethiopia, 76, 131, 141, 159, 196, 205

Euthanasia Program (*Aktion T4*), 69–70, 78, 107, 136, 154, 165, 175, 185
Evian Conference, 151, 197

family, 1–2, 71–72, 102, 169, 180–81, 232
Faulhaber, Michael, 185
Feder, Gottfried, 64, 66, 72–73, 87, 138, 146
Federal Republic of Germany, 53, 61, 103, 109, 182
"Final Solution," 7, 27, 90, 106, 118, 120, 135–36, 152, 192, 236. *See also* Holocaust
Finland, 15, 147, 148, 172, 194, 210, 239
Flossenbürg, 45, 93, 206
Foch, Ferdinand, 231
Ford, Henry, 132
Fortress Europe, 32, 73–74, 163, 195, 221
Four-Year Plan, 64, 74–75, 80, 85, 90, 110, 152, 182, 198, 201, 236
France, 7, 12, 15–16, 29–30, 32, 37–38, 42, 45, 49, 55–56, 61–62, 75–78, 80, 82, 90, 92, 100, 106, 110–11, 121, 124, 130, 132–33, 135–36, 138, 140–41, 147, 149–51, 160, 163–64, 172–75, 181, 195, 197, 199, 205–6, 208, 210, 219, 223, 231, 240–41
Vichy Regime, 12, 76–78, 164, 175
Franco, Francisco, 12, 14, 46, 75, 77–78, 138, 141, 161, 205, 213
Free French Army, 12
Freikorps, 39, 52, 87, 123, 190, 211, 214
Freisler, Roland, 129
Freyand, John Ernst Von, 20
Frick, Wilhelm, 35, 53, 68, 78–79, 184, 222
Fritsch, Werner Freiherr Von, 38–39, 42, 45, 90, 108, 110–11, 123, 140, 149, 187, 199, 237
Friedrich II, 67
Friedrich Wilhelm I, 161
Fromm, Friedrich, 20–21, 23
Frontbann, 39, 128, 190, 214
Führer myth, 7, 11, 32, 43, 59, 63, 79–80, 87–88, 104, 130, 156, 225, 241
Funk, Walther 39, 80, 108, 110, 114, 220

Galen, Clemens Von, 70
General Government, 106, 136, 174. *See also* Poland
General Plan for the East, 81, 99, 133, 153, 162, 227–28
Geneva, 49, 82

Geneva Disarmament Conference, 82, 149, 181
Genoud, François, 219, 220
German American Bund, 82–84, 119, 203
German Combat League, 34
German Democratic Party (DDP), 65, 86
German Democratic Republic, 21, 53, 56, 58, 103, 105, 182, 217
German Fatherland Party 87
German Labor Front, 5, 64, 84–85, 114, 131, 140, 147, 205, 233
German National Front, 86, 111
German National People's Party (DNVP) 48, 66, 85–87, 94–95, 111, 127, 144, 245–46
German Workers' Party, 2, 33, 63, 73, 84, 86–87, 123, 137, 143, 145, 167, 198, 204, 232
Gestapo, 6, 19, 25, 38, 41, 45–46, 53–54, 90, 93, 97–98, 109, 114, 139, 145, 152, 164–65, 182–83, 195, 205, 208, 213, 237–38
ghetto, 54, 99, 152, 192, 195, 203. *See also* Poland
Godwin, Mike. *See* Godwin's Law
Godwin's Law, 87–88
Goebbels, Joseph, 2, 4, 14, 16, 18–19, 21, 23, 25, 32, 36, 38, 40–41, 43, 47, 49, 51, 59, 66–67, 70, 79–80, 88–90, 94–95, 104, 107, 110, 114, 119, 127, 135, 150–52, 156, 159–63, 170–71, 177, 181, 183–84, 186, 192, 199, 206, 208, 212, 214–18, 221, 224, 230, 236, 239, 241, 245
Goebbels, Magda, 89, 181, 216, 218, 241
Göring, Hermann, 2, 15, 19, 25, 35–36, 38–41, 58, 62, 64, 74–75, 80, 85, 89–91, 96, 106, 110, 114, 120, 127, 131–32, 134–35, 141, 150, 152, 171, 182–84, 198–99, 201, 205, 208, 211, 215, 217, 227–28, 236
Great Britain, 3, 7, 12, 15, 23, 29, 49, 55, 62, 64, 71, 75, 82, 90, 92, 106, 110–11, 113, 117–18, 125, 132–33, 135, 141, 149–50, 156, 172–73, 177, 179, 181, 187, 196, 199, 203, 205–6, 213, 219, 223, 229, 236, 242
Great Depression, 4, 7, 24, 52, 66, 83, 145, 204, 223, 246. *See also* economics
Greece, 12, 17–18, 27, 43–44, 142, 150, 159, 194, 210
Groener, Wilhelm, 237
Gross, Walter, 179
Grynszpan, Herschel, 151–52

Guderian, Heinz, 38, 91–92
Gürtner, Franz, 38

Halder, Franz, 62, 93–94, 125, 140, 161
Halder, Franz Von, 172
Hanfstaengl, Ernst, 13, 35, 94, 170, 235
Hanfstaengl, Helene, 94, 170, 241
Hanisch, Reinhold, 232
Harrer, Karl, 87
Harzburg Front, 66, 86, 94–95, 211, 213, 246
health 61, 95–96, 169
Hearst, William Randolph, 94
Heidemann, Gerd, 58–59
Herbstnebel (Autumn Mist), 16–17. *See also* Ardennes Offensive
Hess, Rudolf, 2, 35–36, 39, 82, 87, 96–97, 107, 128, 180, 184, 224
Heydrich, Reinhard, 25, 41, 45, 56, 90, 97, 99, 106–7, 149, 152, 236
Himmler, Heinrich, 2, 6–7, 21, 32, 36, 38, 54, 57–58, 60, 67, 78–81, 85, 90, 95, 97–100, 107–9, 114, 124, 130, 132–33, 145, 153, 162, 171, 174, 179, 184, 192, 199, 202, 208, 213, 215, 217, 227–28, 236
Hindenburg, Oskar Von, 48–49
Hindenburg, Paul Von, 4, 41, 46–47, 54, 66–68, 79, 86, 95, 100–2, 105, 111, 149, 167–68, 183, 191–92, 208, 224, 237
Hirschbiegel, Oliver. *See* cinema and television, representations in
Hirschfeld, Magnus, 108
Hitler Youth, 5, 54, 75, 102–3, 128, 132, 152, 156, 165, 195, 215. *See also* League of German Girls
Hitler, Paula, 71–72, 102. *See also* family
Hoffmann, Heinrich, 11, 36, 42–43, 63, 103–5, 170, 241, 243
Hohenzollerns, 68, 79, 102, 105
Holocaust, 5–6, 8, 13, 18–19, 21, 23, 26–28, 30, 43, 50, 54, 56, 60, 69, 77, 89, 97, 99, 105–8, 112–13, 117, 120–21, 130, 132–33, 136, 139, 151, 153–54, 156, 162, 165, 171, 174–77, 187, 194–95, 197, 199, 203, 207, 210, 228, 236, 239–40. *See also* "Final Solution"
Homosexuality, 38, 54, 98, 108–109, 190, 192
Horthy, Miklos, 111–12, 175
Hossbach Memorandum, 25, 37, 39, 55, 75, 93, 109–11, 149, 182
Hugenberg, Alfred, 57, 66, 86, 94, 111, 245

INDEX

Hungary, 15, 26, 56, 106, 111–12, 161, 175, 187, 194, 210, 224

Ickes, Harold, 176
Independent Social Democratic Party (USPD), 32
India, 12, 15, 117, 161, 192
International Military Tribunal (IMT), 40, 42, 61, 79–80, 91–93, 96, 103, 111, 113–15, 121, 124, 127, 132, 136, 150, 154–55, 169, 172, 183, 187, 198–200, 202–3, 207, 236, 238
Italian Social Republic, 115, 142, 161
Italy, 15–16, 24, 27, 30, 50, 56, 75–77, 82, 104–5, 110–11, 115, 117, 124–25, 131, 133, 140–42, 148–49, 153, 159, 176, 181, 188, 194–96, 203, 205–6, 210, 223

Jackson, Robert, 114
Japan, 14–15, 23, 30, 50, 82, 110, 117, 131–32, 141, 147, 159, 161, 184, 207, 211, 223, 229, 230, 236
Jetzinger, Franz, 126
Jews, 1–8, 11, 17–8, 22–23, 25–28, 43, 53–54, 57, 63, 69–72, 74, 77, 80–83, 87–90, 97, 99, 102–3, 105–9, 112, 117–20, 126, 129, 132–33, 135–36, 138–39, 141, 146, 148–54, 156–65, 167, 171–76, 184, 187, 190, 192, 194–99, 201, 203, 207–9, 211, 215, 218, 220, 227–28, 230, 232, 236, 239, 244; robbery of, 13, 19, 25, 65, 69, 80, 90, 106, 119–20, 146, 151–52, 156, 165, 175, 194, 201, 208
Jodl, Alfred, 29, 39, 42, 60–61, 120–21, 140, 238, 240
Judeo-Bolshevism, 3, 89, 118, 150. *See also* Anti-Semitism

Kahr, Gustav Von, 34–35, 222–23
Kahr, Ritter Von, 191
Kaltenbrunner, Ernst, 25, 150, 203
Kapp, Wolfgang, 52, 123, 138
Katyń massacre, 114
Keitel, Wilhelm 20–21, 29, 39–40, 42, 60, 76, 120, 123–24, 151, 162, 237–38, 240
Kempner, Robert, 199
Kennedy, John F., 93
Kenya, 120
Kesselring, Albert, 62, 115, 124–25, 199
Kindertransport, 153
Klemperer, Victor, 160

Knopp, Guido. *See* cinema and television, representations in
Konev, Ivan, 28
Kriebel, Hermann, 128, 222
Ku Klux Klan, 83, 229
Kubizek, August Friedrich, 125–26, 169, 232
Kuhn, Fritz, 82–84
Kujau, Konrad, 58–59

La Guardia, Fiorello, 84
LaFarge, John, 175
Lammers, Hans Heinrich, 7, 127
Landsberg Prison, 3, 22, 35, 37, 60, 86, 95, 96, 127–28, 139, 143, 154, 180, 198, 202, 221
Latvia, 27–28, 148
law, 2, 25, 41, 49, 54, 57, 67–69, 78, 83, 87–88, 105, 113–14, 118, 127–30, 139, 146, 149, 151, 154, 156, 173, 191, 199, 218, 222–23, 228–29, 243; international, 60, 114, 121, 195
leadership principle, 5, 40, 66, 107, 129–30, 144
League of German Girls, 5, 54. *See also* Hitler Youth
League of Nations, 14, 49, 75, 76, 82, 102, 130–31, 141, 148–49, 173, 181, 231
Lebensraum, 2–3, 8, 58, 64, 75, 81, 106–7, 109, 132, 139, 146, 161, 203, 211, 239
Lenin, Vladimir, 53
Lennings, Hans-Martin, 183–84
Levin, Ira. *See* cinema and television, representations in
Levy, Dany. *See* cinema and television, representations in
Ley, Robert, 64, 85, 90, 114, 131–32, 217, 233
Libya, 12–13, 30, 141, 164
Liebknecht, Karl, 52
Lindbergh, Charles, 132, 229
List, Guido Von, 218
Lithuania, 27–28, 148
Litvinov, Maxim, 147–48
Louis, Joe, 160
Lubitsch, Ernst. *See* cinema and television, representations in
Ludendorff, Erich, 11, 34–35, 208, 222–23
Luftwaffe, 15–17, 27, 29, 31, 39, 53, 62, 73, 75, 77, 90, 103, 120, 124, 132–34, 140, 163, 174, 181, 194, 205, 213, 217, 224, 232

Luxembourg, 17, 151
Luxemburg, Rosa, 52

Macedonia, 43, 44
Madagascar. *See* Madagascar Plan
Madagascar Plan, 106, 120, 135–36, 163
Majdanek, 99, 107, 174
Manstein, Erich Von, 31, 136–37, 140, 237
Maurice, Emil 128, 180
Mauthausen, 25, 206
May, Karl 137, 203, 228
Mayr, Karl 33, 63, 73, 87, 123, 137–39, 232, 244
McCloy, John J., 127, 154
Mein Kampf, 1, 5, 11, 13, 33, 35, 51, 63, 71, 75, 79, 87, 94, 102, 117–18, 126, 128–29, 133, 139, 145, 161, 169, 177, 179, 184, 203–4, 212, 232, 243–44
Mengele, Josef, 50
Meyjes, Menno. *See* cinema and television, representations in
military commander, 17, 31, 42, 62, 73, 92–93, 95, 131, 137, 139–40, 163–64, 237, 240
Moeller, Arthur van den Bruck, 220
Möhl, Arnold Von, 138
Molotov, Vyacheslav, 147–48, 161, 187
Molotov–Ribbentrop Pact. *See* Nazi–Soviet Nonaggression Pact
Montgomery, Bernard Law, 13, 30
Morell, Theodor, 61, 96
Morocco, 12–13, 30, 77–78, 164
Müller, Alexander Von, 138
Müller, Hans, 219
Murdoch, Rupert, 59, 111
Mussolini, Benito, 3, 12, 14, 16, 18, 22, 24–25, 27, 34–35, 46, 56, 75–78, 80, 110, 115, 140–42, 147, 171, 194, 203, 205, 216, 223–24

National Food Estate (RNS), 5, 57
National Socialist German Workers' Party (NSDAP), 2–4, 11, 13, 17, 21–22, 24, 33–34, 39–41, 46–49, 52–54, 57, 59, 63–66, 68, 73, 78, 80, 82, 84, 86–89, 94, 96, 98, 100–2, 108, 114, 118, 123, 127–29, 131, 138–40, 143–45, 148, 155–56, 167–68, 171, 174, 177, 179–81, 185, 187, 190–91, 195–96, 198–99, 201, 203–4, 206, 209, 211–12, 218–19, 221, 223–24, 232, 236, 245–46

National Socialist Welfare Organization, 144–46, 205
Nazi Party Program (25-Point Program), 64, 66, 73, 75, 87, 118, 141, 143, 145–47, 185, 212, 232
Nazi–Soviet Nonaggression Pact, 7, 14-15, 28–29, 56, 76, 117, 147–48, 161, 173, 187, 194, 209–10
Nero Order, 148–49, 207
Neurath, Konstantin Von, 15, 39, 56, 109–11, 149–50
New Zealand, 120
Niemeyer, Helene, 94
Night and Fog Decree, 124, 151
Night of Broken Glass, 54, 89–90, 106, 119, 132, 151–53, 158, 165, 176, 197, 215, 229
NKVD, 28, 174, 216
Nordwind (North wind), 17. *See also* Ardennes Offensive
Nuremberg Military Tribunal (NMT), 58, 60, 65, 70, 92–93, 115, 128–29, 154–55, 180, 199, 203, 238
Nuremberg Party Rallies, 57, 79, 103, 114, 155–56
Nuremberg Race Laws, 78, 89, 106, 114, 119, 129, 149, 151, 155–59, 165, 171, 218, 236

Odermatt, Urs, *See* cinema and television, representations in
Olbricht, Friedrich, 20
Olympic Games, 74, 83, 89, 119, 132, 151, 157–60, 188, 205
Operation Anthropoid, 97. *See also* Heydrich, Reinhard
Operation Barbarossa 7, 23, 27, 30, 38, 42–43, 53, 73, 79, 81, 92–93, 96, 99, 106, 117, 124, 131, 133, 136, 140, 150–51, 160–62, 174, 194, 195, 199, 227, 230, 240–41. *See also* Einsatzgruppen
Operation Bodyguard, 74, 163
Operation Dragoon, 74, 77
Operation Dynamo, 61
Operation Felix, 77
Operation Husky, 31, 74, 142
Operation Overlord, 32, 50, 74, 77, 160, 162–63, 195, 199, 241
Operation Torch, 12–13, 30, 77, 164
Opposition, 45, 49, 54, 67, 69, 84, 97–98, 103, 105, 124, 136, 151, 162, 164–65, 180, 185, 195, 204, 207, 228, 237

Order Police, 107–8, 152
Oster, Hans, 45
Ottoman Empire, 17, 22
Owens, Jesse, 160

Pacelli, Eugenio (Pope Pius XII), 46, 49, 68, 70, 175–76, 185, 203
Pact of Locarno, 14, 76, 130, 149, 181, 206
Pact of Mutual Assistance, 14
Pact of Paris, 82
Pakistan, 192
Palestine, 22, 30, 120
Pan-German, 1, 3, 12, 24–25, 37, 55, 73, 86–87, 111, 125, 133, 138, 150, 167, 232
Papen, Franz Von, 46–48, 66–67, 78, 102, 111, 114, 125, 149, 167–69, 183, 186, 191,
Pasha, Talat, 17
Paulus, Friedrich, 31–32, 73, 120
personal will and political testament, 40, 60, 89, 99, 106, 171–72, 216, 219
personality, 1, 18, 37, 42, 61, 79, 94, 96, 125–26, 130, 169–71, 181, 219, 222, 235, 241
Petain, Philippe, 76, 175
Phony War, 172–73
Piłsudski, Józef, 173
Pius XI, 46, 175, 185
Poland, 14, 16, 21–23, 27–28, 38, 55–56, 70, 75–76, 81, 90, 92–93, 99, 105, 124, 127, 130, 133, 135, 150–51, 165, 173–75, 195, 203, 210, 213, 223, 240; Holocaust in 8, 99, 106–8, 120, 136, 174–75, 236; invasion of 7, 15, 30, 37, 39, 42, 45, 76, 92, 114, 118, 136, 142, 147–48, 172–74, 195, 199, 223
Portugal, 12
Preysing, Konrad, 175
propaganda, 5, 8, 19, 23, 25, 30, 47, 57, 59–60, 67, 74, 80, 85, 88–89, 102–3, 119, 145, 150, 159–60, 184, 188–89, 207, 212, 214, 218, 220, 224–25, 236; Ministry of, 14, 25, 59, 73, 80, 88, 94, 114, 145, 153, 163, 177, 195, 197, 224, 230
Prophecy, 23, 89, 120, 176–77
Prophecy speech, 59, 89, 90, 106, 236, 171, 176–77
Protocols of the Elders of Zion, 118, 177, 199

Quisling, Vidkun, 153–54, 239

racism, 3, 23, 50, 54, 57, 69, 78, 83, 88, 90, 98, 106–7, 118, 133, 139, 153, 170, 173, 175, 179-80, 192–93, 196, 198, 218, 228–29, 232, 239
Raeder, Erich, 39, 60, 120, 239
Raubal, Angela "Geli," 42, 71, 79, 180–81, 241
rearmament, 7, 14–15, 45, 55, 63–64, 74–75, 82–83, 85, 90, 110, 130–31, 140, 147, 159, 172, 181–82, 186, 191, 196, 199, 201, 203, 205, 215, 221, 230, 232–33, 237
Red Army, 8, 16, 17, 20, 28–29, 31, 40, 43–44, 50, 55, 71, 73, 76, 103, 107, 112–13, 160, 162–64, 173–74, 194, 209–10, 214, 216–18, 228, 236–37, 239–40, 242
Red Cross, 99, 145, 203
Red Front Fighters' League, 52
Reichkommissariat Ostland, 28
Reichstag, 4, 14, 22, 29, 45–48, 65–68, 73, 78–79, 84–86, 90, 95, 101–2, 106, 111, 131, 145, 168, 172, 182–83, 186, 204, 212, 218, 230, 245; elections, 130, 146, 168, 203, 214, 245; fire, 4, 41, 46, 52, 54, 67, 78, 86, 90, 102, 129, 149, 157, 164, 168, 182–84; fire decree, 4, 52, 54, 78
Reichswehr, 33–35, 82, 120, 123–24, 136–38, 181, 190–92, 199, 214, 222, 231, 236–37
religion, 11, 37, 40, 46, 54, 68, 98, 103, 108, 145, 164, 175, 184–86, 191
Rhineland, 7, 14, 56, 69, 76, 80, 88, 131–32, 141, 148–49, 159, 165, 172, 181, 231
remilitarization of, 186, 205
Ribbentrop, Joachim Von 14–16, 36, 39, 60, 78, 111, 117, 148–49, 164, 186–87
Richthofen, Manfred Von, 90
Riefenstahl, Leni, 5, 35, 50, 79, 89, 103, 155, 156, 159, 187–89, 192, 224–25, 241
Röhm purge, 38, 41, 49, 98, 102, 105, 108, 131, 146, 149, 164, 168, 190–91, 199, 202, 213
Röhm, Ernst, 5, 34–35, 87, 108, 128, 190–92, 199, 212, 214–15, 222, 224, 237
Romani, 99, 188, 192–93
Romania, 15, 16, 27, 31, 43, 55, 76, 112, 115, 135, 148, 161, 174, 193–95, 210, 224
Rommel, Erwin, 12–13, 30, 124, 163, 164, 195–96, 237

INDEX

Roosevelt, Franklin D., 16, 23, 30, 49, 83, 94, 106, 108, 113, 132, 153, 161, 173, 176, 196–97, 229–30
Rosenberg, Alfred, 13, 19, 28, 63, 87, 89, 107, 128, 132, 162, 177, 184, 198–99, 221
Royal Air Force, 29, 77, 107, 213, 233, 241
Rundstedt, Gerd Von, 17, 61–62, 124, 136, 140, 163, 199–200, 227
Russia, 2–3, 7, 12–13, 22, 27–29, 31, 37, 40, 43–44, 72, 74–75, 81, 83, 87, 89, 93, 99–100, 106, 110, 118, 120, 132–33, 139, 162–65, 167, 173, 175, 177, 198, 208–10, 217, 231, 243

Sachsenhausen, 67, 152, 206
Salomon, Franz Pfeffer Von, 214–15
Sauckal, Fritz, 207
Schacht, Hjalmar, 15, 39, 58, 65, 73–74, 80, 110, 114, 119, 156, 182, 201–2
Scheidemann, Philipp, 33, 182
Scheubner-Richter, Max Erwin, 22, 132, 198
Schirach, Baldur Von, 103
Schmeling, Max, 160
Schmitt, Carl, 129, 134
Schroeder, Kurt Von, 47
Schuschnigg, Kurt Von, 24–25
Schutzstaffel (SS), 6–8, 13, 17, 20, 25–26, 28, 30, 36–37, 39, 41, 45, 49–50, 53–55, 57, 59, 65, 68, 70, 80–81, 85, 89–90, 93, 97–99, 100, 102–3, 105–7, 109, 112–15, 124–25, 129–30, 133, 135–36, 142, 145, 149, 151–55, 162–65, 174, 177, 179–80, 184, 191–92, 198–99, 202–3, 206, 214–15, 224, 228, 236, 238–39, 242
Seekt, Hans Von, 35
Seldte, Franz, 94, 211
Serbia, 27, 44
Seyss-Inquart, Arthur, 25
Shirer, William, 160
Sicherheitsdienst (SD; SS Security Service), 25, 30, 45, 97, 99, 114
Simon, John, 14
Slovakia, 15, 56, 111, 187, 224
Sobibor, 107, 174
Social Darwinism, 118
Social Democratic Party of Germany (SPD), 32, 41, 45–46, 48, 51, 53, 65, 67, 78, 84–86, 88, 101, 123, 138, 143, 164, 168, 182–83, 204–5, 209
Socialist Unity Party, 53
South Africa, 53, 120

South America, 40, 50, 120, 207. *See also specific countries*
Soviet Union, 3, 7–8, 13–16, 21, 23, 28–30, 42–43, 50, 52, 55–56, 64, 74, 78, 81–82, 92–93, 96, 98–99, 106–7, 110, 112, 117, 120, 124, 131, 133, 147–148, 159, 161–62, 172, 174–75, 177, 181, 187, 194, 196, 203, 205, 209–12, 223, 227, 229–30, 237, 239
Spain, 12, 14–15, 75, 77–78, 161, 188, 203, 205
Spandau Prison, 97, 114, 150, 107, 207
Spanish Civil War, 14, 46, 75, 77, 131, 133, 141, 159, 205–6, 213
Speer, Albert, 32, 36, 40, 42, 46–47, 60, 65, 90, 93, 95, 114, 127, 132–34, 137, 148–49, 153, 155, 184, 189, 197, 206–8, 215, 221, 224, 242
"Stab in the back" myth, 34, 101, 105, 145, 208–9, 231
Stalin, Josef, vii, 15–16, 19, 28–29, 31, 35, 41, 49–50, 52–53, 71, 74, 76, 80–81, 96, 110, 114, 124, 147–48, 159–62, 164, 172, 174–75, 183, 187, 194, 209–211, 216, 224, 228
Stauffenberg, Claus Shenk Graf Von, viii, 20–21, 196, 240
Steel Helmets, 94, 211, 245
Stennes, Walther, 41
Strasser, Gregor, 4, 39, 47–48, 66, 73, 88, 146, 191, 211–13, 221, 245
Strasser, Otto, 94, 180
strategic bombing campaign, 7, 24, 29–30, 32, 50, 61, 70, 78, 89, 103, 107, 133, 162, 182, 207, 213–14, 242
Strauss, Richard, 160
Streicher, Julius, 35, 150, 177
Stresemann, Gustav, 86, 130
Sturmabteilung (SA; Stormtroopers or Brownshirts), 3–5, 22, 34–35, 39–41, 46–47, 49, 52–53, 55, 67–68, 75, 82, 86, 90, 98, 102–3, 105, 108, 111, 119, 128, 143–44, 146, 152, 155–56, 164, 168, 179, 182–84, 190–92, 196, 199, 202, 206, 211, 214–15, 221–22, 224, 237
suicide, 4, 8, 13, 29, 40, 43, 89–90, 95, 106, 114–15, 121, 142, 144, 154, 171, 187, 212, 214–19, 221
swastika, 159, 218
Sweden, 123, 153–54, 236, 239
Switzerland, 19, 26, 67, 94, 177, 221, 236
Szálasi, Ferenc, 112

Table Talk and the Testament of Adolf Hitler, 58, 172, 219–20
Tarantino, Quentin. *See* cinema and television, representations in
Taylor, Telford, 40, 80
Terboven, Josef, 153–54
Thälmann, Ernst, 52, 183
Thierack, Otto Georg, 129
Third Reich, 220–21
Thyssen, Fritz, 64
Todt, Fritz, 73, 207, 221
"total war," 89
Treblinka, 43, 107, 174
Tresckow, Henning Von, 20–21
Trevor-Roper, Hugh, 58–59, 172, 216, 219–20
trial (1924), 221–23
Tripartite Pact, 15, 23, 30, 43, 112, 117, 187, 194, 223–24
Triumph of the Will, 5, 35, 50, 79, 89, 103, 155, 188–89, 224–25, 241
Truman, Harry, 113, 210
Tunisia, 13, 30
Turkish Committee of Union and Progress, 17

Ukraine, 7, 28, 81, 99, 106, 111, 120, 131, 133, 160, 162, 173–74, 195, 227–28, 240
United States, 3, 7, 13, 15, 17, 21, 23, 29–31, 37, 43, 49–51, 56, 64, 66, 71, 75, 78, 82–83, 93–94, 99, 105–6, 115, 117–20, 124, 128, 132–33, 136–37, 150, 153, 155–57, 161–62, 167, 171–72, 176–77, 179–80, 196–97, 199, 203, 205, 207–8, 210, 212, 216, 219, 223–25, 228–31
Universal Declaration of Human Rights, 114

Van der Lubbe, Marinus, 183
Vatican, 46, 68, 108, 175–76, 185, 203
Treaty of Versailles, 2–3, 6–7, 14, 22, 24, 33, 75–76, 82, 130, 138, 146, 149, 181–82, 186, 201, 203, 208, 211–12, 229, 231–32, 235–37, 244, 245
Vinberg, Fyodor, 177
Völkisher Beobachter, 22
Volksgemeinschaft, 6–7, 84–85, 103, 128, 144–46, 198, 214
Volksgerichtshof, 129
Voloshilov, Kliment, 148
Von Below, Nicolaus, 17

Wacht am Rhein, 16. *See also* Ardennes Offensive

Waffen SS, 17, 28, 98, 107, 113, 174, 184, 202–3
Wagner, Richard, 18, 77, 94, 125–26, 169, 184, 212, 232, 235–36
Wagner, Robert, 222
Wagner, Winifred, 170, 241
Waititi, Taiko. *See* cinema and television, representations in
Wehrmacht, 7–8, 13, 16–17, 19, 20, 23, 25, 27–28, 30–32, 38, 42, 45, 60–61, 76, 81, 85, 89–90, 92–93, 98–99, 107, 109, 111, 114–15, 120, 123–25, 131, 136–37, 140, 148, 151, 154, 160–64, 171–72, 174, 186, 196, 198–200, 202–3, 215, 217–19, 224, 227, 229, 232, 236–40
Weimar Republic, 4, 65, 69, 84, 85, 86, 103, 105, 108, 111, 130, 145, 186, 196, 201, 211, 215,
Weinberg, Gerhard, 204
Wels, Otto, 68, 204
Weser Exercise, 29, 38, 76, 80, 105, 117, 153, 173, 239–40
Wessel, Horst, 214–15
Wilson, Woodrow, 23, 82, 231
Wnendt, David, 51. *See* cinema and television, representations in
Wolf's Lair, 7, 20, 37, 161–62, 214, 227, 240
women, 1, 42, 65, 69, 71, 79, 94, 103–4, 108, 125, 143, 147, 153, 165, 169, 181, 218, 237, 240–41
"wonder weapons," 16, 23, 89, 134, 163, 214, 241–43
Wood, Edward, 15
World Jewish Congress, 99
World War I, 11–13, 22, 24, 37, 39, 42, 45, 51, 54–55, 57, 59–60, 63, 64, 69, 71–74, 76, 78–80, 82–83, 85–86, 88, 90–91, 96, 99–100, 102–3, 111, 113, 115, 117–18, 120, 123–25, 131–33, 136, 139, 141, 143–45, 148–49, 160, 167, 169, 173–74, 176, 186, 190, 193, 195–96, 199, 204, 208, 211, 214, 220, 229, 236, 240, 243, 245

Young Plan Referendum, 66, 86, 94, 211, 245–46
Young Turk movement, 17
Young, Owen, 245
Yugoslavia, 27, 44, 111–12, 210

Zhukov, Georgi, 28, 61, 210, 216
Ziegler, Adolf, 18

About the Author

Steven P. Remy is a professor of history at the City University of New York, Brooklyn College and the Graduate Center, where he has taught modern European and German history since 2002. He is the author of *The Malmedy Massacre: The War Crimes Trial Controversy* (2017) and *The Heidelberg Myth: The Nazification and Denazification of a German University* (2003).

www.ingramcontent.com/pod-product-compliance
Lightning Source LLC
Chambersburg PA
CBHW082032300426
44117CB00015B/2453